1999

1

Handbook on Effective Instructional Strategies

Evidence for Decision-Making

Myles I. Friedman
and Steven P. Fisher

THE INSTITUTE FOR EVIDENCE-BASED
DECISION-MAKING IN EDUCATION, INC.

Library of Congress Catalog Card Number: 98-96603
ISBN: 0-9666588-0-9

First published in 1998

The Institute for Evidence-Based Decision-Making in Education, Inc.
A South Carolina non-profit corporation
P.O. Box 122, Columbia, SC 29202

Printed in the United States of America

The paper used in this book complies with the
Permanent Paper Standard issued by the National
Information Standards Organization (Z39.48–1984).

10 9 8 7 6 5 4 3 2 1

Educational administration, school buildings,
counseling, equipment, busing, and other factors
may be essential to schooling, but
INSTRUCTION
has the greatest and most direct impact
on learning.

Contents

Foreword

It isn't often that scholars take the painstaking time and the enormous effort to bring the results of massive amounts of research to the public. In general, scholars are rewarded for their research prowess, and popular writing is normally discounted heavily in academic circles. Carl Sagan, for example, was roundly criticized for spending so much of his time trying to make astronomy understandable to the millions of non-academics in this world.

So we must give a vote of thanks to Professor Myles Friedman and one of his graduate students, Steven Fisher, of the University of South Carolina College of Education, for devoting their attention to the enormously important task of informing teachers, school administrators, school board members, parents, and legislators of the research available on instructional strategies. It is important to thank also the former Dean of Education at the University of South Carolina, Dr. John E. King, for his vision and insistence that this handbook was badly needed in today's political and confrontational educational environment. For how else can sound educational policy be fostered? It needs to be based upon sound research and empirical evidence. This handbook provides just that.

Sound instructional strategies are not always obvious. Some that sound good sometimes turn out to be flawed, and some that do not appeal to common sense sometimes seem to work quite well.

Because this exciting new handbook is research-based and reviews the work of scores of scholars, it is an important contribution to the field of education and a wonderful resource for anyone interested in teaching and learning. It brings a distillation of too-hard-to-read studies into the hands of teachers, administrators, and policy-makers in an easy-to-read/understand format.

The purpose of this handbook is to present effective instructional strategies that can be incorporated into most instructional programs. Instructional strategies are sometimes adopted without evidence of effectiveness, and too many are based on political agendas, special interest groups, or biases. This handbook makes possible a quick and easy understanding of a wide variety of instructional strategies and the research evidence behind the effectiveness or lack thereof.

The handbook covers three types of instructional strategies: those that have been found to be effective in improving academic achievement, those that show they are promising but are not yet proven, and those that have shown promise in only very specialized or restricted venues and may well not be generally effective even though they may be in common use. For example, strategies such as the matching of student–teacher cognitive styles or ability grouping of students or whole language instruction have not been found to be generally useful in improving student achievement.

Some of the findings appeal to common sense: repetition can be a powerful, successful teaching strategy. Other ideas that many people take for granted, such as rewarding behavior as an instructional strategy, seem to be less effective than commonly thought.

This book is for everyone interested in teaching and learning. Teachers and policy-makers will appreciate the plain-English explanations of what would otherwise be complex and tedious research findings. And researchers will appreciate the additional sections on statistical findings and extensive bibliographies. Industrial and military trainers can benefit from these findings as well, since successful instructional strategies cut across all forms of instruction and audiences.

The authors employ a common format which helps readers more quickly digest the important aspects. For each instructional strategy, the authors present: which students seem to benefit, where learning is enhanced, instructional tactics used, cautions and comments, generalizations that can be drawn, and a description of the supporting research.

In addition to providing access to otherwise hard-to-find research and reducing it to a more readable form, the authors promise to keep the book up to date by publishing periodic revisions which will incorporate new and developing research findings.

Martin B. Solomon, Ph.D.

Acknowledgments

We are deeply indebted to the PSARAS Fund for financing the publication of this handbook. We want to thank Dr. Jesse Coles, Jr. for recognizing the importance of the instructional strategies in the handbook and for his leadership and effort to make them a part of classroom practice. In addition, we want to thank Dr. Sam Griswold and James Konduros for their support and assistance.

We are very grateful to Dr. John King and Dr. Marvin Efron for guiding, nurturing, and investing in the development of the handbook, and to Drs. Lorin Anderson, Jere Brophy, Carolyn Evertson, and Greta Morine-Dershimer for critiquing and improving the first draft. Also, we wish to acknowledge Dr. Teri Kuhs's insight concerning the titles of the instructional strategies. We would like to acknowledge Ron Leslie for his work in developing the Teamwork and Reminders generalizations. We also would like to acknowledge the contribution of Betty Friedman in preparing the manuscript.

User's Guide

BENEFITING FROM THE HANDBOOK

The *Handbook on Effective Instructional Strategies* is unique in many ways, and if used appropriately can have a very beneficial effect on education. In this guide the reader is acquainted with the handbook and how to use it to greatest advantage.

PURPOSE OF THE HANDBOOK

The purpose of the handbook is to present effective instructional strategies that can be incorporated into most instructional programs being planned or presently being used in schools and other educational settings, and to provide evidence of the effectiveness of the instructional strategies in enhancing learning. Evidence is described in plain English. Technical data such as statistical tables and footnotes are presented in a separate chapter for those who are interested and prepared to interpret it. All too often, instructional strategies are adopted without evidence of their effectiveness being considered. Pressure for change tends to accelerate the number of unproven instructional innovations that are adopted. Too many instructional decisions are based on political agendas, special interest group pressures, the biases of educational executives, and commercial sales pitches, ignoring available evidence. The handbook makes it possible to consider instructional strategies that work and to understand the evidence that demonstrates their effectiveness in enhancing learning.

THE IMPORTANCE OF THE HANDBOOK

A handbook that describes effective instructional strategies and shows educators how to use them is sorely needed. First, educators need to focus their efforts on improving instruction because all educational institutions are established to instill desired learning in students, and instruction is the means of producing desired learning. Other educational factors, such as building, administration, facilities, and busing, are less central.

Second, educators need to focus more on adopting and adapting particular instructional strategies that have been proven to work than on adopting entire instructional programs and texts. Sales promotions of publishers and manufacturers of instructional texts and programs urge educators to buy their extensive programs and textbook series, which tends to structure and dominate education in America. Yet there is little if any research evidence that these mega-instructional programs in total are effective in producing desired learning. Rather, when comprehensive programs that do have a desirable effect are analyzed, they have common instructional strategies. And it appears that it is the instructional strategies that are responsible for their effectiveness, rather than the programs as a whole. The evidence indicates that particular instructional strategies enhance learning, and that those instructional programs that enhance learning incorporate them.

The effective instructional strategies described in the handbook can be incorporated into most instructional programs presently in use (or planned) without undue inconvenience. The evidence that supports their adoption should be reviewed and their adoption should be seriously considered. Neither present instructional objectives nor the subject matter students are to learn need to be changed.

WHO BENEFITS FROM THE HANDBOOK

The handbook is written for practitioners and decision-makers rather than researchers. Instructional planners, teachers, and trainers of instructional planners and teachers will benefit directly from the handbook. Instructional planners can incorporate the strategies in the instructional programs they are presently designing and introduce them into existing instructional programs that are under their supervision; teachers can incorporate them in their lesson plans and apply them during teaching to guide their interactions with students; and trainers of instructional planners and teachers can teach them in both pre-service and in-service training. Unfortunately, teachers and instructional planners are frequently persuaded, if not coerced, to adopt instructional programs and ploys that are in vogue without being provided with evidence of their effectiveness. The pressure to improve instruction through innovation results in the introduction of one fad after another. It is time to base instructional decisions on evidence.

The handbook will also be of value to educational administrators and school board members who want to become more familiar with effective instructional strategies. Since the primary goal of education is to enhance learning, and instruction has a direct and primary effect on learning, administrators and school board members need to know more about effective instruction in general.

The ultimate beneficiaries of the handbook are the students themselves, who learn more because of the strategies, and the societies that sponsor education and benefit from more learned, competent citizens. In essence, the evidence provided in the handbook enables educators to make more informed, cogent instructional decisions that will result in increased student achievement.

FEATURES AND FOCUS OF THE HANDBOOK

Effective Rather Than Efficient Strategies

The focus of the handbook is solely on the *effectiveness of instruction* in generating desired learning, rather than on the efficiency of instruction. To be considered an effective strategy, the findings of at least 50 research studies must support its effectiveness in improving academic achievement. The primary aim is to identify instructional strategies that work. After desired learning has been produced, efficiency factors such as time and money can become the focus of inquiry. What good is it to use efficient instructional strategies that don't work? It is not uncommon in research reports to find instructional strategies recommended because they are more efficient, without considering the effectiveness of the strategies. Effective instruction produces desired learning, not efficient instruction. Even if effective instruction is costly at first, its efficiency may be improved over time. Almost all strategies are more costly when they are first introduced and become more efficient to administer with experience over time.

Generalizable Strategies

The primary concern is with instructional strategies that are more generalizable. Instructional strategies are more valuable when they can be applied across more academic disciplines, types of students, and edcuational settings such as military, industrial, higher education, elementary, and secondary institutions as well as to home schooling. Instructional strategies that have been shown to work only in a very limited situation are simply not as useful and cannot be recommended as general practice.

All Methods of Instruction

Teachers, teaching apparatus, and combinations of the two are of interest. Advances in technology are rapidly increasing instructional alternatives. Education needs to be able to profit from what works and adjust traditional instruction accordingly.

For the Practitioner

Many, if not most, research reports are written using symbols that are understood by academicians with a sophisticated knowledge of research. As a result, many practitioners are not able to benefit from the research findings, so researchers and practitioners tend to go their separate ways and valuable research findings all too seldom benefit practice. The handbook is written for practitioners in plain English so they may derive maximum benefit from the research findings. Research findings in a professional field are of little value if they are not translated into an effective practice.

Teaching Rather Than Teachers

The focus is on teaching rather than teachers, because research has failed to establish that teacher characteristics have a direct impact on student achievement. Teacher personality characteristics do not appear to directly affect student achievement (Getzels & Jackson, 1963); nor does teacher knowledge (Shulman, 1986). It appears that teacher characteristics have the most significant impact on student achievement, as they affect teaching. Teaching has a more direct impact on achievement. Similarly, the physical classroom environment does not appear to have a direct impact on student achievement (Loughlin, 1992). However, it may have an indirect impact as it affects teaching. Therefore, the physical instructional environment will be a concern only as it affects teaching.

Evidence-Based Decision-Making

Many decisions made in education are not evidence-based decisions. And this may be a primary cause of educational failures. As indicated, educational decisions are often made because of the bias of administrators or special interest group pressures, a convincing sales pitch, or to meet political agendas. Businesses and industries that do not base their decisions on evidence go bankrupt. Educational institutions that do not base their decisions on evidence continue on and on despite their failures. The decision to recommend the instructional strategies in the handbook is based solely on scientific evidence, which is presented for the reader's consideration.

THE PRESENTATION FORMAT

The following format will be used in presenting each instructional strategy.

Description of Each Instructional Strategy

Title of the Strategy

Introduction. An orientation to the strategy.

Student Beneficiaries. Types of students who have benefited from the strategy and their ages or grade levels are described.

Learning Achieved. The learning or academic achievement enhanced by the instructional strategies in the content areas covered are described.

Instructional Tactics. Tactics used in different studies to apply the strategy are integrated and summarized.

Cautions and Comments. Constraints in applying the strategy are discussed, and comments are made to further clarify the presentation.

Discretion was required in distinguishing among strategies. Lines of demarcation among strategies were not always obvious. Moreover, different researchers tended to define different strategies in different ways. These differences needed to be reconciled in order to derive a parsimonious number of strategies that overlapped as little as possible. Every effort was made to allow evidence rather than personal opinion or logic to influence decision making. However, in the handbook the statistical findings supporting the use of particular tactics are presented in a separate chapter, Chapter 18, so that readers may determine the implications of the evidence for themselves. Hopefully, readers will apprise the Institute of their determinations so that the handbook can be refined in subsequent editions.

GENERALIZATIONS

A generalization is provided highlighting the essence of the strategy. The generalization clarifies the common characteristics of the different tactics that were used in different studies to apply the strategy.

DESCRIPTIONS OF SUPPORTING RESEARCH

Studies are described that provide evidence supporting the use of the strategy. The following format is used to describe the research.

Author(s) of the research.

Students included in the research.

Learning achieved in the research.

Instructional Tactics used in the research. Occasionally, purely research procedures are included under instructional tactics to clarify how instructional tactics were employed in the study.

Findings of the research. Technical findings, such as statistical data, will be presented in Chapter 18 of the handbook.

Research integrating *groups* of studies will be presented first. Then *individual* studies will be presented.

Extensive references follow the presentation of each effective instructional strategy. The references provide access to additional detail and corroboration. Extensive references are provided because the handbook is intended to serve as a reference book as well. When research integrating groups of studies is reported, the individual studies included in the group are cued by symbols so that they can be easily identified in the references.

Instructional tactics are presented in outline form. First, a summary outline of tactics is presented for each strategy. Afterward, the tactics used in each study from which the summary is derived are outlined, and occasionaly include research procedures to clarify how the instructional tactics were employed in the study. This enables instructional planners and teachers to use the outlines as guides in creating their own instructional plans, adapted to their own students and educational setting. Although the strategies are generalizable, their effectiveness can be improved if they are adapted to the particular students and educational milieu where they are being applied by instructional planners and teachers familiar with the characteristics of the students and milieu.

Effective instructional strategies are presented in Parts I and Part II of the handbook. Part II, "The Time Dimension," includes instructional strategies that pertain to beneficial ways of allotting and using time. These strategies are distinctive and can be best understood and used in combination with other strategies if they are presented separately.

PROMISING INSTRUCTIONAL STRATEGIES

In this section, instructional strategies that bear watching are discussed. There is some evidence to suggest that the instructional strategies may be effective, but not sufficient evidence to warrant their adoption as generalizations at this time. Additional research is needed to determine their effectiveness, and should be encouraged and supported. If proven effective, these strategies have the potential to enhance instruction in the future. Readers might wish to pilot test one of the strategies to assess its effectiveness in their locale for their purposes.

QUESTIONABLE INSTRUCTIONAL STRATEGIES

In addition to effective instructional strategies and promising instructional strategies, there are questionable strategies. There is evidence indicating that the questionable strategies are not effective in enhancing learning and/or can have deleterious side effects. Some of these questionable strategies are in common use. In this section, questionable strategies are reviewed and evidence is presented to caution against their use.

Promising and questionable strategies are presented in Part III, "Instructional Alerts."

STATISTICAL FINDINGS

After all of the strategies have been presented, statistical findings that support conclusions pertaining to promising, questionable, and effective instructional strategies described are presented in Chapter 18. Statistical findings are cross-referenced with the particular strategies they pertain to so that they can be readily accessed.

GUIDELINES FOR INSTRUCTIONAL DECISION-MAKING

In this section of the handbook, key instructional decision-making points are identified and the decisions made at each point are discussed. This is done for both instructional planning in preparation for instruction and for the instructional process. In addition, failures in instructional planning and the instructional process are described. This section highlights major components of instruction and their relationship, providing a context for understanding the instructional strategies presented in the book. However, the instructional strategies can be understood in other instructional contexts, provided that they are sufficiently comprehensive and tenable.

GLOSSARY

The glossary defines the key terms used in the handbook for the reader's convenience and to reduce ambiguity.

Guidelines for instructional decision-making and the glossary are presented in Part IV, "Instructional Aids."

The table of contents and indexes provide additional guidance for efficiently using and benefiting from the handbook. Two indexes are provided. One is the usual alphabetical index of the content of the book; the other is an index of the researchers cited in the book.

SUGGESTIONS FOR USING THE HANDBOOK

The handbook is a reference book, and there are many ways in which the information in the handbook can be accessed and utilized, depending on your purpose at a particular time. Hence, there is no standard or right way to use the handbook. However, there is an inherent logic in the way the handbook is organized to enable you to glean information about strategies to the degree or depth required at the time. Consider the following suggestions to see if they might be helpful to you in any way.

Considering Instructional Strategies for Adoption

There are fifteen effective strategies that can be advantageously incorporated into your present instructional program or an instructional program you may be planning. You are probably aware of many of them to a greater or lesser extent. You can become more familiar with all fifteen effective instructional strategies by reading the *Introduction* to each of them at the beginning of the first fifteen chapters. Very little reading is required to acquaint yourself with the entire repertoire of effective instructional strategies in the handbook.

You can learn more about an instructional strategy you might wish to adopt by reading a very few pages further at the beginning of a chapter. You will learn about (1) students who have benefited from the strategy under the heading *Student Beneficiaries*, (2) the subject areas in which the strategy was used effectively under the heading *Learning Achieved*, (3) tactics that are used to implement the strategy in brief summary form under the heading *Instructional Tactics*, and (4) limitations and nuances that should be considered when employing the strategy, which are discussed under the heading *Cautions and Comments*. All of the above are presented in approximately two to four pages at the beginning of each chapter.

Should you wish to probe further into the implementation of an instructional strategy, you can continue on in a chapter and read about the various studies conducted to demonstrate the effectiveness of the instructional strategy. Those studies are summarized in easy-to-understand language, devoid of statistics.

Should you wish to learn more about a particular effective instructional strategy, a detailed reference list is provided at the end of each chapter. The reference list includes all of the studies that could be found pertaining to an instructional strategy.

Those interested in inspecting the statistical evidence that supports the effectiveness of an instructional strategy can find the evidence in Chapter 18, "Statistical Findings." The page number where statistical evidence can be found for each effective strategy is given in the table of contents for Chapter 18. An effort was made to make the statistical tables clear and understandable. However, if you have not studied statistics, anyone familiar with statistics can interpret the findings for you.

In considering the fifteen instructional strategies for adoption, it is well to understand that they are not totally independent of each other. There is some overlap among them, and they are used for different purposes. For example, some strategies facilitate rapid recall; others facilitate rather slow, methodical deliberation. Some pertain to the presentation of information to students; others pertain to knowledge and skills that are to be taught to students. Many of the strategies can be used advantageously in combination. For instance, strategies listed in the table of contents for Part II, "The Time Dimension," pertain to the effective allocation and utilization of time. These strategies can be combined with many other strategies that deal with instructional issues other than time.

Keep in mind that the effective instructional strategies described in the handbook were derived inductively from research findings. They were not conceptualized as discrete parts of a logical system of instructional strategies. The research evidence shows that each of the strategies works. It is up to educators to determine how the strategies might best be utilized for their purposes in their educational setting.

Considering Questionable Instructional Strategies

You can quickly identify questionable instructional strategies by reading their names listed in the table of contents for Chapter 17. Reading the introductions to them in Chapter 17 will further acquaint you with the questionable strategies.

If you are presently using or planning to use any of the questionable strategies, you should read the entire description of the strategies and the evidence that challenges their use. You should then reconsider using them. Not all of the questionable strategies described are ineffective under all conditions for all purposes. You need to reconsider using them for your purpose.

Considering Promising Instructional Strategies

The promising strategies described in the handbook are included because they are distinct from and complementary to the fifteen effective instructional strategies reviewed in the first fifteen chapters. Although there is evidence indicating that they are effective, the evidence is insufficient. Their effectiveness needs to be further tested before considering them for adoption. You might want to read about *The Control Motive* in Chapter 16 if you are interested in pilot testing a strategy to enlist student motivation to enhance learning. You might want to read about *Predictive Ability Instruction* if you are interested in pilot testing a generic problem-solving strategy that students can learn to increase their ability to solve most problems that confront them in school and in their daily lives.

Following the preceding suggestions enables you to avail yourself of most of the benefits that can be gleaned from the book. Should you need to clarify the meaning of key terms used in the book as you consider the suggestions, consult the glossary.

The handbook, however, has more to offer in Chapter 19, "Guidelines for Making Instructional Decisions." In this chapter a simple rendition of the instructional process is derived, within which major instructional decision-making points are identified. The rendition of the instructional process provides a context for relating instructional strategies to the instructional process and for defining key terms that are used consistently in discussions of the different strategies. You might find the renditions useful and clarifying if you have not already subscribed to one of the many renditions of instruction that have been promulgated over the years. However, it is well to remember that the effective instructional strategies in the handbook are empirically derived and validated and can be understood in the context of any rendition of the instructional process that is congruent with scientific evidence. You will need to determine the extent to which the rendition in the handbook is helpful to you.

Identifying major decision-making points within our rendition of the instructional process provides a basis for specifying guidelines for instructional decision-making. The guidelines enable you to consider and utilize the fifteen effective instructional strategies described in the book to make evidence-based instructional decisions. The strategies need to be considered in instructional decision-making if they are to benefit instructional practice and, therefore, student learning.

Next, instructional failures are systematically reviewed in the context of the decision-making process, highlighting possible breakdowns in the process that can result from inept decision-making. Finally, a summary of both the instructional decision-making points and the fifteen instructional strategies is presented, specifying the decision-making points at which a strategy should be considered.

Keep in mind that this is a resource and reference book designed to help you make more effective instructional decisions, however you may decide to tap and utilize its resources.

In conclusion, the effective instructional strategies described in the handbook are generalizable in that they are generalizable (1) across many research studies, that is, from 50 to over 200 research studies support the effectiveness of each strategy in enhancing learning; (2) across many content areas, that is, they have been effectively applied in a variety of academic disciplines; (3) across students of varying ages in various educational settings. For these reasons, teachers, teacher educators, instructional planners, and educational administrators should consider incorporating them in instructional programs presently in use or being planned. When adapted to local conditions they may well increase student achievement, although all of them may not be suitable for a particular educational setting. The presentation of each effective instructional strategy includes a description of the number of research studies that support the effectiveness of the strategy, the content areas in which the strategy was shown to be effective, and the types of students that have benefited from each strategy. This information enables teachers, instructional planners, teacher educators, and administrators to ascertain the suitability of a particular strategy for their purposes in their educational setting.

Although the effective instructional strategies to be described can be expected to enhance student achievement under many educational conditions, they should not be regarded as a panacea. The generalizations derived for each strategy have not been proven to be as invariant as the universal laws found in physical sciences such as physics: for example, Boyle's Law and Charles's Law. Such laws may be more than we can expect to achieve in education, at least at this time. Nevertheless, the effective strategies described are generalizable, and the extent of their generalizability is discussed. They can be expected to enhance student achievement in a variety of circumstances, as specified. There is little doubt that teachers, teacher educators, instructional planners, and educational administrators can make more informed and effective instructional decisions if they take the strategies into account in their decision-making.

REFERENCE LIST

Getzels, J. W., & Jackson, P. W. (1963). The teacher's personality and characteristics. In N. L. Gage (Ed.), *Handbook of research on teaching* (pp. 506–582). Chicago: Rand McNally.

Loughlin, C. E. (1992). Classroom physical environments. In M. C. Alkin (Ed.), *Encyclopedia of educational research* (6th ed.) (pp. 161–164), vol. 1. New York: Macmillan.

Shulman, L. S. (1986). Paradigms and research programs in the study of teaching: A contemporary perspective. In M. C. Wittrock (Ed.), *Handbook of research on teaching* (3rd ed.) (pp. 1–36). New York: Macmillan.

Effective
Instructional Strategies

Part I of the handbook consists of descriptions of twelve instructional strategies that can be incorporated into existing instructional programs and instructional programs being planned to enhance learning. Four of the strategies pertain to teaching skills to students that will enhance their learning and adaptation. Chapter 8, "Providing Reminders Instruction," teaches students how to create and use memory joggers to increase their recall of information they are assigned to learn; Chapter 10, "Providing Transfer of Learning Instruction," teaches students how to more effectively transfer and use information they have already learned in new situations to solve novel problems that may confront them; Chapter 12, "Providing Decision-Making Instruction," teaches students how to make more effective decisions by means of reflective thought and deliberation; and Chapter 11, "Providing Teamwork Instruction," teaches students how to participate in groups to improve group achievement. Although success in civilized societies depends in large measure on people's ability to cooperate with others to achieve group goals, teamwork is not often taught as a part of the academic curriculum.

The other eight instructional strategies described in Part I cover a variety of strategies that educators can use to increase learning. "Taking Student Readiness into Account" (Chapter 1) is important in planning instruction, evaluating student performance, assigning tasks to students, and in teaching, or instruction cannot possibly be effective. "Defining Instructional Expectations" (Chapter 2) involves educators in defining and clarifying educational objectives and the means of achieving them prior to instruction so that students know what they are expected to achieve and how they are expected to achieve it at the outset to facilitate learning. "Providing Effective Evaluation and Remediation" (Chapter 3) must be used judiciously in tandem if learning is to be enhanced. Evaluation is the means of acquiring information needed to prescribe effective remediation. "Providing Contiguity" (Chapter 4) must be considered in instruction to enhance learning. Much of learning involves association, and association is facilitated when the events to be associated are perceived close together in time and space, that is, contiguously. "Utilizing Repetition

Effectively" (Chapter 5), like contiguity, has long been recognized as fundamental to learning. Educators must repeat to-be-learned information strategically to facilitate its assimilation, and students must repeat to-be-learned skills to perfect them. "Clarifying Communication" (Chapter 6) too has long been known to enhance learning. Educators need to know tactics they can apply to clarify their communication. "Reducing Student/Teacher Ratio" (Chapter 7) also affects learning. Educators need to know more about how student/teacher ratio can be adjusted to improve learning. Finally, educators need to know how "Providing Subject Matter Unifiers" (Chapter 9) in their instruction can increase academic achievement. They also need to know how to teach students to use unifiers on their own.

The above twelve strategies by no means exhaust the instructional strategies that can be used to enhance learning. Three additional effective instructional strategies are presented in Part II, "The Time Dimension." And as the continuing review of research reveals additional effective instructional strategies, they will be presented in future editions of the handbook.

FORMAT

The presentation of effective instructional strategies to be described in Parts I and II will adhere to the following format.

Introduction

The purpose of the introduction is to introduce and orient readers to the instructional strategy being described.

Student Beneficiaries

No instructional strategy can be proven to enhance the learning of all students without exception. In this section, students whom research shows have benefited from the strategy are described. And only strategies that have been shown to be broadly generalizable across students are included in the handbook. The various characteristics of the students are described: for example, grade level, age, and type of educational setting. This enables readers to determine the extent to which a strategy is applicable to students of interest to them.

Learning Achieved

Here the subject areas in which the strategy has been shown to be effective are described: for instance, math, science, social studies, language arts, and more specific designations. This enables readers to determine the extent to which a strategy has been shown to be effective in subject areas of interest to them. Only instructional strategies research has shown to be effective in a wide variety of subject areas are included in the handbook.

INSTRUCTIONAL TACTICS

In this section, the tactics that research shows have been effective are highlighted in summary form. The summary is extracted from various research studies that include tactics that have been shown to enhance learning. Not all of the tactics in the summary are extracted from a single research study. Tactics are presented in summary form so that readers can become familiar with the tactics essential to the strategy. This enables them to adapt the strategy to the setting and students of interest to them.

CAUTIONS AND COMMENTS

Here limitations pertaining to a particular strategy are brought to readers' attention so that they may better assess the applicability of the strategy. In addition, comments pertaining to theory may be made, and on occasion a personal opinion may be offered.

GENERALIZATION

Here an attempt is made to encapsulate the strategy in a concise generalization to capture the essence of the strategy. The generalizations are subject to revision based on subsequent research findings. At present it is helpful to establish a list of generalizations that describe what research has shown to be effective instructional strategies for enhancing learning. As we clarify and add to them it should be possible to make instruction more effective.

SUPPORTIVE RESEARCH

In this section, research studies are reported that provide evidence of the effectiveness of the strategy in enhancing academic achievement. Some of the studies are a synthesis of a group or groups of studies that support the effectiveness of an instructional strategy. These are presented first. Then individual studies that support the effectiveness of the instructional strategy are described.

The following information is presented for each study: (1) author, (2) students in the study, (3) learning that was achieved, (4) relevant instructional tactics that were employed, and (5) findings of the study. In the description of the instructional tactics, readers can see some of the tactics that were used in the summary of instructional tactics described earlier. In addition, readers may derive information that will clarify the strategy and enable them to elaborate and adapt the strategy to particular students in particular educational settings of interest to them.

The findings are written in easy-to-understand language that readers can readily interpret. Those interested in statistical evidence that supports the findings can find it in Chapter 18. The appropriate page number is designated in the table of contents.

Supportive research varies in the kind and the extent to which it demonstrates the effectiveness of a strategy in enhancing learning. In some cases a number of individual studies designed to test the effectiveness of a strategy support its effectiveness. In other cases a synthesis is achieved logically, sometimes statistically. In some instances a number of complex instructional programs shown to be effective in enhancing learning are cited to support the effectiveness of a particular strategy. Although each program may include more than one strategy, they all feature the particular strategy being described. Hopefully, studies will be designed in the future to test more directly the effectiveness of the particular strategy. Studies supporting the effectiveness of a strategy range in number from 50 to over 200 studies.

REFERENCE LIST

An extensive reference list is provided, covering the studies that are cited in the text. For studies that synthesize a group of individual studies pertaining to a particular instructional strategy, references are provided for both the individual studies and the synthesis as well. The references enable readers to obtain additional detail and corroboration.

Although there may be overlap between instructional strategies, for the most part the strategies are distinct. They can be incorporated in existing instructional programs or programs being planned, individually or in combination, to enhance learning.

Taking Student Readiness into Account

INTRODUCTION

Readiness is defined as student knowledge, skills, and dispositions necessary to perform a task. To achieve learning objectives, readiness characteristics of students must be taken into account while planning instruction. In planning tasks, entry-level tasks should be designed for students with particular readiness capabilities, and succeeding tasks in a sequence leading to the achievement of the learning objective should be designed so that mastery of preceding tasks in the sequence provides students with the readiness capabilities necessary to perform subsequent tasks. Readiness characteristics of students must enable students to perform the assigned tasks. In addition, readiness characteristics must be taken into account when teaching. Teaching should continue until students have mastered the performance of an assigned task and are ready to perform the next task in a sequence. Finally, in the evaluation process, evaluation instruments must be designed to indicate the readiness level of students so the appropriate task assignments can be made.

STUDENT BENEFICIARIES

The evidence indicates that taking into consideration student readiness when planning, teaching, assigning, and evaluating performance of tasks enhances the academic achievement of students in kindergarten, elementary, secondary, college, and adult learning classrooms. Moreover, academic achievement was improved in a wide range of content areas. No evidence could be found to suggest that student readiness should not be stressed in all subject areas for all types of students.

LEARNING ACHIEVED

Achievement in the content areas of mathematics, history, foreign languages, English, reading, social sciences, sciences, social studies, business, and occupational areas is enhanced when student readiness is taken into consideration in the planning, teaching, assigning, and evaluating performance of tasks. In studies reviewed, student readiness was positively related to student achievement.

INSTRUCTIONAL TACTICS

The evidence well supports the need to consider student readiness when planning, teaching, assigning, and evaluating performance of tasks. The following tactics are derived from studies that demonstrate the benefits of considering student readiness when planning, teaching, assigning, and evaluating performance of tasks. Discretion has been used to interpret and reduce overlap in tactics used in different studies and to elaborate tactics.

Tactics employed are:

Planning: Tasks leading to the achievement of a learning objective should be sequenced so that earlier tasks in the sequence provide students with the skills and knowledge they need to perform subsequent tasks. The number of tasks planned in a sequence should be based on the difficulty level of the learning objective to be achieved. A greater number of tasks should be planned to achieve a more difficult learning objective.

Evaluation: Accurately evaluating the students' current knowledge and skills should be a basis for assigning tasks to students.

Assigning Tasks: In assigning tasks, the knowledge and skills of the students must be sufficient to meet the demands of the tasks.

Teaching: A mastery level of performance should be attained for each task so that students who learn to perform a task are ready to perform the next task in the sequence.

Elaborations of the above summary of tactics can be obtained from reading the studies that are to follow. To be most effective, the instructional tactics need to be integrated into the particular instructional program being planned or presently in use.

CAUTIONS AND COMMENTS

The preeminence of readiness in determining student success in achieving learning objectives cannot be overemphasized. Students who do not have the knowledge and skills necessary to perform the tasks that enable the achievement of a learning objective are not likely to achieve the objective, even if other effective strategies are employed in teaching the students. With respect to group instruction, it would be helpful to find out the extent to which heterogeneity of readiness impairs group achievement, instructional planning, and teaching.

GENERALIZATION: ON STUDENT READINESS

Achievement of learning objectives is enhanced when students possess the readiness capabilities necessary to achieve the learning objectives.

Supportive Research on Student Readiness
Total number of studies covered: 171

Groups of Studies

Author: Anderson (1994): Synthesis of seven meta-analyses

Students: Kindergarten, elementary, secondary, college, and other adult students

Learning: Achievement

Instructional Tactics: The following tactics associated with readiness and Mastery Learning are also presented in Bloom (1985), Block (1980), and others. Other tactics associated with Mastery Learning are applicable to other generalizations and are covered in the appropriate chapters.

- Accurate diagnosis of the students' current level of knowledge in relation to that required for the material to be learned.
- Division of the material to be learned into units with each unit providing prerequisite skills for subsequent units.
- Determine a mastery level the student must achieve prior to moving on to the next unit.

Findings: Positive achievement gains associated with Mastery Learning were seen in 64–93 percent of the studies reviewed in the seven meta-analyses.

Individual studies analyzed by these meta-analyses are identified in the reference list by the following symbols:

Kulik et al. (1990a) *

Kulik et al. (1990b) #

Slavin (1990) @

Guskey & Pigott (1988) $

Guskey & Gates (1985) &

Block & Burns (1976) +

It was not possible to determine the individual studies for which readiness was an instructional tactic for the Willett et al. (1983) analysis.

Author: Rosenshine & Stevens (1986)

Students: Elementary and secondary

Learning: Mathematics, English, science, history, and reading achievement

Instructional Tactics:

- Begin a lesson with a short review of previous, prerequisite learning.
- Skills are taught in a step-by-step manner, with skills learned in one step being applicable to the learning of skills in a subsequent step or steps.

Other instructional tactics are employed in these studies that are applicable to other generalizations and will be presented in the appropriate chapters.

Findings: These tactics were found to be related to greater achievement.

Groups of studies reviewed in this logical synthesis of research did not provide statistical evidence. However, many of the individual studies included in the logical synthesis of research do contain statistical evidence. In the event that a reader wishes to view this evidence, an extensive listing of the individual studies reviewed is provided in the reference list at the end of the chapter (the studies are identified by the symbol %).

Individual Studies

Author: Obando & Hymel (1991)

Students: Grade 9

Learning: Spanish language achievement

Instructional Tactics:

- Accurate diagnosis of the students' current level of knowledge in relation to that required for the material to be learned.
- Division of the material to be learned into units with each unit providing prerequisite skills for subsequent units.
- Determine a mastery level the student must achieve prior to moving on to the next unit.

Other instructional tactics are employed in this study that are applicable to other generalizations and will be presented in the appropriate chapters.

Findings: Achievement was significantly higher for students who benefited from these tactics on unit exams and the National Spanish Examination as compared to students who did not.

REFERENCE LIST

*+Abraham, F. J., & Newton, J. M. (1974). *The interview technique as a personalized system of instruction for economics: The Oregon experience.* Paper presented at the National Conference on Personalized Instruction in Higher Education, Washington, DC.

$Anania, J. (1981). *The effects of quality of instruction on the cognitive and affective learning of students.* Unpublished doctoral dissertation, University of Chicago.

%Anderson, L. M., Evertson, C. M., & Brophy, J. E. (1979). An experimental study of effective teaching in first-grade reading groups. *The Elementary School Journal 79,* 193–222.

%Anderson, L. M., Evertson, C. M., & Brophy, J. E. (1982). *Principles of small group instruction* (Occasional paper no. 32). East Lansing: Michigan State University, Institute for Research on Teaching.

+Anderson, L. W. (1973). *Time and school learning.* Unpublished doctoral dissertation, University of Chicago.

*$&Anderson, L. W. (1975a). Student involvement in learning and school achievement. *California Journal of Educational Research 26,* 53–62.

$&Anderson, L. W. (1975b). *Time to criterion: An experimental study.* Paper presented at the annual meeting of the American Educational Research Association, Washington, DC. (ERIC Document Reproduction Service No. ED 108 006)

*$&+Anderson, L. W. (1976). An empirical investigation of individual differences in time to learn. *Journal of Educational Psychology 68,* 226–233.

*#@$&Anderson, L. W., Scott, C., & Hutlock, N. (1976, April). *The effects of a mastery learning program on selected cognitive, affective, and ecological variables in grades 1 through 6.* Paper presented at the annual meeting of the American Educational Research Association, San Francisco.

+Anderson, O. T., & Artman, R. A. (1972). A self-paced independent study, introductory physics sequence-description and evaluation. *American Journal of Physics 40,* 1737–1742.

Anderson, S. A. (1994). *Synthesis of research on mastery learning* (Information Analysis). (ERIC Document Reproduction Service No. ED 382 567)

*$&%Arlin, M., & Webster, J. (1983). Time costs of mastery learning. *Journal of Educational Psychology 75,* 187–195.

*Austin, S. M., & Gilbert, K. E. (1973). Student performance in a Keller-Plan course in introductory electricity and magnetism. *American Journal of Physics 41,* 12–18.

*Badia, P., Stutts, C., & Harsh, J. (1978). Do methods of instruction and measures of different abilities and study habits interact? In J. G. Sherman, R. S. Ruskin, & R. M. Lazar (Eds.), *Personalized instruction in education today* (pp. 113–128). San Francisco: San Francisco Press.

%Becker, W. C. (1977). Teaching reading and language to the disadvantaged—What we have learned from field research. *Harvard Educational Review 47,* 518–543.

*Benson, J. S., & Yeany, R. H. (1980, April). *Generalizability of diagnostic-prescriptive teaching strategies across student locus of control and multiple instructional units.* Paper presented at the annual meeting of the American Educational Research Association, Boston. (ERIC Document Reproduction Service No. 187 534)

*+Billings, D. B. (1974). PSI versus the lecture course in the principles of economics: A quasi-controlled experiment. In R. S. Ruskin & S. F. Bono (Eds.), *Personalized*

instruction in higher education (pp. 30–37). Washington, DC: Center for Personalized Instruction.

*$Blackburn, K. T., & Nelson, D. (1985, April). *Differences between a group using a traditional format with mastery learning and a group using a traditional format only in developmental mathematics courses at the university level: Implications for teacher education programs.* Paper presented at the annual meeting of the American Educational Research Association, Chicago. (ERIC Document Reproduction Service No. ED 258 948)

*Blasingame, J. W. (1975). Student attitude and performance in a personalized system of instruction course in business administration—Correlates performance with personality traits. *Dissertation Abstracts International 36*, 3840. (University Microfilms No. 75-2834)

$&+Block, J. H. (1972). Student learning and the setting of mastery performance standards. *Educational Horizons 50*, 183–191.

+Block, J. H. (1973). *Mastery performance standards and student learning.* Unpublished study, University of California, Santa Barbara.

Block, J. H. (1980). Success rate. In C. Denham & A. Lieberman (Eds.), *Time to learn* (pp. 95–106). Washington, DC: U.S. Government Printing Office.

Block, J. H., & Burns, R. B. (1976). Mastery learning. In L. Schulman (Ed.), *Review of research in education* (Vol. 4, pp. 3–49). Itasca, IL: F. E. Peacock.

$+Block, J. H., & Tierney, M. (1974). An exploration of two correction procedures used in mastery learning approaches to instruction. *Journal of Educational Psychology 66*, 962–967.

Bloom, B. S. (1985). Learning for mastery. In C. W. Fisher & D. C. Berliner (Eds.), *Perspectives on instructional time.* White Plains, NY: Longman.

*+Born, D. G., & Davis, M. L. (1974). Amount and distribution of study in a personalized instruction course and in a lecture course. *Journal of Applied Behavior Analysis 7*, 365–375.

*+Born, D. G., Gledhill, S. M., & Davis, M. L. (1972). Examination performance in lecture-discussion and personalized instruction courses. *Journal of Applied Behavior Analysis 5*, 33–43.

*+Breland, N. S., & Smith, M. P. (1974). A comparison of PSI and traditional methods of instruction for teaching introduction to psychology. In R. S. Ruskin & S. F. Bono (Eds.), *Personalized instruction in higher education* (pp. 21–25). Washington, DC: Center for Personalized Instruction.

*$Bryant, N. D., Fayne, H. R., & Gettinger, M. (1982). Applying the mastery model to sight word instruction for disabled readers. *Journal of Experimental Education 50*, 116–121.

$Burke, A. (1983). *Students' potential for learning contrasted under tutorial and group approaches to instruction.* Unpublished doctoral dissertation, University of Chicago.

$&+Burrows, C. K., & Okey, J. R. (1975, March–April). *The effects of a mastery learning strategy on achievement.* Paper presented at the annual meeting of the American Educational Research Association, Washington, DC.

*#@$Cabezon, E. (1984). *The effects of marked changes in student achievement pattern on the students, their teachers, and their parents: The Chilean case.* Unpublished doctoral dissertation, University of Chicago.

$Chiappetta, E. L., & McBride, J. W. (1980). Exploring the effects of general remediation on ninth-graders' achievement of the mole concept. *Science Education 6*, 609–614.

*$Clark, C. P., Guskey, T. P., & Benninga, J. S. (1983). The effectiveness of mastery learning

strategies in undergraduate education courses. *Journal of Educational Research 76*, 210–214.

*Clark, S. G. (1975). An innovation for introductory sociology: Personalized system of instruction. In J. M. Johnston (Ed.), *Behavior research and technology in higher education* (pp. 117–124). Springfield, IL: Charles C. Thomas.

*+Coldeway, D. O., Santowski, M., O'Brien, R., & Lagowski, V. (1975). Comparison of small group contingency management with the personalized system of instruction and the lecture system. In J. M. Johnston (Ed.), *Research and technology in college and university teaching* (pp. 215–224). Gainesville: University of Florida.

*+Cole, C., Martin, S., & Vincent, J. (1975). A comparison of two teaching formats at the college level. In J. M. Johnston (Ed.), *Behavior research and technology in higher education* (pp. 61–74). Springfield, IL: Charles C. Thomas.

*Condo, P. (1974, April). *The analysis and evaluation of a self-paced course in calculus.* Paper presented at the National Conference on Personalized Instruction in Higher Education, Washington, DC.

*+Cooper, J. L., & Greiner, J. M. (1971). Contingency management in an introductory psychology course produces better retention. *Psychological Record 21*, 391–400.

*Corey, J. R., & McMichael, J. S. (1974). Retention in a PSI introductory psychology course. In J. G. Sherman (Ed.), *PSI germinal papers* (pp. 17–19). Washington, DC: Center for Personalized Instruction.

+Corey, J. R., McMichael, J. S., & Tremont, P. J. (1970, April). *Long-term effects of personalized instruction in an introductory psychology course.* Paper presented at the meeting of the Eastern Psychology Association, Atlantic City.

*Cote, J. D. (1976). Biology by PSI in a community college. In B. A. Green, Jr. (Ed.), *Personalized instruction in higher education.* Washington, DC: Center for Personalized Instruction.

*Cross, M. Z., & Semb, G. (1976). An analysis of the effects of personalized instruction on students at different initial performance levels in an introductory college nutrition course. *Journal of Personalized Instruction 1*, 47–50.

*Decker, D. F. (1976). *Teaching to achieve learning mastery by using retesting techniques.* (ERIC Document Reproduction Service No. ED 133 002)

$Denton, W. L., Ory, J. C., Glassnap, D. R., & Poggio, J. P. (1976). *Grade expectations within a mastery learning strategy.* Paper presented at the annual meeting of the American Educational Research Association, San Francisco. (ERIC Document Reproduction Service No. ED 126 105)

*$Dillashaw, F. G., & Okey, J. R. (1983). Effects of a modified mastery learning strategy on achievement, attitudes, and on-task behavior of high school chemistry students. *Journal of Research in Science Teaching 20*, 203–211.

$Duby, P. B. (1981). *Attributions and attribution change: Effects of a mastery learning instructional approach.* Paper presented at the annual meeting of the American Educational Research Association, Los Angeles. (ERIC Document Reproduction Service No. ED 200 640)

%Emmer, E. T., Evertson, C., Sanford, J., & Clements, B. (1982). *Improving classroom management: An experimental study in junior high classrooms.* Austin: Research and Development Center for Teacher Education, University of Texas.

%Evertson, C. M., Emmer, E. T., Sanford, J. P., & Clements, B. S. (1983). Improving classroom management: An experiment in elementary classrooms. *Elementary School Journal 84*, 173–188.

*#@Fagan, J. S. (1976). Mastery learning: The relationship of mastery procedures and

aptitude to the achievement and retention of transportation-environment concepts by seventh grade students. *Dissertation Abstracts International 36*, 5981. (University Microfilms No. 76-6402)

*Fehlen, J. E. (1976). Mastery learning techniques in the traditional classroom setting. *School Science and Mathematics 76*, 241–245.

*Fernald, P. S., & DuNann, D. H. (1975). Effects of individualized instruction upon low- and high-achieving students' study behavior and students' evaluation of mastery. *Journal of Experimental Education 43*, 27–34.

$&+Fiel, R. L., & Okey, J. R. (1974). The effects of formative evaluation and remediation on mastery of intellectual skill. *Journal of Educational Research 68*, 253–255.

%Fisher, C. W., Berliner, D. C., Filby, N. N., Marliave, R., Cahen, L. S., & Dishaw, M. M. (1980). Teaching behaviors, academic learning time, and student achievement: An overview. In C. Denham & A. Lieberman (Eds.), *Time to learn* (pp. 7–32). Washington, DC: U.S. Government Printing Office.

%Fitzpatrick, K. A. (1981). *An investigation of secondary classroom material strategies for increasing student academic engaged time.* Doctoral dissertation, University of Illinois at Urbana–Champaign.

%Fitzpatrick, K. A. (1982). *The effect of a secondary classroom management training program on teacher and student behavior.* Paper presented at the annual meeting of the American Educational Research Association, New York.

$&Fitzpatrick, K. A. (1985, April). *Group-based mastery learning: A Robin Hood approach to instruction?* Paper presented at the annual meeting of the American Educational Research Association, Chicago.

+Glassnapp, D. R., Poggio, J. P., & Ory, J. C. (1975, March–April). *Cognitive and affective consequences of mastery and non-mastery instructional strategies.* Paper presented at the annual meeting of the American Educational Research Association, Washington, DC.

*Goldwater, B. C., & Acker, L. E. (1975). Instructor-paced, mass-testing for mastery performance in an introductory psychology course. *Teaching of Psychology 2*, 152–155.

%Good, T. L., & Grouws, D. A. (1979). The Missouri mathematics effectiveness project. *Journal of Educational Psychology 71*, 355–362.

*Gregory, I., Smeltzer, D. J., Knopp, W., & Gardner, M. (1976). *Teaching of psychiatry by PSI: Impact on National Board Examination scores.* Unpublished manuscript, Ohio State University, Columbus.

*$&Guskey, T. R. (1982). The effects of staff development on teachers' perceptions about effective teaching. *Journal of Educational Research 76*, 378–381.

*$&Guskey, T. R. (1984). The influence of changes in instructional effectiveness upon the affective characteristics of teachers. *American Educational Research Journal 21*, 245–259.

$Guskey, T. R. (1985). The effects of staff development on teachers' perceptions about effective teaching. *Journal of Educational Research 79*, 378–381.

*$Guskey, T. R., Benninga, J. S., & Clark, C. B. (1984). Mastery learning and students' attributions at the college level. *Research in Higher Education 20*, 491–498.

Guskey, T. R., & Gates, S. L. (1986). Synthesis of research on the effects of mastery learning in elementary and secondary classrooms. *Educational Leadership 33*(8), 73–80.

*$Guskey, T. R., & Monsaas, J. A. (1979). Mastery learning: A model for academic success in urban junior colleges. *Research in Higher Education 11*, 263–274.

Guskey, T. R., & Pigott, T. D. (1988). Research on group-based mastery learning programs: A meta-analysis. *Journal of Educational Research 81*(4), 197–216.

*Hardin, L. D. (1977). A study of the influence of a physics personalized system of instruction versus lecture on cognitive reasoning, achievement, attitudes and critical thinking. *Dissertation Abstracts International 38*, 4711A–4712A. (University Microfilms No. 77-30826)

*Hecht, L. W. (1980, April). *Stalking mastery learning in its natural habitat.* Paper presented at the annual meeting of the American Educational Research Association, Boston.

*Heffley, P. D. (1974). The implementation of the personalized system of instruction in the freshman chemistry course at Censius College. In R. S. Ruskin & S. F. Bono (Eds.), *Personalized instruction in higher education* (pp. 140–145). Washington, DC: Center for Personalized Instruction.

*Herring, B. G. (1975, December). *Cataloguing and classification.* Austin: University of Texas.

*Herring, B. G. (1977). *The written PSI study guide in a non-PSI course.* Austin: University of Texas.

*Herrmann, T. (1984, August). *TELIDON as an enhancer of student interest and performance.* Paper presented at the annual meeting of the American Psychological Association, Toronto. (ERIC Document Reproduction Service No. ED 251 004)

*Hindman, C. D. (1974). Evaluation of three programming techniques in introductory psychology courses. In R. S. Ruskin & S. F. Bono (Eds.), *Personalized instruction in higher education* (pp. 38–42). Washington, DC: Center for Personalized Instruction.

*Honeycutt, J. K. (1974, April). *The effect of computer managed instruction on content learning of undergraduate students.* Paper presented at the annual meeting of the American Educational Research Association, Chicago. (ERIC Document Reproduction Service No. ED 089 682)

*Hymel, G. M. (1974). *An investigation of John B. Carrol's model of school learning as a theoretical basis for the organizational structuring of schools* (Final Report, NIE Project No. 3-1359). University of New Orleans, New Orleans, LA.

*Hymel, G. M., & Mathews, G. (1980). Effects of a mastery approach on social studies achievement and unit evaluation. *Southern Journal of Educational Research 14*, 191–204.

*Jackman, L. E. (1982). Evaluation of a modified Keller method in a biochemistry laboratory course. *Journal of Chemical Education 59*, 225–227.

*Jacko, E. J. (1974). Lecture instruction versus a personalized system of instruction: Effects on individuals with differing achievement anxiety and academic achievement. *Dissertation Abstracts International 35*, 3521. (University Microfilms No. AAD 74-27211)

+Johnston, J. M., & Pennypacker, H. S. (1971). A behavioral approach to college teaching. *American Psychologist 26*, 219–244.

*#@$&Jones, B. F., Monsaas, J. A., & Katims, M. (1979, April). *Improving reading comprehension: Embedding diverse learning strategies within a mastery learning instructional framework.* Paper presented at the annual meeting of the American Educational Research Association, San Francisco. (ERIC Document Reproduction Service No. ED 170 698)

+Jones, F. G. (1974). *The effects of mastery and aptitude on learning, retention, and time.* Unpublished doctoral dissertation, University of Georgia.

$+Jones, E. L., Gordon, H. A., & Stectman, G. L. (1975). *Mastery learning: A strategy for academic success in a community college.* Los Angeles: ERIC Clearinghouse for Junior Colleges. (ERIC Document Reproduction Service No. ED 115 315)

+Karlin, B. M. (1972). *The Keller method of instruction compared to the traditional method of instruction in a Lafayette College history course.* Unpublished paper, Lafayette College, Lafayette, PA.

*#@Katims, M., Smith, J. K., Steele, C., & Wick, J. W. (1977, April). *The Chicago mastery learning reading program: An interim evaluation.* Paper presented at the annual meeting of the American Educational Research Association, New York. (ERIC Document Reproduction Service No. ED 137 737)

*#@Kersh, M. E. (1970). *A strategy of mastery learning in fifth grade arithmetic.* Unpublished doctoral dissertation, University of Chicago.

+Kim, Y., Cho, G., Park, J., & Park, M. (1974). *An application of a new instructional model* (Research Report No. 8). Seoul, Korea: Korean Educational Development Institute.

*Knight, J. M., Williams, J. D., & Jardon, M. L. (1975). The effects of contingency avoidance on programmed student achievement. *Research in Higher Education 3,* 11–17.

*Kulik, C., & Kulik, J. (1976). PSI and the mastery model. In B. A. Green, Jr. (Ed.), *Personalized instruction in higher education* (pp. 155–159). Washington, DC: Center for Personalized Instruction.

Kulik, C., Kulik, J., & Bangert-Drowns, R. (1990a). Effectiveness of mastery learning programs: A meta-analysis. *Review of Educational Research 60*(2), 265–269.

Kulik, J., Kulik, C., & Bangert-Drowns, R. (1990b). Is there better evidence on mastery learning? A response to Slavin. *Review of Educational Research 60*(2), 303–307.

+Kulik, J. A., Kulik, C., & Carmichael, K. (1974). The Keller Plan in science teaching. *Science 183,* 379–383.

+Lee, Y. D., Kim, C. S., Kim, H., Park, B. Y., Yoo, H. K., Chang, S. M., & Kim, S. C. (1971). *Interaction improvement studies of the Mastery Learning Project* (Final Report on the Mastery Learning Project, April–November 1971). Seoul, Korea: Educational Research Center, Seoul National University.

*Leppmann, P. K., & Herrman, T. F. (1981, August). *PSI—What are the critical elements?* Paper presented at the annual meeting of the American Psychological Association, Los Angeles. (ERIC Document Reproduction Service No. ED 214 502)

$+Levin, T. (1975). *The effect of content prerequisites and process-oriented experiences on application ability in the learning of probability.* Unpublished doctoral dissertation, University of Chicago.

*Lewis, E. W. (1984). The effects of a mastery learning strategy and an interactive computerized quiz strategy on student achievement and attitude in college trigonometry. *Dissertation Abstracts International 45,* 2430A. (University Microfilms No. DA84-24589)

*Leyton, F. S. (1983). *The extent to which group instruction supplemented by mastery of initial cognitive prerequisites approximates the learning effectiveness of one-to-one tutorial methods.* Unpublished doctoral dissertation, University of Chicago.

*Locksley, N. (1977). The Personalized System of Instruction (PSI) in a university mathematics class. *Dissertation Abstracts International 37,* 4194. (University Microfilms No. ADD76-28194)

#@Long, J. C., Okey, J. R., & Yeany, R. H. (1978). The effects of diagnosis with teacher on student directed remediation on science achievement and attitudes. *Journal of Research in Science Teaching 15,* 505–511.

*Lu, M. C. (1976). The retention of material learned by PSI in a mathematics course. In B. A. Green, Jr. (Ed.), *Personalized instruction in higher education* (pp. 151–154). Washington, DC: Center for Personalized Instruction.

*Lu, P. H. (1976). Teaching human growth and development by the Personalized System for Instruction. *Teaching of Psychology 3*, 127–128.

*Lubkin, J. L. (1974). Engineering statistics: A Keller Plan course with novel problems and novel features. In R. S. Ruskin and S. F. Bono (Eds.), *Personalized instruction in higher education* (pp. 153–161). Washington, DC: Center for Personalized Instruction.

*#@Lueckmeyer, C. L., & Chiappetta, W. L. (1981). An investigation into the effects of a modified mastery learning strategy on achievement in a high school human physiology unit. *Journal of Research in Science Teaching 18*, 269–273.

*Malec, M. A. (1975). PSI: A brief report and reply to Francis. *Teaching Sociology 2*, 212–217.

*Martin, R. R., & Srikameswaran, K. (1974). Correlation between frequent testing and student performance. *Journal of Chemical Education 51*, 485–486.

$Mathews, G. S. (1982). *Effects of a mastery learning strategy on the cognitive knowledge and unit evaluation of students in high school social studies.* Unpublished doctoral dissertation, University of Southern Mississippi.

*McFarland, B. (1976). An individualized course in elementary composition for the marginal student. In B. A. Green, Jr. (Ed.), *Personalized instruction in higher education* (pp. 45–52). Washington, DC: Center for Personalized Instruction.

*+McMichael, J., & Corey, J. R. (1969). Contingency management in an introductory psychology course produces better learning. *Journal of Applied Behavior Analysis 2*, 79–83.

*#@Mevarech, Z. R. (1980). *The role of teaching-learning strategies and feedback-corrective procedures in developing higher cognitive achievement.* Unpublished doctoral dissertation, University of Chicago.

$&Mevarech, Z. R. (1981, April). *Attaining mastery on higher cognitive achievement.* Paper presented at the annual meeting of the American Educational Research Association, Los Angeles.

*Mevarech, Z. R. (1985). The effects of cooperative mastery learning strategies on mathematical achievement. *Journal of Educational Research 78*, 372–377.

*#@Mevarech, Z. R. (1986). The role of feedback corrective procedure in developing mathematics achievement and self-concept in desegregated classrooms. *Studies in Educational Evaluation 12*, 197–203.

*Mevarech, Z. R., & Werner, S. (1985). Are mastery learning strategies beneficial for developing problem solving skills? *Higher Education 14*, 425–432.

*Meyers, R. R. (1976). The effects of mastery and aptitude on achievement and attitude in an introductory college geography course. *Dissertation Abstracts International 36*, 5874. (University Microfilms No. 76-6436)

*+Morris, C., & Kimbrill, G. (1972). Performance and attitudinal effects of the Keller method in an introductory psychology course. *Psychological Record 22*, 523–530.

*Nation, J. R., Knight, J. M., Lamberth, J., & Dyck, D. (1974). Programmed student achievement: A test of the avoidance hypothesis. *Journal of Experimental Education 42*, 57–61.

*Nation, J. R., Massad, P., & Wilkerson, P. (1977). Student performance in introductory psychology following termination of the programmed achievement contingency at mid-semester. *Teaching of Psychology 4*, 116–119.

*Nation, J. R., & Roop, S. S. (1975). A comparison of two mastery approaches to teaching introductory psychology. *Teaching of Psychology 2*, 108–111.

*+Nazzaro, J. R., Todorov, J. C., & Nazzaro, J. N. (1972). Student ability and individualized instruction. *Journal of College Science Teaching 2*, 29–30.

*Nord, S. B. (1975). Comparative achievement and attitude in individualized and class instructional settings. *Dissertation Abstracts International 35*, 5129A. (University Microfilms No. 75-02314)

$Nordin, A. B. (1979). *The effects of different qualities of instruction on selected cognitive, affective, and time variables.* Unpublished doctoral dissertation, University of Chicago.

Obando, L. T., & Hymel, G. M. (1991 March). *The effect of mastery learning instruction on the entry-level Spanish proficiency of secondary school students.* Paper presented at the annual meeting to the American Educational Research Association, New Orleans. (ERIC Document Reproduction Service No. ED 359 253)

*$+Okey, J. R. (1974). Altering teacher and pupil behavior with mastery teaching. *Social Science and Mathematics 74*, 530–535.

+Okey, J. R. (1975). *Development of mastery teaching materials* (Final Evaluation Report, USOE G-74-2990). Bloomington: Indiana University.

$&Okey, J. R. (1977). The consequences of training teachers to use a mastery learning strategy. *Journal of Teacher Education 28*(5), 57–62.

*$Omelich, C. L., & Covington, M. V. (1981). *Do the learning benefits of behavioral instruction outweigh the psychological costs?* Paper presented at the annual meeting of the Western Psychological Association, Los Angeles.

*Pascarella, E. T. (1977, April). *Aptitude-treatment interaction in a college calculus course taught in personalized system of instruction and conventional formats.* Paper presented at the annual meeting of the American Educational Research Association, New York. (ERIC Document Reproduction Service No. ED 137 137)

*Peluso, A., & Baranchik, A. J. (1977). Self-paced mathematics instruction: A statistical comparison with traditional teaching. *The American Mathematical Monthly 84*, 124–129.

*+Phillippas, M. A., & Sommerfeldt, R. W. (1972). Keller vs. lecture method in general physics instruction. *American Journal of Physics 40*, 1800.

+Poggio, (1976, April). *Long-term cognitive retention resulting from the mastery learning paradigm.* Paper presented at the annual meeting of the American Educational Research Association, San Francisco.

*Pollack, N. F., & Roeder, P. W. (1975). Individualized instruction in an introductory government course. *Teaching Political Science 8*, 18–36.

%Reid, E. R. (1978-1982). *The Reader Newsletter.* Salt Lake City: Exemplary Center for Reading Instruction.

*+Rosati, P. A. (1975). A comparison of the personalized system of instruction with the lecture method in teaching elementary dynamics. In J. M. Johnston (Ed.), *Behavior research and technology in higher education.* Springfield, IL: Charles C. Thomas.

Rosenshine, B., & Stevens, R. (1986). Teaching functions. In M. C. Wittrock (Ed.), *Handbook of research on teaching.* New York: Macmillan.

+Roth, C. H., Jr. (1973). Continuing effectiveness of personalized self-paced instruction in digital systems engineering. *Engineering Education 63*(6), 447–450.

*Roth, C. H., Jr. (1975, December). *Electrical engineering laboratory I* (One of a series of reports on the projects titled Expansion of Keller Plan Instruction in Engineering and Selected Other Disciplines). Austin: University of Texas.

*Saunders-Harris, R. L., & Yeany, R. H. (1981). Diagnosis, remediation, and locus of control: Effects of immediate and retained achievement and attitude. *Journal of Experimental Education 49*, 220–224.

*Schielack, V. P., Jr. (1983). A personalized system of instruction versus a conventional method in a mathematics course for elementary education majors. *Dissertation Abstracts International 43*, 2267. (University Microfilms No. 82-27717)

*Schimpfhauser, F., Horrocks, L., Richardson, K., Alben, J., Schumm, D., & Sprecher, H. (1974). The personalized system of instruction as an adaptable alternative within the traditional structure of medical basic sciences. In R. S. Ruskin and S. F. Bono (Eds.), *Personalized instruction in higher education* (pp. 61–69). Washington, DC: Center for Personalized Instruction.

*Schwartz, P. L. (1981). Retention of knowledge in clinical biochemistry and the effect of the Keller Plan. *Journal of Medical Education 56*, 778–781.

*Sharples, D. K., Smith, D. J., & Strasler, G. M. (1976). *Individually-paced learning in civil engineering technology: An approach to mastery*. Columbia: South Carolina State Board for Technical and Comprehensive Education. (ERIC Document Reproduction Service No. ED 131 870)

*$Sheldon, M. S., & Miller, E. D. (1973). *Behavioral objectives and mastery learning applied to two areas of junior college instruction*. Los Angeles: University of California at Los Angeles. (ERIC Document Reproduction Service No. ED 082 730)

*Sheppard, W. C., & MacDermott, H. G. (1970). Design and evaluation of a programmed course in introductory psychology. *Journal of Applied Behavior Analysis 3*, 5–11.

*Siegfried, J. J., & Strand, S. H. (1976). An evaluation of the Vanderbilt-JCEE experimental PSI course in elementary economics. *The Journal of Economic Education 8*, 9–26.

*+Silberman, R., & Parker, B. (1974). Student attitudes and the Keller Plan. *Journal of Chemical Education 51*, 393.

Slavin, R. E. (1990). Mastery learning re-considered. *Review of Educational Research 60*(2), 300–302.

*#@$&Slavin, R. E., & Karweit, N. L. (1984). Mastery learning and student teams: A factorial experiment in urban general mathematics classes. *American Educational Research Journal 21*, 725–736.

*Smiernow, G. A., & Lawley, A. (1980). Decentralized sequenced instruction (DSI) at Drexel. *Engineering Education 70*, 423–426.

*Smith, J. E. (1976). A comparison of the traditional method and a personalized system of instruction in college mathematics. *Dissertation Abstracts International 37*, 904. (University Microfilms No. AAD76-18370)

*Spector, L. C. (1976). The effectiveness of personalized system of instruction in economics. *Journal of Personalized Instruction 1*, 118–122.

*Spevack, H. M. (1976). A comparison of the personalized system of instruction with the lecture recitation system for nonscience oriented chemistry students at an open enrollment community college. *Dissertation Abstracts International 36*, 4385A–4386A. (University Microfilms No. 76-01757)

*Steele, W. F. (1974). *Mathematics 101 at Heileberg College—PSI vs. tradition*. Paper presented at the National Conference on Personalized Instruction in Higher Education, Washington, DC.

*Stout, L. J. (1978). A comparison of four different pacing strategies of personalized system of instruction and a traditional lecture format. *Dissertation Abstracts International 38*, 6205. (University Microfilms No. AAD78-08600)

*$Strasler, G. M. (1979, April). *The process of transfer in a learning for mastery setting*.

Paper presented at the annual meeting of the American Educational Research Association, San Francisco. (ERIC Document Reproduction Service No. ED 174 642)

*$&Swanson, D. H., & Denton, J. J. (1976). Learning for Mastery versus Personalized System of Instruction: A comparison of remediation strategies with secondary school chemistry students. *Journal of Research in Science Teaching 14*, 515–524.

*Taylor, V. (1977, April). *Individualized calculus for the "life-long" learner: A two semester comparison of attitudes and effectiveness.* Paper presented at the Fourth National Conference of the Center for Personalized Instruction, San Francisco.

$Tenenbaum, G. (1982). *A method of group instruction which is as effective as one-to-one tutorial instruction.* Unpublished doctoral dissertation, University of Chicago.

*&Thompson, S. B. (1980). Do individualized mastery and traditional instructional systems yield different course effects in college calculus? *American Educational Research Journal 17*, 361–375.

*Tietenberg, T. H. (1975). Teaching intermediate microeconomics using the personalized system of instruction. In J. M. Johnston (Ed.), *Behavior research and technology in higher education* (pp. 75–89). Springfield, IL: Charles C. Thomas.

*Toepher, C., Shaw, D., & Moniot, D. (1972). *The effect of item exposure in a contingency management system.* Paper presented at the annual meeting of the American Psychological Association, Honolulu, HI.

*Vandenbroucke, A. C., Jr. (1974, April). *Evaluation of the use of a personalized system of instruction in general chemistry.* Paper presented at the National Conference on Personalized Instruction in Higher Education, Washington, DC.

*Van Verth, J. E., & Dinan, F. J. (1974). A Keller Plan course in organic chemistry. In R. S. Ruskin and S. F. Bono (Eds.), *Personalized instruction in higher education* (pp. 162–168). Washington, DC: Center for Personalized Instruction.

*Walsh, R. G., Sr. (1977). The Keller Plan in college introductory physical geology: A comparison with the conventional teaching method. *Dissertation Abstracts International 37*, 4257. (University Microfilms No. AAD76-30292)

$&+Wentling, T. L. (1973), Mastery versus nonmastery instruction with varying test item feedback treatments. *Journal of Educational Psychology 65*, 50–58.

*White, M. E. (1974). Different equations by PSI. In R. S. Ruskin and S. F. Bono (Eds.), *Personalized instruction in higher education* (pp. 169–171). Washington, DC: Center for Personalized Instruction.

Willent, J., Yamashita, J., & Anderson, R. (1983). A meta-analysis of instructional systems applied in science teaching. *Journal of Research in Science Teaching 20*(5), 405–417.

$Wire, D. R. (1979). *Mastery learning program at Durham College: Report on progress during the first year, September 1, 1978–August 31, 1979.* Durham, NC. (ERIC Document Reproduction Service No. ED 187 387)

*Witters, D. R., & Kent, G. W. (1972). Teaching without lecturing—Evidence in the case for individualized instruction. *The Psychological Record 22*, 169–175.

$Wortham, S. C. (1980). *Mastery learning in secondary schools: A first year report.* San Antonio, TX. (ERIC Document Reproduction Service No. ED 194 453)

*Yeany, R. H., Dost, R. J., & Matthew, R. W. (1980). The effects of diagnostic-prescriptive instruction and locus of control on the achievement and attitudes of university students. *Journal of Research in Science Teaching 17*, 537–545.

$Yildren, G. (1977). *The effects of level of cognitive achievement on selected learning criteria under mastery learning and normal classroom instruction.* Unpublished doctoral dissertation, University of Chicago.

2

Defining Instructional Expectations

INTRODUCTION

In order for students to accomplish a learning objective, it is necessary that they know prior to instruction (1) what the learning objective is, (2) what procedures are necessary to perform the tasks required to achieve the learning objective, and (3) what the criteria are for successful accomplishment of the learning objective. In the absence of this knowledge the student may not be able to process the available information to determine what is relevant and what is not; may not be able to determine the appropriate procedures needed to accomplish the learning objective; and may have difficulty in determining when they have successfully achieved the objective. They may flounder, become frustrated, and perform poorly.

STUDENT BENEFICIARIES

The evidence indicates that defining instructional expectations enhances the academic achievement of students in kindergarten, elementary, secondary, and college classrooms. No evidence could be found to suggest that defining instructional expectations should not be stressed for all types of students.

LEARNING ACHIEVED

Achievement in the content areas of reading, mathematics, history, language arts, social sciences, sciences, and social studies is enhanced when instructional expectations are defined prior to instruction. In studies reviewed, defining instructional expectations was positively related to student achievement. Moreover, academic achievement was improved in a wide range of content areas.

INSTRUCTIONAL TACTICS

The evidence well supports the need to define instructional expectations prior to instruction and student performance of tasks. The following tactics are derived from studies that demonstrate the benefits of defining instructional expectations. Discretion has been used to interpret and reduce overlap in tactics used in different studies and to elaborate tactics.

Tactics employed are:

- The learning objective must be defined. This is necessary for the student to understand the learning objective. In essence, defining the learning objective assists the student in processing the available information. For instance, if the learning objective is adding fractions, "the learner must be able to identify 2/5 as a fraction and .4 as not a fraction" (Gagné 1962a).

- How the student is to achieve the learning objective must be defined. Students need to know what procedures they are to employ in achieving the learning objectives. In the foregoing example by Gagné (1962a), if the student does not know that the learning objective is to add fractions, they may take the easier route and add decimals. The student may need to know that they are to convert decimals to fractions and then add. In the absence of instructions on how and what they are to do in order to accomplish the learning objective, they may quite simply not know what to do.

- Performance criteria must be defined. The student needs to know what the criteria are for achieving mastery of the learning objective. "For example, if the task is adding fractions, it may be necessary for the learner to identify 15 3/4 as an adequate answer, and 6 3/4 as an inadequate one" (Gagné 1962a). Additionally, if letter grades are used, the student needs to know what task performance level is required to achieve that grade.

CAUTIONS AND COMMENTS

Defining instructional expectations may be seen as orienting the student to the learning goals and the means of achieving them. Although the examples used under instructional tactics to orient the student are seen as one way of accomplishing the orientation of the student, there are other means and examples available in the 169 reference list citations. Should one wish to view other specific examples, it is recommended that readers review some of the many studies cited in the reference list.

GENERALIZATION: ON DEFINING INSTRUCTIONAL EXPECTATIONS

Student achievement of learning objectives is enhanced when prior to instruction, (1) learning objectives are defined for students, (2) procedures to be used in the performance of tasks to achieve the objectives are identified, and (3) student outcomes designating achievement of the objectives are defined.

Supportive Research on Defining Instructional Expectations
Total number of studies covered: 169

Groups of Studies

Author: Anderson (1994): Synthesis of seven meta-analyses

Students: Kindergarten, elementary, secondary, college, and other adult students

Learning: Mathematics, history, language arts, social sciences, sciences, social studies achievement

Instructional Tactics: The following tactics associated with defining instructional expectations and Mastery Learning are also presented in Bloom (1985), Block (1980), and others. Other tactics associated with learning for mastery are applicable to other generalizations and are covered in the appropriate chapters.

Prior to instruction, students are oriented as to:

- Procedures to be used
- What they are expected to learn
- To what level they are expected to learn

Findings: Positive achievement gains associated with Mastery Learning were seen in 64–93 percent of the studies reviewed in the seven meta-analyses.

Individual studies analyzed by these meta-analyses are identified in the reference list at the end of the chapter by the following symbols:

Kulik et al. (1990a) *

Kulik et al. (1990b) #

Slavin (1990) @

Guskey & Pigott (1988) $

Guskey & Gates (1985) &

Block & Burns (1976) +

It was not possible to determine the individual studies for which defining instructional expectations was an instructional tactic for the Willett et al. (1983) analysis.

Author: Rosenshine & Stevens (1986)

Students: Elementary and secondary

Learning: Mathematics, English, science, history, and reading achievement

Instructional Tactics:

• Begin a lesson with a short statement of goals and objectives.

• Demonstrate what is to be learned, giving explicit step-by-step directions.

Other instructional tactics are employed in these studies that are applicable to other generalizations and are presented in the appropriate chapters.

Findings: The above tactics were found to be related to enhanced student achievement.

Groups of studies reviewed in this logical synthesis of research did not provide statistical evidence. However, many of the individual studies included in the logical synthesis of research do contain statistical evidence. In the event that a reader wishes to view this evidence, an extensive listing of the individual studies reviewed is provided in the reference list (the studies are identified by the symbol %).

REFERENCE LIST

*+Abraham, F. J., & Newton, J. M. (1974). *The interview technique as a personalized system of instruction for economics: The Oregon experience.* Paper presented at the National Conference on Personalized Instruction in Higher Education, Washington DC.

$Anania, J. (1981). *The effects of quality of instruction on the cognitive and affective learning of students.* Unpublished doctoral dissertation, University of Chicago.

%Anderson, L. M., Evertson, C. M., & Brophy, J. E. (1979). An experimental study of effective teaching in first-grade reading groups. *The Elementary School Journal 79*, 193–222.

%Anderson, L. M., Evertson, C. M., & Brophy, J. E. (1982). *Principles of small group instruction* (Occasional paper no. 32). East Lansing: Michigan State University, Institute for Research on Teaching.

+Anderson, L. W. (1973). *Time and school learning.* Unpublished doctoral dissertation, University of Chicago.

*$&Anderson, L. W. (1975a). Student involvement in learning and school achievement. *California Journal of Educational Research 26*, 53–62.

$&Anderson, L. W. (1975b). *Time to criterion: An experimental study.* Paper presented at the annual meeting of the American Educational Research Association, Washington, DC. (ERIC Document Reproduction Service No. ED 108 006)

*$&+Anderson, L. W. (1976). An empirical investigation of individual differences in time to learn. *Journal of Educational Psychology 68*, 226–233.

*#@$&Anderson, L. W., Scott, C., & Hutlock, N. (1976, April). *The effects of a mastery learning program on selected cognitive, affective, and ecological variables in grades 1 through 6.* Paper presented at the annual meeting of the American Educational Research Association, San Francisco.

+Anderson, O. T., & Artman, R. A. (1972). A self-paced independent study, introductory physics sequence-description and evaluation. *American Journal of Physics 40*, 1737–1742.

Anderson, S. A. (1994). *Synthesis of research on mastery learning* (Information Analysis). (ERIC Document Reproduction Service No. ED 382 567)

*$&%Arlin, M., & Webster, J. (1983). Time costs of mastery learning. *Journal of Educational Psychology 75*, 187–195.

*Austin, S. M., & Gilbert, K. E. (1973). Student performance in a Keller-Plan course in introductory electricity and magnetism. *American Journal of Physics 41*, 12–18.

*Badia, P., Stutts, C., & Harsh, J. (1978). Do methods of instruction and measures of different abilities and study habits interact? In J. G. Sherman, R. S. Ruskin, & R. M. Lazar (Eds.), *Personalized instruction in education today* (pp. 113–128). San Francisco: San Francisco Press.

%Becker, W. C. (1977). Teaching reading and language to the disadvantaged—What we have learned from field research. *Harvard Educational Review 47*, 518–543.

*Benson, J. S., & Yeany, R. H. (1980, April). *Generalizability of diagnostic-prescriptive teaching strategies across student locus of control and multiple instructional units.* Paper presented at the annual meeting of the American Educational Research Association, Boston. (ERIC Document Reproduction Service No. 187 534)

*+Billings, D. B. (1974). PSI versus the lecture course in the principles of economics: A quasi-controlled experiment. In R. S. Ruskin & S. F. Bono (Eds.), *Personalized instruction in higher education* (pp. 30–37). Washington, DC: Center for Personalized Instruction.

*$Blackburn, K. T., & Nelson, D. (1985, April). *Differences between a group using a traditional format with mastery learning and a group using a traditional format only in developmental mathematics courses at the university level: Implications for teacher education programs.* Paper presented at the annual meeting of the American Educational Research Association, Chicago. (ERIC Document Reproduction Service No. ED 258 948)

*Blasingame, J. W. (1975). Student attitude and performance in a personalized system of instruction course in business administration—Correlates performance with personality traits. *Dissertation Abstracts International 36*, 3840. (University Microfilms No. 75-2834)

$&+Block, J. H. (1972). Student learning and the setting of mastery performance standards. *Educational Horizons 50*, 183–191.

+Block, J. H. (1973). *Mastery performance standards and student learning.* Unpublished study, University of California, Santa Barbara.

Block, J. H. (1980). Success rate. In C. Denham & A. Lieberman (Eds.), *Time to learn* (pp. 95–106). Washington, DC: U.S. Government Printing Office.

Block, J. H., & Burns, R. B. (1976). Mastery learning. In L. Schulman (Ed.), *Review of research in education* (Vol. 4, pp. 3–49). Itasca, IL: F. E. Peacock.

$+Block, J. H., & Tierney, M. (1974). An exploration of two correction procedures used in mastery learning approaches to instruction. *Journal of Educational Psychology 66*, 962–967.

Bloom, B. S. (1985). Learning for mastery. In C. W. Fisher & D. C. Berliner (Eds.), *Perspectives on instructional time.* White Plains, NY: Longman.

*+Born, D. G., & Davis, M. L. (1974). Amount and distribution of study in a personalized instruction course and in a lecture course. *Journal of Applied Behavior Analysis 7*, 365–375.

*+Born, D. G., Gledhill, S. M., & Davis, M. L. (1972). Examination performance in lecture-

discussion and personalized instruction courses. *Journal of Applied Behavior Analysis 5*, 33–43.

*+Breland, N. S., & Smith, M. P. (1974). A comparison of PSI and traditional methods of instruction for teaching introduction to psychology. In R. S. Ruskin & S. F. Bono (Eds.), *Personalized instruction in higher education* (pp. 21–25). Washington, DC: Center for Personalized Instruction.

*$Bryant, N. D., Fayne, H. R., & Gettinger, M. (1982). Applying the mastery model to sight word instruction for disabled readers. *Journal of Experimental Education 50*, 116–121.

$Burke, A. (1983). *Students' potential for learning contrasted under tutorial and group approaches to instruction.* Unpublished doctoral dissertation, University of Chicago.

$&+Burrows, C. K., & Okey, J. R. (1975, March–April). *The effects of a mastery learning strategy on achievement.* Paper presented at the annual meeting of the American Educational Research Association, Washington, DC.

*#@$Cabezon, E. (1984). *The effects of marked changes in student achievement pattern on the students, their teachers, and their parents: The Chilean case.* Unpublished doctoral dissertation, University of Chicago.

$Chiappetta, E. L., & McBride, J. W. (1980). Exploring the effects of general remediation on ninth-graders' achievement of the mole concept. *Science Education 6*, 609–614.

*$Clark, C. P., Guskey, T. P., & Benninga, J. S. (1983). The effectiveness of mastery learning strategies in undergraduate education courses. *Journal of Educational Research 76*, 210–214.

*Clark, S. G. (1975). An innovation for introductory sociology: Personalized system of instruction. In J. M. Johnston (Ed.), *Behavior research and technology in higher education* (pp. 117–124). Springfield, IL: Charles C. Thomas.

*+Coldeway, D. O., Santowski, M., O'Brien, R., & Lagowski, V. (1975). Comparison of small group contingency management with the personalized system of instruction and the lecture system. In J. M. Johnston (Ed.), *Research and technology in college and university teaching* (pp. 215–224). Gainesville: University of Florida.

*+Cole, C., Martin, S., & Vincent, J. (1975). A comparison of two teaching formats at the college level. In J. M. Johnston (Ed.), *Behavior research and technology in higher education* (pp. 61–74). Springfield, IL: Charles C. Thomas.

*Condo, P. (1974, April). *The analysis and evaluation of a self-paced course in calculus.* Paper presented at the National Conference on Personalized Instruction in Higher Education, Washington, DC.

*+Cooper, J. L., & Greiner, J. M. (1971). Contingency management in an introductory psychology course produces better retention. *Psychological Record 21*, 391–400.

*Corey, J. R., & McMichael, J. S. (1974). Retention in a PSI introductory psychology course. In J. G. Sherman (Ed.), *PSI germinal papers* (pp. 17–19). Washington, DC: Center for Personalized Instruction.

+Corey, J. R., McMichael, J. S., & Tremont, P. J. (1970, April). *Long-term effects of personalized instruction in an introductory psychology course.* Paper presented at the meeting of the Eastern Psychology Association, Atlantic City.

*Cote, J. D. (1976). Biology by PSI in a community college. In B. A. Green, Jr. (Ed.), *Personalized instruction in higher education.* Washington, DC: Center for Personalized Instruction.

*Cross, M. Z., & Semb, G. (1976). An analysis of the effects of personalized instruction on students at different initial performance levels in an introductory college nutrition course. *Journal of Personalized Instruction 1*, 47–50.

*Decker, D. F. (1976). *Teaching to achieve learning mastery by using retesting techniques.* (ERIC Document Reproduction Service No. ED 133 002)

$Denton, W. L., Ory, J. C., Glassnap, D. R., & Poggio, J. P. (1976). *Grade expectations within a mastery learning strategy.* Paper presented at the annual meeting of the American Educational Research Association, San Francisco. (ERIC Document Reproduction Service No. ED 126 105)

*$Dillashaw, F. G., & Okey, J. R. (1983). Effects of a modified mastery learning strategy on achievement, attitudes, and on-task behavior of high school chemistry students. *Journal of Research in Science Teaching 20*, 203–211.

$Duby, P. B. (1981). *Attributions and attribution change: Effects of a mastery learning instructional approach.* Paper presented at the annual meeting of the American Educational Research Association, Los Angeles. (ERIC Document Reproduction Service No. ED 200 640)

%Emmer, E. T., Evertson, C., Sanford, J., & Clements, B. (1982). *Improving classroom management: An experimental study in junior high classrooms.* Austin: Research and Development Center for Teacher Education, University of Texas.

%Evertson, C. M., Emmer, E. T., Sanford, J. P., & Clements, B. S. (1983). Improving classroom management: An experiment in elementary classrooms. *Elementary School Journal 84*, 173–188.

*#@Fagan, J. S. (1976). Mastery learning: The relationship of mastery procedures and aptitude to the achievement and retention of transportation-environment concepts by seventh grade students. *Dissertation Abstracts International 36*, 5981. (University Microfilms No. 76-6402)

*Fehlen, J. E. (1976). Mastery learning techniques in the traditional classroom setting. *School Science and Mathematics 76*, 241–245.

*Fernald, P. S., & DuNann, D. H. (1975). Effects of individualized instruction upon low- and high-achieving students' study behavior and students' evaluation of mastery. *Journal of Experimental Education 43*, 27–34.

$&+Fiel, R. L., & Okey, J. R. (1974). The effects of formative evaluation and remediation on mastery of intellectual skill. *Journal of Educational Research 68*, 253–255.

%Fisher, C. W., Berliner, D. C., Filby, N. N., Marliave, R., Cahen, L. S., & Dishaw, M. M. (1980). Teaching behaviors, academic learning time, and student achievement: An overview. In C. Denham & A. Lieberman (Eds.), *Time to learn* (pp. 7–32). Washington, DC: U.S. Government Printing Office.

%Fitzpatrick, K. A. (1981). *An investigation of secondary classroom material strategies for increasing student academic engaged time.* Doctoral dissertation, University of Illinois at Urbana–Champaign.

%Fitzpatrick, K. A. (1982). *The effect of a secondary classroom management training program on teacher and student behavior.* Paper presented at the annual meeting of the American Educational Research Association, New York.

$&Fitzpatrick, K. A. (1985, April). *Group-based mastery learning: A Robin Hood approach to instruction?* Paper presented at the annual meeting of the American Educational Research Association, Chicago.

Gagné, R. M. (1962a). The acquisition of knowledge. *Psychological Review 69*(4), 355–365.

Gagné, R. M. (1962b). Military training and principles of learning. *American Psychologist 17*, 83–91.

+Glassnapp, D. R., Poggio, J. P., & Ory, J. C. (1975, March–April). *Cognitive and affective consequences of mastery and non-mastery instructional strategies.* Paper presented at the annual meeting of the American Educational Research Association, Washington, DC.

*Goldwater, B. C., & Acker, L. E. (1975). Instructor-paced, mass-testing for mastery performance in an introductory psychology course. *Teaching of Psychology 2*, 152–155.

%Good, T. L., & Grouws, D. A. (1979). The Missouri mathematics effectiveness project. *Journal of Educational Psychology 71*, 355–362.

*Gregory, I., Smeltzer, D. J., Knopp, W., & Gardner, M. (1976). *Teaching of psychiatry by PSI: Impact on National Board Examination scores.* Unpublished manuscript, Ohio State University, Columbus.

*$&Guskey, T. R. (1982). The effects of staff development on teachers' perceptions about effective teaching. *Journal of Educational Research 76*, 378–381.

*$&Guskey, T. R. (1984). The influence of changes in instructional effectiveness upon the affective characteristics of teachers. *American Educational Research Journal 21*, 245–259.

$Guskey, T. R. (1985). The effects of staff development on teachers' perceptions about effective teaching. *Journal of Educational Research 79*, 378–381.

*$Guskey, T. R., Benninga, J. S., & Clark, C. B. (1984). Mastery learning and students' attributions at the college level. *Research in Higher Education 20*, 491–498.

Guskey, T. R., & Gates, S. L. (1986). Synthesis of research on the effects of mastery learning in elementary and secondary classrooms. *Educational Leadership 33*(8), 73–80.

*$Guskey, T. R., & Monsaas, J. A. (1979). Mastery learning: A model for academic success in urban junior colleges. *Research in Higher Education 11*, 263–274.

Guskey, T. R., & Pigott, T. D. (1988). Research on group-based mastery learning programs: A meta-analysis. *Journal of Educational Research 81*(4), 197–216.

*Hardin, L. D. (1977). A study of the influence of a physics personalized system of instruction versus lecture on cognitive reasoning, achievement, attitudes and critical thinking. *Dissertation Abstracts International 38*, 4711A–4712A. (University Microfilms No. 77-30826)

*Hecht, L. W. (1980, April). *Stalking mastery learning in its natural habitat.* Paper presented at the annual meeting of the American Educational Research Association, Boston.

*Heffley, P. D. (1974). The implementation of the personalized system of instruction in the freshman chemistry course at Censius College. In R. S. Ruskin & S. F. Bono (Eds.), *Personalized instruction in higher education* (pp. 140–145). Washington, DC: Center for Personalized Instruction.

*Herring, B. G. (1975, December). *Cataloguing and classification.* Austin: University of Texas.

*Herring, B. G. (1977). *The written PSI study guide in a non-PSI course.* Austin: University of Texas.

*Herrmann, T. (1984, August). *TELIDON as an enhancer of student interest and performance.* Paper presented at the annual meeting of the American Psychological Association, Toronto. (ERIC Document Reproduction Service No. ED 251 004)

*Hindman, C. D. (1974). Evaluation of three programming techniques in introductory psychology courses. In R. S. Ruskin & S. F. Bono (Eds.), *Personalized instruction in higher education* (pp. 38–42). Washington, DC: Center for Personalized Instruction.

*Honeycutt, J. K. (1974, April). *The effect of computer managed instruction on content learning of undergraduate students.* Paper presented at the annual meeting of the

American Educational Research Association, Chicago. (ERIC Document Reproduction Service No. ED 089 682)

*Hymel, G. M. (1974). *An investigation of John B. Carrol's model of school learning as a theoretical basis for the organizational structuring of schools* (Final Report, NIE Project No. 3-1359). University of New Orleans, New Orleans, LA.

*Hymel, G. M., & Mathews, G. (1980). Effects of a mastery approach on social studies achievement and unit evaluation. *Southern Journal of Educational Research 14*, 191–204.

*Jackman, L. E. (1982). Evaluation of a modified Keller method in a biochemistry laboratory course. *Journal of Chemical Education 59*, 225–227.

*Jacko, E. J. (1974). Lecture instruction versus a personalized system of instruction: Effects on individuals with differing achievement anxiety and academic achievement. *Dissertation Abstracts International 35*, 3521. (University Microfilms No. AAD 74-27211)

+Johnston, J. M., & Pennypacker, H. S. (1971). A behavioral approach to college teaching. *American Psychologist 26*, 219–244.

*#@$&Jones, B. F., Monsaas, J. A., & Katims, M. (1979, April). *Improving reading comprehension: Embedding diverse learning strategies within a mastery learning instructional framework.* Paper presented at the annual meeting of the American Educational Research Association, San Francisco. (ERIC Document Reproduction Service No. ED 170 698)

$+Jones, E. L., Gordon, H. A., & Stectman, G. L. (1975). *Mastery learning: A strategy for academic success in a community college.* Los Angeles: ERIC Clearinghouse for Junior Colleges. (ERIC Document Reproduction Service No. ED 115 315)

+Jones, F. G. (1974). *The effects of mastery and aptitude on learning, retention, and time.* Unpublished doctoral dissertation, University of Georgia.

+Karlin, B. M. (1972). *The Keller method of instruction compared to the traditional method of instruction in a Lafayette College history course.* Unpublished paper, Lafayette College, Lafayette, PA.

*#@Katims, M., Smith, J. K., Steele, C., & Wick, J. W. (1977, April). *The Chicago mastery learning reading program: An interim evaluation.* Paper presented at the annual meeting of the American Educational Research Association, New York. (ERIC Document Reproduction Service No. ED 137 737)

*#@Kersh, M. E. (1970). *A strategy of mastery learning in fifth grade arithmetic.* Unpublished doctoral dissertation, University of Chicago.

+Kim, Y., Cho, G., Park, J., & Park, M. (1974). *An application of a new instructional model* (Research Report No. 8). Seoul, Korea: Korean Educational Development Institute.

*Knight, J. M., Williams, J. D., & Jardon, M. L. (1975). The effects of contingency avoidance on programmed student achievement. *Research in Higher Education 3*, 11–17.

*Kulik, C., & Kulik, J. (1976). PSI and the mastery model. In B. A. Green, Jr. (Ed.), *Personalized instruction in higher education* (pp. 155–159). Washington, DC: Center for Personalized Instruction.

Kulik, C., Kulik, J., & Bangert-Drowns, R. (1990a). Effectiveness of mastery learning programs: A meta-analysis. *Review of Educational Research 60*(2), 265–269.

Kulik, J., Kulik, C., & Bangert-Drowns, R. (1990b). Is there better evidence on mastery learning? A response to Slavin. *Review of Educational Research 60*(2), 303–307.

+Kulik, J. A., Kulik, C., & Carmichael, K. (1974). The Keller Plan in science teaching. *Science 183*, 379–383.

+Lee, Y. D., Kim, C. S., Kim, H., Park, B. Y., Yoo, H. K., Chang, S. M., & Kim, S. C. (1971). *Interaction improvement studies of the Mastery Learning Project* (Final Report on the Mastery Learning Project, April–November 1971). Seoul, Korea: Educational Research Center, Seoul National University.

*Leppmann, P. K., & Herrman, T. F. (1981, August). *PSI—What are the critical elements?* Paper presented at the annual meeting of the American Psychological Association, Los Angeles. (ERIC Document Reproduction Service No. ED 214 502)

$+Levin, T. (1975). *The effect of content prerequisites and process-oriented experiences on application ability in the learning of probability.* Unpublished doctoral dissertation, University of Chicago.

*Lewis, E. W. (1984). The effects of a mastery learning strategy and an interactive computerized quiz strategy on student achievement and attitude in college trigonometry. *Dissertation Abstracts International 45*, 2430A. (University Microfilms No. DA84-24589)

*Leyton, F. S. (1983). *The extent to which group instruction supplemented by mastery of initial cognitive prerequisites approximates the learning effectiveness of one-to-one tutorial methods.* Unpublished doctoral dissertation, University of Chicago.

*Locksley, N. (1977). The Personalized System of Instruction (PSI) in a university mathematics class. *Dissertation Abstracts International 37*, 4194. (University Microfilms No. ADD76-28194).

#@Long, J. C., Okey, J. R., & Yeany, R. H. (1978). The effects of diagnosis with teacher on student directed remediation on science achievement and attitudes. *Journal of Research in Science Teaching 15*, 505–511.

*Lu, M. C. (1976). The retention of material learned by PSI in a mathematics course. In B. A. Green, Jr. (Ed.), *Personalized instruction in higher education* (pp. 151–154). Washington, DC: Center for Personalized Instruction.

*Lu, P. H. (1976). Teaching human growth and development by the Personalized System for Instruction. *Teaching of Psychology 3*, 127–128.

*Lubkin, J. L. (1974). Engineering statistics: A Keller Plan course with novel problems and novel features. In R. S. Ruskin and S. F. Bono (Eds.), *Personalized instruction in higher education* (pp. 153–161). Washington, DC: Center for Personalized Instruction.

*#@Lueckmeyer, C. L., & Chiappetta, W. L. (1981). An investigation into the effects of a modified mastery learning strategy on achievement in a high school human physiology unit. *Journal of Research in Science Teaching 18*, 269–273.

*Malec, M. A. (1975). PSI: A brief report and reply to Francis. *Teaching Sociology 2*, 212–217.

*Martin, R. R., & Srikameswaran, K. (1974). Correlation between frequent testing and student performance. *Journal of Chemical Education 51*, 485–486.

$Mathews, G. S. (1982). *Effects of a mastery learning strategy on the cognitive knowledge and unit evaluation of students in high school social studies.* Unpublished doctoral dissertation, University of Southern Mississippi.

*McFarland, B. (1976). An individualized course in elementary composition for the marginal student. In B. A. Green, Jr. (Ed.), *Personalized instruction in higher education* (pp. 45–52). Washington, DC: Center for Personalized Instruction.

*+McMichael, J., & Corey, J. R. (1969). Contingency management in an introductory psychology course produces better learning. *Journal of Applied Behavior Analysis 2*, 79–83.

*#@Mevarech, Z. R. (1980). *The role of teaching-learning strategies and feedback-corrective procedures in developing higher cognitive achievement.* Unpublished doctoral dissertation, University of Chicago.

$&Mevarech, Z. R. (1981, April). *Attaining mastery on higher cognitive achievement.* Paper presented at the annual meeting of the American Educational Research Association, Los Angeles.

*Mevarech, Z. R. (1985). The effects of cooperative mastery learning strategies on mathematical achievement. *Journal of Educational Research 78,* 372–377.

*#@Mevarech, Z. R. (1986). The role of feedback corrective procedure in developing mathematics achievement and self-concept in desegregated classrooms. *Studies in Educational Evaluation 12,* 197–203.

*Mevarech, Z. R., & Werner, S. (1985). Are mastery learning strategies beneficial for developing problem solving skills? *Higher Education 14,* 425–432.

*Meyers, R. R. (1976). The effects of mastery and aptitude on achievement and attitude in an introductory college geography course. *Dissertation Abstracts International 36,* 5874. (University Microfilms No. 76-6436)

*+Morris, C., & Kimbrill, G. (1972). Performance and attitudinal effects of the Keller method in an introductory psychology course. *Psychological Record 22,* 523–530.

*Nation, J. R., Knight, J. M., Lamberth, J., & Dyck, D. (1974). Programmed student achievement: A test of the avoidance hypothesis. *Journal of Experimental Education 42,* 57–61.

*Nation, J. R., Massad, P., & Wilkerson, P. (1977). Student performance in introductory psychology following termination of the programmed achievement contingency at mid-semester. *Teaching of Psychology 4,* 116–119.

*Nation, J. R., & Roop, S. S. (1975). A comparison of two mastery approaches to teaching introductory psychology. *Teaching of Psychology 2,* 108–111.

*+Nazzaro, J. R., Todorov, J. C., & Nazzaro, J. N. (1972). Student ability and individualized instruction. *Journal of College Science Teaching 2,* 29–30.

*Nord, S. B. (1975). Comparative achievement and attitude in individualized and class instructional settings. *Dissertation Abstracts International 35,* 5129A. (University Microfilms No. 75-02314)

$Nordin, A. B. (1979). *The effects of different qualities of instruction on selected cognitive, affective, and time variables.* Unpublished doctoral dissertation, University of Chicago.

Obando, L. T., & Hymel, G. M. (1991, March). *The effect of mastery learning instruction on the entry-level Spanish proficiency of secondary school students.* Paper presented at the annual meeting to the American Educational Research Association, New Orleans. (ERIC Document Reproduction Service No. ED 359 253)

*$+Okey, J. R. (1974). Altering teacher and pupil behavior with mastery teaching. *Social Science and Mathematics 74,* 530–535.

+Okey, J. R. (1975). *Development of mastery teaching materials* (Final Evaluation Report, USOE G-74-2990). Bloomington: Indiana University.

$&Okey, J. R. (1977). The consequences of training teachers to use a mastery learning strategy. *Journal of Teacher Education 28(5),* 57–62.

*$Omelich, C. L., & Covington, M. V. (1981). *Do the learning benefits of behavioral instruction outweigh the psychological costs?* Paper presented at the annual meeting of the Western Psychological Association, Los Angeles.

*Pascarella, E. T. (1977, April). *Aptitude-treatment interaction in a college calculus course* *taught in personalized system of instruction and conventional formats.* Paper presented at the annual meeting of the American Educational Research Association, New York. (ERIC Document Reproduction Service No. ED 137 137)

*Peluso, A., & Baranchik, A. J. (1977). Self-paced mathematics instruction: A statistical comparison with traditional teaching. *The American Mathematical Monthly 84*, 124–129.

*+Phillippas, M. A., & Sommerfeldt, R. W. (1972). Keller vs. lecture method in general physics instruction. *American Journal of Physics 40*, 1800.

+Poggio, (1976, April). *Long-term cognitive retention resulting from the mastery learning paradigm.* Paper presented at the annual meeting of the American Educational Research Association, San Francisco.

*Pollack, N. F., & Roeder, P. W. (1975). Individualized instruction in an introductory government course. *Teaching Political Science 8*, 18–36.

%Reid, E. R. (1978-1982). *The Reader Newsletter.* Salt Lake City: Exemplary Center for Reading Instruction.

*+Rosati, P. A. (1975). A comparison of the personalized system of instruction with the lecture method in teaching elementary dynamics. In J. M. Johnston (Ed.), *Behavior research and technology in higher education.* Springfield, IL: Charles C. Thomas.

Rosenshine, B., & Stevens, R. (1986). Teaching functions. In M. C. Wittrock (Ed.), *Handbook of research on teaching.* New York: Macmillan.

+Roth, C. H., Jr. (1973). Continuing effectiveness of personalized self-paced instruction in digital systems engineering. *Engineering Education 63*(6), 447–450.

*Roth, C. H., Jr. (1975, December). *Electrical engineering laboratory I* (One of a series of reports on the projects titled Expansion of Keller Plan Instruction in Engineering and Selected Other Disciplines). Austin: University of Texas.

*Saunders-Harris, R. L., & Yeany, R. H. (1981). Diagnosis, remediation, and locus of control: Effects of immediate and retained achievement and attitude. *Journal of Experimental Education 49*, 220–224.

*Schielack, V. P., Jr. (1983). A personalized system of instruction versus a conventional method in a mathematics course for elementary education majors. *Dissertation Abstracts International 43*, 2267. (University Microfilms No. 82-27717)

*Schimpfhauser, F., Horrocks, L., Richardson, K., Alben, J., Schumm, D., & Sprecher, H. (1974). The personalized system of instruction as an adaptable alternative within the traditional structure of medical basic sciences. In R. S. Ruskin and S. F. Bono (Eds.), *Personalized instruction in higher education* (pp. 61–69). Washington, DC: Center for Personalized Instruction.

*Schwartz, P. L. (1981). Retention of knowledge in clinical biochemistry and the effect of the Keller Plan. *Journal of Medical Education 56*, 778–781.

*Sharples, D. K., Smith, D. J., & Strasler, G. M. (1976). *Individually-paced learning in civil engineering technology: An approach to mastery.* Columbia: South Carolina State Board for Technical and Comprehensive Education. (ERIC Document Reproduction Service No. ED 131 870)

*$Sheldon, M. S., & Miller, E. D. (1973). *Behavioral objectives and mastery learning applied to two areas of junior college instruction.* Los Angeles: University of California at Los Angeles. (ERIC Document Reproduction Service No. ED 082 730)

*Sheppard, W. C., & MacDermott, H. G. (1970). Design and evaluation of a programmed course in introductory psychology. *Journal of Applied Behavior Analysis 3*, 5–11.

*Siegfried, J. J., & Strand, S. H. (1976). An evaluation of the Vanderbilt-JCEE experimental PSI course in elementary economics. *The Journal of Economic Education 8*, 9–26.

*+Silberman, R., & Parker, B. (1974). Student attitudes and the Keller Plan. *Journal of Chemical Education 51*, 393.

Slavin, R. E. (1990). Mastery learning re-considered. *Review of Educational Research 60*(2), 300–302.

*#@$&Slavin, R. E., & Karweit, N. L. (1984). Mastery learning and student teams: A factorial experiment in urban general mathematics classes. *American Educational Research Journal 21*, 725–736.

*Smiernow, G. A., & Lawley, A. (1980). Decentralized sequenced instruction (DSI) at Drexel. *Engineering Education 70*, 423–426.

*Smith, J. E. (1976). A comparison of the traditional method and a personalized system of instruction in college mathematics. *Dissertation Abstracts International 37*, 904. (University Microfilms No. AAD76-18370)

*Spector, L. C. (1976). The effectiveness of personalized system of instruction in economics. *Journal of Personalized Instruction 1*, 118–122.

*Spevack, H. M. (1976). A comparison of the personalized system of instruction with the lecture recitation system for nonscience oriented chemistry students at an open enrollment community college. *Dissertation Abstracts International 36*, 4385A–4386A. (University Microfilms No. 76-01757)

*Steele, W. F. (1974). *Mathematics 101 at Heileberg College–PSI vs. tradition.* Paper presented at the National Conference on Personalized Instruction in Higher Education, Washington, DC.

*Stout, L. J. (1978). A comparison of four different pacing strategies of personalized system of instruction and a traditional lecture format. *Dissertation Abstracts International 38*, 6205. (University Microfilms No. AAD78-08600)

*$Strasler, G. M. (1979, April). *The process of transfer in a learning for mastery setting.* Paper presented at the annual meeting of the American Educational Research Association, San Francisco. (ERIC Document Reproduction Service No. ED 174 642)

*$&Swanson, D. H., & Denton, J. J. (1976). Learning for Mastery versus Personalized System of Instruction: A comparison of remediation strategies with secondary school chemistry students. *Journal of Research in Science Teaching 14*, 515–524.

*Taylor, V. (1977, April). *Individualized calculus for the "life-long" learner: A two semester comparison of attitudes and effectiveness.* Paper presented at the Fourth National Conference of the Center for Personalized Instruction, San Francisco.

$Tenenbaum, G. (1982). *A method of group instruction which is as effective as one-to-one tutorial instruction.* Unpublished doctoral dissertation, University of Chicago.

*&Thompson, S. B. (1980). Do individualized mastery and traditional instructional systems yield different course effects in college calculus? *American Educational Research Journal 17*, 361–375.

*Tietenberg, T. H. (1975). Teaching intermediate microeconomics using the personalized system of instruction. In J. M. Johnston (Ed.), *Behavior research and technology in higher education* (pp. 75–89). Springfield, IL: Charles C. Thomas.

*Toepher, C., Shaw, D., & Moniot, D. (1972). *The effect of item exposure in a contingency management system.* Paper presented at the annual meeting of the American Psychological Association, Honolulu, HI.

*Vandenbroucke, A. C., Jr. (1974, April). *Evaluation of the use of a personalized system of* *instruction in general chemistry.* Paper presented at the National Conference on Personalized Instruction in Higher Education, Washington, DC.

*Van Verth, J. E., & Dinan, F. J. (1974). A Keller Plan course in organic chemistry. In R. S. Ruskin and S. F. Bono (Eds.), *Personalized instruction in higher education* (pp. 162–168). Washington, DC: Center for Personalized Instruction.

*Walsh, R. G., Sr. (1977). The Keller Plan in college introductory physical geology: A comparison with the conventional teaching method. *Dissertation Abstracts International 37*, 4257. (University Microfilms No. AAD76-30292)

$&+Wentling, T. L. (1973), Mastery versus nonmastery instruction with varying test item feedback treatments. *Journal of Educational Psychology 65*, 50–58.

*White, M. E. (1974). Different equations by PSI. In R. S. Ruskin and S. F. Bono (Eds.), *Personalized instruction in higher education* (pp. 169–171). Washington, DC: Center for Personalized Instruction.

Willent, J., Yamashita, J., & Anderson, R. (1983). A meta-analysis of instructional systems applied in science teaching. *Journal of Research in Science Teaching 20*(5), 405–417.

$Wire, D. R. (1979). *Mastery learning program at Durham College: Report on progress during the first year, September 1, 1978–August 31, 1979.* Durham, NC. (ERIC Document Reproduction Service No. ED 187 387)

*Witters, D. R., & Kent, G. W. (1972). Teaching without lecturing—Evidence in the case for individualized instruction. *The Psychological Record 22*, 169–175.

$Wortham, S. C. (1980). *Mastery learning in secondary schools: A first year report.* San Antonio, TX. (ERIC Document Reproduction Service No. ED 194 453)

*Yeany, R. H., Dost, R. J., & Matthew, R. W. (1980). The effects of diagnostic-prescriptive instruction and locus of control on the achievement and attitudes of university students. *Journal of Research in Science Teaching 17*, 537–545.

$Yildren, G. (1977). *The effects of level of cognitive achievement on selected learning criteria under mastery learning and normal classroom instruction.* Unpublished doctoral dissertation, University of Chicago.

3

Providing Effective Evaluation and Remediation

INTRODUCTION

In the present context, evaluation can be defined as (1) assessing student task performance for the purpose of certifying student competence in performing the tasks being evaluated and (2) diagnosing causes of inadequacy. Remediation is the correction of inadequate task performance. Evaluation and remediation are presented together since they tend to be closely linked in the research studies reviewed. Remediation is based on evaluation and, when indicated, is to be prescribed and initiated immediately following evaluation. When evaluations are conducted, students are to be given immediate feedback on the competence of their task performance and new tasks are assigned to students based on evaluation results. Students whose task performance is judged to be competent are assigned more advanced tasks. Students who have not as yet achieved competence are assigned remedial tasks to correct inadequacies diagnosed during evaluation. This could be seen as a diagnostic and prescriptive cycle or loop, with feedback occurring between or linking the two. Evaluations serve as diagnostic tools for determining competent or inadequate task performance. In the case of inadequacy, the evaluations should provide for the diagnosis of the cause as well as the inadequacy itself. Once the inadequacy and causes are identified, appropriate remedial tasks leading to competence can be prescribed. In the case of competence, the prescription is for the student to exit the current cycle and move on to more complex tasks and a new evaluation-feedback-remediation cycle.

Far too many evaluation procedures provide for the assessment of competency without providing for the diagnosis of causes of inadequate task performance. This neglect prevents the remediation of inadequate task performance. In such cases, feedback of evaluation results can convey to students only that their performance is competent or inadequate. When students are told that evaluation results indicate that their task performance is inadequate, they must suffer the insult. There is no cogent basis for remediating their inadequacy. Instruction is ineffective and student achievement of learning objectives is severely impaired when evaluation procedures do not diagnose the causes of students' inadequate task performance.

Since most students do not often achieve competent task performance without making and correcting inadequacies along the way, effective remediation, as well as diagnostic procedures, must be provided for beforehand. When evaluation results indicate the need for remediation, remedial action must be taken without delay so that students do not wallow in their failure and become discouraged. Excessive failure to learn is frustrating and can generate perceptions of helplessness and dissuade students from trying to learn.

STUDENT BENEFICIARIES

The evidence indicates that the academic achievement of students in kindergarten, elementary, secondary, college, and adult learning classrooms is enhanced when student performance of assigned tasks is evaluated, feedback on the correctness of performance is provided, and incorrect performance is remediated. Moreover, academic achievement was improved in a wide range of content areas. No evidence could be found to suggest that remedial tactics should not be utilized in all subject areas for all types of students.

LEARNING ACHIEVED

Achievement in the content areas of mathematics, history, foreign languages, English, reading, social sciences, sciences, social studies, business, and occupational areas is enhanced when student performance of tasks is evaluated, feedback on the correctness of performance is provided, and the student is afforded the information and opportunity to correct his or her errors. In studies reviewed, instruction incorporating effective evaluation and remedial tactics was positively associated with enhanced student achievement.

INSTRUCTIONAL TACTICS

The following tactics are derived from studies that demonstrate their benefit on student achievement. Discretion has been used in interpreting, elaborating, and reducing overlap in tactics used in different studies.

Tactics employed are:

Planning: Procedures for evaluating and remediating student performance need to be planned beforehand. Tasks need to be sufficiently short to enable frequent evaluation of student performance and to avoid excessive task complexity so that it is possible for students to perform tasks correctly on their first attempt.

Evaluation: Frequent quizzes, tests, and other forms of performance evaluation should be employed. Evaluation procedures should enable the diagnosis of student inadequacies as well as the assessment of student progress.

Feedback: Students are to be informed of the correctness of their performance on assigned tasks. Their achievements and/or efforts are to be acknowledged, as appropriate, and they are to be encouraged to undertake their next challenge with expectations of success.

Remediating: Remedial tasks are to be assigned to correct inadequate student performance. Students who need remediation are to be assured that they will receive all the help they need and that their concerted efforts will ultimately result in success. Their success, however, depends on their receiving task assignments they have the readiness ability to perform, and that they are given the help they need to be successful.

Elaborations of the above summary of tactics can be obtained from reading the studies that follow. To be most effective, the instructional tactics need to be integrated into the particular instructional program being planned or presently in use.

CAUTIONS AND COMMENTS

The importance of remediation on student success in achieving learning objectives cannot be overemphasized. Students who consistently fail in their attempts to achieve the learning objectives eventually tire of trying to learn. They become frustrated and feel helpless, at times even angry. Eventually they may become "dropouts" and burdens on society. It is equally important that evaluation instruments provide diagnostic information that can be used as the basis for prescribing effective remedial tactics.

GENERALIZATION: ON EVALUATION AND REMEDIATION

Achievement of learning objectives is enhanced when appropriate remediation is provided: (1) evaluation procedures and remedial tasks are formulated when task sequences are planned; (2) student task performance is frequently evaluated; (3) feedback on evaluation is given to students without delay; and (4) incorrect performance is immediately remediated, based on evaluation results.

Supportive Research on Evaluation and Remediation
Total number of studies covered: 219

Groups of Studies

Author: Anderson (1994): Synthesis of seven meta-analyses

Students: Kindergarten, elementary, secondary, college, and other adult students

Learning: Achievement

Instructional Tactics: The following tactics associated with readiness and Mastery Learning are also presented in Bloom (1985), Block (1980), and others. Other tactics associated with Mastery Learning are applicable to other generalizations and are covered in the appropriate chapters.

- Subject matter should be divided into small units of learning in order to enhance the possibilities for student success, and student learning should be tested at the end of each unit.
- Alternative instructional materials, procedures, or correctives are developed by the teacher for each item on a test that is designed to reteach the material tested in ways different from the original instruction.
- The teacher provides feedback to the students on their errors after each test.
- The teacher assigns the developed alternative learning materials, procedures, or correctives to be accomplished either inside or outside of the class as they diagnose to be appropriate for each student.

Findings: Positive achievement gains associated with Mastery Learning were seen in 64–93 percent of the studies reviewed in the seven meta-analyses.

Individual studies analyzed by these meta-analyses are identified in the reference list at the end of the chapter by the following symbols:

Kulik et al. (1990a) *
Kulik et al. (1990b) #
Slavin (1990) @
Guskey & Pigott (1988) $
Guskey & Gates (1985) &
Block & Burns (1976) +

It was not possible to determine the individual studies for which readiness was an instructional tactic for the Willett et al. (1983) analysis.

Author: Rosenshine & Stevens (1986)

Students: Elementary and secondary

Learning: Mathematics, English, science, history, and reading achievement

Instructional Tactics:

- The teacher prepares a large number of questions relevant to the to-be-learned material.

- During instruction and student practice the teacher asks a large number of questions to check for student understanding.
- Frequent tests are given.
- Correct responses to questions are acknowledged as correct.
- The teacher should simply provide the correct response to the student if an incorrect response is determined by the teacher to be a careless error on the part of the student.
- When a student's incorrect response is due to a lack of knowledge or understanding, the teacher has one of two options to pursue as deemed most appropriate: (1) provide students with prompts or hints to lead them to the correct answer or (2) reteach the material to the students who do not understand.
- The teacher provides praise for correct responses and encouragement for incorrect responses.

Other instructional tactics are employed in these studies that are applicable to other generalizations and will be presented in the appropriate chapters.

Findings: Use of these tactics was found to be related to greater levels of student achievement.

Groups of studies reviewed in this logical synthesis of research did not provide statistical evidence. However, many of the individual studies included in the logical synthesis of research do contain statistical evidence. In the event that a reader wishes to view this evidence, an extensive listing of the individual studies reviewed is provided in the reference list (the studies are identified by the symbol %).

Author: Brophy & Good (1986)

Students: Elementary and secondary

Learning: Reading, mathematics, English, and biology achievement

Instructional Tactics:

- The teacher asks questions that focus on academic content in ordered turns to ensure that all students have an opportunity to respond.
- The teacher acknowledges correct responses.
- When incorrect responses are made the teacher ensures that the correct response is revealed. The teacher might provide the correct response or continue questioning until the correct response emerges as discretion indicates.
- The teacher then provides additional instruction or opportunity for practice as deemed appropriate.
- The teacher provides encouragement and reinforces correct responses.

Other instructional tactics are employed in these studies that are applicable to other generalizations and will be presented in the appropriate chapters.

Individual studies included in this research synthesis are identified by the symbol ! in the reference list.

Findings: Use of the preceding instructional tactics was found to be positively related to student achievement.

Individual Studies

Author: Obando & Hymel (1991)

Students: Grade 9

Learning: Spanish language achievement

Instructional Tactics:

- Diagnostic formative trial tests are administered to the students.
- Students are provided feedback on their performance on the formative tests.
- The teacher provides learning correctives in the form of additional assignments and tutoring sessions when necessary.

Other instructional tactics are employed in this study that are applicable to other generalizations and will be presented in the appropriate chapters.

Findings: Achievement was significantly higher for students who benefited from these tactics on unit exams and the National Spanish Examination as compared to students who did not.

REFERENCE LIST

*+Abraham, F. J., & Newton, J. M. (1974). *The interview technique as a personalized system of instruction for economics: The Oregon experience.* Paper presented at the National Conference on Personalized Instruction in Higher Education, Washington, DC.

!Acland, H. (1976). Stability of teacher effectiveness: A replication. *Journal of Educational Research 69*, 289–292.

$Anania, J. (1981). *The effects of quality of instruction on the cognitive and affective learning of students.* Unpublished doctoral dissertation, University of Chicago.

!%Anderson, L. M., Evertson, C. M., & Brophy, J. E. (1979). An experimental study of effective teaching in first-grade reading groups. *The Elementary School Journal 79*, 193–222.

!%Anderson, L. M., Evertson, C. M., & Brophy, J. E. (1982). *Principles of small group instruction* (Occasional paper no. 32). East Lansing: Michigan State University, Institute for Research on Teaching.

+Anderson, L. W. (1973). *Time and school learning.* Unpublished doctoral dissertation, University of Chicago.

*$&Anderson, L. W. (1975a). Student involvement in learning and school achievement. *California Journal of Educational Research 26,* 53–62.

$&Anderson, L. W. (1975b). *Time to criterion: An experimental study.* Paper presented at the annual meeting of the American Educational Research Association, Washington, DC. (ERIC Document Reproduction Service No. ED 108 006)

*$&+Anderson, L. W. (1976). An empirical investigation of individual differences in time to learn. *Journal of Educational Psychology 68,* 226–233.

*#@$&Anderson, L. W., Scott, C., & Hutlock, N. (1976, April). *The effects of a mastery learning program on selected cognitive, affective, and ecological variables in grades 1 through 6.* Paper presented at the annual meeting of the American Educational Research Association. San Francisco.

+Anderson, O. T., & Artman, R. A. (1972). A self-paced independent study, introductory physics sequence-description and evaluation. *American Journal of Physics 40,* 1737–1742.

Anderson, S. A. (1994). *Synthesis of research on mastery learning* (Information Analysis). (ERIC Document Reproduction Service No. ED 382 567)

!Arehart, J. (1979). Student opportunity to learn related to student achievement of objectives in a probability unit. *Journal of Educational Research 72,* 253–269.

*$&%Arlin, M., & Webster, J. (1983). Time costs of mastery learning. *Journal of Educational Psychology 75,* 187–195.

*Austin, S. M., & Gilbert, K. E. (1973). Student performance in a Keller-Plan course in introductory electricity and magnetism. *American Journal of Physics 41,* 12–18.

*Badia, P., Stutts, C., & Harsh, J. (1978). Do methods of instruction and measures of different abilities and study habits interact? In J. G. Sherman, R. S. Ruskin, & R. M. Lazar (Eds.), *Personalized instruction in education today* (pp. 113–128). San Francisco: San Francisco Press.

%Becker, W. C. (1977). Teaching reading and language to the disadvantaged—What we have learned from field research. *Harvard Educational Review 47,* 518–543.

*Benson, J. S., & Yeany, R. H. (1980, April). *Generalizability of diagnostic-prescriptive teaching strategies across student locus of control and multiple instructional units.* Paper presented at the annual meeting of the American Educational Research Association, Boston. (ERIC Document Reproduction Service No. 187 534)

!Berliner, D., Fisher, C., Filby, N., & Marliave, R. (1978). *Executive summary of Beginning Teacher Evaluation Study.* San Francisco: Far West Laboratory.

*+Billings, D. B. (1974). PSI versus the lecture course in the principles of economics: a quasi-controlled experiment. In R. S. Ruskin & S. F. Bono (Eds.), *Personalized instruction in higher education* (pp. 30–37). Washington, DC: Center for Personalized Instruction.

*$Blackburn, K. T., & Nelson, D. (1985, April). *Differences between a group using a traditional format with mastery learning and a group using a traditional format only in developmental mathematics courses at the university level: Implications for teacher education programs.* Paper presented at the annual meeting of the American Educational Research Association, Chicago. (ERIC Document Reproduction Service No. ED 258 948)

*Blasingame, J. W. (1975). Student attitude and performance in a personalized system of instruction course in business administration—Correlates performance with personality traits. *Dissertation Abstracts International 36*, 3840. (University Microfilms No. 75-2834)

$&+Block, J. H. (1972). Student learning and the setting of mastery performance standards. *Educational Horizons 50*, 183–191.

+Block, J. H. (1973). *Mastery performance standards and student learning.* Unpublished study, University of California, Santa Barbara.

Block, J. H. (1980). Success rate. In C. Denham & A. Lieberman (Eds.), *Time to learn* (pp. 95–106). Washington, DC: U.S. Government Printing Office.

Block, J. H., & Burns, R. B. (1976). Mastery learning. In L. Schulman (Ed.), *Review of research in education* (Vol. 4, pp. 3–49). Itasca, IL: F. E. Peacock.

$+Block, J. H., & Tierney, M. (1974). An exploration of two correction procedures used in mastery learning approaches to instruction. *Journal of Educational Psychology 66*, 962–967.

Bloom, B. S. (1985). Learning for mastery. In C. W. Fisher & D. C. Berliner (Eds.), *Perspectives on instructional time.* White Plains, NY: Longman.

*+Born, D. G., & Davis, M. L. (1974). Amount and distribution of study in a personalized instruction course and in a lecture course. *Journal of Applied Behavior Analysis 7*, 365–375.

*+Born, D. G., Gledhill, S. M., & Davis, M. L. (1972). Examination performance in lecture-discussion and personalized instruction courses. *Journal of Applied Behavior Analysis 5*, 33–43.

*+Breland, N. S., & Smith, M. P. (1974). A comparison of PSI and traditional methods of instruction for teaching introduction to psychology. In R. S. Ruskin & S. F. Bono (Eds.), *Personalized instruction in higher education* (pp. 21–25). Washington, DC: Center for Personalized Instruction.

!Brophy, J. (1973). Stability of teacher effectiveness. *American Educational Research Journal 10*, 245–252.

!Brophy, J., & Evertson, C. (1974a). *Process–product correlations in the Texas Teacher Effectiveness Study: Final report* (Research Report 74-4). Austin: Research and Development Center for Teacher Education, University of Texas. (ERIC Document Reproduction No. ED 091 094)

!Brophy, J., & Evertson, C. (1974b). *The Texas Teacher Effectiveness Project: Presentation of non-linear relationships and summary discussion* (Research Report 74-6). Austin: Research and Development Center for Teacher Education, University of Texas. (ERIC Document Reproduction No. ED 099 345)

!%Brophy, J., & Evertson, C. (1976). *Learning from teaching: A developmental perspective.* Boston: Allyn and Bacon.

Brophy, J., & Good, T. (1986). Teacher behavior and student achievement. In M. C. Wittrock (Ed.), *Handbook of research on teaching* (pp. 328–375). New York: Macmillan.

*$Bryant, N. D., Fayne, H. R., & Gettinger, M. (1982). Applying the mastery model to sight word instruction for disabled readers. *Journal of Experimental Education 50*, 116–121.

$Burke, A. (1983). *Students' potential for learning contrasted under tutorial and group approaches to instruction.* Unpublished doctoral dissertation, University of Chicago.

$&+Burrows, C. K., & Okey, J. R. (1975, March–April). *The effects of a mastery learning strategy on achievement.* Paper presented at the annual meeting of the American Educational Research Association, Washington, DC.

*#@$Cabezon, E. (1984). *The effects of marked changes in student achievement pattern on the students, their teachers, and their parents: The Chilean case.* Unpublished doctoral dissertation, University of Chicago.

$Chiappetta, E. L., & McBride, J. W. (1980). Exploring the effects of general remediation on ninth-graders' achievement of the mole concept. *Science Education 6*, 609–614.

*$Clark, C. P., Guskey, T. P., & Benninga, J. S. (1983). The effectiveness of mastery learning strategies in undergraduate education courses. *Journal of Educational Research 76*, 210–214.

*Clark, S. G. (1975). An innovation for introductory sociology: Personalized system of instruction. In J. M. Johnston (Ed.), *Behavior research and technology in higher education* (pp. 117–124). Springfield, IL: Charles C. Thomas.

!Coker, H., Medley., & Soar, R. (1980). How valid are expert opinions about effective teaching? *Phi Delta Kappan 62*, 131–134, 149.

*+Coldeway, D. O., Santowski, M., O'Brien, R., & Lagowski, V. (1975). Comparison of small group contingency management with the personalized system of instruction and the lecture system. In J. M. Johnston (Ed.), *Research and technology in college and university teaching* (pp. 215–224). Gainesville: University of Florida.

*+Cole, C., Martin, S., & Vincent, J. (1975). A comparison of two teaching formats at the college level. In J. M. Johnston (Ed.), *Behavior research and technology in higher education* (pp. 61–74). Springfield, IL: Charles C. Thomas.

*Condo, P. (1974, April). *The analysis and evaluation of a self-paced course in calculus.* Paper presented at the National Conference on Personalized Instruction in Higher Education, Washington, DC.

*+Cooper, J. L., & Greiner, J. M. (1971). Contingency management in an introductory psychology course produces better retention. *Psychological Record 21*, 391–400.

*Corey, J. R., & McMichael, J. S. (1974). Retention in a PSI introductory psychology course. In J. G. Sherman (Ed.), *PSI germinal papers* (pp. 17–19). Washington, DC: Center for Personalized Instruction.

+Corey, J. R., McMichael, J. S., & Tremont, P. J. (1970, April). *Long-term effects of personalized instruction in an introductory psychology course.* Paper presented at the meeting of the Eastern Psychology Association, Atlantic City.

*Cote, J. D. (1976). Biology by PSI in a community college. In B. A. Green, Jr. (Ed.), *Personalized instruction in higher education.* Washington, DC: Center for Personalized Instruction.

!Crawford, J. (1983). A study of instructional processes in Title I classes: 1981–82. *Journal of Research and Evaluation of the Oklahoma City Public Schools 13*(1).

*Cross, M. Z., & Semb, G. (1976). An analysis of the effects of personalized instruction on students at different initial performance levels in an introductory college nutrition course. *Journal of Personalized Instruction 1*, 47–50.

*Decker, D. F. (1976). *Teaching to achieve learning mastery by using retesting techniques.* (ERIC Document Reproduction Service No. ED 133 002)

$Denton, W. L., Ory, J. C., Glassnap, D. R., & Poggio, J. P. (1976). *Grade expectations within a mastery learning strategy.* Paper presented at the annual meeting of the American Educational Research Association, San Francisco. (ERIC Document Reproduction Service No. ED 126 105)

*$Dillashaw, F. G., & Okey, J. R. (1983). Effects of a modified mastery learning strategy on achievement, attitudes, and on-task behavior of high school chemistry students. *Journal of Research in Science Teaching 20*, 203–211.

$Duby, P. B. (1981). *Attributions and attribution change: Effects of a mastery learning instructional approach.* Paper presented at the annual meeting of the American Educational Research Association, Los Angeles. (ERIC Document Reproduction Service No. ED 200 640)

!Dunkin, M. J. (1978). Student characteristics, classroom processes, and student achievement. *Journal of Educational Psychology 70,* 998–1009.

!Ebmier, H., & Good, T. (1979). The effects of instructing teachers about good teaching on mathematics achievement of fourth grade students. *American Educational Research Journal 16,* 1–16.

!Emmer, E., Evertson, C., & Anderson, L. (1980). Effective classroom management at the beginning of the school year. *Elementary School Journal 80,* 219–231.

!Emmer, E., Evertson, C., & Brophy, J. (1979). Stability of teacher effects in junior high classrooms. *American Educational Research Journal 16,* 71–75.

!%Emmer, E. T., Evertson, C., Sanford, J., & Clements, B. (1982). *Improving classroom management: An experimental study in junior high classrooms.* Austin: Research and Development Center for Teacher Education, University of Texas.

%Evertson, C. (1982). Differences in instructional activities in higher and lower achieving junior high English and mathematics classrooms. *Elementary School Journal 82,* 329–351.

!%Evertson, C., Anderson, C., Anderson, L., & Brophy, J. (1980). Relationships between classroom behaviors and student outcomes in junior high mathematics and English classes. *American Educational Research Journal 17,* 43–60.

!Evertson, C., Anderson, L., & Brophy, J. (1978). *Texas Junior High School Study: Final report of process–outcome relationship* (Report No. 4061). Austin: Research and Development Center for Teacher Education, University of Texas.

!Evertson, C., & Brophy, J. (1973). High-inference behavioral ratings as correlates of teacher effectiveness. *JSAS Catalog of Selected Documents in Psychology 3,* 97.

!Evertson, C., & Brophy, J. (1974). *Texas Teacher Effectiveness Project: Questionnaire and interview data* (Research Report No. 74-5). Austin: Research and Development Center for Teacher Education, University of Texas.

!%Evertson, C., Emmer, E., & Brophy, J. (1980). Predictors of effective teaching in junior high mathematics classrooms. *Journal for Research in Mathematics Education 11,* 167–178.

%Evertson, C. M., Emmer, E. T., Sanford, J. P., & Clements, B. S. (1983). Improving classroom management: An experiment in elementary classrooms. *Elementary School Journal 84,* 173–188.

*#@Fagan, J. S. (1976). Mastery learning: The relationship of mastery procedures and aptitude to the achievement and retention of transportation-environment concepts by seventh grade students. *Dissertation Abstracts International 36,* 5981. (University Microfilms No. 76-6402)

*Fehlen, J. E. (1976). Mastery learning techniques in the traditional classroom setting. *School Science and Mathematics 76,* 241–245.

*Fernald, P. S., & DuNann, D. H. (1975). Effects of individualized instruction upon low- and high-achieving students' study behavior and students' evaluation of mastery. *Journal of Experimental Education 43,* 27–34.

$&+Fiel, R. L., & Okey, J. R. (1974). The effects of formative evaluation and remediation on mastery of intellectual skill. *Journal of Educational Research 68,* 253–255.

!%Fisher, C. W., Berliner, D. C., Filby, N. N., Marliave, R., Cahen, L. S., & Dishaw, M. M.

(1980). Teaching behaviors, academic learning time, and student achievement: An overview. In C. Denham & A. Lieberman (Eds.), *Time to learn* (pp. 7–32). Washington, DC: U.S. Government Printing Office.

!%Fitzpatrick, K. A. (1981). *An investigation of secondary classroom material strategies for increasing student academic engaged time.* Doctoral dissertation, University of Illinois at Urbana–Champaign.

!%Fitzpatrick, K. A. (1982). *The effect of a secondary classroom management training program on teacher and student behavior.* Paper presented at the annual meeting of the American Educational Research Association, New York.

$&Fitzpatrick, K. A. (1985, April). *Group-based mastery learning: A Robin Hood approach to instruction?* Paper presented at the annual meeting of the American Educational Research Association, Chicago.

+Glassnapp, D. R., Poggio, J. P., & Ory, J. C. (1975, March–April). *Cognitive and affective consequences of mastery and non-mastery instructional strategies.* Paper presented at the annual meeting of the American Educational Research Association, Washington, DC.

*Goldwater, B. C., & Acker, L. E. (1975). Instructor-paced, mass-testing for mastery performance in an introductory psychology course. *Teaching of Psychology 2*, 152–155.

!Good, T., Ebmeier, H., & Beckerman, T. (1978) Teaching mathematics in high and low SES classrooms: An empirical comparison. *Journal of Teacher Education 29*, 85–90.

!Good, T., Grouws, D., & Beckerman, T. (1978). Curriculum pacing: Some empirical data in mathematics. *Journal of Curriculum Studies 10*, 75–81.

!%Good, T., Grouws, D., & Ebmeier, M. (1983). *Active mathematics teaching.* New York: Longman.

!%Good, T. L., & Grouws, D. A. (1977). Teaching effects: a process-product study in fourth grade mathematics classrooms. *Journal of Teacher Education 28*(3), 49–54.

!Good, T. L., & Grouws, D. A. (1979a). *Experimental study of mathematics instruction in elementary schools* (Final Report, National Institute of Education Grant No. NIE-G-79-0103). Columbia: University of Missouri, Center for the Study of Social Behavior.

!%Good, T. L., & Grouws, D. A. (1979b). The Missouri mathematics effectiveness project. *Journal of Educational Psychology 71*, 355–362.

!Good, T. L., & Grouws, D. A. (1981). *Experimental research in secondary mathematics* (Final Report, National Institute of Education Grant No. NIE-G-79-0103). Columbia: University of Missouri, Center for the Study of Social Behavior.

*Gregory, I., Smeltzer, D. J., Knopp, W., & Gardner, M. (1976). *Teaching of psychiatry by PSI: Impact on National Board Examination scores.* Unpublished manuscript, Ohio State University, Columbus.

*$&Guskey, T. R. (1982). The effects of staff development on teachers' perceptions about effective teaching. *Journal of Educational Research 76*, 378–381.

*$&Guskey, T. R. (1984). The influence of changes in instructional effectiveness upon the affective characteristics of teachers. *American Educational Research Journal 21*, 245–259.

$Guskey, T. R. (1985). The effects of staff development on teachers' perceptions about effective teaching. *Journal of Educational Research 79*, 378–381.

*$Guskey, T. R., Benninga, J. S., & Clark, C. B. (1984). Mastery learning and students' attributions at the college level. *Research in Higher Education 20*, 491–498.

Guskey, T. R., & Gates, S. L. (1986). Synthesis of research on the effects of mastery learning in elementary and secondary classrooms. *Educational Leadership 33*(8), 73–80.

*$Guskey, T. R., & Monsaas, J. A. (1979). Mastery learning: A model for academic success in urban junior colleges. *Research in Higher Education 11*, 263–274.

Guskey, T. R., & Pigott, T. D. (1988). Research on group-based mastery learning programs: A meta-analysis. *Journal of Educational Research 81*(4), 197–216.

*Hardin, L. D. (1977). A study of the influence of a physics personalized system of instruction versus lecture on cognitive reasoning, achievement, attitudes and critical thinking. *Dissertation Abstracts International 38*, 4711A–4712A. (University Microfilms No. 77-30826)

*Hecht, L. W. (1980, April). *Stalking mastery learning in its natural habitat.* Paper presented at the annual meeting of the American Educational Research Association, Boston.

*Heffley, P. D. (1974). The implementation of the personalized system of instruction in the freshman chemistry course at Censius College. In R. S. Ruskin & S. F. Bono (Eds.), *Personalized instruction in higher education* (pp. 140–145). Washington, DC: Center for Personalized Instruction.

*Herring, B. G. (1975, December). *Cataloguing and classification.* Austin: University of Texas.

*Herring, B. G. (1977). *The written PSI study guide in a non-PSI course.* Austin: University of Texas.

*Herrmann, T. (1984, August). *TELIDON as an enhancer of student interest and performance.* Paper presented at the annual meeting of the American Psychological Association, Toronto. (ERIC Document Reproduction Service No. ED 251 004)

*Hindman, C. D. (1974). Evaluation of three programming techniques in introductory psychology courses. In R. S. Ruskin & S. F. Bono (Eds.), *Personalized instruction in higher education* (pp. 38–42). Washington, DC: Center for Personalized Instruction.

*Honeycutt, J. K. (1974, April). *The effect of computer managed instruction on content learning of undergraduate students.* Paper presented at the annual meeting of the American Educational Research Association, Chicago. (ERIC Document Reproduction Service No. ED 089 682)

!Hughes, D. (1973). An experimental investigation of the effect of pupil responding and teacher reacting on pupil achievement. *American Educational Research Journal 10*, 21–37.

*Hymel, G. M. (1974). *An investigation of John B. Carrol's model of school learning as a theoretical basis for the organizational structuring of schools* (Final Report, NIE Project No. 3-1359). University of New Orleans, New Orleans, LA.

*Hymel, G. M., & Mathews, G. (1980). Effects of a mastery approach on social studies achievement and unit evaluation. *Southern Journal of Educational Research 14*, 191–204.

*Jackman, L. E. (1982). Evaluation of a modified Keller method in a biochemistry laboratory course. *Journal of Chemical Education 59*, 225–227.

*Jacko, E. J. (1974). Lecture instruction versus a personalized system of instruction: Effects on individuals with differing achievement anxiety and academic achievement. *Dissertation Abstracts International 35*, 3521. (University Microfilms No. AAD 74-27211)

+Johnston, J. M., & Pennypacker, H. S. (1971). A behavioral approach to college teaching. *American Psychologist 26*, 219–244.

*#@$&Jones, B. F., Monsaas, J. A., & Katims, M. (1979, April). *Improving reading*

comprehension: Embedding diverse learning strategies within a mastery learning instructional framework. Paper presented at the annual meeting of the American Educational Research Association, San Francisco. (ERIC Document Reproduction Service No. ED 170 698)

$+Jones, E. L., Gordon, H. A., & Stectman, G. L. (1975). *Mastery learning: A strategy for academic success in a community college.* Los Angeles: ERIC Clearinghouse for Junior Colleges. (ERIC Document Reproduction Service No. ED 115 315)

+Jones, F. G. (1974). *The effects of mastery and aptitude on learning, retention, and time.* Unpublished doctoral dissertation, University of Georgia.

+Karlin, B. M. (1972). *The Keller method of instruction compared to the traditional method of instruction in a Lafayette College history course.* Unpublished paper, Lafayette College, Lafayette, PA.

*#@Katims, M., Smith, J. K., Steele, C., & Wick, J. W. (1977, April). *The Chicago mastery learning reading program: An interim evaluation.* Paper presented at the annual meeting of the American Educational Research Association, New York. (ERIC Document Reproduction Service No. ED 137 737)

*#@Kersh, M. E. (1970). *A strategy of mastery learning in fifth grade arithmetic.* Unpublished doctoral dissertation, University of Chicago.

+Kim, Y., Cho, G., Park, J., & Park, M. (1974). *An application of a new instructional model* (Research Report No. 8). Seoul, Korea: Korean Educational Development Institute.

*Knight, J. M., Williams, J. D., & Jardon, M. L. (1975). The effects of contingency avoidance on programmed student achievement. *Research in Higher Education 3*, 11–17.

!Kounin, J. (1970). *Discipline and group management in classrooms.* New York: Holt, Reinhart, & Winston.

*Kulik, C., & Kulik, J. (1976). PSI and the mastery model. In B. A. Green, Jr. (Ed.), *Personalized instruction in higher education* (pp. 155–159). Washington, DC: Center for Personalized Instruction.

Kulik, C., Kulik, J., & Bangert-Drowns, R. (1990a). Effectiveness of mastery learning programs: A meta-analysis. *Review of Educational Research 60*(2), 265–269.

Kulik, J., Kulik, C., & Bangert-Drowns, R. (1990b). Is there better evidence on mastery learning? A response to Slavin. *Review of Educational Research 60*(2), 303–307.

+Kulik, J. A., Kulik, C., & Carmichael, K. (1974). The Keller Plan in science teaching. *Science 183*, 379–383.

!Larrivee, B., & Algina, J. (1983, April). *Identification of teaching behaviors which predict success for mainstream students.* Paper presented at the annual meeting of the American Educational Research Association. Montreal, Canada. (ERIC Document Reproduction Service No. ED 232 362)

+Lee, Y. D., Kim, C. S., Kim, H., Park, B. Y., Yoo, H. K., Chang, S. M., & Kim, S. C. (1971). *Interaction improvement studies of the Mastery Learning Project* (Final Report on the Mastery Learning Project, April–November 1971). Seoul, Korea: Educational Research Center, Seoul National University.

*Leppmann, P. K., & Herrman, T. F. (1981, August). *PSI—What are the critical elements?* Paper presented at the annual meeting of the American Psychological Association, Los Angeles. (ERIC Document Reproduction Service No. ED 214 502)

$+Levin, T. (1975). *The effect of content prerequisites and process-oriented experiences on application ability in the learning of probability.* Unpublished doctoral dissertation, University of Chicago.

*Lewis, E. W. (1984). The effects of a mastery learning strategy and an interactive computerized quiz strategy on student achievement and attitude in college trigonometry. *Dissertation Abstracts International 45*, 2430A. (University Microfilms No. DA84-24589)

*Leyton, F. S. (1983). *The extent to which group instruction supplemented by mastery of initial cognitive prerequisites approximates the learning effectiveness of one-to-one tutorial methods.* Unpublished doctoral dissertation, University of Chicago.

*Locksley, N. (1977). The Personalized System of Instruction (PSI) in a university mathematics class. *Dissertation Abstracts International 37*, 4194. (University Microfilms No. ADD76-28194)

#@Long, J. C., Okey, J. R., & Yeany, R. H. (1978). The effects of diagnosis with teacher on student directed remediation on science achievement and attitudes. *Journal of Research in Science Teaching 15*, 505–511.

*Lu, M. C. (1976). The retention of material learned by PSI in a mathematics course. In B. A. Green, Jr. (Ed.), *Personalized instruction in higher education* (pp. 151–154). Washington, DC: Center for Personalized Instruction.

*Lu, P. H. (1976). Teaching human growth and development by the Personalized System for Instruction. *Teaching of Psychology 3*, 127–128.

*Lubkin, J. L. (1974). Engineering statistics: A Keller Plan course with novel problems and novel features. In R. S. Ruskin and S. F. Bono (Eds.), *Personalized instruction in higher education* (pp. 153–161). Washington, DC: Center for Personalized Instruction.

*#@Lueckmeyer, C. L., & Chiappetta, W. L. (1981). An investigation into the effects of a modified mastery learning strategy on achievement in a high school human physiology unit. *Journal of Research in Science Teaching 18*, 269–273.

*Malec, M. A. (1975). PSI: A brief report and reply to Francis. *Teaching Sociology 2*, 212–217.

*Martin, R. R., & Srikameswaran, K. (1974). Correlation between frequent testing and student performance. *Journal of Chemical Education 51*, 485–486.

$Mathews, G. S. (1982). *Effects of a mastery learning strategy on the cognitive knowledge and unit evaluation of students in high school social studies.* Unpublished doctoral dissertation, University of Southern Mississippi.

!McConnell, J. (1977). *Relationship between selected teacher behaviors and attitudes/achievements of algebra classes.* Paper presented at the annual meeting of the American Educational Research Association. New York. (ERIC Document Reproduction Service No. ED 141 118)

!McDonald, F. (1976). Report on Phase II of the Beginning Teacher Evaluation Study. *Journal of Teacher Education 27*(1), 39–42.

!McDonald, F. (1977). Research on teaching: Report on Phase II of the Beginning Teacher Evaluation Study. In G. Borich and K. Fenton (Eds.), *The appraisal of teaching: Concepts and process.* Reading, MA: Addison-Wesley.

!McDonald, F., & Elias, P. (1976). *Executive Summary Report: Beginning Teacher Evaluation Study, Phase II.* Princeton, NJ: Educational Testing Service.

*McFarland, B. (1976). An individualized course in elementary composition for the marginal student. In B. A. Green, Jr. (Ed.), *Personalized instruction in higher education* (pp. 45–52). Washington, DC: Center for Personalized Instruction.

*+McMichael, J., & Corey, J. R. (1969). Contingency management in an introductory psychology course produces better learning. *Journal of Applied Behavior Analysis 2*, 79–83.

*#@Mevarech, Z. R. (1980). *The role of teaching-learning strategies and feedback-corrective*

procedures in developing higher cognitive achievement. Unpublished doctoral dissertation, University of Chicago.

$&Mevarech, Z. R. (1981, April). *Attaining mastery on higher cognitive achievement.* Paper presented at the annul meeting of the American Educational Research Association, Los Angeles.

*Mevarech, Z. R. (1985). The effects of cooperative mastery learning strategies on mathematical achievement. *Journal of Educational Research 78*, 372–377.

*#@Mevarech, Z. R. (1986). The role of feedback corrective procedure in developing mathematics achievement and self-concept in desegregated classrooms. *Studies in Educational Evaluation 12*, 197–203.

*Mevarech, Z. R., & Werner, S. (1985). Are mastery learning strategies beneficial for developing problem solving skills? *Higher Education 14*, 425–432.

*Meyers, R. R. (1976). The effects of mastery and aptitude on achievement and attitude in an introductory college geography course. *Dissertation Abstracts International 36*, 5874. (University Microfilms No. 76-6436)

*+Morris, C., & Kimbrill, G. (1972). Performance and attitudinal effects of the Keller method in an introductory psychology course. *Psychological Record 22*, 523–530.

*Nation, J. R., Knight, J. M., Lamberth, J., & Dyck, D. (1974). Programmed student achievement: A test of the avoidance hypothesis. *Journal of Experimental Education 42*, 57–61.

*Nation, J. R., Massad, P., & Wilkerson, P. (1977). Student performance in introductory psychology following termination of the programmed achievement contingency at mid-semester. *Teaching of Psychology 4*, 116–119.

*Nation, J. R., & Roop, S. S. (1975). A comparison of two mastery approaches to teaching introductory psychology. *Teaching of Psychology 2*, 108–111.

*+Nazzaro, J. R., Todorov, J. C., & Nazzaro, J. N. (1972). Student ability and individualized instruction. *Journal of College Science Teaching 2*, 29–30.

*Nord, S. B. (1975). Comparative achievement and attitude in individualized and class instructional settings. *Dissertation Abstracts International 35*, 5129A. (University Microfilms No. 75-02314)

$Nordin, A. B. (1979). *The effects of different qualities of instruction on selected cognitive, affective, and time variables.* Unpublished doctoral dissertation, University of Chicago.

!Nuthall, G., & Church, J. (1973). Experimental studies of teaching behavior. In G. Chanan (Ed.), *Towards a science of teaching.* London: National Foundation for Educational Research.

Obando, L. T., & Hymel, G. M. (1991 March). *The effect of mastery learning instruction on the entry-level Spanish proficiency of secondary school students.* Paper presented at the annual meeting to the American Educational Research Association, New Orleans. (ERIC Document Reproduction Service No. ED 359 253)

*$+Okey, J. R. (1974). Altering teacher and pupil behavior with mastery teaching. *Social Science and Mathematics 74*, 530–535.

+Okey, J. R. (1975). *Development of mastery teaching materials* (Final Evaluation Report, USOE G-74-2990). Bloomington: Indiana University.

$&Okey, J. R. (1977). The consequences of training teachers to use a mastery learning strategy. *Journal of Teacher Education 28*(5), 57–62.

*$Omelich, C. L., & Covington, M. V. (1981). *Do the learning benefits of behavioral instruction outweigh the psychological costs?* Paper presented at the annual meeting of the Western Psychological Association, Los Angeles.

*Pascarella, E. T. (1977, April). *Aptitude-treatment interaction in a college calculus course* *taught in personalized system of instruction and conventional formats.* Paper presented at the annual meeting of the American Educational Research Association, New York. (ERIC Document Reproduction Service No. ED 137 137)

*Peluso, A., & Baranchik, A. J. (1977). Self-paced mathematics instruction: A statistical comparison with traditional teaching. *The American Mathematical Monthly 84*, 124–129.

*+Phillippas, M. A., & Sommerfeldt, R. W. (1972). Keller vs. lecture method in general physics instruction. *American Journal of Physics 40*, 1800.

+Poggio, (1976, April). *Long-term cognitive retention resulting from the mastery learning paradigm.* Paper presented at the annual meeting of the American Educational Research Association, San Francisco.

*Pollack, N. F., & Roeder, P. W. (1975). Individualized instruction in an introductory government course. *Teaching Political Science 8*, 18–36.

!%Reid, E. R. (1978–1982). *The Reader Newsletter.* Salt Lake City: Exemplary Center for Reading Instruction.

*+Rosati, P. A. (1975). A comparison of the personalized system of instruction with the lecture method in teaching elementary dynamics. In J. M. Johnston (Ed.), *Behavior research and technology in higher education.* Springfield, IL: Charles C. Thomas.

Rosenshine, B., & Stevens, R. (1986). Teaching functions. In M. C. Wittrock (Ed.), *Handbook of research on teaching.* New York: Macmillan.

+Roth, C. H., Jr. (1973). Continuing effectiveness of personalized self-paced instruction in digital systems engineering. *Engineering Education 63*(6).

*Roth, C. H., Jr. (1975, December). *Electrical engineering laboratory I* (One of a series of reports on the projects titled Expansion of Keller Plan Instruction in Engineering and Selected Other Disciplines). Austin: University of Texas.

*Saunders-Harris, R. L., & Yeany, R. H. (1981). Diagnosis, remediation, and locus of control: Effects of immediate and retained achievement and attitude. *Journal of Experimental Education 49*, 220–224.

*Schielack, V. P., Jr. (1983). A personalized system of instruction versus a conventional method in a mathematics course for elementary education majors. *Dissertation Abstracts International 43*, 2267. (University Microfilms No. 82-27717)

*Schimpfhauser, F., Horrocks, L., Richardson, K., Alben, J., Schumm, D., & Sprecher, H. (1974). The personalized system of instruction as an adaptable alternative within the traditional structure of medical basic sciences. In R. S. Ruskin and S. F. Bono (Eds.), *Personalized instruction in higher education* (pp. 61–69). Washington, DC: Center for Personalized Instruction.

!Schuck, R. (1981). The impact of set induction on student achievement and retention. *Journal of Educational Research 74*, 227–232.

*Schwartz, P. L. (1981). Retention of knowledge in clinical biochemistry and the effect of the Keller Plan. *Journal of Medical Education 56*, 778–781.

*Sharples, D. K., Smith, D. J., & Strasler, G. M. (1976). *Individually-paced learning in civil engineering technology: An approach to mastery.* Columbia: South Carolina State Board for Technical and Comprehensive Education. (ERIC Document Reproduction Service No. ED 131 870)

*$Sheldon, M. S., & Miller, E. D. (1973). *Behavioral objectives and mastery learning applied to two areas of junior college instruction.* Los Angeles: University of California at Los Angeles. (ERIC Document Reproduction Service No. ED 082 730)

*Sheppard, W. C., & MacDermott, H. G. (1970). Design and evaluation of a programmed course in introductory psychology. *Journal of Applied Behavior Analysis 3*, 5–11.

*Siegfried, J. J., & Strand, S. H. (1976). An evaluation of the Vanderbilt-JCEE experimental PSI course in elementary economics. *The Journal of Economic Education 8*, 9–26.

*+Silberman, R., & Parker, B. (1974). Student attitudes and the Keller Plan. *Journal of Chemical Education 51*, 393.

Slavin, R. E. (1990). Mastery learning re-considered. *Review of Educational Research 60*(2), 300–302.

*#@$&Slavin, R. E., & Karweit, N. L. (1984). Mastery learning and student teams: A factorial experiment in urban general mathematics classes. *American Educational Research Journal 21*, 725–736.

*Smiernow, G. A., & Lawley, A. (1980). Decentralized sequenced instruction (DSI) at Drexel. *Engineering Education 70*, 423–426.

*Smith, J. E. (1976). A comparison of the traditional method and a personalized system of instruction in college mathematics. *Dissertation Abstracts International 37*, 904. (University Microfilms No. AAD76-18370)

!Soar, R. S. (1966). *An integrative approach to classroom learning* (Report for NIMH Projects No. 5-R11 MH 01096 and R-11 MH 02045). Philadelphia: Temple University. (ERIC Document Reproduction Service No. ED 033 749)

!Soar, R. S. (1968). Optimum teacher-pupil interaction for pupil growth. *Educational Leadership 26*, 275–280.

!Soar, R. S. (1973). *Follow-Through classroom process measurement and pupil growth (1970–1971) final report.* Gainesville: College of Education, University of Florida.

!Soar, R. S. (1977). An integration of findings from four studies of teacher effectiveness. In G. Borich and K. Fenton (Eds.), *The appraisal of teaching: Concepts and process.* Reading, MA: Addison-Wesley.

!Soar, R. S., & Soar, R. M. (1972). An empirical analysis of selected Follow Through Programs: An appraisal of a process approach to evaluation. In G. Borich and K. Fenton (Eds.), *The appraisal of teaching: Concepts and process.* Reading, MA: Addison-Wesley.

!Soar, R. S., & Soar, R. M. (1973). Classroom behavior, pupil characteristics, and pupil growth for the school year and the summer. Gainesville: University of Florida, Institute for Development of Human Resources.

!Soar, R. S., & Soar, R. M. (1978). *Setting variables, classroom interaction, and multiple pupil outcomes* (Final Report, Project No. 6-0432, Grant No. NIE-G-76-0100). Washington, DC: National Institute of Education.

!Soar, R. S., & Soar, R. M. (1979). Emotional climate and management. In P. Peterson and H. Walberg (Eds.), *Research on teaching: Concepts, findings, and implications.* Berkeley, CA: McCutchan.

!Solomon, D., & Kendall, A. (1979). *Children in classrooms: An investigation person-environment interaction.* New York: Praeger.

*Spector, L. C. (1976). The effectiveness of personalized system of instruction in economics. *Journal of Personalized Instruction 1*, 118–122.

*Spevack, H. M. (1976). A comparison of the personalized system of instruction with the lecture recitation system for nonscience oriented chemistry students at an open enrollment community college. *Dissertation Abstracts International 36*, 4385A–4386A. (University Microfilms No. 76-01757)

!Stallings, J. (1980). Allocated academic learning time revisited, or beyond time on task. *Educational Researcher 8*(11), 11–16.

!%Stallings J., Corey, R., Fairweather, J., & Needles, M. (1977). *Early Childhood Education classroom evaluation.* Menlo Park, CA: SRI International.

!%Stallings, J., Needles, M., & Staybrook, N. (1979). *The teaching of basic reading skills in secondary schools, Phase II and Phase III.* Menlo Park, CA: SRI International.

!%Stallings, J. A., & Kaskowitz, D. (1974). *Follow-Through Classroom Observation.* Menlo Park, CA: SRI International.

*Steele, W. F. (1974). *Mathematics 101 at Heileberg College—PSI vs. tradition.* Paper presented at the National Conference on Personalized Instruction in Higher Education, Washington, DC.

*Stout, L. J. (1978). A comparison of four different pacing strategies of personalized system of instruction and a traditional lecture format. *Dissertation Abstracts International 38,* 6205. (University Microfilms No. AAD78-08600)

*$Strasler, G. M. (1979, April). *The process of transfer in a learning for mastery setting.* Paper presented at the annual meeting of the American Educational Research Association, San Francisco. (ERIC Document Reproduction Service No. ED 174 642)

*$&Swanson, D. H., & Denton, J. J. (1976). Learning for Mastery versus Personalized System of Instruction: A comparison of remediation strategies with secondary school chemistry students. *Journal of Research in Science Teaching 14,* 515–524.

*Taylor, V. (1977, April). *Individualized calculus for the "life-long" learner: A two semester comparison of attitudes and effectiveness.* Paper presented at the Fourth National Conference of the Center for Personalized Instruction, San Francisco.

$Tenenbaum, G. (1982). *A method of group instruction which is as effective as one-to-one tutorial instruction.* Unpublished doctoral dissertation, University of Chicago.

*&Thompson, S. B. (1980). Do individualized mastery and traditional instructional systems yield different course effects in college calculus? *American Educational Research Journal 17,* 361–375.

*Tietenberg, T. H. (1975). Teaching intermediate microeconomics using the personalized system of instruction. In J. M. Johnston (Ed.), *Behavior research and technology in higher education* (pp. 75–89). Springfield, IL: Charles C. Thomas.

!Tobin, K., & Caple, W. (1982). Relationships between classroom process variables and middle-school science achievement. *Journal of Educational Psychology 74,* 441–454.

*Toepher, C., Shaw, D., & Moniot, D. (1972). *The effect of item exposure in a contingency management system.* Paper presented at the annual meeting of the American Psychological Association, Honolulu, HI.

*Vandenbroucke, A. C., Jr. (1974, April). *Evaluation of the use of a personalized system of instruction in general chemistry.* Paper presented at the National Conference on Personalized Instruction in Higher Education, Washington, DC.

*Van Verth, J. E., & Dinan, F. J. (1974). A Keller Plan course in organic chemistry. In R. S. Ruskin and S. F. Bono (Eds.), *Personalized instruction in higher education* (pp. 162–168). Washington, DC: Center for Personalized Instruction.

*Walsh, R. G., Sr. (1977). The Keller Plan in college introductory physical geology: A comparison with the conventional teaching method. *Dissertation Abstracts International 37,* 4257. (University Microfilms No. AAD76-30292)

$&+Wentling, T. L. (1973), Mastery versus nonmastery instruction with varying test item feedback treatments. *Journal of Educational Psychology 65,* 50–58.

*White, M. E. (1974). Different equations by PSI. In R. S. Ruskin and S. F. Bono (Eds.), *Personalized instruction in higher education* (pp. 169–171). Washington, DC: Center for Personalized Instruction.

Willent, J., Yamashita, J., & Anderson, R. (1983). A meta-analysis of instructional systems applied in science teaching. *Journal of Research in Science Teaching 20*(5), 405–417.

$Wire, D. R. (1979). *Mastery learning program at Durham College: Report on progress during the first year, September 1, 1978–August 31, 1979.* Durham, NC. (ERIC Document Reproduction Service No. ED 187 387)

*Witters, D. R., & Kent, G. W. (1972). Teaching without lecturing—Evidence in the case for individualized instruction. *The Psychological Record 22*, 169–175.

$Wortham, S. C. (1980). *Mastery learning in secondary schools: A first year report.* San Antonio, TX. (ERIC Document Reproduction Service No. ED 194 453)

*Yeany, R. H., Dost, R. J., & Matthew, R. W. (1980). The effects of diagnostic-prescriptive instruction and locus of control on the achievement and attitudes of university students. *Journal of Research in Science Teaching 17*, 537–545.

$Yildren, G. (1977). *The effects of level of cognitive achievement on selected learning criteria under mastery learning and normal classroom instruction.* Unpublished doctoral dissertation, University of Chicago.

4

Providing Contiguity

INTRODUCTION

When the relationship between events is being demonstrated to students, the events must appear sufficiently close together in time and space for their relationship to be perceived. For instance, students' understanding of the relationship between planting a bulb and the blooming of a flower can be facilitated by using time-lapse photography to shorten the time between the two events. It is also easier for a student to associate correction and remediation activities with their incorrect responses if remediation is provided sooner, rather than later, after the incorrect response. When young children misbehave, it is more likely that they will associate any corrective action with their misbehavior if the corrective action is taken soon after the misbehavior occurs.

STUDENT BENEFICIARIES

The evidence indicates that making events contiguous when teaching, assigning, evaluating, and remediating performance of tasks enhances the academic achievement of students in kindergarten, elementary, secondary, college, and adult learning classrooms. Moreover, academic achievement was improved in a wide range of content areas. No evidence could be found to suggest that contiguity should not be stressed in all subject areas for all types of students.

LEARNING ACHIEVED

Achievement in the content areas of mathematics, history, foreign languages, English, reading, social sciences, sciences, social studies, business, and occupational areas is enhanced when events are made contiguous in the teaching, assigning, evaluating, and remediation of performance tasks. In studies reviewed, contiguity was positively related to student achievement.

INSTRUCTIONAL TACTICS

The evidence supports the need to make events contiguous when teaching, assigning, evaluating, and remediating performance of tasks. The following tactics are derived from studies that demonstrate the benefits of contiguity when teaching, assigning, evaluating, and remediating performance of tasks. Discretion has been used to interpret and reduce overlap in tactics used in different studies and to elaborate tactics.

Tactics employed are:

- *Instructional Planning*: The tasks students are to perform to achieve the learning objective should be broken down into small increments so that they will be performed as close together as possible.

- *Teaching*: To-be-associated events should be presented to students as close together as possible. This applies to the association of to-be-associated subject matter and to consequences that are to be associated with student behavior. Teaching devices that can be used to promote contiguity among to-be-associated events include: (1) focusing attention on and highlighting relationships: for example, focusing students' attention on a constellation in the sky, say the Big Dipper, and pointing out the configuration of stars in it; (2) condensing time: for example, using time-lapse photography to show the relationship between a newborn and an adult animal; (3) condensing space: for example, drawing a map to show the relationship among places that are far away from one another.

- *During the Instructional Process*: Student task performance should follow instruction as soon as possible; evaluation of student task performance should occur during or immediately after student task performance; feedback to students on the correctness of their task performance should occur immediately, or very soon, after evaluation; and remediation should occur immediately following feedback.

CAUTIONS AND COMMENTS

Much of the supportive research to be cited highlights the importance of contiguity during the instructional process as described above. For the most part this research was conducted in the classroom setting in the late 1900s. However, contiguity has long been known to be a condition of associative learning dating back to the 1800s. It was the cornerstone of Edwin R. Guthrie's (1886–1959) theory of contiguous conditioning. In addition, the Gestalt psychologists' "Law of Proximity" emphasizes the importance of contiguity in perception. Many other learning theorists have recognized the importance of contiguity, and a sizable amount of research has accumulated over the years attesting to its validity. The book *Theories of Learning* by Bower and Hilgard (Prentice-Hall, 1981) provides additional information on contiguity.

GENERALIZATION: ON CONTIGUITY

Achievement of learning objectives is enhanced when events students are to associate are presented to them close together in time and space.

Supportive Research on Contiguity
Total number of studies covered: 178

Groups of Studies

Author: Rosenshine & Stevens (1986)

Students: Elementary, secondary

Learning: Mathematics, science, reading, history, and English achievement

Instructional Tactics:

- Divide to-be-learned material into smaller segments, with each succeeding segment being related to the previous segment, and following the preceding segment as closely as possible.
- Student instruction, student practice of assigned tasks, and evaluation of student performance of assigned tasks are incorporated in each segment.
- Student practice immediately follows instruction.
- Evaluation of student practice, whether written or verbal, occurs during or immediately following student practice.
- Feedback on evaluations and corrections is given immediately following evaluation.

Findings: Use of the above tactics was found to be associated with higher student achievement. Teaching to-be-learned material in its entirety as one lesson, discontinuity in the form of allowing too much time to pass between instruction and student practice, not evaluating student task performance during or immediately after student practice, and delays in or lack of feedback and corrections were found to be associated with lower student achievement.

Other instructional tactics are employed in these studies that are applicable to other generalizations and will be presented in the appropriate chapters.

Groups of studies reviewed in this logical synthesis of research did not provide statistical evidence. However, many of the individual studies included in the logical synthesis of research do contain statistical evidence. In the event that a reader wishes to view this evidence, an extensive listing of the individual studies reviewed is provided in the reference list at the end of the chapter (the studies are identified by the symbol %).

Author: Anderson (1994): Synthesis of seven meta-analyses

Students: Kindergarten, elementary, secondary, college, and other adult students

Learning: Achievement

Instructional Tactics: The following tactics associated with readiness and Mastery Learning are also presented in Bloom (1985), Block (1980), and others. Other tactics associated with Mastery Learning are applicable to other generalizations and are covered in the appropriate chapters.

- To-be-learned knowledge and skills are divided into smaller units, with each succeeding unit being related to the previous unit and following the preceding unit as closely as possible.
- Student task performance occurs immediately or as closely as possible following instruction on needed knowledge and skills.
- Evaluation of student task performance occurs as soon as possible following task performance.
- Ideally, feedback to students and corrections should immediately follow evaluation of their task performance.

Findings: Use of the above tactics was found to be related to enhanced student achievement.

Individual studies analyzed by these meta-analyses are identified in the reference list by the following symbols:

Kulik et al. (1990a) *

Kulik et al. (1990b) #

Slavin (1990) @

Guskey & Pigott (1988) $

Guskey & Gates (1985) &

Block & Burns (1976) +

It was not possible to determine the individual studies for which readiness was an instructional tactic for the Willett et al. (1983) analysis.

REFERENCE LIST

*+Abraham, F. J., & Newton, J. M. (1974). *The interview technique as a personalized system of instruction for economics: The Oregon experience.* Paper presented at the National Conference on Personalized Instruction in Higher Education. Washington, DC.

$Anania, J. (1981). *The effects of quality of instruction on the cognitive and affective learning of students.* Unpublished doctoral dissertation, University of Chicago.

%Anderson, L. M., Evertson, C. M., & Brophy, J. E. (1979). An experimental study of effective teaching in first-grade reading groups. *The Elementary School Journal 79*, 193–222.

%Anderson, L. M., Evertson, C. M., & Brophy, J. E. (1982). *Principles of small group instruction* (Occasional paper no. 32). East Lansing: Michigan State University, Institute for Research on Teaching.

+Anderson, L. W. (1973). *Time and school learning.* Unpublished doctoral dissertation, University of Chicago.

*$&Anderson, L. W. (1975a). Student involvement in learning and school achievement. *California Journal of Educational Research 26*, 53–62.

$&Anderson, L. W. (1975b). *Time to criterion: An experimental study.* Paper presented at the annual meeting of the American Educational Research Association, Washington, DC. (ERIC Document Reproduction Service No. ED 108 006)

*$&+Anderson, L. W. (1976). An empirical investigation of individual differences in time to learn. *Journal of Educational Psychology 68*, 226–233.

*#@$&Anderson, L. W., Scott, C., & Hutlock, N. (1976, April). *The effects of a mastery learning program on selected cognitive, affective, and ecological variables in grades 1 through 6.* Paper presented at the annual meeting of the American Educational Research Association. San Francisco.

+Anderson, O. T., & Artman, R. A. (1972). A self-paced independent study, introductory physics sequence-description and evaluation. *American Journal of Physics 40*, 1737–1742.

Anderson, S. A. (1994). *Synthesis of research on mastery learning* (Information Analysis). (ERIC Document Reproduction Service No. ED 382 567)

*$&%Arlin, M., & Webster, J. (1983). Time costs of mastery learning. *Journal of Educational Psychology 75*, 187–195.

*Austin, S. M., & Gilbert, K. E. (1973). Student performance in a Keller-Plan course in introductory electricity and magnetism. *American Journal of Physics 41*, 12–18.

*Badia, P., Stutts, C., & Harsh, J. (1978). Do methods of instruction and measures of different abilities and study habits interact? In J. G. Sherman, R. S. Ruskin, & R. M. Lazar (Eds.), *Personalized instruction in education today* (pp. 113–128). San Francisco: San Francisco Press.

%Becker, W. C. (1977). Teaching reading and language to the disadvantaged—What we have learned from field research. *Harvard Educational Review 47*, 518–543.

*Benson, J. S., & Yeany, R. H. (1980, April). *Generalizability of diagnostic-prescriptive teaching strategies across student locus of control and multiple instructional units.* Paper presented at the annual meeting of the American Educational Research Association, Boston. (ERIC Document Reproduction Service No. 187 534)

*+Billings, D. B. (1974). PSI versus the lecture course in the principles of economics: a quasi-controlled experiment. In R. S. Ruskin & S. F. Bono (Eds.), *Personalized instruction in higher education* (pp. 30–37). Washington, DC: Center for Personalized Instruction.

*$Blackburn, K. T., & Nelson, D. (1985, April). *Differences between a group using a traditional format with mastery learning and a group using a traditional format only in developmental mathematics courses at the university level: Implications for teacher education programs.* Paper presented at the annual meeting of the American Educational Research Association, Chicago. (ERIC Document Reproduction Service No. ED 258 948)

*Blasingame, J. W. (1975). Student attitude and performance in a personalized system of instruction course in business administration—Correlates performance with personality traits. *Dissertation Abstracts International 36*, 3840. (University Microfilms No. 75-2834)

$&+Block, J. H. (1972). Student learning and the setting of mastery performance standards. *Educational Horizons 50*, 183–191.

+Block, J. H. (1973). *Mastery performance standards and student learning.* Unpublished study, University of California, Santa Barbara.

Block, J. H. (1980). Success rate. In C. Denham & A. Lieberman (Eds.), *Time to learn* (pp. 95–106). Washington, DC: U.S. Government Printing Office.

Block, J. H., & Burns, R. B. (1976). Mastery learning. In L. Schulman (Ed.), *Review of research in education* (Vol. 4, pp. 3–49). Itasca, IL: F. E. Peacock.

$+Block, J. H., & Tierney, M. (1974). An exploration of two correction procedures used in mastery learning approaches to instruction. *Journal of Educational Psychology 66*, 962–967.

Bloom, B. S. (1985). Learning for mastery. In C. W. Fisher & D. C. Berliner (Eds.), *Perspectives on instructional time.* White Plains, NY: Longman.

*+Born, D. G., & Davis, M. L. (1974). Amount and distribution of study in a personalized instruction course and in a lecture course. *Journal of Applied Behavior Analysis 7*, 365–375.

*+Born, D. G., Gledhill, S. M., & Davis, M. L. (1972). Examination performance in lecture-discussion and personalized instruction courses. *Journal of Applied Behavior Analysis 5*, 33–43.

*+Breland, N. S., & Smith, M. P. (1974). A comparison of PSI and traditional methods of instruction for teaching introduction to psychology. In R. S. Ruskin & S. F. Bono (Eds.), *Personalized instruction in higher education* (pp. 21–25). Washington, DC: Center for Personalized Instruction.

%Brophy, J., & Evertson, C. (1976). *Learning from teaching: A developmental perspective.* Boston: Allyn and Bacon.

*$Bryant, N. D., Fayne, H. R., & Gettinger, M. (1982). Applying the mastery model to sight word instruction for disabled readers. *Journal of Experimental Education 50*, 116–121.

$Burke, A. (1983). *Students' potential for learning contrasted under tutorial and group approaches to instruction.* Unpublished doctoral dissertation, University of Chicago.

$&+Burrows, C. K., & Okey, J. R. (1975, March–April). *The effects of a mastery learning strategy on achievement.* Paper presented at the annual meeting of the American Educational Research Association, Washington, DC.

*#@$Cabezon, E. (1984). *The effects of marked changes in student achievement pattern on the students, their teachers, and their parents: The Chilean case.* Unpublished doctoral dissertation, University of Chicago.

$Chiappetta, E. L., & McBride, J. W. (1980). Exploring the effects of general remediation on ninth-graders' achievement of the mole concept. *Science Education 6*, 609–614.

*$Clark, C. P., Guskey, T. P., & Benninga, J. S. (1983). The effectiveness of mastery learning strategies in undergraduate education courses. *Journal of Educational Research 76*, 210–214.

*Clark, S. G. (1975). An innovation for introductory sociology: Personalized system of instruction. In J. M. Johnston (Ed.), *Behavior research and technology in higher education* (pp. 117–124). Springfield, IL: Charles C. Thomas.

*+Coldeway, D. O., Santowski, M., O'Brien, R., & Lagowski, V. (1975). Comparison of small group contingency management with the personalized system of instruction and the lecture system. In J. M. Johnston (Ed.), *Research and technology in college and university teaching* (pp. 215–224). Gainesville: University of Florida.

*+Cole, C., Martin, S., & Vincent, J. (1975). A comparison of two teaching formats at the college level. In J. M. Johnston (Ed.), *Behavior research and technology in higher education* (pp. 61–74). Springfield, IL: Charles C. Thomas.

*Condo, P. (1974, April). *The analysis and evaluation of a self-paced course in calculus.* Paper presented at the National Conference on Personalized Instruction in Higher Education, Washington, DC.

*+Cooper, J. L., & Greiner, J. M. (1971). Contingency management in an introductory psychology course produces better retention. *Psychological Record 21*, 391–400.

*Corey, J. R., & McMichael, J. S. (1974). Retention in a PSI introductory psychology course. In J. G. Sherman (Ed.), *PSI germinal papers* (pp. 17–19). Washington, DC: Center for Personalized Instruction.

+Corey, J. R., McMichael, J. S., & Tremont, P. J. (1970, April). *Long-term effects of personalized instruction in an introductory psychology course.* Paper presented at the meeting of the Eastern Psychology Association, Atlantic City.

*Cote, J. D. (1976). Biology by PSI in a community college. In B. A. Green, Jr. (Ed.), *Personalized instruction in higher education.* Washington, DC: Center for Personalized Instruction.

*Cross, M. Z., & Semb, G. (1976). An analysis of the effects of personalized instruction on students at different initial performance levels in an introductory college nutrition course. *Journal of Personalized Instruction 1*, 47–50.

*Decker, D. F. (1976). *Teaching to achieve learning mastery by using retesting techniques.* (ERIC Document Reproduction Service No. ED 133 002)

$Denton, W. L., Ory, J. C., Glassnap, D. R., & Poggio, J. P. (1976). *Grade expectations within a mastery learning strategy.* Paper presented at the annual meeting of the American Educational Research Association, San Francisco. (ERIC Document Reproduction Service No. ED 126 105)

*$Dillashaw, F. G., & Okey, J. R. (1983). Effects of a modified mastery learning strategy on achievement, attitudes, and on-task behavior of high school chemistry students. *Journal of Research in Science Teaching 20*, 203–211.

$Duby, P. B. (1981). *Attributions and attribution change: Effects of a mastery learning instructional approach.* Paper presented at the annual meeting of the American Educational Research Association, Los Angeles. (ERIC Document Reproduction Service No. ED 200 640)

%Emmer, E. T., Evertson, C., Sanford, J., & Clements, B. (1982). *Improving classroom management: An experimental study in junior high classrooms.* Austin: Research and Development Center for Teacher Education, University of Texas.

%Evertson, C. (1982). Differences in instructional activities in higher and lower achieving junior high English and mathematics classrooms. *Elementary School Journal 82*, 329–351.

%Evertson, C., Anderson, C., Anderson, L., & Brophy, J. (1980). Relationships between classroom behaviors and student outcomes in junior high mathematics and English classes. *American Educational Research Journal 17*, 43–60.

%Evertson, C., Emmer, E., & Brophy, J. (1980). Predictors of effective teaching in junior high mathematics classrooms. *Journal for Research in Mathematics Education 11*, 167–178.

%Evertson, C. M., Emmer, E. T., Sanford, J. P., & Clements, B. S. (1983). Improving classroom management: An experiment in elementary classrooms. *Elementary School Journal 84*, 173–188.

*#@Fagan, J. S. (1976). Mastery learning: The relationship of mastery procedures and aptitude to the achievement and retention of transportation-environment concepts by seventh grade students. *Dissertation Abstracts International 36*, 5981. (University Microfilms No. 76-6402)

*Fehlen, J. E. (1976). Mastery learning techniques in the traditional classroom setting. *School Science and Mathematics 76*, 241–245.

*Fernald, P. S., & DuNann, D. H. (1975). Effects of individualized instruction upon low- and high-achieving students' study behavior and students' evaluation of mastery. *Journal of Experimental Education 43*, 27–34.

$&+Fiel, R. L., & Okey, J. R. (1974). The effects of formative evaluation and remediation on mastery of intellectual skill. *Journal of Educational Research 68*, 253–255.

%Fisher, C. W., Berliner, D. C., Filby, N. N., Marliave, R., Cahen, L. S., & Dishaw, M. M. (1980). Teaching behaviors, academic learning time, and student achievement: An overview. In C. Denham & A. Lieberman (Eds.), *Time to learn* (pp. 7–32). Washington, DC: U.S. Government Printing Office.

%Fitzpatrick, K. A. (1981). *An investigation of secondary classroom material strategies for increasing student academic engaged time.* Doctoral dissertation, University of Illinois at Urbana–Champaign.

%Fitzpatrick, K. A. (1982). *The effect of a secondary classroom management training program on teacher and student behavior.* Paper presented at the annual meeting of the American Educational Research Association, New York.

$&Fitzpatrick, K. A. (1985, April). *Group-based mastery learning: A Robin Hood approach to instruction?* Paper presented at the annual meeting of the American Educational Research Association, Chicago.

+Glassnapp, D. R., Poggio, J. P., & Ory, J. C. (1975, March–April). *Cognitive and affective consequences of mastery and non-mastery instructional strategies.* Paper presented at the annual meeting of the American Educational Research Association, Washington, DC.

*Goldwater, B. C., & Acker, L. E. (1975). Instructor-paced, mass-testing for mastery performance in an introductory psychology course. *Teaching of Psychology 2*, 152–155.

%Good, T., Grouws, D., & Ebmeier, M. (1983). *Active mathematics teaching.* New York: Longman.

%Good, T. L., & Grouws, D. A. (1977). Teaching effects: a process-product study in fourth grade mathematics classrooms. *Journal of Teacher Education 28*(3), 49–54.

%Good, T. L., & Grouws, D. A. (1979). The Missouri mathematics effectiveness project. *Journal of Educational Psychology 71*, 355–362.

*Gregory, I., Smeltzer, D. J., Knopp, W., & Gardner, M. (1976). *Teaching of psychiatry by PSI: Impact on National Board Examination scores.* Unpublished manuscript, Ohio State University, Columbus.

*$&Guskey, T. R. (1982). The effects of staff development on teachers' perceptions about effective teaching. *Journal of Educational Research 76*, 378–381.

*$&Guskey, T. R. (1984). The influence of changes in instructional effectiveness upon the affective characteristics of teachers. *American Educational Research Journal 21*, 245–259.

$Guskey, T. R. (1985). The effects of staff development on teachers' perceptions about effective teaching. *Journal of Educational Research 79*, 378–381.

*$Guskey, T. R., Benninga, J. S., & Clark, C. B. (1984). Mastery learning and students' attributions at the college level. *Research in Higher Education 20*, 491–498.

Guskey, T. R., & Gates, S. L. (1986). Synthesis of research on the effects of mastery learning in elementary and secondary classrooms. *Educational Leadership 33*(8), 73–80.

*$Guskey, T. R., & Monsaas, J. A. (1979). Mastery learning: A model for academic success in urban junior colleges. *Research in Higher Education 11*, 263-274.

Guskey, T. R., & Pigott, T. D. (1988). Research on group-based mastery learning programs: A meta-analysis. *Journal of Educational Research 81*(4), 197–216.

*Hardin, L. D. (1977). A study of the influence of a physics personalized system of instruction versus lecture on cognitive reasoning, achievement, attitudes and critical thinking. *Dissertation Abstracts International 38*, 4711A–4712A. (University Microfilms No. 77-30826)

*Hecht, L. W. (1980, April). *Stalking mastery learning in its natural habitat.* Paper presented at the annual meeting of the American Educational Research Association, Boston.

*Heffley, P. D. (1974). The implementation of the personalized system of instruction in the freshman chemistry course at Censius College. In R. S. Ruskin & S. F. Bono (Eds.), *Personalized instruction in higher education* (pp. 140–145). Washington, DC: Center for Personalized Instruction.

*Herring, B. G. (1975, December). *Cataloguing and classification.* Austin: University of Texas.

*Herring, B. G. (1977). *The written PSI study guide in a non-PSI course.* Austin: University of Texas.

*Herrmann, T. (1984, August). *TELIDON as an enhancer of student interest and performance.* Paper presented at the annual meeting of the American Psychological Association, Toronto. (ERIC Document Reproduction Service No. ED 251 004)

*Hindman, C. D. (1974). Evaluation of three programming techniques in introductory psychology courses. In R. S. Ruskin & S. F. Bono (Eds.), *Personalized instruction in higher education* (pp. 38–42). Washington, DC: Center for Personalized Instruction.

*Honeycutt, J. K. (1974, April). *The effect of computer managed instruction on content learning of undergraduate students.* Paper presented at the annual meeting of the American Educational Research Association, Chicago. (ERIC Document Reproduction Service No. ED 089 682)

*Hymel, G. M. (1974). *An investigation of John B. Carrol's model of school learning as a theoretical basis for the organizational structuring of schools* (Final Report, NIE Project No. 3-1359). University of New Orleans, New Orleans, LA.

*Hymel, G. M., & Mathews, G. (1980). Effects of a mastery approach on social studies achievement and unit evaluation. *Southern Journal of Educational Research 14*, 191–204.

*Jackman, L. E. (1982). Evaluation of a modified Keller method in a biochemistry laboratory course. *Journal of Chemical Education 59*, 225–227.

*Jacko, E. J. (1974). Lecture instruction versus a personalized system of instruction: Effects on individuals with differing achievement anxiety and academic achievement.

Dissertation Abstracts International 35, 3521. (University Microfilms No. AAD 74-27211)

+Johnston, J. M., & Pennypacker, H. S. (1971). A behavioral approach to college teaching. *American Psychologist 26*, 219–244.

*#@$&Jones, B. F., Monsaas, J. A., & Katims, M. (1979, April). *Improving reading comprehension: Embedding diverse learning strategies within a mastery learning instructional framework.* Paper presented at the annual meeting of the American Educational Research Association, San Francisco. (ERIC Document Reproduction Service No. ED 170 698)

$+Jones, E. L., Gordon, H. A., & Stectman, G. L. (1975). *Mastery learning: A strategy for academic success in a community college.* Los Angeles: ERIC Clearinghouse for Junior Colleges. (ERIC Document Reproduction Service No. ED 115 315)

+Jones, F. G. (1974). *The effects of mastery and aptitude on learning, retention, and time.* Unpublished doctoral dissertation, University of Georgia.

+Karlin, B. M. (1972). *The Keller method of instruction compared to the traditional method of instruction in a Lafayette College history course.* Unpublished paper, Lafayette College, Lafayette, PA.

*#@Katims, M., Smith, J. K., Steele, C., & Wick, J. W. (1977, April). *The Chicago mastery learning reading program: An interim evaluation.* Paper presented at the annual meeting of the American Educational Research Association, New York. (ERIC Document Reproduction Service No. ED 137 737)

*#@Kersh, M. E. (1970). *A strategy of mastery learning in fifth grade arithmetic.* Unpublished doctoral dissertation, University of Chicago.

+Kim, Y., Cho, G., Park, J., & Park, M. (1974). *An application of a new instructional model* (Research Report No. 8). Seoul, Korea: Korean Educational Development Institute.

*Knight, J. M., Williams, J. D., & Jardon, M. L. (1975). The effects of contingency avoidance on programmed student achievement. *Research in Higher Education 3*, 11–17.

*Kulik, C., & Kulik, J. (1976). PSI and the mastery model. In B. A. Green, Jr. (Ed.), *Personalized instruction in higher education* (pp. 155–159). Washington, DC: Center for Personalized Instruction.

Kulik, C., Kulik, J., & Bangert-Drowns, R. (1990a). Effectiveness of mastery learning programs: A meta-analysis. *Review of Educational Research 60*(2), 265–269.

Kulik, J., Kulik, C., & Bangert-Drowns, R. (1990b). Is there better evidence on mastery learning? A response to Slavin. *Review of Educational Research 60*(2), 303–307.

+Kulik, J. A., Kulik, C., & Carmichael, K. (1974). The Keller Plan in science teaching. *Science 183*, 379–383.

+Lee, Y. D., Kim, C. S., Kim, H., Park, B. Y., Yoo, H. K., Chang, S. M., & Kim, S. C. (1971). *Interaction improvement studies of the Mastery Learning Project* (Final Report on the Mastery Learning Project, April–November 1971). Seoul, Korea: Educational Research Center, Seoul National University.

*Leppmann, P. K., & Herrman, T. F. (1981, August). *PSI—What are the critical elements?* Paper presented at the annual meeting of the American Psychological Association, Los Angeles. (ERIC Document Reproduction Service No. ED 214 502)

$+Levin, T. (1975). *The effect of content prerequisites and process-oriented experiences on application ability in the learning of probability.* Unpublished doctoral dissertation, University of Chicago.

*Lewis, E. W. (1984). The effects of a mastery learning strategy and an interactive computerized quiz strategy on student achievement and attitude in college trigonometry. *Dissertation Abstracts International 45*, 2430A. (University Microfilms No. DA84-24589)

*Leyton, F. S. (1983). *The extent to which group instruction supplemented by mastery of initial cognitive prerequisites approximates the learning effectiveness of one-to-one tutorial methods.* Unpublished doctoral dissertation, University of Chicago.

*Locksley, N. (1977). The Personalized System of Instruction (PSI) in a university mathematics class. *Dissertation Abstracts International 37*, 4194. (University Microfilms No. ADD76-28194)

#@Long, J. C., Okey, J. R., & Yeany, R. H. (1978). The effects of diagnosis with teacher on student directed remediation on science achievement and attitudes. *Journal of Research in Science Teaching 15*, 505–511.

*Lu, M. C. (1976). The retention of material learned by PSI in a mathematics course. In B. A. Green, Jr. (Ed.), *Personalized instruction in higher education* (pp. 151–154). Washington, DC: Center for Personalized Instruction.

*Lu, P. H. (1976). Teaching human growth and development by the Personalized System for Instruction. *Teaching of Psychology 3*, 127–128.

*Lubkin, J. L. (1974). Engineering statistics: A Keller Plan course with novel problems and novel features. In R. S. Ruskin and S. F. Bono (Eds.), *Personalized instruction in higher education* (pp. 153–161). Washington, DC: Center for Personalized Instruction.

*#@Lueckmeyer, C. L., & Chiappetta, W. L. (1981). An investigation into the effects of a modified mastery learning strategy on achievement in a high school human physiology unit. *Journal of Research in Science Teaching 18*, 269–273.

*Malec, M. A. (1975). PSI: A brief report and reply to Francis. *Teaching Sociology 2*, 212–217.

*Martin, R. R., & Srikameswaran, K. (1974). Correlation between frequent testing and student performance. *Journal of Chemical Education 51*, 485–486.

$Mathews, G. S. (1982). *Effects of a mastery learning strategy on the cognitive knowledge and unit evaluation of students in high school social studies.* Unpublished doctoral dissertation, University of Southern Mississippi.

*McFarland, B. (1976). An individualized course in elementary composition for the marginal student. In B. A. Green, Jr. (Ed.), *Personalized instruction in higher education* (pp. 45–52). Washington, DC: Center for Personalized Instruction.

*+McMichael, J., & Corey, J. R. (1969). Contingency management in an introductory psychology course produces better learning. *Journal of Applied Behavior Analysis 2*, 79–83.

*#@Mevarech, Z. R. (1980). *The role of teaching-learning strategies and feedback-corrective procedures in developing higher cognitive achievement.* Unpublished doctoral dissertation, University of Chicago.

$&Mevarech, Z. R. (1981, April). *Attaining mastery on higher cognitive achievement.* Paper presented at the annual meeting of the American Educational Research Association, Los Angeles.

*Mevarech, Z. R. (1985). The effects of cooperative mastery learning strategies on mathematical achievement. *Journal of Educational Research 78*, 372–377.

*#@Mevarech, Z. R. (1986). The role of feedback corrective procedure in developing mathematics achievement and self-concept in desegregated classrooms. *Studies in Educational Evaluation 12*, 197–203.

*Mevarech, Z. R., & Werner, S. (1985). Are mastery learning strategies beneficial for developing problem solving skills? *Higher Education 14*, 425–432.

*Meyers, R. R. (1976). The effects of mastery and aptitude on achievement and attitude in an introductory college geography course. *Dissertation Abstracts International 36*, 5874. (University Microfilms No. 76-6436)

*+Morris, C., & Kimbrill, G. (1972). Performance and attitudinal effects of the Keller method in an introductory psychology course. *Psychological Record 22*, 523–530.

*Nation, J. R., Knight, J. M., Lamberth, J., & Dyck, D. (1974). Programmed student achievement: A test of the avoidance hypothesis. *Journal of Experimental Education 42*, 57–61.

*Nation, J. R., Massad, P., & Wilkerson, P. (1977). Student performance in introductory psychology following termination of the programmed achievement contingency at mid-semester. *Teaching of Psychology 4*, 116–119.

*Nation, J. R., & Roop, S. S. (1975). A comparison of two mastery approaches to teaching introductory psychology. *Teaching of Psychology 2*, 108–111.

*+Nazzaro, J. R., Todorov, J. C., & Nazzaro, J. N. (1972). Student ability and individualized instruction. *Journal of College Science Teaching 2*, 29–30.

*Nord, S. B. (1975). Comparative achievement and attitude in individualized and class instructional settings. *Dissertation Abstracts International 35*, 5129A. (University Microfilms No. 75-02314)

$Nordin, A. B. (1979). *The effects of different qualities of instruction on selected cognitive, affective, and time variables*. Unpublished doctoral dissertation, University of Chicago.

*$+Okey, J. R. (1974). Altering teacher and pupil behavior with mastery teaching. *Social Science and Mathematics 74*, 530–535.

+Okey, J. R. (1975). *Development of mastery teaching materials* (Final Evaluation Report, USOE G-74-2990). Bloomington: Indiana University.

$&Okey, J. R. (1977). The consequences of training teachers to use a mastery learning strategy. *Journal of Teacher Education 28*(5), 57–62.

*$Omelich, C. L., & Covington, M. V. (1981). *Do the learning benefits of behavioral instruction outweigh the psychological costs?* Paper presented at the annual meeting of the Western Psychological Association, Los Angeles.

*Pascarella, E. T. (1977, April). *Aptitude-treatment interaction in a college calculus course taught in personalized system of instruction and conventional formats*. Paper presented a the annual meeting of the American Educational Research Association, New York. (ERIC Document Reproduction Service No. ED 137 137)

*Peluso, A., & Baranchik, A. J. (1977). Self-paced mathematics instruction: A statistical comparison with traditional teaching. *The American Mathematical Monthly 84*, 124–129.

*+Phillippas, M. A., & Sommerfeldt, R. W. (1972). Keller vs. lecture method in general physics instruction. *American Journal of Physics 40*, 1800.

+Poggio, (1976, April). *Long-term cognitive retention resulting from the mastery learning paradigm*. Paper presented at the annual meeting of the American Educational Research Association, San Francisco.

*Pollack, N. F., & Roeder, P. W. (1975). Individualized instruction in an introductory government course. *Teaching Political Science 8*, 18–36.

*+Rosati, P. A. (1975). A comparison of the personalized system of instruction with the lecture method in teaching elementary dynamics. In J. M. Johnston (Ed.), *Behavior research and technology in higher education*. Springfield, IL: Charles C. Thomas.

Rosenshine, B. & Stevens, R. (1986). Teaching functions. In M. C. Wittrock (Ed.), *Handbook of research on teaching*. New York: Macmillan.

+Roth, C. H., Jr. (1973). Continuing effectiveness of personalized self-paced instruction in digital systems engineering. *Engineering Education 63*(6), 447–450.

*Roth, C. H., Jr. (1975, December). *Electrical engineering laboratory I* (One of a series of reports on the projects titled Expansion of Keller Plan Instruction in Engineering and Selected Other Disciplines). Austin: University of Texas.

*Saunders-Harris, R. L., & Yeany, R. H. (1981). Diagnosis, remediation, and locus of control: Effects of immediate and retained achievement and attitude. *Journal of Experimental Education 49*, 220–224.

*Schielack, V. P., Jr. (1983). A personalized system of instruction versus a conventional method in a mathematics course for elementary education majors. *Dissertation Abstracts International 43*, 2267. (University Microfilms No. 82-27717)

*Schimpfhauser, F., Horrocks, L., Richardson, K., Alben, J., Schumm, D., & Sprecher, H. (1974). The personalized system of instruction as an adaptable alternative within the traditional structure of medical basic sciences. In R. S. Ruskin and S. F. Bono (Eds.), *Personalized instruction in higher education* (pp. 61–69). Washington, DC: Center for Personalized Instruction.

*Schwartz, P. L. (1981). Retention of knowledge in clinical biochemistry and the effect of the Keller Plan. *Journal of Medical Education 56*, 778–781.

*Sharples, D. K., Smith, D. J., & Strasler, G. M. (1976). *Individually-paced learning in civil engineering technology: An approach to mastery.* Columbia: South Carolina State Board for Technical and Comprehensive Education. (ERIC Document Reproduction Service No. ED 131 870)

*$Sheldon, M. S., & Miller, E. D. (1973). *Behavioral objectives and mastery learning applied to two areas of junior college instruction.* Los Angeles: University of California at Los Angeles. (ERIC Document Reproduction Service No. ED 082 730)

*Sheppard, W. C., & MacDermott, H. G. (1970). Design and evaluation of a programmed course in introductory psychology. *Journal of Applied Behavior Analysis 3*, 5–11.

*Siegfried, J. J., & Strand, S. H. (1976). An evaluation of the Vanderbilt-JCEE experimental PSI course in elementary economics. *The Journal of Economic Education 8*, 9–26.

*+Silberman, R., & Parker, B. (1974). Student attitudes and the Keller Plan. *Journal of Chemical Education 51*, 393.

Slavin, R. E. (1990). Mastery learning re-considered. *Review of Educational Research 60*(2), 300–302.

*#@$&Slavin, R. E., & Karweit, N. L. (1984). Mastery learning and student teams: A factorial experiment in urban general mathematics classes. *American Educational Research Journal 21*, 725–736.

*Smiernow, G. A., & Lawley, A. (1980). Decentralized sequenced instruction (DSI) at Drexel. *Engineering Education 70*, 423–426.

*Smith, J. E. (1976). A comparison of the traditional method and a personalized system of instruction in college mathematics. *Dissertation Abstracts International 37*, 904. (University Microfilms No. AAD76-18370)

*Spector, L. C. (1976). The effectiveness of personalized system of instruction in economics. *Journal of Personalized Instruction 1*, 118–122.

*Spevack, H. M. (1976). A comparison of the personalized system of instruction with the lecture recitation system for nonscience oriented chemistry students at an open enrollment community college. *Dissertation Abstracts International 36*, 4385A–4386A. (University Microfilms No. 76-01757)

%Stallings J., Corey, R., Fairweather, J., & Needles, M. (1977). *Early Childhood Education classroom evaluation.* Menlo Park, CA: SRI International.

%Stallings, J. A., & Kaskowitz, D. (1974). *Follow-Through Classroom Observation.* Menlo Park, CA: SRI International.

%Stallings, J., Needles, M., & Staybrook, N. (1979). *The teaching of basic reading skills in secondary schools, Phase II and Phase III.* Menlo Park, CA: SRI International.

*Steele, W. F. (1974). *Mathematics 101 at Heileberg College—PSI vs. tradition.* Paper presented at the National Conference on Personalized Instruction in Higher Education, Washington, DC.

*Stout, L. J. (1978). A comparison of four different pacing strategies of personalized system of instruction and a traditional lecture format. *Dissertation Abstracts International 38*, 6205. (University Microfilms No. AAD78-08600)

*$Strasler, G. M. (1979, April). *The process of transfer in a learning for mastery setting.* Paper presented at the annual meeting of the American Educational Research Association, San Francisco. (ERIC Document Reproduction Service No. ED 174 642)

*$&Swanson, D. H., & Denton, J. J. (1976). Learning for Mastery versus Personalized System of Instruction: A comparison of remediation strategies with secondary school chemistry students. *Journal of Research in Science Teaching 14*, 515–524.

*Taylor, V. (1977, April). *Individualized calculus for the "life-long" learner: A two semester comparison of attitudes and effectiveness.* Paper presented at the Fourth National Conference of the Center for Personalized Instruction, San Francisco.

$Tenenbaum, G. (1982). *A method of group instruction which is as effective as one-to-one tutorial instruction.* Unpublished doctoral dissertation, University of Chicago.

*&Thompson, S. B. (1980). Do individualized mastery and traditional instructional systems yield different course effects in college calculus? *American Educational Research Journal 17*, 361–375.

*Tietenberg, T. H. (1975). Teaching intermediate microeconomics using the personalized system of instruction. In J. M. Johnston (Ed.), *Behavior research and technology in higher education* (pp. 75–89). Springfield, IL: Charles C. Thomas.

%Tobias, S. (1982). When do instructional methods make a difference? *Educational Researcher 11*, 4–10.

*Toepher, C., Shaw, D., & Moniot, D. (1972). *The effect of item exposure in a contingency management system.* Paper presented at the annual meeting of the American Psychological Association, Honolulu, HI.

*Vandenbroucke, A. C., Jr. (1974, April). *Evaluation of the use of a personalized system of instruction in general chemistry.* Paper presented at the National Conference on Personalized Instruction in Higher Education, Washington, DC.

*Van Verth, J. E., & Dinan, F. J. (1974). A Keller Plan course in organic chemistry. In R. S. Ruskin and S. F. Bono (Eds.), *Personalized instruction in higher education* (pp. 162–168). Washington, DC: Center for Personalized Instruction.

*Walsh, R. G., Sr. (1977). The Keller Plan in college introductory physical geology: A comparison with the conventional teaching method. *Dissertation Abstracts International 37*, 4257. (University Microfilms No. AAD76-30292)

$&+Wentling, T. L. (1973), Mastery versus nonmastery instruction with varying test item feedback treatments. *Journal of Educational Psychology 65*, 50–58.

*White, M. E. (1974). Different equations by PSI. In R. S. Ruskin and S. F. Bono (Eds.), *Personalized instruction in higher education* (pp. 169–171). Washington, DC: Center for Personalized Instruction.

Willent, J., Yamashita, J., & Anderson, R. (1983). A meta-analysis of instructional systems applied in science teaching. *Journal of Research in Science Teaching 20*(5), 405–417.

$Wire, D. R. (1979). *Mastery learning program at Durham College: Report on progress during the first year, September 1, 1978–August 31, 1979.* Durham, NC. (ERIC Document Reproduction Service No. ED 187 387)

*Witters, D. R., & Kent, G. W. (1972). Teaching without lecturing—Evidence in the case for individualized instruction. *The Psychological Record 22*, 169–175.

$Wortham, S. C. (1980). *Mastery learning in secondary schools: A first year report.* San Antonio, TX. (ERIC Document Reproduction Service No. ED 194 453)

*Yeany, R. H., Dost, R. J., & Matthew, R. W. (1980). The effects of diagnostic-prescriptive instruction and locus of control on the achievement and attitudes of university students. *Journal of Research in Science Teaching 17*, 537--45.

$Yildren, G. (1977). *The effects of level of cognitive achievement on selected learning criteria under mastery learning and normal classroom instruction.* Unpublished doctoral dissertation, University of Chicago.

5

Utilizing Repetition Effectively

INTRODUCTION

Most people are at least vaguely familiar with the benefits of repetition to learning. They have heard that "practice makes perfect" and have memorized a poem or a part in a play by repeating the lines. Or they have mastered typing, a musical instrument, or a sport such as tennis by practicing it. The challenge is to apply the benefits of repetition in instruction to improve learning.

Two modes of repetition enhance learning:

1. The repeated presentation of to-be-learned information to students enhances their learning of the information: for example, the repeated presentation of names, numbers, or instructions.

2. Students' repetition of assigned tasks or student practice enhances their learning of the tasks: for instance, students repeatedly practicing their handwriting or multiplication tables. The importance and application of these modes of repetition to learning will become clearer as we proceed through the chapter.

STUDENT BENEFICIARIES

Student achievement over a wide range of content areas in elementary classrooms, secondary classrooms, college classrooms, and military training situations will be enhanced by repetition in instruction and tasks students are assigned to perform. Students in adult, community, and business education and training settings may also experience the beneficial achievement effects of repetition.

LEARNING ACHIEVED

Achievement in the content areas of mathematics, science, English, foreign languages, and reading is enhanced by instructional strategies which provide for repetition in instruction and tasks students are assigned to perform. It may be reasonable to expect that achievement may be enhanced in other content areas as well. In studies reviewed, student achievement was shown to be enhanced by repetition.

INSTRUCTIONAL TACTICS

The studies to be presented indicate that repetition will enhance learning if the following tactics are employed.

- To-be-learned information is repeatedly presented to students.
- To-be-learned tasks are repeated or practiced by students.
- Repetition is frequent. In general, frequent repetition enhances learning more than infrequent repetition.
- There is variation with repetitions to avoid boredom. Presentations of the same information can be varied with respect to the media used: for example, oral, written, and pictorial presentation of the same information can be made. Also, examples, applications, and demonstrations can vary from one presentation to the next, and repeated performance of the same task can be varied. For instance, in learning to write, students might write in different contexts, such as "My Favorite Pastime," a newspaper article, or a letter.
- Repeatedly testing students on to-be-learned information enhances their learning of the information.

The following format for incorporating repetition in instruction in order to achieve learning objectives was inferred from the studies to be presented shortly.

Instructional Period 1
- Present the to-be-learned information
- Assign homework on the information
- Quiz the students on the information

Instructional Period 2
- Review the to-be-learned information presented during Period 1
- Present new to-be-learned information
- Assign homework on the new information
- Quiz students on the information presented in Periods 1 and 2

Instructional Period 3
- Review the to-be-learned information presented during Periods 1 and 2
- Present new to-be-learned information

- Assign homework on the new information
- Quiz students on the information presented during Periods 1, 2, and 3

And so on. Progress is made in this way to take advantage of the benefits of repetition in teaching and testing while progressing toward the achievement of the learning objectives being pursued. Progress must be planned in addition to repetition to avoid boredom. The format is intended to be only one illustration of the appropriate use of repetition in instruction.

Elaborations of the above summary of tactics can be obtained from reading the studies that are to follow. To be most effective, the instructional tactics need to be integrated into the particular instructional program being planned or presently in use.

CAUTIONS AND COMMENTS

Research indicates that too much repetition may interfere with learning of to-be-learned material and recall of previously learned material (Rosenshine 1986) and others. Once a student has mastered the material, additional repetition and elaboration may result in the student becoming bored.

GENERALIZATION: ON REPETITION

Achievement of learning objectives is enhanced when there is repetition in instruction and in tasks students are assigned to perform.

Supportive Research on Repetition
Total number of studies covered: 66

Groups of Studies

Author: Kulik et al. (1984)

Students: Elementary, secondary, and postsecondary students

Learning: Achievement

Instructional Tactics: Practice on identical and parallel tests prior to taking the criterion test.

Findings: The review of parallel forms and identical forms of criterion measures found that there was a significant relationship between performance on a criterion measure and the number of practice tests taken. It was found that as the number of the practice tests taken increased, the size of the effect on the criterion measure increased. The effect for taking seven practice tests of the identical form was 4.5 times that for taking one practice test of the identical form. The effect for taking seven practice tests of a parallel form was 3.2 times that for taking one practice test of the parallel form. Findings indicate the effect for practice on identical forms of the criterion measure was 1.8 times the effect found for practice on parallel forms of the criterion measure when the number of practice tests was one. When the number of practice tests increased to seven, the effect for practice on identical forms was 2.5 times the effect for practice on parallel forms of the criterion measure.

Studies associated with this meta-analysis are identified by the symbol * in the reference list at the end of the chapter.

Author: Rosenshine (1986)

Students: Elementary, secondary, and postsecondary

Learning: Mathematics, science, reading, and English achievement

Instructional Tactics:

- The teacher reviews relevant previous learning daily with the students.
- The teacher reviews homework daily with the students.
- The teacher reviews prerequisite skills and knowledge for the lesson with the students.
- The teacher provides for frequent practice by the students of newly acquired knowledge and skills.
- Every Monday the teacher reviews the previous week's work with the students.
- Every fourth Monday the teacher reviews the previous month's work with the students.
- Frequent quizzes (provides students with review and practice for exams that evaluate achievement of the learning objectives pursued).

Findings: For all studies reviewed, teachers of classes with high achievement levels for the students provided practice and review. An important finding was that it is the frequency of practice and review that enhances student achievement.

Studies associated with this logical synthesis are identified by the symbol # in the reference list.

Individual Studies

Author: Ausubel & Youseff (1965)

Students: College

Learning: Endocrinology recall

Instructional Tactics: During a 25-minute first session, the experimental group read and studied a passage on the endocrinology of pubescence, and the control group read an unrelated passage. During a second 25-minute session two days later, both groups read and studied the endocrinology passage utilized in session one. Both groups of students were administered a multiple-choice test of the content of the endocrinology passage two days after session two.

Findings: The average test score for the group that read the endocrinology passage twice was 19% higher than the average test score for the group that read the endocrinology passage once.

Author: Peterson et al. (1935)

Students: College

Learning: History achievement and retention

Instructional Tactics: All students studied a historical passage on monasticism in western Europe, followed by an immediate recall test. Four control groups received no additional study or review of the original content studied prior to being tested at two-, three-, six-, or eighteen-week intervals following instruction. Four experimental groups received one review of the original content studied prior to testing at two-, three-, six-, or eighteen-week intervals. Two experimental groups received two reviews of the original content studied prior to testing at six- or eighteen-week intervals.

Findings: Retention for the one-review groups as compared to the no-review groups was 47% higher at two and three weeks, 28% higher at six weeks, and 18% higher at eighteen weeks. Retention for the two-review groups as compared to the no-review groups was 75% at six weeks and 57% at eighteen weeks. Ratios of retention scores to immediate recall scores, expressed as percentages, indicate that for the no-review groups, at two and three weeks performance on retention was about 60% of that on the day of immediate recall testing. Although not reported, observation of given graphs seems to indicate that performance for all four no-review groups on retention was between 50% and 60% of that on the day of immediate recall testing. The one-review group is reported to have "had almost as much as they had on the day of learning" (p. 67). Review of the provided graphs, under Statistical Evidence on Repetition, indicates that the one-review group's ratio of retention to immediate recall ranged from about 90% at week 2 to 70% at week 18, with gradual declines over the four testing intervals. The two-review group's ratios were slightly over 100% at six weeks and about 90% at eighteen weeks.

Author: Nelson (1977)

Students: College

Learning: Word recall

Instructional Tactics:

Experiment 1: Twenty unrelated words (concrete nouns) were randomly divided into five blocks of four words. The words were ordered randomly within each block, and the blocks were then ordered randomly to form the first list of words. The process was repeated to form a second list of words. The two word lists contained the same words in a different order.

Students were visually presented the words individually from either one or both word lists. Following presentation of the word list(s) the students were given a sheet of paper with 20 lines on it. Students were allowed three minutes to write down as many of the 20 words they could recall from list(s) of words they had seen.

Experiment 2: Twelve words were selected from the list of words used in experiment 1. The twelve words were formed into word lists in the following formats:

1. No repetition (i.e., "A, B, C, . . . , K, L, M") (p. 156);

2. Back-to-back repetition (i.e., "A, A, B, B, . . . , K, K, L, L") (p. 156);

3. Two-spaced repetitions with four words being repeated at an interval of every seventh word, four words repeated at an interval of every eleventh word, and four words being repeated at an interval of every fifteenth word. The word list was constructed in two blocks, with each block containing two words for each of the three interval appearances (i.e., "A, B, C, D, E, F, G, H, I, J, K, L, E(7), F(7), C(11), D(11), A(15), B(15), K(7), L(7), I(11), J(11), G(15), H(15)") (p. 156).

Students were assigned in equal numbers to three groups, with each group being assigned to view one of the preceding arrangements of words. Students in each group viewed their respective word lists individually. Each group saw the words for their respective list presented in a continuous fashion, with the student being allowed to view the word for five seconds. Following the word list presentations the students were given a piece of paper. They were allowed three minutes to write down as many of the twelve words they had viewed as they could recall.

Experiment 3: A procedure similar to that for Experiment 1 was used to form two lists of 30 words. The two lists contained the same words ordered differently in each list. Students were visually presented the words individually from either one or both word lists.

Findings:

Experiment 1: Findings indicated that the groups that saw the same words twice (both word lists) recalled significantly more words than did the groups that saw the words only once (one word list). The average percentages of words recalled for the two groups that saw the same words twice (both word lists) were 7% to 10% higher than average percentage of words recalled by the two groups that saw the words once (one word list).

Experiment 2: Students in the two-repetition conditions recalled a significantly higher percentage of words than the students in the one-repetition condition. The average percentage of words recalled for students who viewed words in the back-to-back two-repetition word list was 16% higher than the average percentage of words recalled for students who saw each word only once. The average percentage of words recalled for students who viewed the spaced-repetition word lists was 24% higher than the average percentage of words recalled for students who saw each word only once.

Experiment 3: Findings indicate that recall was significantly higher for students seeing each word twice as compared to the level of recall for students seeing each word only once.

Author: Petros & Hoving (1980)

Students: Second grade

Learning: Prose main idea retention

Instructional Tactics:

1. One group of students listened to the same stories a second time one week after hearing the stories the first time.

2. One week after hearing the stories for the first time, the teacher led a review session for students in another group. The teacher used leading questions and prompts to elicit verbal responses from the students on the main ideas of the stories (i.e., "What kind of boy did the story say [name] was? Tell me as much as you can remember about what [name] did in the story. Can you tell me anything more about the story?") (p. 37). Students were allowed to respond to questions until they indicated that they could not recall any more information about the story.

3. Another group of students reviewed the stories by listening to audio tapes of the teacher-led review session, which included the teacher's questions/ prompts and the students' responses.

4. Another group of students heard the stories once and received no review.

5. One group of students was required to write down as many of the story main idea units as they could recall immediately after hearing the stories once.

All students were tested on recall of story main idea units two weeks after hearing the stories the first time.

Findings: The average percentages of idea units recalled for all types of review were higher than the average percentage of idea units recalled by students who heard the stories only once and had no additional review. The average percentage of idea units recalled by the group that heard the same stories twice was 19% higher than the average percentage of main idea units recalled by the group that heard the stories once with no subsequent review. The average percentage of idea units recalled by the group that was required to recall as many idea units as they could immediately after hearing the stories was 10% higher than the average percentage of main idea units recalled by the group that heard the stories once with no subsequent review. The average percentage of idea units recalled by the group that reviewed the stories in a teacher-led session was 8% higher than the average percentage of main idea units recalled by the group that heard the stories once with no subsequent review. The average percentage of idea units recalled by the group that heard the audiotape of the teacher-led review session was 7% higher than the average percentage of main idea units recalled by the group that heard the stories once with no subsequent review.

Author: Watkins & Kerkar (1985)

Students: College

Learning: Word recall

Instructional Tactics:

Experiment 1: Word lists were created containing 20 bisyllabic words. Ten words appeared only once on the list and five words appeared twice. Students viewed the 20 words individually on cards held up by the experimenter. The students were allowed to view each word for a two-second time period. Following presentation of all of the words, students were then allowed one minute to write down as many words as they could recall.

Experiment 2: A list of 24 nouns paired with 24 different adjectives was used for this study. Twelve nouns appeared only once and six nouns appeared twice. Students were presented the individual pairs of words on a television screen. The students saw each pair of words for 2.5 seconds. Following the presentation of all of the word pairs, the students were allowed one minute to recall as many of the nouns as they could remember.

Experiment 3: The procedure was the same as for Experiment 2, except that names of famous people were used.

Findings:

Experiment 1: Students recalled 28% more twice-presented words than once-presented words.

Experiment 2: Students recalled 25% more twice-presented nouns than once-presented nouns.

Experiment 3: Students recalled 25% more twice-repeated names than once-repeated names.

Author: Hines et al. (1985)

Students: College

Learning: Mathematics achievement

Instructional Tactics: The tactics employed in this study are as reported in Cruickshank et al. (1979, pp. 28–30). The tactics used in this study are reported under the heading "Clarity of Communication." Others are not relevant to the strategies presented in this handbook.

- Repeating and stressing directions and different points.
- Providing practice.
- Repeating questions and explanations if students do not understand.
- Using verbal repetition.

Findings: Instructional tactics associated with repetition were found to be positively and significantly related to learner achievement.

REFERENCE LIST

#Anderson, L. M., Evertson, C. M., & Brophy, J. E. (1979). An experimental study of effective teaching in first-grade reading groups. *The Elementary School Journal 79*, 193–222.

Ausubel, D. P., & Youseff, M. (1965). The effect of spaced repetition on meaningful retention. *The Journal of General Psychology 73*, 147–150.

*Butler, A. (1954). Test-retest and split-half reliabilities of the Wechsler-Bellvue scales and subtests with mental defectives. *American Journal of Mental Deficiency 59*, 80–84.

*Casey, M. L., Davidson, H. P., & Harter, P. I. (1928). Three studies on the effect of training in similar and identical material upon Stanford-Binet test scores. *Twenty-seventh Yearbook of the National Society for the Study of Education 1*, 431–439.

*Catron, D. W. (1978). Immediate test-retest changes in WAIS scores among college males. *Psychological Reports 43*, 279–290.

*Catron, D. W., & Thompson, C. C. (1979). Test-retest gains in WAIS scores after four retest intervals. *Journal of Clinical Psychology 35*, 352–357.

#Coker, H., Lorentz, C. W., & Coker, J. (1980). *Teacher behavior and student outcomes in the Georgia study*. Paper presented at the annual meeting of the American Educational Research Association, Boston.

*Colver, R. M., & Spielberger, C. D. (1961). Further evidence of a practice effect on the Miller Analogies Test. *Journal of Applied Psychology 50*, 126–127.

#Cook, L. K., & Meyer, R. E. (1983). Reading strategies training for meaningful learning from prose. In M. Preseley and J. Levin (Eds.), *Cognitive strategies training and research*. New York: Springer-Verlag.

Cruickshank, D. R., Kennedy, J. J., Bush, A., & Myers, B. (1979). Clear teaching: What is it? *British Journal of Teacher Education 5*(1), 27–32.

*Curr, W., & Gourlay, N. (1960). The effect of practice on performance in scholastic tests. *British Journal of Educational Psychology 30*, 155–167.

*Droege, R. C. (1966). Effects of practice on aptitude scores. *Journal of Applied Psychology 50*, 306–310.

*Evans, F. R. (1977). *The GRE-Q Coaching/Instruction Study*. Princeton, NJ: Graduate Record Examinations, Educational Testing Service. (ERIC Document Reproduction Service No. ED 163 088)

*Evans, F. R., & Pike, L. W. (1973). The effects of instruction for three mathematics item formats. *Journal of Educational Measurement 10*, 257–272.

Evertson, C., Anderson, C., Anderson, L., & Brophy, J. (1980). Relationships between classroom behaviors and student outcomes in junior high mathematics and English classes. *American Educational Research Journal 17*, 43–60.

#Evertson, C., Emmer, E., & Brophy, J. (1980). Predictors of effective teaching in junior high mathematics classrooms. *Journal for Research in Mathematics Education 11*, 167–178.

#Fisher, C. W., Berliner, D. C., Filby, N. N., Marliave, R., Cahen, L. S., & Dishaw, M. M. (1980). Teaching behaviors, academic learning time, and student achievement: An overview. In C. Denham & A. Lieberman (Eds.), *Time to learn* (pp. 7–32). Washington, DC: U.S. Government Printing Office.

*Frankel, E. (1960). Effects of growth, practice, and coaching on Scholastic Aptitude Test scores. *Personnel Guidance Journal 33*, 713–719.

*Goldsmith, R. P. (1980). The effects of training in test taking skills and test anxiety: Mexican American students' aptitude test performance. *Dissertation Abstracts International 40*, 5790A. (University Microfilms No. 80-09863)

#Good, T. L., & Grouws, D. A. (1979). The Missouri mathematics effectiveness project. *Journal of Educational Psychology 71*, 355–362.

*Greene, K. B. (1928). The influence of specialized training on tests of general intelligence. *Twenty-seventh Yearbook of the National Society for the Study of Education 1*, 421–428.

*Heim, A. W., & Wallace, J. G. (1949). The effects of repeatedly retesting the same group on the same intelligence test: I. Normal adults. *Quarterly Journal of Experimental Psychology 1*, 151–159.

*Heim, A. W., & Wallace, J. G. (1950). The effects of repeatedly retesting the same group on the same intelligence test: II. High grade mental defectives. *Quarterly Journal of Experimental Psychology 2*, 19–32.

Hines, C. V., Cruickshank, D. R., & Kennedy, J. J. (1985). Teacher clarity and its relationship to student achievement and satisfaction. *American Educational Research Journal 22* (1), 87–99.

*Holloway, H. D. (1954). Effects of training on the SRA Primary Mental Abilities (Primary) and the WISC. *Child Development 25*, 253–63.

*Jefferson, J. L. (1975). The effects of anxiety on the achievement of black graduate students taking standardized achievement tests. *Dissertation Abstracts International 35*, 5121A. (University Microfilms No. 75-3105)

*Klutch, M. I. (1976). The influence of test sophistication on standardized test scores. *Dissertation Abstracts International 37*, 809A. (University Microfilms No. 75-10,058)

*Kreit, L. H. (1968). The effects of test-taking practice on pupil test performance. *American Educational Research Journal 5*, 616–625.

#Kulik, J. A., & Kulik, C. C. (1979). College teaching. In P. L. Peterson and H. J. Walberg (Eds.), *Research on teaching: Concepts, findings, and implications* (pp. 70–93). Berkeley, CA: McCutchan.

Kulik, J. A., Kulik, C. C., & Bangert, R. L. (1984). Effects of practice on aptitude and achievement test scores. *American Educational Research Journal 21*(2), 434–447.

*MacNamara, J. (1964). Zero error an practice effects in Moray House English Quotients. *British Journal of Educational Psychology 34*, 315–320.

*McIntosh, D. M. (1944). Effects of practice on intelligence test results. *British Journal of Educational Psychology 14*, 44–45.

*Melametsa, L. (1965). The influence of training on the level of test performance and the factor structure of intelligence tests. *Scandinavian Journal of Psychology 6*, 19–25.

*Merriman, C. (1927). Coaching for mental tests. *Educational Administration and Supervision 13*, 59–64.

*Messick, S., & Jungeblut, A. (1981). Time and method in coaching SAT. *Psychological Bulletin 89*, 191–216.

Nelson, T. O. (1977). Repetition and depth of processing. *Journal of Verbal Learning and Verbal Behavior 16*, 151–171.

*Netley, C., Rachman, S., & Turner, R. K. (1965). The effect of practice on performance in reading attainment tests. *British Journal of Educational Psychology 35*, 1–8.

*Oakland, T. (1972). The effects of test-wiseness materials on standardized test performance of preschool disadvantaged children. *Journal of School Psychology 10*, 355–260.

#Palincsar, A. S. (1984). *Reciprocal teaching*. Paper presented at the annual meeting of the American Educational Research Association, New Orleans.

*Peel, E. A. (1951). A note on practice effects in intelligence tests. *British Journal of Educational Psychology 69*, 122–125.

Peterson, H. A., Ellis, M., Toohill, N., & Kloess, P. (1935). Some measurements of the effects of reviews. *The Journal of Educational Psychology 26*(2), 65–72.

Petros, T., & Hoving, K. (1980). The effects of review on young children's memory for prose. *Journal of Experimental Child Psychology 30*, 33–43.

*Petty, N. E., & Harrell, E. H. (1977). Effects of programmed instruction related to motivation, anxiety, and test wiseness on group IQ test performance. *Journal of Educational Psychology 69*, 630–635,

*Quereshi, M. Y. (1968). Practice effects on the WISC subtest scores and IQ estimates. *Journal of Clinical Psychology 24*, 79–85.

#Raphael, T. E. (1980). *The effective metacognitive awareness training on students' question and answer behavior*. Doctoral dissertation, University of Illinois.

*Richardson, F., & Robinson, E. S. (1921). Effects of practice upon the scores and predictive value of the Alpha Intelligence Examination. *Journal of Experimental Psychology 4*, 300–317.

*Roberts, S. O., & Oppenheim, D. B. (1966). *The effects of specialized instruction upon test performance of high school students*. Princeton, NJ: Educational Testing Service. (ERIC Document Reproduction Service No. ED 053 158)

*Rodgers, A. G. (1936). The application of six group intelligence tests to the same children, and the effects of practice. *British Journal of Educational Psychology 6*, 291–305.

Rosenshine, B. V. (1986). Synthesis of research on explicit teaching. *Educational Leadership 43*(7), 60–69.

*Rutan, P. C. (1979). Test sophistication training: A program level intervention for the school

psychologist. *Dissertation Abstracts International 40*, 171A. (University Microfilms No. 79-14,135)

*Slaughter, B. A. (1976). An examination of the effects of teaching and practice in test-retest skills on student performance on a standardized achievement test. *Dissertation Abstracts International 37*, 1505A. (University Microfilms No. 76-19,931)

#Smith, L., & Land, M. (1981). Low-inference verbal behaviors related to teacher clarity. *Journal of Classroom Interaction 17*, 37–42.

#Soar, R. S. (1973). *Follow-Through Classroom Process Measurement and Pupil Growth (1970–1971) Final Report*. Gainesville: College of Education, University of Florida.

*Spielberger, C. D. (1959). Evidence of a practice effect on the Miller Analogies Test. *Journal of Applied Psychology 43*, 259–263.

#Spiro, R. J., & Meyers, A. (1984). Individual differences and underlying cognitive process. In P. D. Pearson, R. Barr, M. L. Kamil, & P. Mosenthal (Eds.), *Handbook of reading research*. New York: Longman.

#Stallings J., Corey, R., Fairweather, J., & Needles, M. (1977). *Early Childhood Education classroom evaluation*. Menlo Park, CA: SRI International.

#Stallings, J. A., & Kaskowitz, D. (1974). *Follow-Through Classroom Observation*. Menlo Park, CA: SRI International.

#Stallings, J., Needles, M., & Staybrook, N. (1979). *The teaching of basic reading skills in secondary schools, Phase II and Phase III*. Menlo Park, CA: SRI International.

*Steisel, I. M. (1951). The relation between test and retest scores on the Wechsler-Bellvue Scale (Form 1) for selected college students. *Journal of Genetic Psychology 79*, 155–162.

*Throne, F. M., Schulman, J. L., & Kaspar, J. C. (1962). Reliability and stability of the WISC for a group of mentally retarded boys. *American Journal of Mental Deficiency 67*, 455–457.

*Tinney, R. E. (1969). The effect of training in test-taking skills on the reading test scores of fifth grade children of high and low socioeconomic levels. *Dissertation Abstracts International 30*, 595A. (University Microfilms No. 69-11,505)

#Tobias, S. (1982). When do instructional methods make a difference? *Educational Researcher 11*, 4–10.

*Vernon, P. E. (1954). Practice and coaching effects in intelligence tests. *Educational Forum 18*, 269–280.

Watkins, M. J., & Kerkar, S. P. (1985). Recall of twice-presented item without recall of either presentation: Generic memory for events. *Journal of Memory and Language 24*, 666–678.

*Whitely, S. E., & Dawn, R. V. (1974). Effects of cognitive intervention on latent ability measured from analogy items. *Journal of Educational Psychology 66*(5), 710–717.

*Wideman, S., & Wrigley, J. (1953). The comparative effects of coaching and practice on the results of verbal intelligence tests. *British Journal of Educational Psychology 44*, 83–94.

6

Clarifying Communication

INTRODUCTION

An essential aspect of instruction is the clear communication of information to students to facilitate their understanding of (1) the learning objectives they are assigned to pursue, (2) the tasks they are assigned to perform to enhance their achievement of the learning objectives, and (3) the means of evaluating their performance. Although educators may appreciate the importance of clear communication in conversation and in professions such as "newscaster" and "trial lawyer," the following explicates the relevance of clear communication to instruction, elements of clear communication, and tactics for achieving clear communication. Clarity of communication has a distinct application to instruction and learning.

STUDENT BENEFICIARIES

The evidence indicates that clarity of communication enhances the academic achievement of students in elementary, secondary, and college classrooms. Moreover, clarity of communication improves academic achievement in a wide range of content areas. No evidence could be found to suggest that clarity of communication should not be stressed in all subject areas for all types of students, including students in military, community, business, and adult education settings.

LEARNING ACHIEVED

Achievement in the content areas of mathematics, science, social studies, and the social sciences is enhanced when clear communication tactics are incorporated in instruction. It may be reasonable to expect that achievement may be enhanced in other content areas as well. In studies reviewed, student achievement was shown to be positively related to clarity of communication during instruction. Some studies indicated that students exposed to clear communication during instruction achieved at a rate one and one-half to three times higher than students exposed to instruction which lacked clarity.

INSTRUCTIONAL TACTICS

The benefits of clear communication to students are well supported by the evidence. However, there is a need for instructional planners and teachers to know the particular tactics that can be used to ensure clear communication. The following tactics are derived from the studies that demonstrate the benefits of clear communication. Discretion has been used to interpret and reduce overlap in tactics used in different studies and to elaborate tactics.

Tactics that ensure clear communication are:

- Providing examples and illustrations of concepts being taught.
- When speaking, avoiding the use of "er," "um," "uh," "ah," "you know," and other halts in the flow of speech.
- Avoiding irrelevant interjections of subject matter and relevant interjections at inappropriate times.
- Being precise in statements, including sufficient detail in presentations to avoid vagueness.
- Using transitional terms such as "next," "the last item is," "this concludes," "tomorrow we will," "these were the four causes of . . . 1, 2, 3, 4," "first we will . . . ," "second we will . . . ," "third we will."
- Providing explanations to clarify cause-effect relations. This is necessary in answering the question "why."
- Describing the tasks students are to perform, explaining and demonstrating how to perform tasks, and defining performance standards.
- Showing the relevancy of concepts being taught to students' lives.
- Using multiple and diverse approaches to clarify a concept: for instance, using a number of different illustrations or using media that involve a number of senses, such as sight and hearing.
- Providing for question-and-answer instruction. Questioning students and correcting their answers, as well as answering student-initiated questions, sharpens their understanding and corrects misconceptions. Question-and-answer instruction may be incorporated in textbooks and in lesson plans, or teachers can encourage students to ask questions at any time.
- Using simple language. Rarely used and excessively complex terminology are to be avoided.

Elaboration of the above summary of tactics can be obtained from reading the studies that follow. To be most effective, the instructional tactics need to be integrated into the particular instructional program being planned or presently in use.

CAUTIONS AND COMMENTS

The second tactic, "avoiding halts in speech," pertains to speaking. Most of the other tactics pertain to any mode of communication: for example, "using simple language." Some tactics pertain most particularly to instruction: for instance, "describing the task students are to perform, explaining and demonstrating how to perform tasks," and "defining performance standards," as well as "providing question-and-answer instruction." Question-and-answer instruction has been shown to be especially effective in enhancing achievement. More research needs to be done to determine the most effective types of question-and-answer instruction: for example, teacher questioning, students asking questions, a combination of the two, Socratic method, and so on. It would also be helpful to know when during the instructional process it is most effective to conduct question and answer instruction.

GENERALIZATION: ON CLARIFYING COMMUNICATION

Achievement of learning objectives is enhanced when information on learning objectives, tasks, and evaluations is clearly communicated to students over time.

Supportive Research on Clarifying Communication
Total number of studies covered: 111

Groups of Studies

Authors: Land (1985)

Students: Elementary, high school, and college

Learning: Social studies, science, mathematics, and psychology achievement

Instructional Tactics: Some of the tactics used in studies summarized by Land (1985) to enhance learning involved avoiding low-clarity instructional communication, which has been identified as possibly having a negative effect on student achievement. They were vagueness terms, mazes, "uhs," specification of selected content, extra content, and signals of transition and discontinuity. Vagueness terms are words or phrases which lack clarity or may indicate a lack of assurance on the part of the teacher. Mazes relate to the teacher speaking correctly, avoiding false starts or halts in speech, redundantly stated words, tangles of words, and "uhs," "ahs," and "ums." Specification of selected content includes descriptions, explanations, and providing specific details. Clear transition is the presence of such transitional terms as "now" and "the last item was." Discontinuity is defined as interruption of the flow of the lesson, with irrelevant interjections of subject matter and relevant interjections at inappropriate times.

The following are examples of clear and unclear instruction as provided by Land (1979):

Clear: "A concept is a word or phrase (but not a complete statement) or symbol that refers to a group of one or more objects, qualities, actions, or things possessing common characteristics. Here are three examples of concepts. Bacteria is an example because it is a word that refers to a group of common organisms. Parts of speech is an example because it is a phrase that refers to a group of things with common characteristics. HCl is an example because it is a symbol" (p. 797).

Unclear: "A concept is a word or phrase, phrase (but not, uh, a complete statement) or symbol that refers to a group of some objects, qualities, actions, or things possessing common characteristics. Bacteria. Parts of speech. HCl. Concepts can be classified as concrete versus abstract and as conjunctive, disjunctive, and relational" (p. 797).

The following are examples of clear instruction and unclear instruction for a geometry lesson as provided by Smith & Cotton (1980):

No vagueness, no discontinuity (Clear): "The first theorem involves two chords intersecting at one point in a circle. Look at figure 1. AB intersects CD at point E. Look at figure 2. The length of line segment AE is 4 units. The length of line segment EB is 3 units. The length of line segment ED is 6 units. The length of line segment EC is 2 units. Notice that $4 \times 3 = 2 \times 6$. Look at figure 7. The third theorem means that $AE \times AD = AF \times GA$. The length of the secant AE is 8 units. The length of the external segment is 3 units. The length of the secant AF is 6 units. We can determine the length of the external segment GA" (p. 672).

Vagueness, no discontinuity: "The first theorem sort of involves a couple of chords intersecting at one point in a circle. I guess we probably should look at figure 1. AB intersects CD at point E you see. Look at figure 2. The length of line segment AE is 4 units. The length of line segment EB is 3 units. The length of line segment ED is 6 units, you see. The length of line segment EC, you know, is 2 units. You might notice that $4 \times 3 = 2 \times 6$. Look at figure 7 a few seconds. The third theorem ordinarily means that $AE \times AD = AF \times GA$. The length of the secant AE is 8 units. The length of the external segment is 3 units. The length of the secant AF is 6 units, as you know. Chances are we can determine the length of the external segment GA" (p. 672).

Discontinuity, no vagueness: The first theorem involves two chords intersecting at one point in a circle. Look at figure 1. Did you know that the word geometry is derived from the Greek words for earth and measure? AB intersects CD at point E. Look at figure 2. It is shaped somewhat like a baseball diamond. The length of line segment AE is 4 units. The length of line segment EB is 3 units. The length of line segment ED is 6 units. The length of the line segment EC is 2 units. From your work with areas, you will recall that area is represented in terms of square units. Notice that $4 \times 3 = 2 \times 6$. Look at figure 7. Although the word geometry is a noun, the word geometrize is a verb. The third theorem means that $AE \times AD = AF \times GA$. The length of the secant AE is 8 units. The length of the external segment is 3 units. If you square 3 and subtract 1, the result is 8. This is a coincidence, but it is interesting. The length of the secant AF is 6 units. We can determine the length of the external segment GA. Try to remember that the second theorem involved tangents" (p. 672).

The vagueness and discontinuity lesson contained all of the vagueness terms and instances of discontinuity present in the previous examples.

Findings: In eight of the ten studies involving multiple variables associated with teacher clarity of communication, students exposed to clear teacher behaviors performed significantly higher on achievement tests than did students exposed to unclear teacher behaviors. In five experimental studies on the effects of vagueness terms on student achievement, students exposed to instruction containing many vagueness terms performed at a significantly lower level than did students not exposed to instruction containing vagueness terms. The same findings were found in three of the five correlational studies reviewed.

Individual studies reviewed in this logical synthesis of research are identified by the symbol # in the reference list at the end of the chapter.

Author: Brophy & Good (1986)

Students: Elementary and secondary

Learning: Reading and mathematics achievement

Instructional Tactics: The following tactics were derived from the review of studies:

- Give clear and detailed instructions.
- Ask many clear and relevant academic questions and check for student understanding.
- Ask questions one at a time, be clear, and present them at an appropriate level of difficulty so that students can understand them.
- Wait for answers to questions.

- Explain answers when necessary.
- Encourage student questions.
- Answer all student questions.
- Use examples and illustrations to clarify concepts.
- Show analogies between new material and events and what students are already familiar with.
- Present material in a systematic and structured manner.
- Avoid vague words and phrases such as "all of this," "somewhere," "not many," "not very," "almost," "pretty much," "anyway," "of course," "excuse me," "not sure," "some," "a few," "sorts," "factors," "may," "could be," "sometimes," "often," "some things," "usually," "probably," "as you know."
- Avoidance of using "um," "uh," "ah."
- Avoid interjecting irrelevant content.

Other instructional tactics are employed in these studies that are applicable to other generalizations and will be presented in the appropriate chapters.

Groups of studies reviewed in this logical synthesis of research did not provide statistical evidence. However, many of the individual studies included in the logical synthesis of research do contain statistical evidence. In the event that a reader wishes to view this evidence, an extensive listing of the individual studies reviewed is provided in the reference list (the studies are identified by the symbol *).

Findings: Use of the above tactics was related to enhanced achievement across the relevant studies included in these reviews.

Individual Studies

Author: Hines et al. (1985)

Students: College

Learning: Mathematics achievement

Instructional Tactics: The Hines et al. (1982) study summarized by Land (1985) and the Hines et al. (1985) study used the following teaching clarity behaviors reported in Cruickshank et al. (1979).

- Communicate so the students can understand.
- Explain the work to be done and how to do it.
- Repeat questions and explanations if students do not understand.
- Ask students before they start work if they know what to do and how to do it.

- Give explanations that the students understand.
- Provide for student understanding.
- Demonstrate a high degree of verbal fluency.

Findings: Teacher clarity was found to be positively and significantly related to learner achievement.

REFERENCE LIST

*Acland, H. (1976). Stability of teacher effectiveness: A replication. *Journal of Educational Research 69*, 289–292.

*Adams, A., Carnine, D., & Gersten, R. (1982). Instructional straties for studying content area texts in the intermediate grades. *Reading Research Quarterly 18*, 27–55.

*Amarel, M. (1981, April). *Literacy: The personal dimension*. Paper presented at the annual meeting of the American Educational Research Association, Los Angeles.

*Anderson, L. M., Evertson, C. M., & Brophy, J. E. (1979). An experimental study of effective teaching in first-grade reading groups. *The Elementary School Journal 79*, 193–222.

*Anderson, L. M., Evertson, C. M., & Brophy, J. E. (1982). *Principles of small group instruction* (Occasional paper no. 32). East Lansing: Michigan State University, Institute for Research on Teaching.

*Arehart, J. (1979). Student opportunity to learn related to student achievement of objectives in a probability unit. *Journal of Educational Research 72*, 253–269.

*Bennett, N. (1976). *Teaching styles and pupil progress*. London: Open Books.

*Bennett, N., Desforges, C., Cockburn, A., & Wilkinson, B. (1981). *The quality of pupil learning experiences: Interim report*. Lancaster, England: University of Lancaster, Centre for Educational Research and Development.

*Berliner, D. (1979). Tempus Educare. In P. Peterson & H. Walberg (Eds.), *Research on teaching: Concepts, findings, and implications* (pp. 120–135). Berkeley, CA: McCutchan.

*Blank, M. (1973). *Teaching learning in the preschool: A dialogue approach*. Columbus, OH: Charles Merrill.

*Borich, G., & Fenton, K. (Eds.) (1977). *The appraisal of teaching: Concepts and process*. Reading, MA: Addison-Wesley.

*Bossert, S. (1979). *Task and social relationships in classrooms: A study of classroom organization and its consequences*. American Psychological Association, Arnold and Caroline Rose Monograph Series. New York: Cambridge University Press.

Brophy, J., & Good, T. L. (1986). Teacher behavior and student achievement. In M. C. Wittrock (Ed.), *Handbook of research on teaching* (3rd ed., pp. 328–375). New York: Macmillan.

*Bush, A., Kennedy, J., & Cruickshank, D. (1977). An empirical investigation of teacher clarity. *Journal of Teacher Education 28*, 53–58.

*#Clark, C., Gage, N., Marx, R., Peterson, P., Staybrook, N., & Winne, P. (1979). A factorial experiment on teacher structuring, soliciting, and reacting. *Journal of Educational Psychology 71*, 534–552.

Coker, H., Lorentz, C. W., & Coker, J. (1980). *Teacher behavior and student outcomes in the Georgia study*. Paper presented at the annual meeting of the American Educational Research Association, Boston.

Cook, L. K., & Meyer, R. E. (1983). Reading strategies training for meaningful learning from prose. In M. Preseley and J. Levin (Eds.), *Cognitive strategies training and research* (pp. 87–131). New York: Springer-Verlag.

Cruickshank, D. (1976). Synthesis of selected recent research on teacher effects. *Journal of Teacher Education 27*(1), 57–60.

*Cruickshank, D. R., Kennedy, J. J., Bush, A., & Myers, B. (1979). Clear teaching: What is it? *British Journal of Teacher Education 5*(1), 27–32.

#Demham A., & Land, M. L. (1981). Research brief: Effect of teacher verbal fluency and clarity on student achievement. *The Technical Journal of Education 8*, 227–229.

*Doyle, W. (1983). Academic work. *Review of Educational Research 53*, 159–199.

*#Dunkin, M. J. (1978). Student characteristics, classroom processes, and student achievement. *Journal of Educational Psychology 70*, 998–1009.

*#Dunkin, M. J., & Doenau, S. J. (1980). A replication study of unique and joint contributions to variance in student achievement. *Journal of Educational Psychology 72*, 394–403.

*Eaton, J., Anderson, C., & Smith, E. (1984). Students' misconceptions interfere with science learning: Case studies of fifth-grade students. *Elementary School Journal 84*, 365–379.

*Ebmier, H. & Good, T. (1979). The effects of instructing teachers about good teaching on mathematics achievement of fourth grade students. *American Educational Research Journal 16*, 1–16.

*Emmer, E., Evertson, C., & Anderson, L. (1980). Effective classroom management at the beginning of the school year. *Elementary School Journal 80*, 219–231.

*Emmer, E., Evertson, C., & Brophy, J. (1979). Stability of teacher effects in junior high classrooms. *American Educational Research Journal 16*, 71–75.

*Evertson, C. (1979). *Student behavior, student achievement, and student attitudes: Descriptions of selected classrooms* (Report No. 4063). Austin: Research and Development Center for Teacher Education, University of Texas.

*Evertson, C., Anderson, C., Anderson, L., & Brophy, J. (1980). Relationships between classroom behaviors and student outcomes in junior high mathematics and English classes. *American Educational Research Journal 17*, 43–60.

*Evertson, C., Anderson, L., & Brophy, J. (1978). *Texas Junior High School Study: Final report of process–outcome relationship* (Report No. 4061). Austin: Research and Development Center for Teacher Education, University of Texas.

*Evertson, C., & Emmer, E. (1982). Effective management at the beginning of the school year in junior high classes. *Journal of Educational Psychology 74*, 485–498.

*Evertson, C., Emmer, E., & Brophy, J. (1980). Predictors of effective teaching in junior high mathematics classrooms. *Journal for Research in Mathematics Education 11*, 167–178.

*Fisher, C. W., Berliner, D. C., Filby, N. N., Marliave, R., Cahen, L. S., & Dishaw, M. M. (1980). Teaching behaviors, academic learning time, and student achievement: An overview. In C. Denham & A. Lieberman (Eds.), *Time to learn* (pp. 7–32). Washington, DC: U.S. Government Printing Office.

*Flanders, N. (1965). *Teacher influence, pupil attitudes, and achievement* (Cooperative Research Monograph No. 12). Washington, DC: U.S. Office of Education.

*Flanders, N. (1970). *Analyzing teacher behavior.* Reading MA: Addison-Wesley.

*Fortune, J. (1967). *A study of the generality of presenting behaviors in teaching preschool children* (Final Report for U.S. Office of Education Project No. 6-8468). Memphis,

TN: Memphis State University. (ERIC Document Reproduction Service No. ED 016 285)

*Gall, M., Ward, B., Berliner, D., Cahen, L., Winne, P., Elashoff, J., & Stanton, G. (1978). Effects of questioning techniques and recitation on student learning. *American Educational Research Journal 15*, 175–199.

*Good, T. (1979). Teacher effectiveness in the elementary school: What we know about it now. *Journal of Teacher Education 30*, 52–64.

*Good, T., Biddle, B., & Brophy, J. (1975). *Teachers make a difference*. New York: Holt, Rinehart & Winston.

*Good, T., & Brophy, J. (1984). *Looking in classrooms* (3rd ed.). New York: Harper & Row.

*Good, T., Ebmeier, H., & Beckerman, T. (1978) Teaching mathematics in high and low SES classrooms: An empirical comparison. *Journal of Teacher Education 29*, 85–90.

*Good, T., Grouws, D., & Beckerman, T. (1978). Curriculum pacing: Some empirical data in mathematics. *Journal of Curriculum Studies 10*, 75–81.

*Good, T., Grouws, D., & Ebmeier, M. (1983). *Active mathematics teaching*. New York: Longman.

*Good, T. L., & Grouws, D. A. (1977). Teaching effects: a process-product study in fourth grade mathematics classrooms. *Journal of Teacher Education 28*(3), 49–54.

*Good, T. L., & Grouws, D. A. (1979a). *Experimental study of mathematics instruction in elementary schools* (Final Report, National Institute of Education Grant No. NIE-G-79-0103). Columbia: University of Missouri, Center for the Study of Social Behavior.

*Good, T. L., & Grouws, D. A. (1979b). The Missouri mathematics effectiveness project. *Journal of Educational Psychology 71*, 355–362.

*Good, T. L., & Grouws, D. A. (1981). *Experimental research in secondary mathematics* (Final Report, National Institute of Education Grant No. NIE-G-79-0103). Columbia: University of Missouri, Center for the Study of Social Behavior.

*Hamilton, S. (1983). The social side of schooling: Ecological studies of classrooms and schools. *Elementary School Journal 83*, 313–334.

#Hiller J. H. (1968). *An experimental investigation of the effects of conceptual vagueness on speaking behavior*. Paper presented at the annual meeting of the American Educational Research Association, Chicago.

#Hiller, J. H. (1971). Verbal response indicators of conceptual vagueness. *American Educational Research Journal 8*, 151–161.

*#Hiller, J., Fisher, G., & Kaess, W. (1969). A computer investigation of verbal characteristics of effective classroom lecturing. *American Educational Research Journal 6*, 661–675.

#Hines, C. V., Cruickshank, D. R., & Kennedy, J. J. (1982). *Measures of teacher clarity and their relationships to student achievement and satisfaction*. Paper presented at the annual meeting of the American Educational Research Association, New York.

Hines, C. V., Cruickshank, D. R., & Kennedy, J. J. (1985). Teacher clarity and its relationship to student achievement and satisfaction. *American Educational Research Journal 22* (1), 87–99.

*Husen, T. (Ed.). (1967). *International study of achievement in mathematics* (Vol. 1). New York: John Wiley.

*Kulik, J. A., & Kulik, C. C. (1979). College teaching. In P. L. Peterson and H. J. Walberg (Eds.), *Research on teaching: Concepts, findings, and implications* (pp. 70–93). Berkeley, CA: McCutchan.

*#Land, M., & Smith, L. (1979). The effect of low inference teacher clarity inhibitors on student achievement. *Journal of Teacher Education 31*, 55–57.

#Land, M., & Smith, L. (1981). College student ratings and teacher behavior: An experimental study. *Journal of Social Studies Research 5*, 19–22.

*#Land, M. L. (1979). Low-inference variables of teacher clarity effects on student concept learning. *Journal of Educational Psychology 71*(6), 795–799.

#Land, M. L. (1980). Teacher clarity and cognitive level of questions: Effects on learning. *Journal of Experimental Education 49*, 48–51.

#Land, M. L. (1981). Combined effects of two teacher clarity variables on student achievement. *Journal of Experimental Education 50*, 14-17.

Land, M. L. (1985). Vagueness and clarity in the classroom. In T. Husen & T. N. Postlethwaite (Eds.), *The International Encyclopedia of Education Research and Studies* (Vol. 9, pp. 5405–5410). Oxford, England: Pergamon Press.

#Land, M. L., & Combs, A. (1981). *Teacher clarity, student instructional ratings, and student performance*. Paper presented at the annual meeting of the American Educational Research Association, Los Angeles.

#Land, M. L., & Smith, L. R. (1979). Effect of a teacher clarity variable on student achievement. *Journal of Educational Research 73*, 19–22.

*Larrivee, B., & Algina, J. (1983, April). *Identification of teaching behaviors which predict success for mainstream students*. Paper presented at the annual meeting of the American Educational Research Association, Montreal. (ERIC Document Reproduction Service No. ED 232 362)

*MacKay, A. (1979). *Project Quest: Teaching strategies and pupil achievement* (Research Report No. 79-1-3). Edmonton, Canada: University of Alberta, Centre for Research in Teaching, Faculty of Education.

*Madike, F. (1980). Teacher classroom behaviors involved in micro-teaching and student achievement: A regression study. *Journal of Educational Psychology 72*, 265–274.

*McCaleb, J., & White, J. (1980). Critical dimensions in evaluating teacher clarity. *Journal of Classroom Interaction 15*, 27–30.

*McConnell, J. (1977, April). *Relationship between selected teacher behaviors and attitudes/achivements of algebra classes*. Paper presented at the annual meeting of the American Educational Research Association, New York. (ERIC Document Reproduction Service No. ED 141 118)

*Medley, D. (1977). *Teacher competency and teacher effectiveness: A review of process-product research*. Washington, DC: American Association of Colleges for Teacher Education.

*Mitzel, H. (1960). Teacher effectiveness. In C. Harris (Ed.), *Encyclopedia of educational research* (3rd ed., pp. 1481–1485). New York: Macmillan.

*Morsh, J., & Wilder, E. (1954). *Identifying the effective instructor: A review of the quantitative studies, 1900–1952* (Research Bulletin No. AFTRIC-TR-54-44). San Antonio, TX: USAF Personnel Training Research Center, Lackland Air Force Base.

*Nuthall, G., & Church, J. (1973). Experimental studies of teaching behavior. In G. Chanan (Ed.), *Towards a science of teaching* (pp. 9–25). London: National Foundation for Educational Research.

*Palincsar, A. S. (1984). *Reciprocal teaching*. Paper presented at the annual meeting of the American Educational Research Association, New Orleans.

*Peterson, P., & Walberg, H. (Eds.). (1979). *Research on teaching: concepts, findings, and implications*. Berkeley, CA: McCutchan.

*Ramp, E., & Rhine, W. (1981). Behavior analysis model. In W. Rhine (Ed.), *Making schools* *more effective: New directions from Follow Through* (pp. 155–197). New York: Academic Press.

*Raphael, T. E. (1980). *The effective metacognitive awareness training on students' question and answer behavior.* Doctoral dissertation, University of Illinois.

*Redfield, D., & Rousseau, E. (1981). A meta-analysis of experimental research on teacher questioning behavior. *Review of Educational Research 51*, 237–245.

*Romberg, T. (1983). A common curiculum for mathematics. In G. Fenstermacher & J. Goodlad (Eds.), *Individual differences and the common curriculum* (Eighty-second Yearbook of the National Society for the Study of Education, Part 1). Chicago: University of Chicago Press.

*Rosenshine, B. (1968). To explain: A review of research. *Educational Leadership 26*, 275–280.

*Rosenshine, B. (1970a). Evaluation of instruction. *Review of Educational Research 40*, 279–301.

*Rosenshine, B. (1970b). Experimental classroom studies of indirect teaching. *Classroom Interaction Newsletter 5*(2), 7–11.

*#Rosenshine, B. (1971). *Teaching behaviors and student achievement.* London: National Foundation for Educational Research.

*Rosenshine, B. (1976). Classroom instruction. In N. L. Gage (Ed.), *The psychology of teaching methods* (Seventy-seventh Yearbook of the National Society for the Study of Education, pp. 335–371). Chicago: University of Chicago Press.

*Rosenshine, B. (1979). Content, time, and direct instruction. In P. Peterson & H. Walberg (Eds.), *Research on teaching: concepts, findings, and implications* (pp. 28–56). Berkeley, CA: McCutchan.

*Rosenshine, B. (1983). Teaching functions in instructional programs. *Elementary School Journal 83*, 335–351.

*Rosenshine, B., & Berliner, D. (1978). Academic engaged time. *British Journal of Teacher Education 4*, 3–16.

*Rosenshine, B., & Furst, N. (1973). The use of direct observation to study teaching. In R. M. W. Travers (Ed.), *Second handbook of research on teaching* (pp. 37–74). Chicago: Rand McNally.

*Rosenshine, B., & Stevens, R. (1984). Classroom instruction in reading. In D. Pearson (Ed.), *Handbook of research on reading* (pp. 745–798). New York: Longman.

*Rowe, M. (1974). Wait-time and rewards as instructional variables, their influence on language, logic and fate control: Part I. Wait-time. *Journal of Research in Science Teaching 11*, 81–94.

*Ryan, F. (1973). Differentiated effects of levels of questioning on student achievement. *Elementary School Journal 41*, 63–67.

*Ryan, F. (1974). The effects on social studies achievement of multiple students responding to different levels of questioning. *Journal of Experimental Education 42*, 71–75.

*Schuck, R. (1981). The impact of set induction on student achievement and retention. *Journal of Educational Research 74*, 227–232.

*#Smith, L. (1977). Aspects of teacher discourse and student achievement in mathematics. *Journal for Research in Mathematics Education 8*, 195–204.

*Smith, L. (1979). Task-oriented lessons and student achievement. *Journal of Educational Research 73*, 16–19.

*Smith, L., & Land, M. (1981). Low-inference verbal behaviors related to teacher clarity. *Journal of Classroom Interaction 17*, 37–42.

*Smith, L., & Sanders, K. (1981). The effects on student achievement and student perception of varying structure in social studies content. *Journal of Educational Research 74*, 333–336.

#Smith, L. R., & Bramblett, G. H. (1981). The effect of teacher vagueness terms on student performance in high school biology. *Journal of Research in Science Teaching 18*, 353–360.

*#Smith, L. R., & Cotton, M. L. (1980). Effects of lesson vagueness and discontinuity on student achievement and attitudes. *Journal of Educational Psychology 72*(5), 670–675.

#Smith, L. R., & Edmonds, E. M. (1978). Teacher vagueness and pupil participation in mathematics learning. *Journal of Research in Mathematics Education 9*, 228–232.

#Smith, L. R., & Land, M. L. (1980). Student perception of teacher clarity in mathematics. *Journal of Research in Mathematics Education 11*, 137–146.

*Soar, R. S. (1973). *Follow-Through Classroom Process Measurement and Pupil Growth (1970–1971) Final Report.* Gainesville: College of Education, University of Florida.

*Spiro, R. J., and Meyers, A. (1984). Individual differences and underlying cognitive process. In P. D. Pearson, R. Barr, M. L. Kamil, & P. Mosenthal (Eds.), *Handbook of reading research* (pp. 471–501). New York: Longman.

*Stallings, J. (1975). Implimentation and child effects of teaching practices in Follow Through classrooms. *Monographs of the Society for Research in Child Development 40*(7–8, Serial No. 163).

*Stallings J., Corey, R., Fairweather, J., & Needles, M. (1977). *Early Childhood Education classroom evaluation.* Menlo Park, CA: SRI International.

*Stallings, J., Needles, M., & Staybrook, N. (1979). *The teaching of basic reading skills in secondary schools, Phase II and Phase III.* Menlo Park, CA: SRI International.

*Stallings, J. A., & Kaskowitz, D. (1974). *Follow-Through classroom observation.* Menlo Park, CA: SRI International.

*Tobias, S. (1982). When do instructional methods make a difference? *Educational Researcher 11*, 4–10.

*Tobin, K. (1980). The effect of an extended teacher wait-time on science achievement. *Journal of Research in Science Teaching 17*, 469–475.

*Tobin, K., & Capie, W. (1982). Relationships between classroom process variables and middle-school science achievement. *Journal of Educational Psychology 66*, 319–324.

*Winne, P. (1979). Experiments relating teachers' use of higher cognitive questions to student achievement. *Review of Educational Research 49*, 13–50.

*Wright, C., & Nuthall, G. (1970). Relationships between teacher behaviors and pupil achievement in three experimental science lessons. *American Educational Research Journal 7*, 477–491.

7

Reducing Student/Teacher Ratio

INTRODUCTION

Most educators are familiar with different classroom configurations that are dictated by the particular teaching method used. For example, the discussion method is best applied when discussants are in a circle facing each other, and the lecture method is best applied when all students are facing the lecturer. Most educators also are aware that lecture classes can be larger than discussion classes. What many educators may not be fully cognizant of is how class size in general affects student achievement. Generally speaking, larger student-to-teacher ratios are associated with lower student achievement, with a threshold appearing to occur at about the student/teacher ratio of 15:1. That is, as student/teacher ratio increases, academic achievement decreases up to a threshold level of 15:1. As student/teacher ratio increases beyond 15:1, academic achievement is not affected as much. There appear to be several reasons for this. Teachers may need to spend more time on classroom management and less time on teaching. When tasks are formulated to be performed by larger numbers of students at the same time, it is less likely that the readiness capabilities of individual students can be accommodated. In addition, there is more opportunity for off-task behavior, resulting in diminished student focus and performance. However, more is known about the effect on achievement of student-to-teacher ratio than these generalities.

STUDENT BENEFICIARIES

The evidence indicates that reducing the student-to-teacher ratio enhances the academic achievement of students in elementary, secondary, and college classrooms. No evidence could be found to suggest that lower student-to-teacher ratios should not be stressed in all subject areas for all types of students, including students in college, military, community, business, and adult education settings.

LEARNING ACHIEVED

Achievement of learning objectives in the content areas of reading, mathematics, language, psychology, physical sciences, social studies, physical education, composition, art, vocabulary, and history is enhanced when there are smaller student-to-teacher ratios. It may be reasonable to expect that achievement may be enhanced in other content areas as well. In studies reviewed, student achievement was shown to be positively related to student-to-teacher ratio.

INSTRUCTIONAL TACTICS

- To maximize student achievement, conduct one-to-one tutoring. Bloom (1984) has shown that one-to-one tutoring results in as much as twice the achievement when compared to larger student-to-teacher ratios. Group instruction achieves superior results only when teamwork is being taught for the purpose of enhancing group achievement. See the teamwork instructional strategies. The only other justification for group instruction is the saving of money and time.

- In group instruction, keep student-to-teacher ratios below 15:1 and as low as possible. Glass et al. (1982) has shown that student-to-teacher ratios less than 15:1 produce higher levels of achievement. The smaller the group size below 15:1, the higher the academic achievement, with 1:1 producing the highest achievement.

- When conducting group instruction, assess and diagnose student performance often and provide remediation for inadequate performance on an individual basis. Presentations and instructions may be given to the group as a whole, but diagnosis and remediation of inadequate student performance must be done on an individual basis. See remediation instructional strategies.

- Although discussed under the heading "Instructional Tactics," decisions pertaining to student/teacher ratio are not an integral part of the instructional process (according to our definition of instruction and other definitions we are aware of). Most often administrators have more to do with establishing student/teacher ratios, working within policy constraints, than do teachers. Teacher influence is often limited to suggestions and complaints. In the final analysis, it is important to recognize that teachers' failure to achieve the learning objectives they are held responsible for achieving may be due to excessively large classes they are assigned to teach.

CAUTIONS AND COMMENTS

Reducing the student-to-teacher ratio may not enhance student achievement by itself. In addition, the use of other effective instructional tactics, such as those associated with student readiness, remediation, teaching time, and so forth, are required to ensure that higher levels of student achievement are realized. However, it may be that reducing the student-to-teacher ratio may allow the teacher more opportunity to employ other instructional tactics related to higher levels of student achievement. Additionally, the effect of reducing the student-to-teacher ratio will not be the same for classes which primarily involve lecture as opposed to classes with a great deal of student discussion or participation.

Research has demonstrated up to the student/teacher ratio of 15:1 that there is a clear association between increased student/teacher ratio and decreased student achievement. This is not intended to imply linearity. Beyond the student/teacher ratio of 15:1, research has not been able to consistently show an association between higher student/teacher ratio and lower student achievement, which may be indicative of the law of diminishing returns or a curvilinear relationship.

GENERALIZATION: ON STUDENT/TEACHER RATIO

Achievement of learning objectives is enhanced when there is a lower student-to-teacher ratio in teaching situations.

Supportive Research on Student/Teacher Ratio
Total number of studies covered: 101

Groups of Studies

Author: Glass et al. (1982)

Students: Elementary, secondary, and college

Learning: Reading, mathematics, language, psychology, physical sciences, social studies, physical education, and history achievement.

Instructional Tactics:

• Reduction of the student-to-teacher ratio.

Findings: For 98 percent of the comparisons of student-to-teacher ratios of 2:1 and 28:1, the smaller student/teacher ratio had higher levels of achievement regardless of grade level or content area. For 69 percent of the comparisons of student-to-teacher ratios of 18:1 and 28:1, the smaller student-to-teacher ratio had higher levels of achievement regardless of grade level or content area. For about 50 percent of the comparisons of student-to-teacher ratios over 30:1 and over 60:1, the smaller student-to-teacher ratio had higher levels of achievement. For fourteen experimental studies student-to-teacher ratios of 1:1, 2:1, 3:1, and 5:1 had the highest levels of achievement. The student-to-teacher ratio of 1:1 has the largest positive effect on achievement even when compared to a student-to-teacher ratio of 2:1. When the smaller student-to-teacher ratio was 14:1, 15:1, or 16:1, the effect on achievement was much smaller though positive as compared to the smaller student-to-teacher ratios identified above.

Studies analyzed in this meta-analysis are identified by the symbol * in the reference list at the end of the chapter.

Author: Word et al. (1990)

Students: Elementary

Learning: Reading, mathematics, composition, art, and vocabulary achievement

Instructional Tactics:

- Reduction of the student-to-teacher ratio.

Findings: Smaller student-to-teacher ratios lead to higher levels of achievement for students in those classes when compared to students in classes with larger student-to-teacher ratios. Student-to-teacher ratios of less than 20:1 lead to more dramatic increases in student achievement.

Studies reviewed with this logical synthesis are identified by the symbol # in the reference list.

Author: McGivern et al. (1989)

Students: Second grade

Learning: Reading and mathematics achievement

Instructional Tactics:

- Reduction of the student-to-teacher ratio to an average of 19.1, as compared to an average of 26.4 for regular classes.

Findings: Overall, achievement was higher for the smaller student-to-teacher ratio across 24 comparisons. However, the findings were not consistent in favor of the lower student-to-teacher ratio of 19.1:1. Nine of the 24 comparisons indicated higher levels of achievement for the larger student-to-teacher ratio.

Individual Studies

Author: Mosteller (1995)

Students: Kindergarten through third grade

Learning: Reading and mathematics achievement

Instructional Tactics:

- Student-to-teacher ratios were reduced to 13–17:1 from 22–26:1

- Classes with a student-to-teacher ratio of 22–26:1 either had an added teacher's aide or no teacher's aide

Findings: Over the four-year period of the project, reading and mathematics achievement scores were higher for the students in classes with a student-to-teacher ratio of 13–17:1. Percentile ranks for average reading and mathematics scores based on national norms were higher for students in classes with a student-to-teacher ratio of 13–17:1. The addition of a teacher's aide to classes with the larger student-to-teacher ratio had no significant effect on student reading or mathematics achievement.

REFERENCE LIST

*Anderson, F. H., Bedford, F., Clark, V., & Schipper, J. (1963). A report of an experiment at Camelback High School. *The Mathematics Teacher 56*, 155–159.

*Averill, L. A., & Mueller, A. D. (1925). Size of class and reading efficiency. *The Elementary School Journal 25*, 682–691.

*#Balow, I. H. (1969). A longitudinal evaluation of reading achievement in small classes. *Elementary Education 46*, 184–187.

*Bates, D. A. (1928). *The relation of the size of a class to the efficiency of teaching.* Unpublished master's thesis, University of Chicago.

*Bausell, R. B., Moody, W. B., & Walze, F. N. (1972). A factorial study of tutoring versus classroom instruction. *American Educational Research Journal 9*, 591–598.

Bloom, B. (1984). The 2 sigma problem: The search for methods of group instruction as effective as one-to-one tutoring. *Journal of Educational Research 13*, 4–16.

*Bostrom, E. A. (1969). *The effect of class size on critical thinking skills.* Unpublished doctoral thesis, Arizona State University.

*Boyer, P. A. (1914). Class size and school progress. *Psychological Clinic 8*, 82–90.

*Breed, F. S., & McCarthy, G. D. (1916). Size of a class and efficiency of teaching. *School and Society 4*, 965–971.

*Brown, A. E. (1932). The effectiveness of large classes at the college level: An experimental study involving the size variable and size-procedure variable. *University of Iowa Studies in Education 7*, 1–66.

#Cahen, L. S., Filby, N., McCutchen, G., & Kyle, D. W. (1983). *Class size and instruction.* New York: Longman.

*Cammarosano, J. R., & Santopolo, F. A. (1958). Teaching efficiency and class size. *School and Society 86*, 338–340.

#Carrington, A. T., Mounie, J. C., & Lovelace, D. W. (1982). The effects of class-load standards according to a weighted formula of relief upon student achievement and attitude and teacher morale. *Class Size Project 1980–81, Final Report* (pp. 1–8). Virginia Beach, VA Public Schools.

*Christensen, J. J. (1960). *The effects of varying class size and teaching procedures on certain levels of student learning.* Doctoral thesis, Wayne State University (60-2698).

*Clarke, S. C. T., & Richel, S. (1963). The effect of class size and teacher qualifications on achievement. *Research Monograph #5*. Edmonton, Alberta: Alberta Teachers Association.

*Coleman, J. S. et al. (1966). *Equality of educational opportunity.* Washington, DC: U.S. Government Printing Office.

*Cook, J. J., & Blessing, K. R. (1970). *Class size and teacher aides as factors in the achievement of the educable mentally retarded.* Madison: Wisconsin Department of Public Instruction. (ERIC Document Reproduction Service No. ED 047 484)

*Cornman, O. P. (1909). Size of classes and school progress. *The Psychological Clinic 3*, 206–212.

#Counelis, J. S. (1970). *First grade students in the Hunters Point Bayview SEED Project: A diagnostic review.* San Francisco, 63. (ERIC Document Reprocuction Service No. ED 052 905)

*Cram, B. M. (1968). *An investigation of the influence of class size upon academic attainment and student satisfaction.* Doctoral thesis, Arizona State University (68-14988).

*Davis, C. O. (1923). The size of classes and the teaching load in the high schools accredited by the North Central Association. *School Review 31*, 412–429.

*Davis. E., & Goldizen, M. (1930). A study of class size in junior high school history. *The School Review 38*, 360–367.

*Dawe, H. C. (1934). The influence of size of kindergarten group upon performance. *Child Development 5*, 295–303.

*DeCecco, J. P. (1964). Class size and co-ordinated instruction. *British Journal of Educational Psychology 34*, 65–74.

#Dennis, B. D. (1986). *Effects of small class size (1:15) on the teaching/learning process in grade two.* Doctoral dissertation, Tennessee State University.

*Eash, M. J., & Bennet, C. M. (1964). The effects of class size on achievement and attitudes. *American Educational Research Journal 1*, 229–239.

* Eastburn, L. A. (1937). Report of class size investigations in the Phoenix Union High School, 1933–34 to 1935–36. *Journal of Educational Research 31*, 107–117.

*Edmonson, J. B., & Mulder, F. U. (1924). Size of class as a factor in university instruction. *Journal of Educational Research 9*, 1–12.

*Ellson, D. G., Barber, L., Engle, R. L., & Kampwerth, L. (1965). Programmed tutoring: A teaching aid and a research tool. *Reading Research Quarterly 1*, 77–127.

*Ellson, D. G., Harris, P., & Barber, L. (1968). A field test of programmed and directed tutoring. *Reading Research Quarterly 3*, 307–367.

*Feldhusen, J. F. (1963). The effects of small and large group instruction on learning of subject matter, attitudes, and interests. *Journal of Psychology 55*, 357–362.

#Filby, N., Cahen, L., McCutcheon, G., & Kyle, D. (1980). *What happens in smaller classes? A summary report of a field study.* San Francisco: Far West Laboratory for Research and Development, 1–21.

*Flinker, I. (1972). Optimum class size: What is the magic number? *Clearing House 8*, 471–473.

*Flynn, D. L., Haas, A. E., & Al-Salam, N. A. (1976). *An evaluation of the cost effectiveness of alternative compensatory reading programs. Vol. III: Cost-effectiveness analysis.* Bethesda, MD: RMC Research Corporation.

#Fox, D. (1967). *Expansion of More Effective Schools Program.* New York: Center for Urban Education.

*Frymier, J. R. (1964). The effect of class size upon reading achievement in first grade. *The Reading Teacher 18*, 90–93.

*#Furno, O., & Collins, G. J. (1967). *Class size and pupil learning.* Baltimore City Public Schools. (ERIC Document Reproduction Service No. ED 025 003)

*Glass, G. V. et al. (1970). *Data analysis of the 1968–69 Survey of Compensatory Education.* Boulder: Laboratory of Educational Research, University of Colorado.

Glass, G. V., Cahen, L. S., Smith, M. L., & Filby, N. N. (1982). *School class size: Research and policy*. Beverly Hills, CA: Sage Publications.

*Haertter, L. D. (1928). An experiment of the efficiency of instruction in large and small classes in plane geometry. *Educational Administration and Supervision 14*, 580–590.

*Harlan, C. L. (1915). Size of class as a factor in schoolroom efficiency. *Educational Administration and Supervision 1*, 195–214.

*Haskell, S. (1964). Some observations on the effects of class size upon pupil achievement in geometrical drawing. *Journal of Educational Research 58*, 27–30.

*Holland, B. G. (1928). The effect of class size on scholastic acquirement in educational psychology. *School and Society 27*, 668–670.

*Hoover, K. H., Baumann, V. H., & Shafer, S. M. (1970). The influence of class-size variations on cognitive and affective learning of college freshmen. *Journal of Experimental Education 38*, 39–43.

*Horne, K. (1970). Optimum class size for intensive language instruction. *Modern Language Journal 54*, 189–195.

*Husen, T. (1967). *International study of achievement in mathematics* (Vol. II). Stockholm: Almquist & Wiskell.

#Indiana State Department of Pupil Instruction. (1983). *Project PRIMETIME: 1982–83 Report*. Bethesda, MD. (ERIC Document Reproduction Service No. ED 239 765)

*Jeffs, G. A., & Cram, B. M. (1968). *The influence of class size on academic attainment and student satisfaction*. Las Vegas: Edward W. Clark High School. (ERIC Document Reproduction Service No. ED 021 252)

*Johnson, M., & Scriven, E. (1967). Class size and achievement gains in seventh and eighth grade English and mathematics. *The School Review 75*, 300–310.

* Judd, C. H. (1929). Report of the consultative committee. *Bulletin: Department of Secondary School Principals 25*, 49–61.

*Kirk, J. R. (1929). A study of class size, teaching efficiency, and student achievement. *Phi Delta Kappan 12*, 59–61.

*#Little, A., Mabey, C., & Russell, J. (1971). Do small classes help a pupil? *New Society 18*, 769–771.

*Lundberg, L. D. (1947). Effects of smaller classes. *The Nation's Schools 39*, 20–22.

*Macomber, F. G., & Siegel, L. (1957). A study in large-group teaching procedures. *The Educational Record 38*, 220–229.

*Martin, G. M. (1969). *The effect of class size on the development of several abilities involved in critical thinking*. Doctoral thesis, Temple University (71-10853).

*Mayeske, G. W. et al. (n.d.). *A study of our nation's schools*. Washington, DC: U.S. Office of Education.

McGivern, J., Gilman, D., & Tillitski, C. (1989). A meta-analysis of the relation between class size and achievement. *The Elementary School Journal 90*(1), 47–56.

*#Meredith, V. H., Johnson, L. M., & Garcia-Quintana, R. A. (1978). *South Carolina First Grade Pilot Project 1976–77: The effects of class size on reading and mathematics achievement*. Columbia: South Carolina Department of Education.

*Metzner, A. B., & Berry, C. (1926). Size of class for mentally retarded children. *Training School Bulletin 23*, 241–251.

*Miller, P. S. (1929). A quantitative investigation of the efficiency of instruction in high school physics. *Journal of Educational Research 19*, 119–127.

*Moody, W. B. et al. (1973). The effect of class size on the learning of mathematics: A parametric study. *Journal of Research in Mathematics 4*, 170–176.

*Moss, F. A., Loman, W., & Hunt, T. (1929). Impersonal measurement of teaching. *Educational Record 10*(1), 40–50.

Mosteller, F. (1995). The Tennessee study of class size in the early school grades. *The Future of Children 5*(2), 113–127.

#Murnane, R. J. (1975). *The impact of school resources on the learning of inner-city children.* Cambridge, MA, 120. (ERIC Document Reproduction Service No. ED 121 905)

*Nachman, M., & Opochinsky, S. (1958). The effects of different teaching methods: A methodological study. *Journal of Educational Psychology 49*, 245–249.

*Nelson, W. B. (1959). An experiment with class size in the teaching of elementary economics. *Educational Record 40*, 330–341.

*Perry, R. F. (1957). A teaching experiment in geography. *Journal of Geography 56*, 133–135.

*Rivera, L. R. D. (1976). *The effects of increasing class size on achievement and the reactions of students and faculty toward this practice at the Catholic University of Puerto Rico.* Doctoral thesis, Lehigh University (77-10,706).

*Robinson, J. S. (1963). *A study of the relationship of selected school and teacher characteristics to student performance on the BSCS Comprehensive Final Examination 1961–62.* Boulder, CO: BSCS.

*Rohrer, J. H. (1957). Larger and small sections in college classes. *The Journal of Higher Education 28*, 275–279.

*Ronshausen, N. L. (1975). *The programmed math tutorial—Paraprofessionals provide one-to-one instruction in primary school mathematics.* Paper presented at the annul meeting of the American Educational Research Association, Washington, DC. (ERIC Document Reproduction Service No. ED 106 743)

*#Shapson, S. M., Wright, E. N., Eason, G., & Fitzgerald, J. (1980). An experimental study of the effects of class size. *American Educational Research Journal 17*, 141–152.

*Shaver, J. P., & Nuhn, D. (1971). The effectiveness of tutoring under-achievers in reading and writing. *Journal of Educational Research 65*, 107–112.

*Siegel, L., Macomber, F. G., & Adams, J. F. (1959). The effectiveness of large group instruction at the university level. *Harvard Educational Review 29*, 216–226.

*Silver, A. B. (1970). *English department, large-small class study: English 50-60.* (ERIC Document Reproduction Service No. ED 041 586)

*Simmons, H. F. (1959). Achievement in intermediate algebra associated with class size at the University of Wichita. *College and University 34*, 309–315.

#Sindelar, P. T., Rosenberg, M. S., Wilson, R. J., & Bursuck, W. D. (1984). The effects of class size and instructional method on the acquisition of mathematical concepts by fourth grade students. *Journal of Educational Research 77*, 178–183.

*Smith, D. I. (1974). *Effects of class size and individualized instruction on the writing of high school juniors.* Doctoral thesis, Florida State University (74-25461).

*Smith, D. V. (1925). *Class size in high school English.* Minneapolis: The University of Minnesota Press.

*#Spitzer, H. F. (1954). Class size and pupil achievement in elementary schools. *Elementary School Journal 55*, 82–86.

*Stevenson, P. R. (1925). *Class-size in the elementary school.* Bureau of Educational Research Monographs No. 3. Ohio State University Studies, Vol. 2, No. 10. Columbus: Ohio State University.

*Summers, A. A., & Wolfe, B. L. (1975). *Equality of educational opportunity quantified: A* *production function approach.* Philadelphia: Department of Research, Federal Reserve Bank of Philadelphia.

#Taylor, D., & Fleming, M. (1972). *More Effective Schools Program, Disadvantaged Pupil Program Fund, 1971–72 Evaluation (Year 3).* Cleveland: Cleveland Public Schools Division of Research. (ERIC Document Reproduction Service No. ED 076 742)

*Tope, R. E, Groom, E., & Beeson, M. F. (1924). Size of class and school efficiency. *Journal of Educational Research 9,* 126–132.

*Verducci, F. (1969). Effects of class size upon the learning of a motor skill. *Research Quarterly 40,* 391–395.

#Wagner, E. (1981). *The effects of reduced class size upon the acquisition of reading skills in grade two.* Doctoral dissertation, University of Toledo.

*Wasson, W. H. (1929). *A controlled experiment in the size of classes.* Master's thesis, University of Chicago.

*Weitzman, D. C. (1965). Effect of tutoring on performance and motivation ratings in secondary school students. *California Journal of Educational Research 16,* 108–115.

*Wetzel, W. A. (1930). Teaching technique and size of class. *School Life 15,* 181–182.

*Whitney, L., & Willey, G. S. (1932). Advantages of small classes. *School Executive's Magazine 51,* 504–506.

#Whittington, E. H. (1985). *Effects of small class size (1:15) on the teaching/learning process in grade one.* Doctoral dissertation, Tennessee State University (105).

*Wilsgberg, M., Castiglione, L. V., & Schwartz, S. L. (1968). *A program to strengthen early childhood education in poverty area schools.* New York: Educational Research Committee, Center for Urban Education. (ERIC Document Reproduction Service No. ED 034 003)

*Woodson, M. S. (1968). Effect of class size as measured by an achievement test criterion. *IAR Research Bulletin 8,* 1-6.

Word, E. R. et al. (1990). *The State of Tennessee's Student/Teacher Achievement Ratio (STAR) Project: Technical Report.* Review of Literature (pp. 199–205). Nashville: Tennessee State University, Center of Excellence for Research in Basic Skills.

*Wright, E. N. et al. (1977). *Effects of class size in the junior grades.* Toronto: Ministry of Education.

8

Providing Reminders Instruction

INTRODUCTION

The use of reminders to remember things is an established everyday practice. People use a number of strategies to remember things. A "string tied around one's finger" might be used to remind someone to do something. A word written on a piece of paper, such as "money" or "bank," might be used to remind someone they need to go to the bank and make a deposit or withdrawal. The phrase "post office" might remind someone they need stamps or need to mail a letter or package. Many people use appointment books or daily planners to remind them of important upcoming events. And the list could go on.

In education there is a continuing need for students to recall words and factual information that must be committed to memory. In order to engage in problem solving or to write an essay, the student must be able to remember and recall factual information. Although there is currently an emphasis on assessing students' higher order thinking skills, and a supposed de-emphasis on memorization of facts and concepts, much of testing, at all levels of education regardless of the format, continues to be closed-book recall of names, dates, places, things, events, definitions, and concepts. Moreover, students take notes to remind themselves of information they need to pass a test. The use of reminders would seem to be a viable tool when properly used in the appropriate situation to facilitate students' remembering.

STUDENT BENEFICIARIES

The evidence indicates that teaching students how to use reminders enhances achievement in elementary, secondary, college, and adult education settings. Moreover, achievement is enhanced in a wide range of content areas. No evidence could be found to suggest that teaching students to use reminders should not be stressed for all types of students in all subject matter areas that require the recall of factual information. However, there is evidence to suggest that more complex reminder tactics may not be beneficial for students in the lower elementary grades.

LEARNING ACHIEVED

Achievement in the content areas of mathematics, English, foreign languages, physical science, life science, spelling, social studies, and art is enhanced when students are taught to use reminders.

INSTRUCTIONAL TACTICS

Reminders have been found to be useful in three types of learning situations requiring variation in the instructional tactics for each situation. They are (1) when to-be-learned material consists of a short list or small group of interrelated objects or concepts; (2) when a larger number of concepts are to be recalled; and (3) when the focus of instruction is English, foreign language vocabulary instruction, science taxonomies, or other more complex learning situations. There are instructional tactics generic to all three situations as well as instructional tactics specific to each situation.

GENERAL INSTRUCTIONAL TACTICS

- Provide instruction on commonly used effective reminders and how to use them: for example, acronyms, mental images, rhyming, note taking, and so forth.
- Provide students instruction on how to formulate and use reminders appropriate to the particular learning situation. (In some situations, such as when students' readiness characteristics are inadequate or the material to be learned is complex, it may be beneficial for the teacher to formulate the reminders to be used rather than leave the students to their own devices.)
- Allow students ample time to practice using the reminder tactics they have been taught.
- Monitor the students' practice. When students are found to be having difficulty employing the instructional tactics, provide guidance as necessary.

Instructional tactics for short lists or small groups of interrelated objects or concepts:

- A question is asked which necessitates recall.
- A keyword is produced by the student or provided by the teacher which directs an association to the to-be-learned material.
- The answer is given by the student.

Example from Belleza (1996):

1. The question might be "What are the names of the Great Lakes?"

2. An appropriate keyword might be "HOMES."

3. The correct answer—Huron, Ontario, Michigan, Erie, Superior.

Instructional tactics to be used when a larger number of concepts are to be recalled:

- The question is asked requiring an answer consisting of multiple responses, such as the reasons for why something happened or a long list of items.
- Rhyming keywords are then produced by the student or provided by the teacher for each of the required responses.
- The student then is to create a mental image of the relationship between the keyword and the required answers.
- The answer is given by the student.

Example from Morrison & Levin (1987):

- For this example the student is asked to provide eight possible reasons for the extinction of the dinosaurs.
- The student uses keywords that rhyme with the number associated with each reason (e.g., 1 is bun, 2 is shoe, 3 is tree, and so on).
- The student then forms a mental image that will remind the student of the correct answer (e.g., for reason number three the keyword is tree, for which the student might form a mental image of a Christmas tree with an exploding star on the tree which will remind the student that exploding stars might be an explanation for the extinction of the dinosaurs).
- The student provides the answer.

Instructional tactics to be used when the focus of instruction is English, foreign language vocabulary instruction, science taxonomies, or other more complex learning situations:

- The teacher asks the question.
- The to-be-learned word is presented to the student, along with a keyword that rhymes with the to-be-learned word.
- The student then uses the sound of the to-be-learned word to recall the rhymed keyword.
- The student then forms a mental image that includes the meaning of the keyword and the meaning of the to-be-learned word.
- The student provides the answer.

Examples taken from Bellezza (1996):

1. Example for the Spanish word carta:

Question: What does the word carta mean? The student might use the keyword cart and form a mental picture of a large postal letter being pushed in a grocery cart. Later, when the word carta is seen or heard, the image of a postal letter being pushed in a cart should be elicited. This image would remind the student that the word carta means letter.

2. Example for a complex learning situation:

Students are asked to recall the five types of vertebrates:
A drawing of a farm is provided with a sign over the entrance reading *FARM-B*, which represents fish, amphibian, reptile, mammal, bird. Five piles of *dirt* are pictured on the farm with *dirt* being the keyword for *vert*-ebrates. On one pile of dirt there is a picture of a fish, on the second a frog wearing a bib, on the third an alligator and tiles, on the fourth a camel, and on the fifth pile a bird. These images help the student recall the five types of vertebrates: fish, am-*phib*-ian, rep-*tiles*, mammal, and bird.

CAUTIONS AND COMMENTS

Reminders supposedly enhance higher mental functions, such as comprehension and problem solving, but this may happen because reminders cue recall of information needed immediately to perform higher mental functions. Many assigned tasks allow students time to look up information they need: for example, library research. Many other assigned tasks require the immediate recall of information: for example, answering questions on a multiple-choice test in the time allotted.

Reviews of studies cited in the "Supportive Research" section of this chapter use the terminology "mnemonics," "mnemotechnics," and other jargon rather than the term "reminders."

GENERALIZATION: ON REMINDERS INSTRUCTION

Achievement of learning objectives is enhanced when reminders are used to cue the recall of information needed to perform assigned tasks.

Supportive Research on Reminders Instruction
Total number of studies covered: 89

Groups of Studies

Author: Bellezza (1996)

Students: Elementary, secondary, college, and adult education

Learning: English, foreign language, physical science, life science, spelling, and mathematics recall

Instructional Tactics:

- The student connects the word to be learned with a keyword and creates a mental image connecting the keyword to the meaning of the word to be learned.

- In the future, when the student sees or hears the word to be learned, he or she should think of the keyword assigned to it and the mental image associated with it.

- For more complex situations, it may be better for the teacher to provide the keyword(s) and imagery.

Findings: These instructional tactics, when used, "have been shown to, at least, double the amount of information retained by regular students."

Individual studies included in this research synthesis are identified by the symbol * in the reference list at the end of the chapter.

Author: Levin (1993)

Students: "Students of all ages" (grade levels are not provided by the author)

Learning: English, science, social studies, and mathematics achievement and retention

Instructional Tactics:

- Provide students instruction in how to use memory strategies that enhance recall of to-be-learned information.

- Have the students recode unfamiliar information into familiar terms such as:

  Keyword—the word "accolade" could be recoded by the student to be "kool-aid," with the student forming a mental picture of a group of people raising their glasses of kool-aid in a toast to someone being honored.

  Pegword—the student transforms the numbers one to ten into rhyming words, such as 1 is bun, 2 is a shoe, . . . and 10 is a hen. The students are then to relate the pegwords to to-be-learned information such as the top ten reasons for. . . .

  Combinations of these and other methods of enhancing students' recall of to-be-learned information may be used.

- Allow students time to practice the newly learned strategies.

The focus of this review was to provide a "report card" for memory enhancing strategies and not to provide a complete list of instructional tactics or how to employ them. For a more complete list of instructional tactics and information on how they were or should be employed, refer to the studies identified by the symbol # in the reference list. Additionally, Joel Levin, as well as many of the other authors listed in the reference list, have published additional information literature on in-structional tactics associated with reminders.

> *Findings*: The above tactics have been found to enhance students' recall and retention of difficult-to-remember factual information, unfamiliar names and terminology, and previously learned information. The tactics have been found to enhance recall and integration of previously learned information for the purposes of problem solving. The tactics have been successfully used to convey hierarchical relationships among concept families and to teach arithmetic operations.

Complex methods, such as those which combine the above-named strategies with other strategies, have led to inconsistent findings, especially for younger children.

Individual studies included in this research synthesis are identified by the symbol # in the reference list.

Author: Carney et al. (1993)

Students: "Ranging from young children to college age adults and the elderly"

Learning: English, foreign vocabulary, reading, social studies, mathematics, and art recall

Instructional Tactics:

- Recode or change an unfamiliar word into a more familiar word, termed a keyword.
- Relate the keyword in some meaningful way to the information to be learned in the form of a mental picture.
- The keyword and the mental picture are put together to recall the new word and the meaning of the new word.

Findings: Use of the preceding tactics have been found to enhance recall of to-be-learned information, recall of information to be used in novel problem-solving situations, and for complex hierarchical concept classifications.

Individual studies included in this research synthesis are identified by the symbol $ in the reference list.

Author: Levin (1988)

Students: Elementary, secondary, college, and adult education

Learning: Recall and retention of information to be learned

Instructional Tactics:

- Provided elaborations (reminders) should be meaningful to the learner.

- Elaborations should integrate the stimulus and response terms: for instance, the telephone (stimulus) is next to the glass (response).
- Elaborations should provide logical connections.

Example for sentences about different people:

(a) The thirsty woman climbed the hill . . .

(b) The embarrassed woman put on the hat . . .

Students are asked to study these in order to answer questions of the following kind:

(a) Who climbed the hill?

(b) Who put on the hat?

Logically appropriate elaborations complete the original sentences:

(a) . . . to look for the oasis.

(b) . . . when her wig blew off.

- Elaborations should prompt active information processing on the part of the learner. The student should have to think about the elaboration in relation to what is to be learned.
- With inefficient learners, it is better for the teacher to provide the elaboration than it is to have the students generate their own.

Findings: Research evidence supports the use of the preceding tactics for enhancing recall of material to be learned.

Individual studies included in this research synthesis are identified by the symbol @ in the reference list.

Author: Griffith (1979)

Students: College and military personnel

Learning: Numeric, word, information, and concept recall

Instructional Tactics: Reminders-only tactics for which empirical evidence was provided are included below.

1. *Numeric Pegword*: "To use this technique the student must first memorize rhyme pegwords for the digits 1–10. For example, 1 is bun, 2 is a shoe, 3 is a tree, 4 is a door, 5 is a hive, 6 is a stick, 7 is heaven, 8 is gate, 9 is wine, and 10 is hen" (p. 5). It should be noted that the technique is not limited to 10 numbers. It could be 20, 50, 100, and so on. These could then be used to learn the following list of words by forming a visual image linked to the rhyme pegword:

1—Helicopter	1—a helicopter wrapped in a bun
2—Rifle	2—a rifle stuck in a shoe
3—Jeep	3—a jeep up in a tree
4—Desk	4—a desk blocking a door

2. *Alphabet Pegwords*: The following pegwords might be developed based on the alphabet:

A—Ape

B—Bum

C—Cat

D—Dog

3. *Linking (Story)*: Each recalled item is used as a retrieval cue for succeeding items to be recalled: "for example, the task of learning the following chain of command: President, Secretary of Defense, Secretary of the Army, Chief of Staff, FORSCOM Commander, Corps Commander, Division Commander, Brigade Commander, Battalion Commander, Company Commander. One could link these elements as follows: the first image could be of the President talking to a secretary who is acting defensively and who has a big 'D' on her sweater (Secretary of Defense); this secretary could, in turn, be pictured speaking to another secretary who is wearing an army uniform (Secretary of the Army); then one could imagine this secretary talking to an Indian Chief holding a staff (Chief of Staff) . . ." (p. 8).

4. *Substitute Word or Keyword*: A substitute word or keyword is developed based on the sound of the vocabulary word to be learned:

Example: "the Spanish word for horse, Cabailo (Pronounced cab'eye o) . . . first a substitute word or phrase (a cab eyeing an "o") or a keyword (eye) would be developed based on the sound of the target word. Next, an image would be generated linking the meaning of the target word to the substitute phrase (a cab eyeing the (o) mark on a horse, or keyword (a cyclopean horse))" (p. 12).

5. *Reminder for Pictorial Symbols*: The Navy uses the following for learning Navy signal flags:

The flag for "B" (Bravo) is red and shaped as follows:

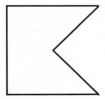

The reminder is that the red flag is a **Bullfighter's** cape and the crowd is yelling BRAVO for him. Or, the flag for "E" (Echo) has a blue top and a red bottom and is shaped as follows:

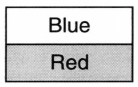

Here the reminder is "Blue sky—Red Earth" (pp. 16–17).

Findings: Twenty experimental studies involving a control group were reviewed. Two studies indicated no significant differences. One study reviewed indicated no difference for longer-term delayed recall between use of mnemonic strategies and not using a mnemonic strategy, but found a significant difference in favor of mnemonics on immediate and shorter-term delayed recall. One study found no significant difference on immediate recall but found a significant difference in favor of the mnemonic group on delayed recall. Eighteen studies reported a significant difference in favor of the use of a mnemonic strategy, with the difference in recall for using a mnemonic strategy as high as four times the level of recall for not using a mnemonic strategy.

Individual studies included in this research synthesis are identified by the symbol & in the reference list.

REFERENCE LIST

*#$@Atkinson, R. C. (1975). Mnemotechnics in second language learning. *American Psychologist 30*, 821–828.

&Atkinson, R. C., & Raugh, M. R. (1975). An application of the mnemonic keyword method to the acquisition of a Russian vocabulary. *Journal of Experimental Psychology: Human Learning and Memory 104*, 120–123.

*Bellezza, F. S. (1996). A mnemonic based on arranging words on visual patterns. *Journal of Educational Psychology 78*, 217–224.

&Berla, E., Persensky, F. F., & Senter, R. J. (1969). Learning time with a mnemonic system. *Psychonomic Science 16*, 207–208.

#Berry, J. K. (1986). *Learning-disabled children's use of mnemonic strategies for vocabulary learning*. Unpublished doctoral dissertation, University of Wisconsin, Madison.

@Beuring, T., & Kee, D. W. (1987). Elaborative propensities during adolescence: The relationships among memory and knowledge, strategy behavior, and memory performance. In M. A. McDaniel & M. Pressley (Eds.), *Imagery and related mnemonic processes* (pp. 257–273). New York: Springer-Verlag.

@Bower, G. H. (1972). Mental imagery and associative learning. In L. Gregg (Ed.), *Cognition in learning and memory*. New York: Wiley.

&Bower, G. H., & Clark, M. C. (1969). Narrative stories as mediators for serial learning. *Psychonomic Science 14*, 181–191.

&Bower, G. H., & Reitman, J. S. (1972). Mnemonic elaboration in multilist learning. *Journal of Verbal Learning and Verbal Behavior 11*, 478–485.

@Bransford, J. D., Stein, B. S., Vye, N. J., Franks, J. J., Auble, P. M., Mezynski, K. J., & Perfetto, G. A. (1982). Differences in approaches to learning: An overview. *Journal of Experimental Psychology: General 3*, 390–398.

&Bugelski, B. R. (1968). Images as mediators in one-trial paired-associate learning II: Self-timing in successive lists. *Journal of Experimental Psychology 77*, 328–334.

&Bugelski, B. R. (1974). The image as mediator in one-trial paired-associate learning III: Sequential functions in serial lists. *Journal of Experimental Psychology 103*, 298–303.

#Carney, R. N., Levin, J. R., & Morrison, C. R. (1988). Mnemonic learning of artists and their paintings. *American Educational Research Journal 25*, 107–125.

#Carney, R. N., Levin, J. R., Willis, D. L., & Smenner, A. D. (1992, August). *Mnemonic artwork learning: Remembering who painted what when.* Paper presented at the annual meeting of the American Psychological Association, Washington, DC.

Carney, R. A., Levin, M. E, & Levin, J. R. (1993). Mnemonic strategies: Instructional techniques worth remembering. *Teaching Exceptional Children 25*(4), 24–30.

&Delprato, D. J., & Baker, E. J. (1974). Concreteness of peg words in two mnemonic systems. *Journal of Experimental Psychology 102*, 520–522.

#Ehri, L. C., Deffner, N. D., & Wilce, L. S. (1984). Pictorial mnemonics for phonics. *Journal of Educational Psychology 76*, 880–893.

@Epstein, W., Rock, I., & Zuckerman, C. B. (1960). Meaning and familiarity in associative learning. *Psychological Monographs*, 74(4, Whole No. 491).

*Fulk, B. M., Mastropieri, M. A., & Scrugss, T. E. (1992). Mnemonic generalization training with learning disabled adolescents. *Learning Disability Quarterly 7*, 2–10.

&Gamst, G., & Freund, J. S. (1978). Effects of subject-generated stories on recall. *Bulletin of the Psychonomic Society 12*, 185–188.

@Ghatala, E. S., Levin, J. R., Pressley, M., & Goodwin, D. (1986). A componential analysis of the effects of derived and supplied strategy-utility information on children's strategy selections. *Journal of Experimental Child Psychology 41*, 76–92.

#$Graves, A. W., & Levin, J. R. (1989). Comparison of monitoring and mnemonic text-processing strategies in learning-disabled students. *Learning Disability Quarterly 12*, 232–236.

Griffith, D. (1979). *A review of the literature on memory enhancement: The potential and relevance of mnemotechnics for military training* (Technical Report No. 436). Fort Hood, TX: U.S. Army Research Unit for the Behavioral and Social Sciences.

&Griffith, D., & Actkinson, T. R. (1978a). International road signs: Interpretability and training techniques (Research Report 1202). Arlington, VA: U.S. Army Research Institute for the Behavioral and Social Sciences.

&Griffith, D., & Actkinson, T. R. (1978b). Mnemonic enhancement and general technical ability (ARI Technical Paper 336). Arlington, VA: U.S. Army Research Institute for the Behavioral and Social Sciences (NTIS No. AD-A061314).

#@Higbee, K. L., & Kunihira, S. (1985). Cross-cultural applications of Yodai mnemonics in education. *Educational Psychologist 20*, 57–64.

&Keppel, G., & Zavortink, B. (1969). Further test of the use of images as mediators. *Journal of Experimental Psychology 82*, 190–192.

@Kuhara-Kohma, K., & Hatang, G. (1985, April). *Dominion general strategy and do-*

main-specific knowledge as determinants of paired associate learning performance. Paper presented at the annual meeting of the American Educational Research Association, Chicago.

Levin, J. (1988). Elaboration-based learning strategies: Powerful theory = powerful application. *Contemporary Educational Psychology 13*, 191–205.

Levin, J. (1993). Mnemonic strategies and classroom learning: A twenty year report card. *The Elementary School Journal 94*(2), 235–244.

@Levin, J. R. (1976). What have we learned about maximizing what children learn? In J. R. Levin & V. L. Allen (Eds.), *Cognitive learning in children: Theories and strategies* (pp. 105–134). New York: Academic Press.

*#@Levin, J. R. (1981). The mnemonic 80's: Keywords in the classroom. *Educational Psychologist 16*, 65–82.

#$@Levin, J. R. (1985). Educational applications of mnemonic pictures: Possibilities beyond your wildest imagination. In A. A. Sheikh & K. S. Sheikh (Eds.), *Imagery in education: Imagery in the educational process* (pp. 63–87). Farmingdale, NY: Baywood.

$Levin, J. R., Dretzke, B. J., McCormick, C. B., Scrugs, T. E., McGivern, J. E., & Mastropieri, M. A. (1983). Learning via mnemonic pictures: Analysis of the presidential process. *Educational Communication and Technology Journal 31*, 161–173.

#Levin, J. R., Johnson, D. D., Pittelman, S. D., Hayes, B. L., Levin, K. M., Shriberg, L. K., & Toms-Bronoski, S. (1984). A comparison of semantic- and mnemonic-based vocabulary-learning strategies. *Reading Psychology 5*, 1–15.

#Levin, J. R., Levin, M. E., Glasman, L. D., & Nordwall, M. B. (1992). Mnemonic vocabulary instruction: Additional effectiveness evidence. *Contemporary Educational Psychology 17*, 156–174.

#Levin, J. R., McCormick, C. B., Miller, G. E., Berry, J. K., & Pressley, M. (1982). Mnemonic versus nonmnemonic vocabulary-learning strategies for children. *American Educational Research Journal 19*, 121–136.

@Levin, J. R., & Pressley, M. (1981). Improving children's prose comprehension: Selected strategies that seem to succeed. In C. M. Santa & B. L. Hayes (Eds.), *Children's prose comprehension: Research and practice* (pp. 44–71). Newark, DE: International Reading Association.

$Levin, J. R., & Pressley, M. (1985). Mnemonic vocabulary instruction: What's fact, what's fiction. In R. F. Dillon (Ed.), *Individual cognitive differences in cognition* (Vol. 2, pp. 145–172). Orlando, FL: Academic Press.

*#$Levin, M. E., & Levin, J. R. (1990). Scientific mnemonomies: Methods for maximizing more than memory. *American Educational Research Journal 27*, 301–321.

#Machida, K., & Carlson, J. (1984). Effects of verbal mediational strategy on cognitive processes in mathematics learning. *Journal of Educational Psychology 76*, 1382–1385.

@Marschark, M., Richman, C. L., Yuille, J. C., & Hunt, R. R. (1987). The role of imagery in memory: On shared and distinctive information. *Psychological Bulletin 102*, 28–41.

@Martin, C. J., Cox, D. L., & Boersma, F. J. (1965). The role of associative strategies in the acquisition of paired-associate material: An alternative approach to meaningfulness. *Psychonomic Science 3*, 463–464.

$Mastropieri, M. A. (1988). Using the keyboard (sic) method. *TEACHING Exceptional Children 20*(2), 4–8.

#$Mastropieri, M. A., & Scruggs, T. E. (1989). Constructing more meaningful relationships: Mnemonic instruction for special populations. *Educational Psychology Review 1*, 83–111.

#Mastropieri, M. A., Scruggs, T. E., & Levin, J. R. (1987a). Learning-disabled students' memory for expository prose: Mnemonic versus nonmnemonic picture. *American Educational Research Journal 24*, 505–519.

#$Mastropieri, M. A., Scruggs, T. E., & Levin, J. R. (1987b). Mnemonic instruction in special education. In M. A. McDaniel & M. Pressley (Eds.), *Imagery and related mnemonic processes: Theories, individual differences, and applications* (pp. 358–376). New York: Springer-Verlag.

#$Mastropieri, M. A., Scruggs, T. E., Levin, J. R., Gaffney, J., & McLoone, B. (1985). Mnemonic vocabulary instruction for learning disabled students. *Learning Disability Quarterly 8*, 57–63.

#$@McCormick, C. B., & Levin, J. R. (1987). Mnemonic prose-learning strategies. In M. A. McDaniel & M. Pressley (Eds.), *Imagery and related mnemonic processes: Theories, individual differences, and applications* (pp. 392–406). New York: Springer-Verlag.

#McDaniel, M. A., & Pressley, M. (1989). Keyword and context instruction of new vocabulary meanings: Effects on text comprehension and memory. *Journal of Educational Psychology 8*, 204–213.

#McGivern, J. E., & Levin, L. R. (1983). The keyword method of vocabulary learning: An interaction with vocabulary knowledge. *Contemporary Educational Psychology 8*, 46–54.

@Milgram, N. A. (1967). Retention of mediation set in paired-associate learning of normal children and retardates. *Journal of Experimental Child Psychology 5*, 341–349.

Morrison, C. R., & Levein, J. (1987). Degree of mnemonic support and students' acquisition of science facts. *Educational Communication and Technology Journal 35*, 67–74.

&Murray, F. S. (1974). Effects of narrative stories on recall. *Bulletin of the Psychonomic Society 100*, 6–8.

$@O'Sullivan, J. T., & Pressley, M. (1984). Completeness of instruction and strategy transfer. *Journal of Experimental Child Psychology 38*, 275–288.

#Ott, C. E., Butler, D. C., Blake, R. S., & Ball, J. P. (1973). The effect of interactive-image elaboration on the acquisition of foreign language vocabulary. *Language Learning 23*, 197–206.

*Patton, G. W., D'Agaro, W. R., & Gaudette, M. D. (1991). The effect of subject-generated and experimenter-supplied code word on the phonetic mnemonic system. *Applied Cognitive Psychology 5*, 135–148.

&Pavio, A. (1968). *Effects of imagery instructions and concreteness of memory pegs in a mnemonic system.* Proceedings of the 76th Annual Convention of the American Psychological Association (pp. 77–78).

@&Pavio, A. (1969). Mental imagery in associative learning and memory. *Psychological Review 76*, 241–263.

&Perensky, J. J., & Senter, R. J. (1969). An experimental investigation of a mnemonic system in recall. *Psychological Record 19*, 491–499.

#Peters, E. E., & Levin, J. R. (1986). Effects of a mnemonic imagery strategy on good and poor readers' prose recall. *Reading Research Quarterly 21*, 179–192.

@Pressley, M. (1982). Elaboration and memory development. *Child Development 53*, 296–309.

*@Pressley, M., Levin, J. R., & Delaney, H. D. (1982). The mnemonic keyword method. *Review of Educational Research 52*, 61–91.

#Pressley, M., Levin, J. R., & McCormick, C. B. (1980). Young children's learning of foreign language vocabulary: A sentence variation of the keyword method. *Contemporary Educational Psychology 5*, 22–29.

$Pressley, M., Levin, J. R., & McDaniel, M. A. (1987). Remembering versus inferring what a word means: Mnemonic and contextual approaches. In M. G. McKeown & M. E. Curtis (Eds.), *The nature of vocabulary acquisition* (pp. 107–127). Hillsdale, NJ: Erlbaum.

*#@Pressley, M., Levin, J. R., & Miller, G. E. (1981). How does the keyword method affect comprehension and usage? *Reading Research Quarterly 16*, 213–226.

@Pressley, M., McDaniel, M. A., Turnure, J. E., Wood, E., & Ahmad, M. (1987). Generation and precision of elaboration: Effects on intentional and incidental learning. *Journal of Experimental Psychology: Learning, Memory, and Cognition 13*, 291–300.

@Pressley, M., Ross, K. A., Levin, J. R., & Ghatala, E. S. (1984). The role of strategy utility knowledge in children's decision making. *Journal of Experimental Child Psychology 38*, 491–504.

&Raugh, M. R., & Atkinson, R. C. (1974). *A mnemonic method for the acquisition of a second-language vocabulary.* Technical Report No. 224. Stanford, CA: Institute for Mathematical Studies in the Social Sciences, Stanford University.

&Raugh, M. R., & Atkinson, R. C. (1975). A mnemonic method for learning a second language vocabulary. *Journal of Educational Psychology 67*, 1–19.

@Roberts, P. (1983). Memory strategy instruction with the elderly: What should memory training be the training of? In M. Pressley & J. R. Levin (Eds.), *Cognitive strategy research: Psychological foundations* (pp. 75–100). New York: Springer-Verlag.

&Robertson-Tchabo, E. A., Hausman, D. P., & Arenberg, D. (1976). A classical mnemonic for older learners: A trip that works! *Educational Gerontology 1*, 215–216.

@Rohwer, W. D., Jr. (1973). Elaboration and learning in childhood and adolescence. In H. W. Reese (Ed.), *Advances in child development and behavior* (Vol. 8, pp. 1–57). New York: Academic Press.

@Rohwer, W. D., Jr., & Levin, J. R. (1968). Action, meaning, and stimulus selection in paired-associate learning. *Journal of Verbal Learning and Verbal Behavior 7*, 137–141.

@Rohwer, W. D., Jr., & Thomas, J. W. (1987). The role of mnemonic strategies in study effectiveness. In M. A. McDaniel & M. Pressley (Eds.), *Imagery and related mnemonic processes: Theories, individual differences, and applications* (pp. 428–450). New York: Springer-Verlag.

@Rosenheck, M. B., Finch, M. E., & Levin, J. R. (1987, April). *Comparison of mnemonic and taxonomic science-learning strategies.* Paper presented at the annual meeting of the American Educational Research Association, Washington, DC.

#$Rosenheck, M. B., Levin, M. E., & Levin, J. R. (1989). Learning botany concepts mnemonically: Seeing the forest *and* the trees. *Journal of Educational Psychology 81*, 196–203.

$Roth, K. J. (1989). Science education: It's not enough to "do" or "relate." *American Educator 13*(4), 16–22, 46–48.

*Scruggs, T. E., & Mastropieri, M. A. (1992). Classroom applications of mnemonic instructions: Acquisition, maintenance, and generalization. *Exceptional Children 58*, 219–229.

$Scruggs, T. E., Mastropieri, M. A., & Levin, J. R. (1985). Vocabulary acquisition by mentally retarded students under direct and mnemonic instruction. *American Journal of Mental Deficiency 89*, 546–551.

@Scruggs, T. E., Mastropieri, M. A., & Levin, J. R. (1987). Implications of mnemonic strategy research for theories of learning disabilities. In H. L. Swanson (Ed.), *Memory and learning disabilities* (pp. 225–244). Greenwich, CT: JAI Press.

$Scruggs, T. E., Mastropieri, M. A., Levin, J. R., & Gaffney, J. (1985). Facilitating the acquisition of science facts in learning disabled students. *American Educational Research Journal 22*, 575–586.

&Senter, R. J., & Hauser, G. K. (1968). An experimental study of a mnemonic system. *Psychonomic Science 10*, 289–290.

#Shriberg, L. K., Levin, J. R., McCormick, C. B., & Pressley, M. (1982). Learning about "famous" people via the keyword method. *Journal of Educational Psychology 74*, 238–247.

&Smith, R. K., & Nobel, C. E. (1965). Effects of a mnemonic technique applied to verbal learning and memory. *Perception and Motor Skills 21*, 123–134.

@Stein, B. S., Littlefield, J., Branford, J. D., & Persampieri, M. (1984). Elaboration and knowledge acquisition. *Memory and Cognition 12*, 522–529.

@Suzki-Slakter, N. (1988). Elaboration and metamemory during adolescence. *Contemporary Educational Psychology 13*, 206–220.

*Sweeney, C. A., & Bellezza, F. S. (1982). Use of the keyword mnemonic in learning English vocabulary words. *Human Learning 1*, 155–163.

@Taylor, A. M., & Turnure, J. E. (1979). Imagery and verbal elaboration with retarded children: Effects on learning and memory. In N. R. Ellis (Ed.), *Handbook of mental deficiency, psychological theory, and research* (pp. 659–697). Hillsdale, NJ: Erlbaum.

@Thomas, J. W. (1988). Proficiency at academic studying. *Contemporary Educational Psychology 13*, 265–275.

@Turnure, J. E. (1971). Types of verbal elaboration in the paired-associate performance of educable mentally retarded children. *American Journal of Mental Deficiency 76*(3), 306–312.

#Velt, D. T., Scruggs, T. E., & Mastropieri, M. A. (1986). Extended mnemonic instruction with learning disabled students. *Journal of Educational Psychology 78*, 300–308.

&Willerman, B. S. (1977). The effect of a keyword mnemonic on the recall of French vocabulary. Unpublished doctoral dissertation, University of Texas at Austin.

&Wood, G. (1967). Mnemonic systems in recall. *Journal of Educational Psychology Monographs 58*(6, Part 2).

&Wortman, P. M., & Sparling, P. B. (1974). Acquisition and retention of mnemonic information in LTM. *Journal of Experimental Psychology 102*, 22–26.

@Yussen, S. R., Mathews, S. R., & Hiebert, E. (1982). Metacognitive aspects of reading. In W. Otto & S. White (Eds.), *Reading expository material* (pp. 189–218). New York: Academic Press.

9

Providing Subject Matter Unifiers

INTRODUCTION

Most people are aware that subject matter tends to be presented in an organized manner. They know that books provide a table of contents; that calendars and clocks organize time into related segments; and that symphonies are organized into movements. What many people may not know is that subject matter, whatever form it may take, is easier to understand and manage when inherent relationships are conveyed. A large number of research studies have attempted to determine how to best convey subject matter relationships. The results of the research have important implications for instruction.

Research shows that highlighting parts/whole relationships in the subject matter students are assigned to learn appreciably enhances their learning of the subject matter. In general, this revelation indicates that parts/whole relationships in subject matter need to be highlighted during instructional planning and conveyed to students during teaching. Specifics are explained in the remainder of the chapter.

STUDENT BENEFICIARIES

The evidence indicates that incorporating the use of unifying schemes in the teaching of subject matter enhances the academic achievement of students in preschool, elementary, secondary, college, and adult learning classrooms. Moreover, academic achievement was improved in a wide range of content areas. No evidence could be found to suggest that the use of unifiers should not be stressed in all subject areas for all types of students.

LEARNING ACHIEVED

Achievement in the content areas of mathematics, history, reading, social sciences, sciences, and social studies is enhanced when subject matter unifiers are used. In studies reviewed, the use of subject matter unifiers led to enhanced student achievement. The evidence indicates that the use of unifiers may elevate student achievement by as much as five times that for students in learning situations where unifiers were not used.

INSTRUCTIONAL TACTICS

- Either the teacher or instructional planner provides a unifying scheme that highlights the parts to whole relationships within the subject matter. The evidence indicates this may be accomplished prior to, during, or after instruction. The evidence is not conclusive on which is best.

- Students are taught to construct their own unifying scheme either during or after instruction. The evidence does not seem to support students' constructing their own unifying scheme prior to instruction.

Unifying schemes employed to highlight relationships in the subject matter in the studies reviewed by the research syntheses incorporated into this chapter were (1) textual summaries, (2) hierarchical tree diagrams, (3) pictorial representations, and (4) subject matter outlines.

The following examples where derived from individual studies incorporated into the research syntheses. Each individual example may be seen as taking the form of one or more of the previously mentioned formats.

Bower et al. (1969)

Students were presented four conceptual hierarchies for minerals presented in the form of a vertical tree diagram.

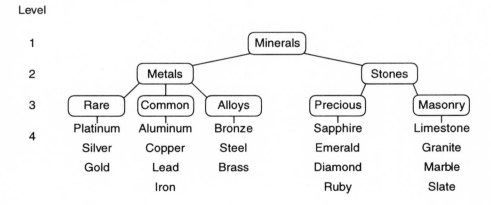

Hawk (1986)

The following unifying schemes are hand-drawn unifiers used to highlight the relationships in chapters to be taught in a sixth- and seventh-grade life sciences course.

UNIT I — The Living World
Chap. 3 "The Variety of Life"

classify	Linnaeus	binomial system

Need for system of classification:
1- same organisms had different names in different languages.
2- common names were misleading.

Method of Classification

KINGDOM
PHYLUM
CLASS
ORDER
FAMILY
GENUS
SPECIES

Binomial System

EXAMPLES

Common Name	Genus	Species
1- lion	Felis	leo
2- tiger	Felis	tigris
3- house cat	Felis	catus

MAJOR CLASSIFICATION

Nonliving   Living

Animal Kingdom   Plant Kingdom   Protist Kingdom

CHARACTISTICS USED IN CLASSIFICATION

Animals
* blood temperature
* type of support system
* adaptation for body functions
* body covering
* shape of body
* type of body openings
* no. of body sections
* no. of apendages
* types of reproduction
* method of birth
* nourishment of young

Plants
* cellular structure
* reproduction
* leaf structure
* roots, stems, leaves

Protists
* Algae
* fungi
* Protozoans
* bacteria
* viruses

© N. McLeod

116

III. Protoplasm

cell

Ex. water
minerals
dissolved gases

INORGANIC

protoplasm

ORGANIC

Protein
(amino acid)
C H N O
builds protoplasm

Carbohydrates
(sugars)
C H O
energy source

fats
C H O
energy storer

nucleic acid
controls cell activity

IV. Levels of organization

Single-celled
organisms

have
specialized parts
to perform
necessary life
functions

Multicellular organisms

organism
Ex.

System
Ex

Levels pp. 81, 86

Organ
Ex.

tissue
Ex

specialized cell
Ex.

© N. McLeod

117

Robinson & Schraw (1994)

The following unifying schemes were used to highlight the relationships in a fictional text on types of fish. One unifier is a matrix presentation of the relationships within the subject matter, and the other unifier employed is an outline of the relationships within the subject matter.

Matrix

Depth:	200 ft		400 ft		600 ft	
Fish:	Hat	Lup	Arch	Bone	Tin	Scale
Social group:	Solitary	Small	Solitary	School	Small	School
Color:	Black	Brown	Blue	Orange	Yellow	White
Size:	30 cm		45 cm		70 cm	
Diet:	Shrimp		Krill		Prawn	

Outline

Depth	*Fish*	*Characteristics*
200 ft	Hat	Social Group—Solitary Color—Black Size—30 cm Diet—Shrimp
	Lup	Social Group—Small Color—Brown Size—30 cm Diet—Shrimp
400 ft	Arch	Social Group—Solitary Color—Blue Size—45 cm Diet—Krill
	Bone	Social Group—School Color—Orange Size—45 cm Diet—Krill
600 ft	Tin	Social Group—Small Color—Yellow Size—70 cm Diet—Prawn
	Scale	Social Group—School Color—White Size—70 cm Diet—Prawn

Simmons et al. (1988)

The following is a graphical unifying scheme highlighting the relationships in an experimental passage on the *Building Blocks of Matter*.

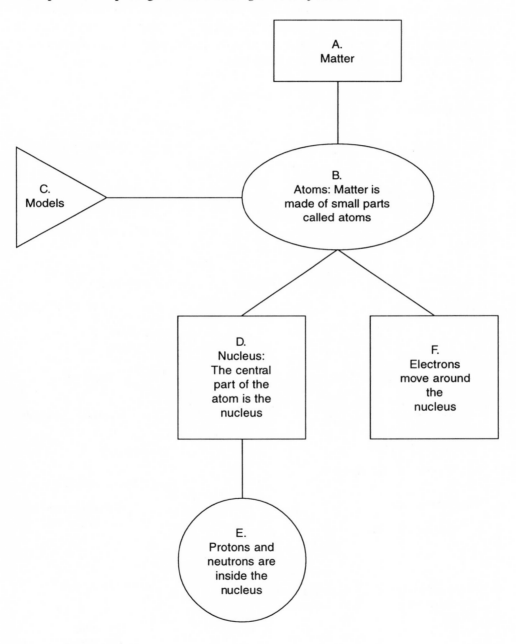

Denner (1986)

The following unifying scheme was used to highlight the relationships within a story passage that describes a locksmith named Horace, who has a mania for old, rare books. Once a year he steals jewels to pay for the books. This time, however, he is caught by a pretty young lady who tricks him into opening a safe. Horace is later arrested for jewel robbery and ends up as the assistant prison librarian because no one believes his story about the young lady.

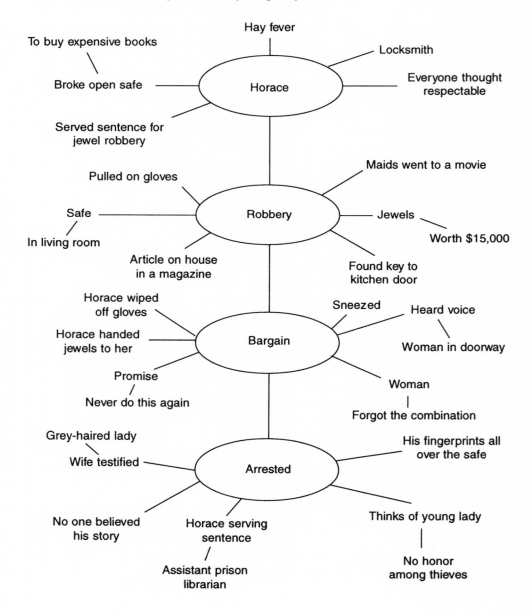

Gillies (1984)

The following textual summary was given to students prior to instruction on peripheral circulatory disorders. The unifying scheme outlines the metabolic consequences of cellular ischemia; possible cardiac, vascular, and humoral causes for ischemia; and proposed principles of ischemia relief.

> Ischemia is inadequate perfusion of tissues with blood of sufficient quantity or quality to meet cellular needs for oxygen and nutrients. Ischemia can result from cardiac pump failure, vascular obstruction, decreased blood volume, or increased blood viscosity. Ischemia impairs cellular metabolism because needed oxygen, nutrients, and hormones fail to reach the cell and toxic wastes are retained in tissues.
>
> When adequate oxygen is available, the cell breaks down each molecule of glucose to CO_2 and H_2O, and forms 38 molecules of high energy ATP. When oxygen is lacking, each molecule of glucose breaks down only to pyruvate, and only two molecules of ATP are formed. Thus, ischemic tissues are deprived of energy both because available glucose yields only part of its energy. Further, the pyruvate resulting from anaerobic glycolysis is converted to lactic acid, which lowers tissue pH and impairs cellular metabolism.
>
> General ischemia and ischemia of highly active tissues (brain, liver, kidney, myocardium) often result from cardiac pump failure. Thus, lowered blood pressure following myocardial infarction may cause stroke, hepatic necrosis, renal tubular necrosis, or a second myocardial infarction. Localized ischemia usually results from vascular obstruction or changes in blood volume or viscosity. In arteriosclerosis subintimal plaques roughen arterial linings and rupture platelets, initiating clot formation and blocking blood flow. Impaired venous blood flow may result from external pressure, varicosities, or phlebothrombosis. In these conditions increased venous pressure is referred backward to capillaries, causing edema formation. Tissue edema compresses capillaries, arterioles, and arteries, producing ischemia. Increased blood viscosity in polycythemia, increased platelet stickiness in disseminated malignancy, and red cell distortion in sickle cell disease may all cause intravascular clotting and tissue ischemia.
>
> Ischemia can be alleviated either by decreasing cellular needs for oxygen and nutrients or by improving arterial blood flow through positioning, removal of external pressure, or use of anticoagulants.

Selinger (1995)

The following are directions given to students to assist them in developing parts/whole summaries of the relationships within subject matter.

1. Read the entire article to get a general impression of what it is about.

2. Write a thesis statement for the entire article on planning paper. (This may be more than one sentence if necessary.)

3. Underneath your thesis statement write a sentence for each topic heading describing what that section is telling the reader. This should be the most general statement you can make about the section. Leave about ten lines between each statement.

4. Look at each section and write down major points that describe in more detail the statements you made in step 3. Write this in the space you left under each statement. You may underline parts of the text if that helps. Remember that often a major point will be the topic sentence of a paragraph, but you cannot rely on this. It may be necessary to write several sentences to describe your major point adequately.

CAUTIONS AND COMMENTS

Research has shown that highlighting the parts/whole relationships within the subject matter enhances student learning. Many textbooks used in instruction continue to do an inadequate job of highlighting parts/whole relationships within the subject matter. It is not unusual for a teacher to have to move from one part of a text to another in order to present the subject matter units in an organized manner. Additionally, organization within the individual units is often inadequate in the highlighting of the relationships within the subject matter and may often contain irrelevant information in the form of pictures or diagrams intended to merely make the text more attractive. As a result, there is a need for instructional planners to consider incorporating the use of unifying schemes into instruction in order to assist students in the identification of the important parts/whole relationships within the subject matter they are to learn. Authors and publishers of texts need to be more cognizant of the importance of highlighting the parts/whole relationships within the subject matter when designing and organizing textbooks. Additionally, the evidence is of sufficient strength to suggest that authors and publishers consider incorporating unifying schemes into each unit of a textbook.

GENERALIZATION: ON UNIFIERS

Achievement of learning objectives is enhanced when a scheme is used to highlight parts/whole relationships in the subject matter students are assigned to learn.

Supportive Research on Unifiers
Total number of studies covered: 50

Groups of Studies

Author: Horton et al. (1993)

Students: Elementary, secondary, and college

Learning: Science achievement

Instructional Tactics:

- Preparation of concept maps for important concepts within the subject matter: these were prepared by the teachers, the students, or both.

- The concept maps produced the greatest achievement when they were prepared in class.

Findings: Use of the above tactics was found to enhance science achievement.

Author: Fisher (1997)

Students: Preschool, elementary, secondary, college, adult

Learning: Mathematics, reading, science, social studies, social science, and history

Instructional Tactics:

- Students were provided with conceptual hierarchies in the form of tree diagrams highlighting relationships within the subject matter.

- Students were provided with partially completed conceptual hierarchies in the form of tree diagrams, which they were required to complete.

- Students were taught how to construct their own conceptual hierarchies in the form of tree diagrams.

- Students were provided textual summaries that highlighted relationships within the subject matter.

- Students were provided outlines that highlighted the relationships within the subject matter.

- Students were provided a pictorial representation that highlighted the relationships within the subject matter.

Findings: Use of the above instructional tactics led to higher levels of student achievement as compared to students for whom the above tactics were not used. Achievement was enhanced regardless of whether the unifying scheme was presented prior to, during, or after instruction.

Individual Studies

Author: Bower et al. (1969)

Students: High school and college

Learning: Vocabulary recall

Instructional Tactics:

Experiment I

- Students were assigned to instructional conditions defined as either a random or blocked condition.
- The blocked condition (organized) consisted of exposure to four word lists presented in hierarchies organized in vertical trees displaying category and subcategory relationships.
- The random condition (unorganized) consisted of the same word lists being scrambled and assigned in an unorganized fashion to four vertical trees.

Experiment II

- Students were assigned to instructional conditions defined as either a random or blocked condition.
- The blocked condition (organized) consisted of exposure to four word lists presented in hierarchies organized in vertical trees displaying category and subcategory relationships.
- The random condition (unorganized) consisted of the same word lists being scrambled and assigned in an unorganized fashion to four vertical trees.

Experiment III

- Students were assigned to either a rest control (Control), irrelevant interpolation (unorganized), or relevant interpolation (organized) condition.
- Initially all three groups were exposed to two trials of word list 1, organized into association level hierarchies.
- While the Irrelevant and Relevant groups studied a second word list, the rest control group then read "Peanuts" cartoons.
- For the Relevant group the words were presented in a tree form relevant for classifying level four words learned in word list 1.
- The list for the Irrelevant group was also presented in tree form, but were not relevant for classifying words from word list 1.
- The three groups were then re-tested on word list 1.

Experiment IV

- Words were listed in an organized way across an associative hierarchy and levels in a manner displaying the parts-to-whole relationship and a condition in which words were scattered randomly throughout an associative hierarchy and its levels.
- The words were presented in the form of trees in written material for both groups.

- Following a study period, both groups then recalled as many words as they could by writing them on a blank sheet of paper.

Findings: In experiments I, II, and IV, the groups exposed to a unifying scheme recalled significantly more words than the groups not employing a unifying scheme. There was no significant difference between groups for experiment III.

Author: Tompkins (1991)

Students: High school

Learning: History achievement

Instructional Tactics:

- Students were instructed on the application of a partially completed graphic organizer, displaying the parts/whole relationships, for textual material to be learned.

Findings: students using a partially completed graphic organizer recalled significantly more information than did students who did not use a graphic organizer.

Author: Alvermann (1982)

Students: Grade 10

Learning: Health science achievement

Instructional Tactics:

- The teacher constructs a graphic organizer showing the main idea units reflecting either a comparison/contrast or cause/effect relationship and empty boxes for subordinate idea units.
- Students are taught how to use a compare and contrast procedure to identify important information in the text. For example, students might be taught how remembering the color, shape, texture, or taste of one fruit might help them identify and recall the same characteristics of a different fruit.
- Students are taught how to search for information in the text to mentally fill in the empty boxes using the compare and contrast procedure they have been taught.

Findings: Students using the graphic organizer exhibited higher levels of recall than did students not using a graphic organizer.

Author: Selinger (1995)

Students: College

Learning: English achievement

Instructional Tactics:

- Students were taught how to use a hierarchical top-down approach (identifying main ideas followed by subordinate ideas) to summarize textual information they were to learn.

Findings: Students who were taught to summarize text in a hierarchical fashion scored significantly higher on a writing posttest than students in a control group not using the procedure.

Author: Dean & Kulhavy (1981)

Students: College

Learning: Text recall

Instructional Tactics:

Experiments I and II

- Students were assigned to read a passage about a mythical African tribe. The passage contained information on the topography of the area, economics, government, and tribal ritual practices.
- Students in the experimental conditions were instructed to construct a map of the territory and events described in the passage after they had read the passage.

Findings: Students who constructed maps of the territories and events scored significantly higher on multiple choice, constructed response, and recall of main idea units tests than did students who did not construct maps.

Author: Corkill et al. (1988)

Experiment I

Students: College

Learning: Science recall

Instructional Tactics:

- Students were assigned to either a concrete organizer, abstract organizer, or control condition.
- The concrete organizer was written in terms, which may be seen as highlighting relationships in the subject matter, specific to an instructional passage on astronomical models.

- The abstract organizers described the use of scientific models in terms not associated with the instructional passage.
- A control group simply read the passage on astronomy.

Findings: Students who employed the concrete organizer scored significantly higher on recall of main idea units than those in the abstract organizer or control conditions. There was no significant difference between the control and abstract organizer conditions.

Experiment II

Students: College

Learning: Linguistics recall

Instructional Tactics:

- Students were assigned to either a concrete organizer, abstract organizer, or control condition.
- The concrete organizer was written in terms, which may be seen as highlighting relationships in the subject matter, specific to an instructional passage on language usage.
- The abstract organizers described the use of scientific models in terms not associated with the instructional passage.
- A control group simply read the passage on language usage.

Findings: Students who employed the concrete organizer scored significantly higher on recall of main idea units than those in the abstract organizer or control conditions. There was no significant difference between the control and abstract organizer conditions.

REFERENCE LIST

Abayomi, B. I. (1988). The effects of concept mapping and cognitive style on science achievement. Doctoral dissertation, Georgia State University. *Dissertation Abstracts International 49*, 1420A.

Alvermann, D. E. (1981). The compensatory effect of graphic organizers on descriptive text. *Journal of Educational Research 75*(1), 44–48.

Alvermann, D. E. (1982). Restructuring text facilitates written recall of main ideas. *Journal of Reading 25*(8), 754–758.

Alvermann, D. E., Boothby, P. R., & Wolfe, J. (1984). The effect of graphic organizer instruction on fourth graders' comprehension of text. *Journal of Social Studies Research 8*(1), 13–20.

Basili, P. A. (1988). Conceptual change strategies within cooperative groups of community college chemistry students: An experiment. Doctoral dissertation, University of Maryland. *Dissertation Abstracts International 49*, 1752A.

Bodolus, J. E. (1986). The use of concept mapping strategy to facilitate meaningful learning for ninth grade students in science. Doctoral dissertation, Temple University. *Dissertation Abstracts International 47*, 3387A.

Boothby, P. R., & Alvermann, D. E. (1984). A classroom training study: The effects of graphic organizer instruction on fourth graders' comprehension. *Reading World 23*, 325–339.

Bower, G. H., Clark, M. C., Lesgold, A. M., & Winzenz, D. (1969). Hierarchical retrieval schemes in recall of categorized word lists. *Journal of Verbal Learning and Verbal Behavior 8*, 323–343.

Cliburn, J. W., Jr. (1985). Concept maps to promote meaningful learning. *Journal of College Science Teaching 19*, 212–217.

Corkill, A. J., Bruning, R. H., & Glover, J. A. (1988). Advance organizers: Concrete versus abstract. *Journal of Educational Research 82*(2), 76–81.

Corkill, A. J., Bruning, R. H., Glover, J. A., & Krug, D. (1988). Advance organizers: Retrieval context hypotheses. *Journal of Educational Psychology 80*(3), 304–311.

Darch, C. B., Carnine, D. W., & Kameenui, E. J. (1986). The role of graphic organizers and social structure in content area instruction. *Journal of Reading Behavior 18*(4), 275–295.

Dean, R. S., & Kulhavy, R. W. (1981). Influence of spatial organization in prose learning. *Journal of Educational Psychology 73*(1), 57–64.

Denner, P. R. (1986, June). *Comparison of the effects of episodic organizers and traditional notetaking on story recall.* Paper submitted to the Faculty Research Committee of Idaho State University. (ERIC ED 270 731)

Dinnel, D., & Glover, J. A. (1985). Advance organizers: Encoding manipulations. *Journal of Educational Psychology 77*(5), 514–521.

Dunston, P. J., & Ridgeway, V. G. (1991) The effect of graphic organizers on learning and remembering information from connected discourse. *Forum for Reading 22*(1), 15–23.

Fisher, S. (1997). *Subject matter unifiers: Synthesis of a body of research.* Unpublished manuscript. Columbia: University of South Carolina.

Gillies, D. A. (1984). Effect of advance organizers on learning medical surgical nursing content by baccalaureate nursing students. *Research in Nursing and Health 7*, 173–180.

Guri-Rosenblit, S. (1989). Effects of a tree diagram on students' comprehension of main ideas in an expository text within multiple themes. *Reading Research Quarterly 24*(2), 236–247.

Hawk, P. P. (1986). Using graphic organizers to increase achievement in middle school life science. *Science Education 70*(1), 81–87.

Heinze-Fry, J. A., & Novak, J. D. (1990). Concept mapping brings long-term movement toward meaningful learning. *Science Education 74*, 461–472.

Horton, P. B., McConney, A. A., Gallo, M., Woods, A. L., Senn, G. J., & Hamlin, D. (1993). An investigation of the effects of concept mapping as an instructional tool. *Science Education 77*(1), 95–111.

Huang, W. (1991). *Concept mapping and chemistry achievement, integrated science process skills, logical thinking abilities, and gender at teachers' colleges in Taiwan.* Unpublished doctoral dissertation, Florida Institute of Technology, Melbourne, FL.

Jegede, O. J., Alaiyemola, F. F., & Okebukola, P. A. (1989). *The effects of a metacognitive strategy on students' anxiety and achievement in biology.* (ERIC Document Reproduction Service No. ED 313 219)

Karahalios, S. M., Tonjes, M. J., & Towner, J. C. (1979). Using advance organizers to improve comprehension of content text. *Journal of Reading 22*, 706–708.

Lawton, J. T., & Fowell, N. (1978). Effects of advance organizer on preschool children's learning of mathematics concepts. *Journal of Experimental Education 47*, 76–81.

Lehman, J. D., Carter, C., & Kahle, J. B. (1985). Concept mapping, vee mapping, and achievement: Results of a field study with black high school students. *Journal of Research in Science Teaching 22*, 663–673.

Loncaric, L. (1986). The effects of a concept mapping strategy program upon the acquisition of social studies concepts. Doctoral dissertation, University of Pittsburgh. *Dissertation Abstracts International 47*, 2006A.

Martin, D. J., & Lucy, E. C. (1992, March). *The effects of concept mapping on biology achievement of field dependent students.* Paper presented at the annual meeting of the National Association for Research in Science Teaching, Boston.

Okebukola, P. A., & Jegede, O. J. (1989). Students' anxiety towards and perception of difficulty of some biological concepts under the concept-mapping heuristic. *Research in Science and Technological Education 7*, 85–92.

Pankratius, W. J. (1987). Building an organized knowledge base: Concept mapping and achievement in secondary school physics. Doctoral dissertation, Georgia State University. *Dissertation Abstracts International 49*, 474A.

Prater, D. L., & Terry, C. A. (1988). Effects of mapping strategies on reading comprehension and writing performance. *Reading Psychology 9*, 101–120.

Robinson, D. H., & Schraw, G. (1994). Computational efficiency through visual argument: Do graphic organizers communicate relations in text too effectively? *Contemporary Educational Psychology 19*, 399–415.

Schmid, R. F., & Telaro, G. (1990). Concept mapping as an instructional strategy for high school biology. *Journal of Educational Research 84*, 78–85.

Selinger, Barry M. (1995). Summarizing text: Developmental students demonstrate a successful method. *Journal of Developmental Education 19*(2), 14–19.

Simmons, D. C., Griffin, C. C., & Kameenui, E. J. (1988). Effects of teacher-constructed pre- and post-graphic organizer instruction on sixth-grade science students' comprehension and recall. *Journal of Educational Research 82*(1), 15–21.

Slock, J. A., Snyder, I. S., & Sharp, W. L. (1980). Evaluation of the effectiveness of an advance organizer in a medical microbiology course. *Journal of Medical Education 55*, 878–880.

Spaulding, D. T. (1989). Concept mapping and achievement in high school biology and chemistry. Doctoral dissertation, Florida Institute of Technology. *Dissertation Abstracts International 50*, 1619A.

Stensvold, M. S., & Wilson, J. T. (1990). Concept maps as a heuristic for science curriculum development: Toward improvement in process and product. *Journal of Research in Science Teaching 27*, 987–1000.

Tompkins, R. S. (1991, April). *The use of a spatial learning strategy to enhance reading comprehension of secondary subject area text.* Paper presented at the Annual Indiana Reading Conference, Indianapolis, IN.

Troyer, S. J. (1994, April). *The effects of three instructional conditions in text structure on upper elementary students' reading comprehension and writing performance.* Paper presented at the Annual Meeting of the American Educational Research Association, New Orleans, LA. (ERIC Document Reproduction Service No. ED 373 315)

Willerman, M., & Mac Harg, R. A. (1991). The concept map as an advance organizer. *Journal of Research in Science Teaching 28*, 705–711.

10

Providing Transfer of Learning Instruction

INTRODUCTION

In our context, transfer of learning is defined as the application of prior learning to enable the performance of new tasks. That people transfer learning is an established fact, manifested in research findings as well as everyday experience. If people did not transfer what they learned to solve new problems that confront them, learning would be useless and adaptation and success in society would be virtually impossible.

The challenge to education is to facilitate the transfer of learning that is necessary for the achievement of learning objectives. Any sequence of tasks students are to perform to achieve a learning objective must be formulated so that the performance of earlier tasks in the sequence enables the performance of subsequent tasks. In essence, this ensures the readiness conditions that facilitate transfer. Under these conditions, to progressively move through the sequence of tasks to the achievement of the learning objective, students are able to transfer what they have learned from performing earlier tasks to successfully complete the subsequent tasks in the sequence.

It is a major responsibility of instruction to facilitate the transfer of learning needed to progress from one assigned task in a sequence to the next. Instruction must be planned and executed so that students acquire the learning they need to transfer in order to successfully perform the next task in the sequence. In addition, students need to be given instruction on how to determine the relevance of prior learning to the performance of the new tasks they are assigned to perform. In other words, students need to be taught the knowledge and skills they need to transfer to perform the new tasks they are assigned to perform. They also need to be taught how to determine the relevance of the knowledge and skills they have learned to the performance of new tasks. In general, it might be said that the more a task successfully performed in the past has in common with a newly assigned task, the more likely it is that the procedures used to perform the old task can be used to successfully perform the newly assigned task.

STUDENT BENEFICIARIES

The evidence indicates that transfer of learning instruction enhances the academic achievement of students in elementary, secondary, college, and vocational classrooms. Additionally, transfer of learning instruction has been shown to enhance achievement in business and industry training situations. No evidence could be found to suggest that transfer of learning instruction should not be stressed in all subject areas for all types of students, including students in military, community, and adult education settings.

LEARNING ACHIEVED

Achievement and transfer of learning in the content areas of reading, mathematics, science, social studies, the social sciences, literature, and vocational education are enhanced when transfer of learning instruction tactics are incorporated into the instruction. It may be reasonable to expect that achievement and transfer may be enhanced in other content areas as well. In studies reviewed, student achievement and transfer was shown to be enhanced when transfer of learning instruction was incorporated into the instruction.

INSTRUCTIONAL TACTICS

The following tactics are derived from the studies that demonstrate the benefits of transfer of learning instruction. Discretion has been used to interpret and reduce overlap in tactics used in different studies and to elaborate tactics.

- Ensure that students possess the readiness characteristics necessary to perform assigned tasks. Students cannot transfer skills they do not possess.
- Teach students to assess the extent to which they are able to perform assigned tasks.
- Teach procedures for performing tasks and the conditions for applying the procedures, relevant to the students' lives.
- Have students determine how procedures they are learning might be applied to perform tasks in the future.
- Teach students to detect correspondence between tasks and procedures.
- Show students how procedures used to perform one task can be used to perform analogous tasks, but not different tasks.
- Teach students to select a procedure to perform an assigned task that has been used successfully to perform analogous tasks.
- Give students practice selecting procedures to perform assigned tasks that have been used successfully to perform analogous tasks. Have students de-

fend their selections based on analogy, then have them test the effectiveness of the procedure they have selected and evaluate the result.

GENERALIZATION: ON TRANSFER OF LEARNING INSTRUCTION

Achievement of learning objectives is enhanced when students are taught beforehand the knowledge and skills needed to perform assigned tasks and how to determine when learned knowledge and skills can be used to perform assigned tasks.

Supportive Research on Transfer of Learning Instruction
Total number of studies covered: 73

Groups of Studies

Author: Misko (1995)

Students: College, vocational school, and business and industry training

Learning: Achievement and transfer of learning

Instructional Tactics: The following instructional tactics that teach students how to achieve transfer of previous learning to current learning or problem-solving situations were derived by the author from studies reviewed:

- Teach facts, strategies, and relevant application of strategies together, prompting students to use previously acquired knowledge to solve current problems.

- Initially teachers should focus on the facts; then, once the student has acquired the facts, focus on the underlying principles.

- Alert students to take note of how information, facts, and principles currently being learned can be analogous to other contexts.

- Teach students to manipulate information presented to them by redefining the problem, transforming the problem into components that can be better dealt with, and looking for patterns and comparisons.

- Teach students to group items into smaller groups, rather than leaving them in one large group. When successful, the students are then asked to describe what they had done. This should be followed by a reminder from the teacher that the strategy can be used for new tasks in the future.

- Teach students to use analogies by teacher modeling and giving students ample time to practice using analogies to answer questions.

- Allow students time to practice looking for analogies and providing their reasons for their selection.

- Provide students relevant hands-on analogous tasks to practice on.

Specific examples of the above tactics were not provided by the author. Many of the individual studies reviewed in this synthesis of research do provide specific information. These studies appear in the reference list at the end of the chapter (the studies are identified by the symbol *).

Findings: Use of the above tactics was found to enhance learning and transfer of prior learning to new learning situations within and beyond the classroom.

Groups of studies reviewed in this logical synthesis of research did not provide statistical evidence. However, many of the individual studies included in the logical synthesis of research do contain statistical evidence. In the event that a reader wishes to view this evidence, an extensive listing of the individual studies reviewed is provided in the reference list (the studies are identified by the symbol *).

Author: Prawat (1989)

Students: Elementary, secondary, college

Learning: Reading, mathematics, science, vocabulary, literature, and social studies achievement and transfer

Instructional Tactics: The following instructional tactics that facilitate knowledge acquisition and utilization were derived by the author from studies reviewed for this synthesis of research. The author divides these tactics into those associated with organization and those associated with student awareness.

Organization

- Develop comparisons between various ways of representing concepts and procedures through the use of concrete materials of various sorts.
- The teacher should use and teach students to use analogies to foster connections between objects and events in the real world and their symbolic connections.
- Teach in a way that makes explicit how important elements of the knowledge base, such as mathematics concepts and procedures, can be compared to one another.

Awareness

- Teach students to be aware of what they know and do not know.
- Provide students with information on other contexts in which known concepts or procedures may be used.
- Teach strategies in the context of analogous real situations.

Findings: Utilization of the above tactics was reported to enhance achievement and transfer.

Groups of studies reviewed in this logical synthesis of research did not provide statistical evidence. However, many of the individual studies included in the logical synthesis of research do contain statistical evidence. In the event that a reader wishes to view this evidence, an extensive listing of the individual studies reviewed is provided in the reference list (the studies are identified by the symbol #).

Individual Studies

Author: Marzolf & DeLoach (1994)

Experiment 1

Students: 2 1/2-year-old preschool

Learning: Transfer of learning to similar and dissimilar tasks

Instructional Tactics:

- Children in the experimental group were exposed to the easier similar task before being exposed to the more difficult dissimilar task. Children in the control group were exposed to the more difficult dissimilar task on two subsequent trials.

- The similar task involved the child watching the researcher hide a small plastic toy dog (3 cm) in some location within a small model of a room. The researcher then hid a slightly larger plastic toy dog (7 cm) in a location within a slightly larger room (2:1 scale) corresponding to the location in which the smaller toy dog was hidden in the smaller room. The appearance and location of the furnishings, appearance of the room, and appearance of the toy dog were the same except for the size difference. The child was told that the larger toy dog was hiding in the same place in the larger room that the smaller toy dog was hiding in for the smaller room. The child was then instructed to try to find the larger toy dog in the larger room.

- For the dissimilar task, the same small model of a room and 3 cm plastic toy dog were used to show the child where the toy dog was hiding. For this task, the larger room was much larger (16:1) than the smaller room. The larger toy dog was a 15 cm stuffed toy dog. Otherwise, the room and location and appearance of the furniture was the same as for the smaller room. After showing the child where the smaller toy dog was hiding in the smaller room, the researcher hid the larger toy dog in the larger room in a location that corresponded to the location of the smaller toy dog in the smaller room. The child was then instructed to try to find the larger toy dog in the larger room.

- The children for both groups were shown the toy dogs for each task prior to performing the actual tasks.

Findings: The experimental group performed better on the similar task than the control group did performing the dissimilar task on the first trial without the prior exposure to the similar task. The experimental group was correct 67% of the time on their first try and the control group was correct 27% of the time on their first try. When comparing the experimental group performance on the dissimilar task following performing the similar task to the control group's performance on their first trial on the dissimilar difficult task, without prior benefit of performing the similar or dissimilar tasks, the experimental group was correct 65% of the time on their first try as compared to the control group being correct 27% of the time on their first try. On the comparison of the experimental group's performance on the dissimilar task after completing the similar task to the control group's second trial on the dissimilar task, the experimental group was correct 65% of the time on their first try as compared to the control group being correct 35% of the time on their first try.

Experiment 2

Students: Three-year-old preschool children

Learning: Transfer of learning to similar and dissimilar tasks

Instructional Tactics:

- Children in the experimental group were exposed to an easier similar task before being exposed to a more difficult dissimilar task. Children in the control group were exposed to the more difficult dissimilar task on two subsequent trials. The strategies used in this experiment were similar to those used in experiment 1 with the exceptions that follow.

- The similar task involved the child watching the researcher hide a small toy dog in some location within a small model of a room. The researcher then hid a larger toy dog in a location within a larger room corresponding to the location where the smaller toy dog was hidden in the smaller room. The appearance and location of the furnishings, appearance of the room, and appearance of the toy dog were the same except for the size difference. The child was told that the larger toy dog was hiding in the same place in the larger room that the smaller toy dog was hiding in for the smaller room. The child was then instructed to try to find the larger toy dog in the larger room.

- For the dissimilar task, the same small model of a room and small toy dog were used to show the child where the toy dog was hiding. For this task, the larger room's appearance and location of the furniture was the same as for the smaller room. However, for this task the colors of the furniture in the two rooms differed. After showing the child where the smaller toy dog was hiding in the smaller room, the researcher hid the larger toy dog in the larger room in a location that corresponded to the location where the smaller toy dog was in the smaller room. The child was then instructed to try to find the larger toy dog in the larger room.

Findings: The experimental group performed better on the similar task than the control group did performing the dissimilar task on the first trial without the prior exposure to the similar task. The experimental group was correct 88% of the time on their first try and the control group was correct 30% of the time on their first try. When comparing the experimental group's performance on the dissimilar task following performing the similar task to the control group's performance on their first trial on the dissimilar difficult task, without prior benefit of performing the similar or dissimilar tasks, the experimental group was correct 88% of the time on their first try as compared to the control group being correct 30% of the time on their first try. On the comparison of the experimental group's performance on the dissimilar task after completing the similar task to the control group's second trial on the dissimilar task, the experimental group was correct 88% of the time on their first try as compared to the control group being correct 65% of the time on their first try.

Author: Farrell (1988)

Experiment 1

Students: 8th grade

Learning: Science transfer of learning

Instructional Tactics:

- The students were informed that they would be trying a new way to study science.
- All students were pretested on their knowledge of physical science principles associated with the balance beam, inclined plane, and hydraulic lift.
- They were then randomly assigned to groups to study instructional material associated with either the balance beam, inclined plane, or the hydraulic lift. Each group studied only one topic area.
- Each group was further divided into two groups. One group received traditional science text material to study, and the other group received the traditional text material to study plus additional study on setting up and calculating proportions associated with the topic they were studying.
- Following the study periods, each student was posttested on all three topic areas. The tests required the student to fill in a missing distance or weight number associated with a condition for the balance beam, incline, or hydraulic lift.

Findings: Students' scores for the content area they individually studied were dropped from their posttest. Only scores associated with the content areas they had not studied were analyzed. Students receiving additional instruction in proportions scored on average 67.3% on the posttest as compared to 34.8% for students who had received only the traditional instruction.

Experiment 2

Students: 8th grade students in a different school than for experiment 1

Learning: Science achievement and transfer of learning

Instructional Tactics: The same as for experiment 1

Findings: Students' scores for the content area they individually studied were dropped from their posttest. Only scores associated with the content areas they had not studied were analyzed. Students receiving additional instruction in proportions scored on average 72.4% on the posttest as compared to 50.4% for students who had received only the traditional instruction.

Author: Gott et al. (1995)

Students: U.S. Air Force apprentice and Master technicians

Learning: Avionics achievement and transfer of learning

Instructional Tactics:

- An experimental group received instruction, coaching, tutoring, and postsession feedback in their development of electronics equipment troubleshooting skills via a computer instructional program. "The learning activity is centered in a computer simulated work environment" (p. 2).
- The work environment consisted of computer graphic displays, simulated controls, and icons for diagnostic meter probes.
- The activities involved hands-on practice solving problems in defective avionics equipment associated with the job the student was being trained for.
- The student could request assistance from the computer coach/tutor at any time during the practice session
- Assistance available was computer critique of the student's most recent action, information on what an expert would have done in this situation, and frequent hyper-graphic displays of equipment diagrams with textual definitions associated with the problem the student was working on.
- Reasons behind procedural and strategic steps were made explicit.
- A standard troubleshooting goal structure was used in coaching for all scenarios.
- General terminology was used rather than problem-specific terminology to allow for broader application.
- The student received reflective follow-up from the computer in the form of

a record and critique of the student's solution to the problem and provided a side-by-side expert solution to the problem with an accompanying cost-benefit reasoning for the expert solution.

• The reflective follow-up emphasized general troubleshooting principles.

The control group received a "more traditional academic classroom" (p. 6) form of instruction. The instruction received by both groups related to human controlled manual test stations. The transfer test tested the students' ability to transfer their acquired knowledge to a novel automated computer controlled system, which included technical data for programming information and the programming language.

Findings: 70.6% of the experimental group achieved the correct solution to the novel transfer test as compared to 63.6% for the control group. The experimental group committed 9 violations of the logical troubleshooting sequence, as compared to 21 for the control group. The control group swapped 50 components without testing, as compared to 3 for the experimental group.

REFERENCE LIST

#*Bereiter, C., & Scardamalia, M. (1986). Educational relevance of the study of expertise. *Interchange 17*(2), 10–19.

#Billett, S. (1994). Authenticity in workplace settings. In J. Stevenson (Ed.), *The development of vocational expertise*. Adelaide: NCVER.

#Boldovici, J. A. (1987). Measuring transfer in military settings. In S. M. Cormier (Ed.), *Transfer of learning*. San Diego: Academic Press.

#Bransford, J. D. (1979). *Human cognition: Learning, understanding, and remembering*. Belmont, CA: Wadsworth Publishing.

#Brown, A. L., & Kane, M. J. (1988). Preschool children can learn to transfer: Learning to learn and learning from example. *Cognitive Psychology 20*, 493–523.

#Brown, A. L., & Palinscar, A. S. (1989). Guided, co-operative learning and individual knowledge acquisition. In L. B. Resnick (Ed.), *Knowing, learning, and instruction: Essays in honor of Robert Glaser* (pp. 393–451). Hillsdale, NJ: Erlbaum.

Catrambone, R. (1995). Aiding subgoal learning: Effects on transfer. *Journal of Educational Psychology 87*(1), 5–17.

*Catrambone, R., & Holyoak, K. J. *The function of schemas in analogical problem solving*. Poster presented at the meeting of the American Psychological Association, Los Angeles.

*Charles, R. I., & Lester, F. K., Jr. (1984). An evaluation of a process-oriented instructional program in mathematical problem solving in grades 5 and 7. *Journal of Research in Mathematical Education 15*, 15–34.

#Chase, W. G. (1982). Spatial representations of taxi drivers. *In NATO conference on the acquisition of symbolic skills* (pp. 391–405). New York: Plenum.

#Chase, W. G., & Simon, H. A. (1973). Perception in chess. *Cognitive Psychology 4*, 55–81.

#Chi, M. T. H. (1978). Knowledge structures and memory development. In R. S. Siegler (Ed.), *Children's thinking: What develops?* (pp. 73–96). Hillsdale, NJ: Erlbaum.

#Chi, M. T. H., & Bassok, M. (1989). Learning from examples via self-explanations. In L. B. Resnick (Ed.), *Knowing, learning, and instruction: Essays in honor of Robert Glaser* (pp. 251–282). Hillsdale, NJ: Erlbaum.

*Chi, M. T. H., Feltovich, P., & Glaser, R. (1981). Categorization and representation of physics problems by experts and novices. *Cognitive Science 5*, 121–152.

*Chi, M. T. H., Glaser, R., & Rees, E. (1981). *Expertise in problem solving* (Technical Report No. 5). Pittsburgh, PA: University of Pittsburgh, Learning Research and Development Center.

*Chi, M. T. H., & Koeske, R. D. (1983). Network representation of a child's dinosaur knowledge. *Developmental Psychology 19*, 29–39.

*Clement, J. (1982, March). *Spontaneous analogies in problem solving: The progressive construction of mental models*. Paper presented at the annual meeting of the American Educational Research Association, New York.

*Collins, A., Brown, J. S., & Newman, S. (1989). The new apprenticeship: Teaching students the craft of reading, writing, and mathematics. In L. B. Resnick (Ed.), *Knowing and learning* (pp. 283–305). Hillsdale, NJ: Erlbaum.

*Dansereau, D. F. (1985). Learning strategy research. In J. W. Segal, S. F. Chipman, & R. Glaser (Eds.), *Thinking and learning skills: Vol. 1. Relating instruction to research* (pp. 209–239). Hillsdale, NJ: Erlbaum.

*DeCorte, E., & Verschaffel, L. (1981). Children's solution processes in elementary arithmetic problems. *Journal of Educational Psychology 73*, 765–779.

#de Groot, A. D. (1965). *Thought and choice in chess*. The Hague, Netherlands: Mouton.

*de Jong, T., & Gerguson-Hessler, M. G. M. (1986) Cognitive structures of good and poor novice problem solvers in physics. *Journal of Educational Psychology 78*, 279–288.

*Duncker, K. (1945). On problem solving. *Psychological Monographs 58*(Whole No. 270).

#Egan, D. E., & Schwartz, B. J. (1979). Chunking in recall of symbolic drawings. *Memory & Cognition 7*(2), 149–158.

Farrell, E. (1988). How teaching proportionality affects transfer of learning: Science and math teachers need each other. *School Science and Mathematics 88*(8), 688–695.

*Gentner, D. (1981). Generative analogies as mental models. In *Proceedings of the Third Annual Conference of the Cognitive Science Society* (pp. 97–100). Berkeley, CA: University of California, Institute of Human Learning.

*Gick, M. L. (1986). Problem-solving strategies. *Educational Psychologist 21*, 99–120.

*Gick, M. L., & Holyoak, K. J. (1980). Anological problem solving. *Cognitive Psychology 12*, 306–355.

*Gick, M. L., & Holyoak, K. J. (1983). Schema induction and anological transfer. *Cognitive Psychology 15*, 1–38.

#Gick, M. L., & Holyoak, K. J. (1987). The cognitive basis of knowledge transfer. In S. M. Cormier (Ed.), *Transfer of learning* (pp. 9–47). San Diego: Academic Press.

#Glaser, R., & Chi, M. T. H. (1988). Overview. In M. Chi, R. Glaser, & M. Farr (Eds.), *The nature of expertise*. Hillsdale, NJ: Erlbaum.

Gott, S. P. et al. (1995, February). *Tutoring for transfer of technical competence*. Report from Armstrong Lab, Brooks AFB, TX. (ERIC Document Reproduction Service No. ED 382 817)

*Gould, S. J. (1980). *The panda's thumb*. New York: Norton.

*Hasselhorn, M., & Korkel, J. (1986). Metacognitive versus traditional reading instructions: The mediating role of domain-specific knowledge on children's text processing. *Human Learning 5*, 75–90.

*Hiebert, J. (1984). Children's mathematics learning: The struggle to link form and understanding. *Elementary School Journal 84*, 497–513.

*Holyoak, K. J. (1985). The pragmatics of analogical transfer. In G. Bower (Ed.), *The psychology of learning and motivation* (Vol. 19, pp. 59–87). New York: Academic Press.

*Janvier, C. (1987). Representations and understanding: The notion of function as an example. In C. Janvier (Ed.), *Problems of representation in the teaching and learning of mathematics* (pp. 67–71). Hillsdale, NJ: Erlbaum.

*Kaput, J. J. (1987). Representation systems and mathematics. In C. Janvier (Ed.), *Problems of representation in the teaching and learning of mathematics* (pp. 19–26). Hillsdale, NJ: Erlbaum.

*Lampert, M. (1986). Knowing, doing, and teaching multiplication. *Cognition and Instruction 3*, 305–342.

#Larkin, J. H. (1983). The role of problem representation in physics. In D. Getner & A. L. Stevens (Eds.), *Mental models* (pp. 75–98). Hillsdale, NJ: Erlbaum.

#Lesgold, A., & Lajoie, S. (1991). Complex problem solving in electronics. In R. J. Sternberg & P. A. Frensch (Eds.), *Complex problem solving: Principles and mechanisms* (pp. 287–316). Hillsdale, NJ: Erlbaum.

#Lesgold, A., Rubinson, H., Feltovich, P., Glaser, R., Klopfer, D., & Wang, Y. (1988). Expertise in a complex skill: Diagnosing x-ray pictures. In M. Chi, R. Glaser, & M. Farr (Eds.), *The nature of expertise*. Hillsdale, NJ: Erlbaum.

*Lesh, R., Behr, M., & Post, T. (1987). Rational numbers and proportions. In C. Janvier (Ed.), *Problems of representation in the teaching and learning of mathematics* (pp. 41–58). Hillsdale, NJ: Erlbaum.

*Lesh, R., Post, T., & Behr, M. (1987). Representations and translations among representations in mathematics learning and problem solving. In C. Janvier (Ed.), *Problems of representation in the teaching and learning of mathematics* (pp. 207–214). Hillsdale, NJ: Erlbaum.

*Lester, F. K. (1980). Research on mathematical problem solving. In R. J. Shumway (Ed.), *Research in mathematics education* (pp. 286–323). Reston, VA: National Council of Teachers of Mathematics.

Marzolf, D. P. & DeLoach, J. S. (1994). Transfer in young children's understanding of spatial representations. *Child Development 65*, 1–15.

#*Mayer, R. E. (1975a). Different problem-solving competencies established in learning computer programming with and without meaningful models. *Journal of Educational Psychology 67*, 725–734.

*Mayer, R. E. (1975b). Information processing variables in learning to solve problems. *Review of Educational Research 45*, 525–541.

Misko, J. (1995). *Transfer: Using learning in new contexts*. Leabrook, Australia: National Centre for Vocational Education Research. (ERIC Document Reproduction Service No. ED 383 895)

*Nesher, P. (1986). Are mathematical understanding and algorithmic performance related? *For the Learning of Mathematics 6*, 2–9.

*Nickerson, R. S. (1985). Understanding understanding. *American Journal of Education 93*, 201–239.

*Paige, J. M., & Simon, H. A. (1966). Cognitive processes in solving algebra word problems. In B. Kleinmuntz (Ed.), *Problem solving: Research, method, and theory* (pp. 51–119). New York: Wiley.

*Pea, R. D. (1987). Socializing the knowledge transfer problem. *International Journal of Educational Research 11*, 639–663.

#Pea, R. D., & Kurland, D. M. (1984). On the cognitive effects of learning computer programming. *New Ideas Psychology 2*(2), 137–168.

*Petrie, H. G. (1976). Do you see what I see? The epistemology of interdisciplinary inquiry. *Educational Researcher 5*(2), 9–15.

#Polya, G. (1957). *How to solve it: A new aspect of mathematical method* (2nd ed.). Princeton, NJ: Princeton University Press.

*Porter, A. C., Floden, R. E., Freeman, D. J., Schmidt, W. H., & Schwille, J. R. (1986). *Content determinants* (Research Series No. 179). East Lansing: Michigan State University, Institute for Research on Teaching.

Prawat, R. S. (1989). Promoting access to knowledge, strategy, and disposition in students: A research synthesis. *Review of Educational Research 59*(1), 1–41.

*Pressley, M., Goodchild, F., Fleet, J., Zejchowski, R., & Evans, E. D. (1989). The challenges of classroom strategy instruction. *Elementary School Journal 89*, 301–342.

#Pressley, M., Symons, S., McDaniel, M., Snyder, B., & Turnure, J. (1988). Elaborative interrogation facilitates acquisition of confusing facts. *Journal of Educational Psychology 80*(3), 268–278.

*Resnick, L. B. (1986). The development of mathematical intuition. In M. Perimutter (Ed.), *Perspectives on intellectual development. The Minnesota Symposia on Child Psychology* (Vol. 19, pp. 159–194). Hillsdale, NJ: Erlbaum.

#Resnick, L. B. (1987). Education and learning to think. In *Committee on Mathematics, Science and Technology Education*. Washington, DC: National Academy Press.

*Resnick, L. B., & Omanson, S. F. (1987). Learning to understand arithmetic. In R. Glaser (Ed.), *Advances in instructional psychology* (pp. 41–95). Hillsdale, NJ: Erlbaum.

*Scardamalia, M., & Bereiter, C. (1984). Development of strategies in text processing. In H. Mandl, N. Stein, & T. Trabasso (Eds.), *Learning and comprehension of text* (pp. 379–406). Hillsdale, NJ: Erlbaum.

*Schoenfeld, A. (1982). Measures of problem-solving performance and problem-solving instruction. *Journal for Research in Mathematics Education 13*, 31–49.

*Schoenfeld, A. H. (1986). On having and using geometric knowledge. In J. Heibert (Ed.), *Conceptual and procedural knowledge: The case of mathematics* (pp. 225–264). Hillsdale, NJ: Erlbaum.

*Simon, D. P., & Simon, H. A. (1978). Individual differences in solving physic problems. In R. S. Siegler (Ed.), *Children's thinking: What develops?* (pp. 325–348). Hillsdale, NJ: Erlbaum.

*Skemp, R. R. (1978). Relational understanding and instrumental understanding. *Arithmetic Teacher 26*, 9–15.

*Steinberg, R., Haymore, J., & Marks, R. (1985, April). *Teacher's knowledge and structuring content in mathematics*. Paper presented at the annual meeting of the American Educational Research Association, Chicago.

*Swing, S., Stoiber, K., & Peterson, P. L. (1988). Thinking skills versus learning time: Effects of alternative classroom-based interventions on students' mathematics problem solving. *Cognition and Instruction 5*, 123–191.

*von Glaserfeld, E. (1987). Learning as a constructive activity. In C. Janvier (Ed.), *Problems of representation in the teaching and learning of mathematics* (pp. 3–17). Hillsdale, NJ: Erlbaum.

*Voss, J. F. (1987). Learning and transfer in subject-matter learning: A problem-solving model. *International Journal of Educational Research 11*, 607–622.

*Weiss, I. (1978). *Report of the 1977 National Survey of Science, Mathematics, and Social Studies Education.* Research Triangle Park, NC: Research Triangle Institute, Center for Educational Research and Evaluation.

#Woloshyn, V. E., Pressley, M., & Schneider, W. (1992). Elaborative-interrogation and prior knowledge effects on learning of facts. *Journal of Educational Psychology 82*(1), 115–124.

#Wood, E., Pressley, M., & Winne, P. (1990). Elaborative interrogation effects on children's learning of actual content. *Journal of Educational Psychology 82*(4), 741–748.

11

Providing Teamwork Instruction

INTRODUCTION

Instructing students on teamwork and having students work on task performance in teams seems to be advantageous when the learning objective is team achievement. To be successful in the modern world, students must be able to work as team members to achieve team goals and objectives. In the world of work they will have to know how to perform as team members in problem solving, determination of goals and objectives, and just plain getting along with co-workers if the organization they work for is to be successful and if they are to remain employed. If they are to have successful families as adults, they will have to be able to work as teams with their partners in determining their goals and objectives, appropriately dividing the labors, being able to rationally resolve conflicts, and sharing in their successes and failures. To be productive members of their social communities, they will have to be able to function as team members within the community if they are to address any problems confronting the community. Additionally, participation in team sports and games requires one to participate as a team member.

As the statistical evidence shows, group teaching does not produce the highest individual student academic achievement effects. One-on-one teacher tutoring continues to produce the highest levels of student achievement, as much as two times more than group teaching. The primary benefit of group instruction is that it is the only way to teach teamwork. And since teamwork is essential to success in civilized societies, the teaching of teamwork needs to be emphasized to a much greater extent than it is now.

STUDENT BENEFICIARIES

The evidence indicates that teaching students to function as team members enhances the achievement of the goals the group is pursuing in elementary, secondary, and college classrooms. Moreover, group achievement was improved in a wide range of content areas. No evidence could be found to suggest that the teaching of teamwork should not be stressed when the achievement of group goals is being pursued.

LEARNING ACHIEVED

Group achievement in the content areas of mathematics, history, foreign languages, English, reading, social sciences, sciences, and social studies is enhanced when student teamwork is taught.

INSTRUCTIONAL TACTICS

- Students' readiness capabilities should be diagnosed on the basis of their prior performance and/or pretesting, and only those with the potential to succeed as team members should begin the instructional program.
- Students should be assigned to work in four- to five-member teams.
- Before starting a learning program, team-building exercises should be conducted to allow team members a chance to get to know one another and build rapport. This might take the form of the individuals in the teams interviewing one another to get to know their names, interests, common interests, and background. The importance of group goals and rewards that can be obtained should be stressed at this time.
- Initial presentation of the knowledge and skills to be learned should be made to the entire group, then individual team members should receive the instruction they need to perform their function.
- The group presentation should be followed by team practice, where the entire group works together on tasks assigned. "Brainstorming" within the team and mutual assistance within the team should be encouraged for solving problems.
- Students should be provided assistance any time they need help.
- Evaluation should be conducted of both team and individual performance, with appropriate feedback and opportunity for remediation. Individuals are held accountable for their performance.
- Teams are recognized for their degree of improvement.

Elaborations of the above summary of tactics can be obtained from reading the studies that follow. To be most effective, the instructional tactics need to be integrated into the particular instructional program being planned or presently in use.

CAUTIONS AND COMMENTS

The studies reviewed had many different purposes. The focus of some of the studies was not on group achievement. However, group achievement was assessed in all studies reported, enabling us to conclude that the teaching of teamwork enhances group achievement. Other benefits of group instruction indicated by research studies include individual achievement, integration of people from diverse cultures, and attitudinal changes.

Since teamwork is so important for success in society, more studies need to be conducted that focus directly on the effect of teamwork instruction on group achievement.

Dr. Slavin and many others deserve to be acknowledged for their important contributions on the affective outcomes of group learning, such as student attitudes toward learning and student attitudes toward one another.

GENERALIZATION: ON TEAMWORK INSTRUCTION

Achievement of the learning objective group achievement is enhanced when students are taught to perform complementary tasks as a team in pursuit of the objective.

Supportive Research on Teamwork Instruction
Total number of studies covered: 165

Groups of Studies

Author: Slavin (1995) (A "best evidence synthesis" of cooperative learning methods)

Students: Grades 1–12

Learning: Reading, math, sciences, social studies, spelling, language arts, literature, geography, writing, history, and drafting achievement

Instructional Tactics: The following tactics are associated with the "Learning Together" method:

- Students are assigned to work in four- to five-member groups of mixed composition.
- Each student must learn the names of the other members of the group.
- Each student in the team interviews another team member in a manner that results in all team members being interviewed, and students present the information they have obtained during their interview to the entire team.
- Each team is to decide on team name, logo, or mural.
- The entire group works together on tasks assigned.
- "Brainstorming" within the group is encouraged in problem-solving situations.
- Each team is graded on their task performance.

- Evaluation of each team member's individual mastery of the material to be learned is conducted.

The following instructional tactics are associated with the "Student Teams—Achievement Divisions" (STAD) method:

- Compute a base score for each student in the class based on their prior performance.
- Students are assigned to work in four- to five-member groups of mixed composition in terms of academic performance, sex, and race or ethnicity.
- Before starting the learning program, team-building exercises are conducted to allow team members a chance to get to know one another.
- Learning material is initially presented in a class by teacher or audiovisual presentation.
- The classroom presentation is followed by team practice.
- All team members are responsible for making sure their teammates have learned the material.
- All team members must participate until all teammates have mastered the material to be learned.
- Team members are required to ask questions of their teammates before asking the teacher.
- After one or two class presentations and one or two team practice sessions, students are administered a quiz. This quiz is to be an individual assessment of what the students have learned as individuals.
- Improvement points are calculated for individual students based on their quiz score in relation to their initial base score. These points are then totaled for the team members of each team and divided by the number of team members to come up with a team improvement score.
- Teams are recognized for their degree of improvement.
- The individual base score for determining improvement is recomputed after each quiz.
- Individual grades are to be based on their actual test (quiz) performance.

The following instructional tactics are associated with the "Teams-Games-Tournaments" (TGT) method:

- Instructional tactics are the same as for the STAD method except that quizzes and the individual improvement score system are replaced by academic tournaments, in which a team member of one team competes with a team member of another team of equal ability based on prior performance. The "games" for the tournament consist of content-relevant questions.

The following instructional tactics are associated with the "Team Assisted–Individualization" (TAI) (mathematics) method:

- Students are pretested at the beginning of the program to determine their placement level.
- Students are assigned to four- to five-member heterogeneous teams.
- Each day the teacher works for ten to fifteen minutes with each of two or three small teaching groups of students who are at the same point in the curriculum.
- Students are given a guide page reviewing the concepts introduced by the teacher in the teaching group.
- Students from the teaching groups are given several skill-practice pages consisting of sixteen practice problems broken down into blocks of four problems, with each skill-practice representing a subskill that leads to mastery of the entire skill, two formative tests, and a unit test.
- Students return to their teams, where they are instructed to read their guide pages and ask teammates or the teacher for help when needed.
- Students are formed into pairs or triads for the purpose of checking.
- Each student works on the first block of four problems. When they finish they have a teammate check the problems against a provided answer sheet. If they fail to get all four correct, they must proceed to the next four practice problems for that subskill page and continue to do so until they get four problems correct. If the student gets all four correct, they are allowed to proceed to the first four practice problems for the next subskill practice page.
- Once a student has successfully proceeded through all of the subskill practice pages, they take a ten-question formative test that is graded by a teammate. If the student gets at least eight questions correct, the teammate signs the test certifying it and the student is allowed to take the unit test. If the student does not get at least eight questions correct, the teacher is called in to diagnose the problem and assign additional practice.
- At the end of each week, team recognition is given based on the number of units each team member has completed and the accuracy on unit tests.

Instructional tactics associated with the "Cooperative Integrated Reading and Composition" method are the same as for the "Team Assisted–Individualization" method except that they are tailored to reading.

The following instructional tactics are associated with the "Group Investigation" method:

- The teacher presents a broad problem or issue to the entire class.
- Students meet in groups to determine the subtopics to be investigated.

- Once the subtopics are determined, the students form groups according to the subtopic they are interested in.
- The students in each group plan what and how they will study.
- Each group plans the division of labor.
- Students within the groups gather information, analyze data, and reach conclusions, with each group member contributing to the group effort.
- Students exchange, discuss, clarify, and synthesize ideas.
- Group members plan what they will report and how they will present their findings to the whole class.
- Teachers and students collaborate in evaluating student learning.

The following instructional tactics are associated with "Jigsaw II" and "Jigsaw" methods:

- Team assignment is the same as for other methods, where the teacher makes the assignments.
- Each student in a team is given individual topics and reads assigned material.
- Students from the different teams who were assigned the same topic meet and discuss the topic.
- The students then return to their team and teach the topic to their fellow team members.
- Students take individual quizzes covering all topics.
- Team scores are computed for the purpose of giving team recognition.

Findings: In general, group achievement was higher for teamwork instruction as compared to more traditional methods.

Individual studies included in this "best evidence synthesis" are identified by the symbol * in the reference list at the end of the chapter.

Author: Sharan (1980)

Students: Grades 1–12

Learning: English, mathematics, language arts, reading, and social studies achievement

Instructional Tactics: Instructional tactics are listed following the name of the cooperative learning method reviewed.

Jigsaw Method

- The material to be learned is divided into as many parts as there are group members.

- Each student initially learns only one part of the total material and is responsible for teaching that part to their groupmates.
- Each group member is responsible for learning all of the curriculum.

TGT Method

- The students are formed into four- or five-member teams that reflect a cross-section of the class ability levels, sexes, and racial/ethnic groups.
- The teams prepare their members through peer tutoring for learning-game tournaments.
- For the academic tournaments, a team member of one team competes with a team member of another team of equal ability based on prior performance. The "games" for the tournament consist of content-relevant questions.

STAD Method

- Team given instructions to work together.
- Team reward with an individual task.

A broader and clearer description of instructional tactics associated with this method is available in the Slavin (1995) synthesis.

Group Investigation Method

- Students select specific subtopics within a general problem area presented by the teacher.
- Students and the teacher cooperatively plan specific learning procedures, tasks, and goals.
- Students carry out the plan they have formulated.
- Students analyze and evaluate information.
- Students plan how the information obtained will be summarized for display or presentation.
- Teachers and students collaborate in evaluating student learning.

Findings: Across all team-learning methods, group achievement was superior as compared to traditional classrooms. In the review of TGT and STAD studies, peer-tutoring was found not to produce a positive effect on achievement.

Individual studies included in this research synthesis are identified by the symbol # in the reference list.

Author: Johnson et al. (1981)

Students: Elementary, secondary, and college

Learning: Language arts, reading, mathematics, science, social studies, psychology, and physical education achievement

Instructional Tactics:

- Group cooperation.
- Group cooperation with intergroup competition.
- Interpersonal competition.
- Individualistic efforts.

Findings:

1. There is no difference in achievement for group cooperation without intergroup competition, as compared to group cooperation with intergroup competition.
2. Group cooperation promotes higher achievement than does individual competition.
3. Group cooperation with intergroup competition promotes higher achievement than does interpersonal competition.
4. Group cooperation without intergroup competition promotes higher achievement than does individualistic effort.
5. Group cooperation with intergroup competition promotes higher achievement than does individualistic effort.
6. There was no difference on achievement between individual competition and individualistic effort.

Individual studies included in this meta-analysis are identified by the symbol @ in the reference list.

REFERENCE LIST

*Allen, W. H., & Van Sickle, R. L. (1984). Learning teams and low achievers. *Social Education 48*, 60–64.

@Almack, J. C. (1930). Mental efficiency of consulting pairs. *Educational Research Bulletin 9*, 2–3.

@Anderson, N. H. (1961). Group performance in an anagram task. *Journal of Social Psychology 55*, 67–75.

@Armstrong, B., Johnson, D. W., & Balow, B. (in press). Cooperative goal structures as a means for integrating learning disabled with normal progress elementary pupils. *Contemporary Educational Psychology.*

@Barnlund, D. (1959). A comparative study of individual, majority, and group judgment. *Journal of Abnormal and Social Psychology 58*, 55–60.

@Beach, L. (1974). Self-directed student groups and college learning. *Higher Education 3*, 187–200.

@Beaman, A. L., Diener, A., Fraser, S. C., & Endresen, D. L. (1977). Effects of voluntary and semi voluntary peer-monitoring programs on academic performance. *Journal of Educational Psychology 69*, 109–114.

*Berg, K. F. (1993, April). *Structured cooperative learning and achievement in a high school mathematics class.* Paper presented at the annual meeting of the American Educational Research Association, Atlanta.

@Bodine, R. (1977, April). *The effects of cognitive style, task structure, and task setting on student outcomes—Cognitive and affective.* Paper presented at the annual meeting of the American Educational Research Association, New York.

#Bridgeman, D. (1977). *The influence of cooperative, interdependent learning on role taking and moral reasoning: A theoretical and empirical field study with fifth grade students.* Unpublished doctoral dissertation, University of California, Santa Cruz.

@Bruning, J., Sommer, D., & Jones, B. (1966). The motivational effects of cooperation and competition in the means-independent situation. *Journal of Social Psychology 68*, 269–274.

*Chambers, B., & Abrami, P. C. (1991). The relationship between student team learning outcomes and achievement, causal attributions, and affect. *Journal of Educational Psychology 83*, 140–146.

@Clifford, M. (1971). Motivational effects of competition and goal-setting in reward and non-reward conditions. *Journal of Experimental Education 39*, 11–16.

@Clifford, M. (1972). Effects of competition as a motivational technique in the classroom. *American Educational Research Journal 9*, 123–137.

@D'Antuono, M. (1979). *The implementation and results of peer interaction as a rehearsal technique.* Unpublished master's thesis, University of Maryland.

@DeCharms, R. (1957). Affiliation motivation and productivity in small groups. *Journal of Abnormal and Social Psychology 55*, 222–226.

@Deutch, M. (1949). An experimental study of the effects of cooperation and competition upon group process. *Human Relations 2*, 199–231.

#@DeVries, D., & Edwards, K. (1973). Student teams and learning games: Their effect on classroom process. *American Educational Research Journal 10*, 307–318.

#DeVries, D., & Edwards, K. (1974a). *Expectancy theory and cooperation-competition in the classroom.* Paper presented at the annual convention of the American Psychological Association, New Orleans.

#DeVries, D., & Edwards, K. (1974b). Student teams and learning games: Their effect on cross-race and cross-sex interaction. *Journal of Educational Psychology 66*, 741–749.

@DeVries, D., Lucasse, P. R., & Shackman, S. L. (1979). *Small group vs. individualized instruction: A field test* (Report No. 217). Baltimore: Johns Hopkins University, Center for Social Organization of Schools.

*DeVries, D., Lucasse, P. R., & Shackman, S. L. (1980). *Small group vs. individualized instruction: A field test of relative effectiveness* (Report No. 293). Baltimore: Johns Hopkins University, Center for Social Organization of Schools.

*@DeVries, D., & Mescon, I. T. (1975). *Teams-Games-Tournaments: An effective task and reward structure in the elementary grades* (Report No. 189). Baltimore: Johns Hopkins University, Center for Social Organization of Schools.

*DeVries, D., Mescon, I. T., & Shackman, S. L. (1975a). *Teams-Games-Tournaments (TGT) effects on reading skills in the elementary grades* (Report No. 200). Baltimore: Johns Hopkins University, Center for Social Organization of Schools.

*@DeVries, D., Mescon, I. T., & Shackman, S. L. (1975b). *Teams-Games-Tournaments in the elementary school classroom: A replication* (Report No. 190). Baltimore: Johns Hopkins University, Center for Social Organization of Schools.

*@DeVries, D., Mescon, I. T., & Shackman, S. L. (1976). *Student teams can improve basic skills: TGT applied to reading.* Paper presented at the annual meeting of the American Psychological Association, Washington, DC.

#DeVries, D., & Slavin, R. E. (1978). Team-Games-Tournaments: A research review. *Journal of Research and Development in Education 12,* 28–38.

*@DeVries, D. L., Edwards, K. J., & Wells, E. H. (1974). *Teams-Games-Tournaments in instruction: Effects on academic achievement, student attitudes, cognitive beliefs, and classroom climate* (Report No. 173). Baltimore: Johns Hopkins University, Center for Social Organization of Schools.

*Edwards, K. J., & DeVries, D. (1972). *Learning games and student teams: Their effect on student attitudes and achievement* (Report No. 147). Baltimore: Johns Hopkins University, Center for Social Organization of Schools.

*@Edwards, K. J., & DeVries, D. (1974). *The effects of Teams-Games-Tournaments and two structural variations on classroom process, student attitudes, and student achievement* (Report No. 172). Baltimore: Johns Hopkins University, Center for Social Organization of Schools.

*#@Edwards, K. J., DeVries, D., & Snyder, J. P. (1972). Games and teams: A winning combination. *Simulation and Games 3,* 247–269.

*Fantuzzo, J. W., King, J. A., & Heller, L. R. (1992). Effects of reciprocal peer tutoring on mathematics and school adjustments: A component analysis. *Journal of Educational Psychology 84*(3), 331–339.

@Faust, W. L. (1959). Group versus individual problem solving. *Journal of Abnormal and Social Psychology 59,* 68–72.

*Frantz, L. J. (1979). The effects of the student teams achievement approach in reading on peer attitudes. Norfolk, VA: Master's thesis, Old Dominion University, Norfolk, VA.

@Fraser, S. C., Beaman, A. L., Diener, E., & Kelem, R. T. (1977). Two, three, or four heads are better than one: Modification of college performance by peer monitoring. *Journal of Educational Psychology 69,* 101–108.

@French, D., Brownele, C., Graziano, W., & Hartup, W. (1977). Effects of cooperative, competitive, and individualistic sets on performance in children's groups. *Journal of Experimental Child Psychology 24,* 1–10.

@Garibaldi, A. (1979). The affective contributions of cooperative and group goal structures. *Journal of Educational Psychology 71,* 788–795.

@Goldman, M., Stockbauer, J., & McAuliffe, T. (1977). Intergroup and intragroup competition and cooperation. *Journal of Experimental Social Psychology 13,* 81–88.

@Gordon, K. (1924). Group judgments in the field of lifted weights. *Journal of Experimental Psychology 7,* 398–400.

@Graziano, W., French, D., Brownele, C., & Hartup, W. (1976). Peer interaction in same- and mixed-age triads in relation to chronological age and incentive condition. *Child Development 47,* 707–714.

*Greenwood, C. R., Delquadri, J. C., & Hall, R. V. (1989). Longitudinal effects of classwide peer tutoring. *Journal of Educational Psychology 81,* 371–383.

@Grunee, H. (1937). Maze learning in the collective situation. *Journal of Psychology 13,* 437–443.

@Haines, D., & McKeachie, W. (1967). Cooperative versus competitive discussion methods in teaching introductory psychology. *Journal of Educational Psychology 58*, 386–390.

@Hammond, L., & Goldman, M. (1961). Competition and noncompetition and its relationship to individual and group productivitiy. *Sociometry 24*, 46–60.

*Hawkins, J. D., Doueck, H. J., & Lishner, D. M. (1988). Changing teacher practices in mainstream classrooms to improve bonding and behavior of low achievers. *American Educational Research Journal 25*(1), 31–50.

*Heller, L. R., & Fantuzzo, J. W. (in press). Reciprocal peer tutoring and parent partnership: Does parent involvement make a difference? *School Psychology Review.*

*Hertz-Lasarowitz, R., Sapir, C., & Sharan, S. (1981). Academic and social effects of two cooperative learning methods in desegregated classrooms. Manuscript, Haifa University, Haifa, Israel.

@Horner, M. S. (1974). Performance of men in noncompetitive and interpersonal competitive achievement-oriented situations. In J. Atkinson & J. Raynor (Eds.), *Motivation and Achievement* (pp. 237–254). Washington, DC.

@Hovey, D., Gruber, H., & Terrell, G. (1963). Effects of self-directed study and course achievement, retention, and curiosity. *Journal of Educational Research 56*, 346–351.

@Hudgins, B. Effects of group experience and individual problem solving. *Journal of Educational Psychology 51*, 37–42.

*Hulten, B. H., & DeVries, D. L. (1976). *Team competition and group practice: Effects on student achievement and attitudes* (Report No. 212). Baltimore: Johns Hopkins University, Center for Social Organization of Schools.

@Hulten, G. (1974, April). *Games and teams: An effective combination in the classroom.* Paper presented at the annual meeting of the American Educational Research Association, Chicago.

@Humphreys, B., Johnson, R., & Johnson, D. W. (in press). Cooperation, competition, individualization, and the ninth grade science student. *Journal of Research on Science Teaching.*

@Hurlock, E. (1927). Use of group rivalry as an incentive. *Journal of Abnormal and Social Psychology 22*, 278–290.

@Husband, R. (1940). Cooperation versus solitary problem solving. *Journal of Social Psychology 11*, 405–409.

#@Johnson, D. W., Johnson, R. T., Johnson, J., & Anderson, D. (1976). The effects of cooperative vs. individualized instruction on student prosocial behavior, attitudes toward learning, and achievement. *Journal of Educational Psychology 68*, 446–452.

*#@Johnson, D. W., Johnson, R. T., & Scott, L. (1978). The effects of cooperative and individualized instruction on student attitudes and achievement. *Journal of Social Psychology 104*, 207–216.

@Johnson, D. W., Johnson, R. T., & Skon, L. (1979). Student achievement on different types of tasks under cooperative, competitive, and individualistic conditions. *Contemporary Educational Psychology 4*, 99–106.

@Johnson, D. W., Skon, L., & Johnson, R. T. (1980). The effects of cooperative, competitive and individualistic goal structures on student achievement on different types of tasks. *American Educational Research Journal 17*, 83–93.

Johnson, D. W., Muruyama, G., Johnson, R., Nelson, D., & Skon, L. (1981). Effects of cooperative, competetive, and individualistic goal structures on achievement: A meta-analysis. *Psychological Bulletin 89*(1), 47–62.

*Johnson, L. (1985). The effects of groups of four cooperative learning models on student problem-solving achievement in mathematics. Doctoral dissertation, University of Houston.

*Johnson, L., & Waxman, H. C. (1985, March). *Evaluating the effects of the "groups of four" program.* Paper presented at the annual meeting of the American Educational Research Association, Chicago.

@Johnson, R. T., & Johnson, D. W. (1979). Type of task and student achievement and attitudes in interpersonal cooperation, competition, and individualization. *Journal of Social Psychology 108*, 37–48.

*Johnson, R. T., Johnson, D. W., Scott, L. E., & Romolae, B. A. (1985). Effects of single-sex and mixed-sex cooperative interaction on science achievement and attitudes and cross-handicap and cross-sex relationships. *Journal of Research in Science Teaching 22*, 207–220.

@Johnson, R. T., Johnson, D. W., & Tauer, M. (1979). Effects of cooperative, competitive, and individualistic goal structures on students' achievement and attitudes. *Journal of Psychology 102*, 191–198.

@Jones, S., & Vroom, V. (1964). Division of labor and performance under cooperative-competitive conditions. *Journal of Abnormal Social Psychology 68*, 313–320.

@Julian, J., & Perry, F. (1967). Cooperation contrasted with intra-group competition. *Sociometry 30*, 79–90.

*Kagan, S., Zahn, G. L., Widaman, K. F., Schwarzwald, J., & Tyrell, G. (1985). Classroom structural bias: Impact of cooperative and competitive classroom structures on cooperative and competitive individuals and groups. In R. E. Slavin, S. Sharan, S. Kagan, R. Hertz-Lazarowitz, C. Webb, and R. Schmuck (Eds.), *Learning to cooperate, cooperating to learn* (pp. 277–312). New York: Plenum.

@Kanekar, S., Libley, C., Engels, J., & John, G. (1978). Group performance as a function of group type, task condition, and scholastic level. *European Journal of Social Psychology 8*, 439–451.

@Kelly, R., Rawson, R., & Terry, R. (1973). Interaction effects of achievement need and situational press on performance. *Journal of Social Psychology 89*, 141–145.

*Kinney, J. H. (1989, May). *A study of the effects of a cooperative learning program on the achievement of ninth grade multi-cultural general biology classes.* Paper presented to the Alexandria City, Virginia School Board.

@Klugman, S. (1944). Cooperation versus individual efficiency in problem solving. *Journal of Educational Psychology 35*, 91–100.

*Kosters, A. E. (1990). *The effects of cooperative learning in the traditional classroom on student achievement and attitude.* Unpublished doctoral dissertation, University of South Dakota.

*Lamberights, R., & Diepenbroek, J. W. (1992, July). *Implementation and the effects of an integrated direct and activative instruction in a cooperative classroom setting.* Paper presented at the International Convention on Cooperative Learning, Utrecht, The Netherlands.

@Laughlin, P. (1965). Selection strategies in concept attainment as a function of number of persons and stimulus display. *Journal of Experimental Psychology 70*, 323–327.

@Laughlin, P. (1972). Selection versus reception concept-attainment paradigms for individuals and cooperative pairs. *Journal of Educational Psychology 63*, 116–122.

@Laughlin, P., & Adamopoulos, J. (1980). Social combination processes and individual learning for six person cooperative groups on an intellective task. *Journal of Personality and Social Psychology 38*, 941–947.

@Laughlin, P., & Bitz, D. (1975). Individual versus dyadic performance on a dysjunctive task as a function of initial ability level. *Journal of Personality and Social Psychology 31*, 487–496.

@Laughlin, P., & Branch, L. (1972). Individual versus triadic performance on a complimentary task as a function of initial ability level. *Organizational Behavior and Human Performance 8*, 201–216.

@Laughlin, P., Branch, L., & Johnson, H. (1969). Individual versus triadic performance on a unidimensional complimentary task as a function of initial ability level. *Journal of Personality and Social Psychology 12*, 144–150.

@Laughlin, P., & Jaccard, J. (1975). Social facilitation and obvsevational learning of individuals and cooperative pairs. *Journal of Personality and Social Psychology 32*, 873–879.

@Laughlin, P., & Johnson, H. (1966). Group and individual performance on a complimentary task as a function of initial ability level. *Journal of Experimental Social Psychology 2*, 407–414.

@Laughlin, P., Kalowski, C., Metzler, M., Ostap, K., & Venclovas, S. (1968). Concept identification as a function of sensory modality, information, and number of persons. *Journal of Experimental Psychology 77*, 335–340.

@Laughlin, P., Keer, N., Munch, M., & Haggerty, C. (1976). Social decision schemes of the same four-person groups on two different intellective tasks. *Journal of Personality and Social Psychology 33*, 80–88.

@Laughlin, P., & McGlynn, R. (1967). Cooperative versus competitive concept attainment as a function of sex and stimulus display. *Journal of Personality and Social Psychology 7*, 398–402.

@Laughlin, P., McGlynn, R., Anderson, J., & Jacobsen, E. (1968). Concept attainment by individuals versus cooperative pairs as a function of memory, sex, and concept rule. *Journal of Personality and Social Psychology 8*, 410–417.

*Lazarowitz, R. (1991). Learning biology cooperatively: An Israeli junior high school study. *Cooperative Learning 11*(3), 19–21.

*Lazarowitz, R., & Karsenty, G. (1990). Cooperative learning and students' self-esteem in tenth grade biology classrooms. In S. Sharan (Ed.), *Cooperative learning, theory, and research* (pp. 123–149). New York: Praeger.

#@Lucker, G., Rosenfield, D., Sikes, J., & Aronson, E. (1976). Performance in the interdependent classroom: A field study. *American Educational Research Journal 13*, 115–123.

*Madden, N. A., & Slavin, R. E. (1983). Mainstreaming students with mild academic handicaps: Academic and social outcomes. *Review of Educational Research 53*, 519–569.

@Maller, J. (1929). *Cooperation and competition: An experimental study of motivation.* New York: Columbia University, Teachers College.

*Martinez, L. J. (1990). *The effects of cooperative learning on academic achievement and self-concept with bilingual third-grade students.* Unpublished doctoral dissertation, United States International University.

@Martino, L., & Johnson, D. W. (1979). Cooperative and individualistic experiences among disabled and normal children. *Journal of Social Psychology 107*, 177–183.

*Mattingly, R. M., & Van Sickle, R. L. (1991). Cooperative learning and achievement in social studies: Jigsaw II. *Social Education 55*(6), 392–395.

@McClintock, E., & Sonquist, J. (1976). Cooperative task-oriented groups in a college classroom: A field application. *Journal of Educational Psychology 68*, 588–596.

@McCurdy, H., & Lambert, W. (1952). The efficiency of small human groups in the solution of problems requiring genuine cooperation. *Journal of Personality 20*, 478–494.

@McGlynn, R. (1972). Four-person group concept attainment as a function of interaction format. *Journal of Social Psychology 86*, 89–94.

*Mevarach, Z. R. (1985a, April). *Cooperative mastery learning strategies.* Paper presented at the annual meeting of the American Educational Research Association, Chicago.

*Mevarach, Z. R. (1985b). The effects of cooperative learning strategies on mathematics achievement. *Journal of Educational Research 78*, 372–377.

*Mevarach, Z. R. (1991). Learning mathematics in different mastery environments. *Journal of Educational Research 84*(4), 225–231.

@Michaels, J. (1978). Effects of differential rewarding and sex on math performance. *Journal of Educational Psychology 70*, 565–573.

@Miller, F. (1971). Effects of small group instruction on achievement of technical information by ninth grade industrial arts students. *Dissertation Abstracts International 32*, 5009A. (University Microfilms No. 72–10,559)

@Miller, L., & Hamblin, R. (1963). Interdependence, differential rewarding, and productivity. *American Sociological Review 28*, 768–778.

@Nelson, L., & Madsen, M. C. (1969). Cooperation and competition in four-year-olds as a function of reward contingency and subculture. *Developmental Psychology 1*, 340–344.

@Newcomb, A., Brady, J., & Hartup, W. (1979). Friendship and incentive condition as determinants of children's task-oriented social behavior. *Child Development 50*, 878–881.

@Nogami, G. (1976). Effects of group size, room size, or density? *Journal of Applied Social Psychology 6*, 105–125.

@Nowicki, S., Duke, M., & Crouch, M. (1978). Sex differences in locus of control and performance under competitive and cooperative conditions. *Journal of Educational Psychology 70*, 482–486.

*Okebukola, P. A. (1984). In search of more effective interaction patterns in biology laboratories. *Journal of Biological Education 18*, 305–308.

*Okebukola, P. A. (1985). The relative effectiveness of cooperativeness and competitive interaction techniques in strengthening students' performance in science classes. *Science Education 69*, 501–509.

*Okebukola, P. A. (1986a). Impact of extended cooperative and competitive relationships on the performance of students in science. *Human Relations 39*, 673–682.

*Okebukola, P. A. (1986b). The influence of preferred learning styles on cooperative learning in science. *Science Education 70*, 509–517.

@Okun, M., & Divesta, F. (1975). Cooperation and competition in coacting groups. *Journal of Personality and Social Psychology 31*, 615–620.

@Olson, P., & Davis, J. (1964). Divisible tasks and pooling performance in groups. *Psychological Reports 15*, 511–517.

*Peck, G. L. (1991). *The effects of cooperative learning on the spelling achievement of intermediate elementary students.* Unpublished doctoral dissertation, Ball State University.

*Perrault, R. (1982). *An experimental comparison of cooperative learning to noncooperative learning and their effects on cognitive achievement in junior high industrial arts laboratories.* Doctoral dissertation, University of Maryland.

@Peterson, P. L., & Janicki, T. C. (1979). Individualized characteristics and children's learning in large-group and small-group approaches. *Journal of Educational Psychology 71*, 677–687.

*Phelps, J. D. (1990). *A study of the interrelationships between cooperative team learning, learning preference, friendship patterns, gender, and achievement in middle school students.* Unpublished doctoral dissertation, Indiana University.

@Philip, A. (1940). Strangers and friends as competitors and cooperators. *Journal of Genetic Psychology 57*, 249–258.

@Raven, B., & Eachus, H. (1963). Cooperation and competition in means-interdependent triads. *Journal of Abnormal and Social Psychology 67*, 307–316.

@Richmond, B., & Weiner, G. (1973). Cooperation and competition among young children as a function of ethnic grouping, grade, sex, and reward condition. *Journal of Educational Psychology 64*, 329–334.

@Roberts, G. (1972). Effects of achievement motivation and social environment on performance of a motor task. *Journal of Motor Behavior 4*, 37–46.

*Robertson, L. (1982). *Integrated goal structuring in the elementary school: Cognitive growth in mathematics.* Doctoral dissertation, Rutgers University.

@Rorie, V. (1979). *The effects of cooperative versus competitive goal structure on student achievement among Afro-American students.* Unpublished Educational Specialist Thesis, University of Minnesota, Minneapolis.

@Rosenbaum, M., Groff, B., & Skowronski, J. (1980). Unpublished study cited in M. Rosenbaum, *Cooperation and competition.* In P. Paulus (Ed.), *Psychology of group influence.* Hillsdale, NJ: Erlbaum.

@Rosenbaum, M. E. et al. (1980). Group productivity and process: Pure and mixed reward structure and task interdependence. *Journal of Personality and Social Psychology 39*, 626–642.

@Ryack, B. L. (1965). A comparison of individual and group learning of nonsense syllables. *Journal of Personality and Social Psychology 2*, 296–299.

*Schaedel, B., Hertz-Lasarowitz, R., Walk, A., Lerner, M., Juberan, S., & Sarid, M. (in press). The Israeli CIRC (ALSASH): First year achievements in reading and composition. *Helkat-Lashon* (Journal of Linguistic Education, in Hebrew).

@Scott, W., & Cherrington, D. (1974). Effects of competitive, cooperative, and individualized reinforcement contingencies. *Journal of Personality and Social Psychology 30*, 748–759.

Sharan, S. (1980). Cooperative learning in small groups: Recent methods and effects on achievement, attitudes, and ethnic relations. *Review of Educational Research 50*(2), 241–271.

*Sharan, S., Kussel, P., Hertz-Lazarowitz, R., Bejarano, Y., Raviv, S., & Sharan, Y. (1984). *Cooperative learning in the classroom: Research in desegregated schools.* Hillsdale, NJ: Erlbaum.

*Sharan, S., & Shachar, C. (1988). *Language and learning in the cooperative classroom.* New York: Springer-Verlag.

@Shaw, M. (1958). A comparison of individuals and small groups in the rational solution of complex problems. *Journal of Personality 26*, 155–169.

*Sherman, L. W. (1988). A comparative study of cooperative and competitive achievement in two secondary biology classrooms: The group investigation model versus an individually competitive goal structure. *Journal of Research in Science Teaching 26*(1), 35–64.

*Sherman, L. W., & Thomas, M. (1986). Mathematics achievement in cooperative versus individualistic goal-structured high school classrooms. *Journal of Educational Research 79*, 169–172.

*Sherman, L. W., & Zimmerman, D. (1986, November). *Cooperative versus competitive reward-structured secondary science classroom achievement.* Paper presented at the annual meeting of the School Science and Mathematics Association, Lexington, KY.

@Sims, V. (1928). The relative influence of two types of motivation on improvement. *Journal of Educational Psychology 19*, 480–484.

@Skon, L., Johnson, D. W., & Johnson, R. (1981). Effects of cooperative, competitive, and individualistic learning situations on achievement and reasoning processes. *Journal of Educational Psychology 73*(1), 83–92.

#Slavin, R. E. (1977a). Classroom reward structure: An analytical and practical review. *Review of Educational Research 47*, 633–650.

@Slavin, R. E. (1977b). How student learning teams can integrate the desegregated classroom. *Integrated Education 15*, 56–58.

*@Slavin, R. E. (1977c). A student team approach to teaching adolescents with special emotional and behavioral needs. *Psychology in the Schools 14*(1), 77–84.

@Slavin, R. E. (1978a). *Effects of biracial learning teams on cross-racial friendships and interaction* (Report No. 240). Baltimore: Johns Hopkins University, Center for Social Organization of Schools.

#Slavin, R. E. (1978b). Student teams and achievement divisions. *Journal of Research and Development in Education 12*, 39–49.

*@Slavin, R. E. (1978c). Student teams and comparison among equals: Effects on academic performance and student attitudes. *Journal of Educational Psychology 70*, 532–538.

@Slavin, R. E. (1978d). *Effects of student teams and peer tutoring on academic achievement and time on-task* (Report No. 253). Baltimore: Johns Hopkins University, Center for Social Organization of Schools.

*Slavin, R. E. (1979). Effects of biracial learning teams on cross-racial friendships. *Journal of Educational Psychology 71*, 381–387.

*Slavin, R. E. (1980). Student teams and peer tutoring on academic achievement and time on-task. *Journal of Experimental Education 48*, 252–257.

Slavin, R. E. (1995). *Cooperative learning* (2nd ed.). Boston: Allyn and Bacon.

Slavin, R. E. (1996). *Education for all.* Lisse, The Netherlands: Swets & Zeitlinger.

*Slavin, R. E., & Karweit, N. L. (1981). Cognitive and affective outcomes of an intensive student team learning experience. *Journal of Experimental Education 50*, 29–35.

*Slavin, R. E., & Karweit, N. L. (1984). Mastery learning and student teams: A factorial experiment in urban general mathematics classes. *American Educational Research Journal 21*, 725–736.

*Slavin, R. E., & Karweit, N. L. (1985). Effects of whole-class, ability grouped, and individualized instruction on mathematics achievement. *American Educational Research Journal 22*, 351–367.

*Slavin, R. E., Leavey, M. B., & Madden, M. A. (1984). Combining cooperative learning and individualized instruction: Effects on student mathematics achievement, attitudes, and behaviors. *Elementary School Journal 84*, 409–422.

*Slavin, R. E., Madden, M. A., & Leavey, M. B. (1984). Effects of team assisted individualization on the mathematics achievement of academically handicapped students and nonhandicapped students. *Journal of Educational Psychology 76*, 813–819.

*Slavin, R. E., & Oickle, E. (1981). Effects of cooperative learning on student achievement and race relations: Treatment by race interactions. *Sociology of Education 54*, 174–180.

*Solomon, D., Watson, M. S., Delucchi, K. L., Schaps, E., & Battistich, V. (1988). Enhancing children's prosocial behavior in the classroom. *American Educational Research Journal 25*, 527–554.

*Stevens, R. J., & Durkin, S. (1992). *Using student team reading and student team writing in middle schools: Two evaluations* (Report No. 36). Baltimore: Johns Hopkins University, Center for Research on Effective Schooling for Disadvantaged Students.

*Stevens, R. J., Slavin, R. E., & Farnish, A. M. (1991). The effects of cooperative learning and direct instruction in reading comprehension strategies on main idea identification. *Journal of Educational Psychology 83*(1), 8–16.

*Stevens, R. J., Slavin, R. E., Farnish, A. M., & Madden, N. A. (1988, April). *Effects of cooperative learning and direct instruction in reading comprehension strategies on main idea identification.* Paper presented at the annual meeting of the American Educational Research Association, New Orleans.

*Stevens, R. J., Madden, N. A., Slavin, R. E., & Farnish, A. M. (1987). Cooperative integrated reading and composition: Two field experiments. *Reading Research Quarterly 22*, 433–454.

*Talmage, H., Pascarella, E. T., & Ford, S. (1984). The influence of cooperative learning strategies on teacher practices, student perceptions of the learning environment, and academic achievement. *American Educational Research Journal 21*, 163–179.

*Tomblin, E. A., & Davis, B. R. (1985). *Technical report on the evaluation of the race/ human relations program: A study of cooperative learning environment strategies.* San Diego: San Diego Public Schools.

*Van Oudenhaven, J. P., Van Berkum, G., & Swen-Koopmans, T. (1987). Effects of cooperation and shared feedback on spelling achievement. *Journal of Educational Psychology 79*, 92–94.

*Van Oudenhaven, J. P., Wiersma, B., & Van Yperen, N. (1987). Effects of cooperation and feedback by fellow pupils on spelling achievement. *European Journal of Psychology of Education 2*, 83–91.

*Veder, P. H. (1985). *Cooperative learning: A study on process and effects of cooperation between primary school children.* The Hague, The Netherlands: Stichting Voor Onderzoek Van Het Onderwijs.

12

Providing Decision-Making Instruction

INTRODUCTION

Some of the procedures people use to perform familiar, routine tasks are selected automatically and performed as habits: for example, procedures for brushing one's teeth, bathing, and getting dressed in the morning. Other procedures used primarily to perform less familiar, novel, and complex tasks are selected by means of reflective, deliberative decision-making: for instance, planning a vacation to a foreign country, developing a household budget for the first time, and learning a new subject in school. Whenever people do not know for certain how to proceed to perform a task, they revert to deliberate decision-making, which requires the relatively slow consideration of relevant factors and alternatives as a basis for deciding on a procedure to perform the task.

Assigned tasks are to (1) be based on student readiness capabilities and (2) present students with new challenges so they can extend their learning. Quite often students do not know for certain what procedures to use to accomplish the tasks they are assigned. They need to employ deliberative decision-making tactics to derive a procedure. Research shows that when students are taught how to use decision-making tactics, their academic achievement is enhanced. In this chapter, effective decision-making instruction is described.

STUDENT BENEFICIARIES

The evidence indicates that decision-making instruction enhances the academic achievement of students in elementary, secondary, college, and adult learning situations. No evidence could be found to suggest that decision-making instruction should not be stressed in all subject areas for all types of students, including students in military, business and industry, and community education settings.

LEARNING ACHIEVED

Achievement in the content areas of reading, mathematics, science, social studies, literature, and writing is enhanced when decision-making instruction tactics are incorporated into the instruction. It may be reasonable to expect that achievement may be enhanced in other content areas as well. In studies reviewed, student achievement was shown to be enhanced when decision-making instruction was incorporated into the instruction.

INSTRUCTIONAL TACTICS

The benefits of providing students with decision-making instruction are supported by the evidence. However, there is a need for instructional planners and teachers to know the particular tactics that can be used in decision-making instruction. The following tactics are derived from the studies that demonstrate the benefits of decision-making instruction. A unique feature of the instructional tactics is that they utilize self-questioning to guide the decision-making. Discretion has been used to interpret and reduce overlap in tactics used in different studies and to elaborate tactics.

- Clarify task assignments. Ask, "What outcome am I to achieve? Are there any constraints such as time limits?" Ask for clarification of instruction if need be.

- Analyze the assigned task and instructions for clues that suggest the correct procedure to use. Ask, "What am I required to do to accomplish the assigned task?"

- Consider procedures that have been used to accomplish similar tasks. Ask, "Do I know of procedures that have been used to accomplish similar tasks? How can I find out about other procedures?" Students should be assisted in learning about additional procedures.

- Consider the relative merits of alternative procedures you know about or have found out about for accomplishing assigned tasks. Ask, "Which procedure is most likely to accomplish the assigned task? Do I have the ability and resources to execute the procedure?"

- Tentatively select a procedure for accomplishing the assigned task that can be predicted to succeed and is feasible to execute.

- Reevaluate the tentatively selected procedure and attempt to defend that it is feasible to execute and likely to accomplish the assigned task. Ask, "Am I overlooking any relevant factors or contingencies?"

- Decide on a procedure to test. Ask, "Why do I think the procedure will work?"

Students should be informed that the most considered procedure selected might fail. They can learn from their failure and select a procedure that is likely to succeed on an ensuing attempt.

Students need to be given the opportunity and time to practice decision-making, and teachers should model the correct decision-making behavior for the students.

CAUTIONS AND COMMENTS

It would make little sense to try to teach students to employ decision-making tactics if they do not possess the readiness characteristics necessary to achieve the learning objectives to begin with. Attempts to do so will merely result in frustrated students. Additionally, trying to teach decision-making skills to students who do not want to learn or think they cannot learn may be fruitless.

The reviews of studies, and the individual studies included in these reviews, utilize terms such as metacognition, metamemory, self-monitoring, self-regulation, and other jargon instead of the term decision-making.

GENERALIZATION: ON DECISION-MAKING INSTRUCTION

Achievement of learning objectives is enhanced when students are shown how to use decision-making tactics to consider and select procedures to perform assigned tasks.

Supportive Research on Decision-Making Instruction
Total number of studies covered: 79

Groups of Studies

Additional instructional tactics are employed in the studies cited in the following reviews of research that are applicable to other generalizations and are presented in the appropriate chapters.

Author: Kucan & Beck (1997)

Students: Elementary and secondary

Learning: Reading comprehension

Instructional Tactics:

1. *The teacher models a comprehension monitoring and hypothesis formation strategy.*

   The following example was derived from Collins & Smith (1982) and cited and elaborated on by Kucan & Beck (1997): "The basic idea of the modeling stage is that the teacher reads a story or other text aloud, making comments while reading. . . . As the text is being read, the teacher interrupts maybe once or twice a paragraph to make comments about . . . different aspects of the comprehension process . . . such as generating hypotheses, citing evidence to support or refute a hypothesis, expressing confusion, or making critical comments about text content" (p. 279).

2. *The teacher elicits and guides student participation in the strategy activities.*

The following example was derived from a Kucan & Beck (1997) description of tactics used in studies conducted by Brown & Palincsar: "a teacher supports a small group of students in developing more sophisticated ways of interacting with the text by engaging them in a dialogue about the text that includes a consistent format of asking questions, identifying sections in the text that require clarification, summarizing the text, and making predictions about it" (p. 281).

3. *The students are left to utilize the strategies taught on their own while they read.*

In a study conducted by Miller (1985), students employed the following strategies while reading on their own: "students were taught the use of a set of statements such as: 'First, I am going to decide if this story has any problems.' . . . Second, as I read I will ask myself, 'Is there anything wrong with the story?' " (p. 282).

In a study conducted by Schunk & Rice (1985), students were taught the following strategy to answer questions about text they were assigned to read: Students were taught to verbalize statements such as "What do I have to do? (1) Read the question, (2) Read the story, and (3) Look for key words" (p. 283).

Findings: Use of the above tactics was found to lead to enhanced reading comprehension.

Groups of studies reviewed in this logical synthesis of research did not provide statistical evidence. However, many of the individual studies included in the logical synthesis of research do contain statistical evidence. In the event that a reader wishes to view this evidence, an extensive listing of the individual studies reviewed is provided in the reference list at the end of the chapter (the studies are identified by the symbol @).

Author: Dole et al. (1991)

Students: Elementary and secondary

Learning: Reading comprehension

Instructional Tactics:

• Students receive instruction to promote student-generated questions.

In an example from Singer & Donlan (1982), "students were taught to generate story-specific questions from a list of general questions. . . . 'Who are the main characters in the story? What does the leading character initiate?' to create their own more specific questions about the particular story they were reading" (p. 246).

Findings: Use of the above tactic was found to lead to enhanced reading comprehension.

Groups of studies reviewed in this logical synthesis of research did not provide statistical evidence. However, many of the individual studies included in the logical synthesis of research do contain statistical evidence. In the event that a reader wishes to view this evidence, an extensive listing of the individual studies reviewed is provided in the reference list (the studies are identified by the symbol $).

Author: Rosenshine & Meister (1994)

Students: Elementary and secondary

Learning: Reading comprehension

Instructional Tactics:

- The student receives instruction on and practices *comprehension-fostering* strategies, such as (1) question generation, (2) summarization, (3) prediction, and (4) clarification.
- The teacher models the strategies.
- Students are initially guided in their use of newly learned strategies.
- The teacher encourages students to initiate discussion and to react to other students' statements by (1) suggesting other questions, (2) elaborating on a summary, and (3) commenting on another's predictions.

Specific examples of the above tactics were not provided by the author. Many of the individual studies reviewed in this synthesis of research do provide specific information. These studies appear in the reference list (the studies are identified by the symbol !).

Findings: Use of the above tactics led to enhanced reading comprehension.

Author: Salomon & Perkins (1989)

Students: Elementary, secondary, and adults

Learning: Mathematics, science, and reading achievement

Instructional Tactics:

- Teach students to not jump to conclusions based on their first impulse as to what their correct decision should be.

- Teach students to examine provided information for task-relevant clues or underlying meanings that may help them in determining the correct course of action to take.

- Teach students to question whether or not something they have learned in some other content area, or related prior learning, might assist them in making the correct decision as to the correct procedure to apply to the current learning task.

  The following example is provided: "a student pondering a physics problem . . . might ask, 'Do I know anything from calculus that might address this?' "

- Teach students to question their understanding and their decisions on how to proceed.

- Allow students time to practice decision-making tactics.

Other than the one example cited, specific examples of the above tactics and statistical evidence were not provided by the author. Many of the individual studies reviewed in this synthesis of research do provide specific information. These studies appear in the reference list (the studies are identified by the symbol *).

Findings: Use of the above tactics was found to enhance achievement.

Author: Prawat (1989)

Students: Elementary, secondary, college

Learning: Mathematics, science, reading, literature, and social studies

Instructional Tactics:

- Teach students to examine how important concepts and procedures previously learned might be applied to a current assigned task.

- Teach students to analyze problems in terms of initial goals, available resources, problem limitations, and anticipated outcomes as an aid to deciding on procedures to employ.

- Require students to explain, elaborate, or defend a course of action they have decided on to others.

- Provide students with information on how known concepts or procedures applicable to one content area may be used in other content areas.

Findings: Use of the above tactics was found to enhance achievement.

Specific examples of the above tactics and statistical evidence were not provided by the author. Many of the individual studies reviewed in this synthesis of research do provide specific information. These studies appear in the reference list (the studies are identified by the symbol #).

Author: Rosenshine et al. (1996)

Students: Elementary, secondary, and college

Learning: Reading comprehension

Instructional Tactics: The following instructional tactics, reported as procedural prompts, were identified by the authors in their review of the research:

- *Signal Words*: Students are provided with a list of words for starting questions "such as who, what where, when, why, and how." Students are then taught how to use these words to generate questions about the to-be-learned material.

- *Generic question stems and generic questions*: Students are provided with a list of stems of generic questions or generic questions to aid them in the formulation of their own questions. The following examples are from studies as cited by Rosenshine et al. (1996).

    King (1989, 1990, 1992) used the following generic question stems: "How are . . . and . . . alike?" "What is the main idea of . . .?" "What are the strengths and weaknesses of . . .?" "How does . . . affect . . .?" "How does . . . tie in with what we have learned before?" "What is a new example of . . .?" "What conclusions can you draw about . . .?" "Why is it important that . . .?"

    Weiner (1978) provided students with the following list of generic questions: "How does this passage or chapter relate to what I already know about the topic?" "What is the main idea of this passage or chapter?" "What are five important ideas that the author develops that relate to the main idea?" "How does the author put the ideas in order?" "What are the key vocabulary words? Do I know what they all mean?" "What special things does the passage make me think about?"

- *Main Idea*: Students are taught to identify the main idea of a paragraph an to use the main idea to formulate questions.

Dreher & Gambrell (1985) suggested the following to students: (1) identify the main idea for each paragraph; (2) form questions which ask for new examples of the main idea; (3) if it is difficult to ask for a new instance, then write a question about a concept in the paragraph in a paraphrased form.

Nolte & Singer (1985) taught students to identify four elements of a story and to use the elements to generate questions. The four elements of a story they use were (1) setting, (2) main character, (3) characters' goal, and (4) obstacles. Students were taught that possible questions for the character element might be: "Who is the leading character?" "What action does the character initiate?" "What do you learn about the character from this action?"

Findings: Use of the above tactics was found to enhance reading comprehension.

Additional examples of the above tactics may be provided by the authors of the individual studies reviewed in this synthesis of research. These studies appear in the reference list (the studies are identified by the symbol &).

REFERENCE LIST

@Anderson, V. A., & Roit, M. (1993). Planning and implementing collaborative strategy instruction for delayed readers in grades 6–10. *The Elementary School Journal 94*(2), 121–137.

!$Andre, M. E. D. A., & Anderson, T. H. (1978–1979). The development and evaluation of a self-questioning study technique. *Reading Research Quarterly 14*, 605–623.

*Bandura, A., & Cervone, M. (1986). Differential engagement of self-reactive influences in cognitive motivation. *Organizational Behavior and Human Decision Processes 38*, 92–113.

$Baker, L., & Brown, A. L. (1984). Metacognitive skills and reading. In P. D. Pearson (Ed.), *Handbook of reading research* (pp. 353–394). New York: Longman.

$Baumann, J. F. (1984). The effectiveness of a direct instruction paradigm for teaching main idea comprehension. *Reading Research Quarterly 20*, 93–115.

$Baumann, J. F. (1986). The direct instruction of main idea comprehension ability. In J. F. Baumann (Ed.), *Teaching main idea comprehension* (pp. 133–178). Newark, DE: International Reading Association.

@Beck, I. L., McKeown, M. G., Worthy, J., Sandora, C. A., & Kucan, L. (1996). Questioning the author: A yearlong classroom implementation to engage students with text. *The Elementary School Journal 96*(4), 385–414.

@Bereiter, C., & Bird, M. (1985). Use of thinking aloud in identification and teaching of reading comprehension strategies. *Cognition and Instruction 2*(2), 131–156.

&Blaha, B. A. (1979). *The effects of answering self-generated questions on reading.* Unpublished doctoral dissertation, Boston University School of Education.

!&Brady, P. L. (1990). *Improving the reading comprehension of middle school students through reciprocal teaching and semantic mapping strategies.* Unpublished doctoral dissertation, University of Alaska.

#Bransford, J., Sherwood, R., Vye, N., & Rieser, J. (1986). Teaching thinking and problem solving. *American Psychologist 41*, 1078–1089.

#Brown, A. L. (1985). *Teaching students to think as they read: Implications for curriculum reform* (Reading Rep. No. 58). Champaign: University of Illinois, Center for the Study of Reading.

*Brown, A. L., Bransford, J. D., Ferrara, R. A., & Campione, J. C. (1983). Learning, remembering and understanding. In J. H. Flavell & E. M. Markman (Eds.), *Carmichael handbook of child psychology* (Vol. 3, pp. 515–529). New York: Wiley.

@Brown, A. L., & Campione, J. C. (1994). Guided discovery in a community of learners. In K. McGilly (Ed.), *Classroom lessons: Integrating cognitive theory and classroom practice* (pp. 229–270). Cambridge, MA: MIT Press.

*Brown, A. L., Campione, J. C., & Day, J. D. (1981). Learning to learn: On training students to learn from texts. *Educational Researcher 10*, 14–21.

@Brown, A. L., & Palincsar, A. S. (1982). Inducing strategic learning from texts by means of informed, self-control training. *Topics in Learning and Learning Disabilities 2*(1), 1–17.

$Brown, A. L., & Palincsar, A. S. (1985). *Reciprocal teaching of comprehension strategies:*

A natural history of one program to enhance learning (Tech. Rep. No. 334). Urbana: University of Illinois, Center for the Study of Reading.

@Brown, A. L., & Palincsar, A. S. (1989). Guided, cooperative learning and individual knowledge acquisition. In L. B. Resnick (Ed.), *Knowing, learning, and instruction: Essays in honor of Robert Glaser* (pp. 393–451). Hillsdale, NJ: Erlbaum.

$Brown, A. L., Palincsar, A. S., & Armbruster, B. B. (1984). Instructing comprehension-fostering activities in interactive learning situations. In H. Mandl, N. L. Stein, & T. Trabasso (Eds.), *Learning and comprehension of text* (pp. 255–286). Hillsdale, NJ: Erlbaum.

@Chi, M. T. H., de Leeuw, N., Chiu, M., & LaVancher, C. (1994). Eliciting self-explanations. *Cognitive Science 18*(3), 439–477.

!Cohen, R. (1983). Self-generated questions as an aid to reading comprehension. *The Reading Teacher 36*, 770–775.

&Cohen, R. (1983). Students generate questions as an aid to reading comprehension. *The Reading Teacher 36*, 770–775.

Collins, R., & Smith, E. E. (1982). Teaching the process of reading comprehension. In D. K. Detterman & R. J. Sternberg (Eds.), *How and how much can intelligence be increased* (pp. 173–185). Norwood, NJ: Ablex.

$Craik, F. I. M., & Lockhart, R. S. (1972). Levels of processing: A framework for memory research. *Journal of Verbal Learning and Verbal Behavior 11*, 671–684.

$Cunningham, J. W., & Moore, D. W. (1986). The confused world of main idea. In J. B. Baumann (Ed.), *Teaching main idea comprehension* (pp. 1–17). Newark, DE: International Reading Association.

!&Davey, B., & McBride, S. (1986). Effects of question-generation on reading comprehension. *Journal of Educational Psychology 78*, 256–262.

!&Dermody, M. (1988, February). *Metacognitive strategies for development of reading comprehension for younger children.* Paper presented at the annual meeting of the American Association of Colleges for Teacher Education, New Orleans, LA.

Dole, J. A., Duffy, G. G., Roehler, L. R., & Pearson, P. D. (1991). Moving from the old to the new: Research on reading comprehension instruction. *Review of Educational Research 61*(2), 239–264.

&Dreher, M. J., & Gambrell, L. B. (1985). Teaching children to use a self-questioning strategy for studying expository text. *Reading Improvement 22*, 2–7.

!Fischer-Galbert, J. L. (1989). *An experimental study of reciprocal teaching of expository text with third, fourth, and fifth grade students enrolled in Chapter 1 Reading.* Unpublished doctoral dissertation, Ball State University, Muncie, IN.

#Hasselhorn, M., & Korkel, J. (1986). Metacognitive versus traditional reading instructions: The mediating role of domain-specific knowledge on children's text processing. *Human Learning 5*, 75–90.

&Helfeldt, J. P., & Lalik, R. (1976). Reciprocal student–teacher questioning. *The Reading Teacher 33*, 283–287.

!Jones, M. P. (1987). *Effects of reciprocal teaching method on third graders' decoding and comprehension abilities.* Unpublished doctoral dissertation, Texas A&M University.

*Kane, J. M., & Anderson, R. C. (1978). Depth of processing and inference effects in the learning and remembering of sentences. *Journal of Educational Psychology 70*, 626–635.

*Kerr, B. (1973). Processing demands during mental operations. *Memory & Cognition 1*, 401–412.

&King, A. (1989). Effects of self-questioning training on college students' comprehension of lectures. *Contemporary Educational Psychology 14*, 366–381.

&King, A. (1990). Improving lecture comprehension: Effects of a metacognitive strategy. *Applied Educational Psychology 5*, 331–346.

&King, A. (1992). Comparison of self-questioning, summarizing, and notetaking-review as strategies for learning from lectures. *American Educational Research Journal 29*, 303–325.

*Kintsch, W. (1977). *Memory and cognition.* New York: Wiley.

Kucan, L., & Beck, I. L. (1997). Thinking aloud and reading comprehension research: Inquiry, instruction, and social interaction. *Review of Educational Research 67*(3), 271–299.

!&Labercane, G., & Battle, J. (1987). Cognitive processing strategies, self-esteem, and reading comprehension of learning disabled students. *Journal of Special Education 11*, 167–185.

*Langer, E. J. (1985). Playing the middle against both ends: The influence of adult cognitive activity as a model for cognitive activity in childhood and old age. In S. R. Yussen (Ed.), *The development of reflection* (pp. 267–285). New York: Academic Press.

*Langer, E. J., & Imber, L. E. (1979). When practice makes imperfect: Debilitating effects of overlearning. *Journal of Personality and Social Psychology 37*, 2014–2024.

#Lawson, J. (1984). Being executive about metacognition. In J. R. Kirby (Ed.), *Cognitive strategies and educational performance* (pp. 89–109). New York: Academic Press.

!Levin, M. C. (1989). *An experimental investigation of reciprocal teaching and informed strategies for learning taught to learning-disabled intermediate school learners.* Unpublished doctoral dissertation, Teachers College, Columbia University.

!&Lonberger, R. B. (1988). *The effects of training in a self-generated learning strategy on the prose processing abilities of fourth and sixth graders.* Unpublished doctoral dissertation, State University of New York at Buffalo.

!&Lysybchuk, L., Pressley, M., & Vye, G. (1990). Reciprocal instruction improves reading comprehension performance in poor grade school comprehenders. *Elementary School Journal 40*, 471–484.

&MacGregor, S. K. (1988). Use of self-questioning with a computer-mediated text system and measures of reading performance. *Journal of Reading Behavior 20*, 131–148.

#&Manzo, A. V. (1969). *Improving reading comprehension through reciprocal teaching.* Unpublished doctoral dissertation, Syracuse University.

@Miller, G. E. (1985). The effects of general and specific self-instruction training on children's comprehension monitoring performances during reading. *Reading Research Quarterly 20*(5), 616–628.

&Nolte, R. Y., & Singer, H. (1985). Active comprehension: Teaching a process of reading comprehension and its effects on reading achievement. *The Reading Teacher 39*, 24–31.

!Padron, Y. N. (1985). *Utilizing cognitive reading strategies to improve English reading comprehension of Spanish-speaking bilingual students.* Unpublished doctoral dissertation, University of Houston.

!&Palinscar, A. S. (1987, April). *Collaboration for collaborative learning of text comprehension.* Paper presented at the annual meeting of the American Educational Research Association, Washington, DC.

#!&Palinscar, A. S., & Brown, A. L. (1984). Reciprocal teaching of comprehension-fostering and comprehension-monitoring activities. *Cognition and Instruction 2*, 117–175.

@Palinscar, A. S., & Brown, A. L. (1988). Teaching and practicing thinking skills to promote comprehension in the context of group problem solving. *Remedial and Special Education 9*(1), 53–59.

@Palinscar, A. S., & Klenk, L. (1992). Fostering literacy learning in supportive contexts. *Journal of Learning Disabilities 25*(4), 211–225, 229.

@Palinscar, A. S., & Klenk, L. (1993). Third invited response: Broader visions encompassing literacy, learners, and contexts. *Remedial and Special Education 14*(4), 19–25.

*Pascual-Leone, J. (1984). Attention, dialectic and mental effort: Toward an organismic theory of life stages. In M. L. Commons, F. A. Richards, & C. Armon (Eds.), *Beyond formal operations* (pp. 182–215). New York: Praeger.

#Petrie, H. G. (1976). Do you see what I see? The epistemology of interdisciplinary inquiry. *Educational Researcher 5*(2), 9–15.

Prawat, R. S. (1989). Promotion access to knowledge, strategy, and disposition in students: A research synthesis. *Review of Educational Research 59*(1), 1–41.

*Pressley, M. (1986). The relevance of the good strategy user to the teaching of mathematics. *Educational Psychologist 21*, 139–162.

!Rich, R. Z. (1989). *The effects of training adult poor readers to use text comprehension strategies.* Unpublished doctoral dissertation, Teachers College, Columbia University.

!Risko, V. J., & Feldman, N. (1986). Teaching young remedial readers to use generate questions as they read. *Reading Horizons 27*, 54–64.

&Ritchie, P. (1985). The effects of instruction in main idea and question generation. *Reading Canada Lecture 3*, 139–146.

Rosenshine, B., & Meister, C. (1994). Reciprocal teaching: A review of the research. *Review of Educational Research 64*(4), 479–530.

Rosenshine, B., Meister, C., & Chapman, S. (1996). Teaching students to generate questions: A review of intervention studies. *Review of Educational Research 66*(2), 181–221.

!Rush, R. T., & Milburn, J. L. (1988, November). *The effects of reciprocal teaching on self-regulation of reading comprehension in a postsecondary technical school program.* Paper presented at the annual meeting of the National Reading Conference, Tucson, AZ.

Salomon, G., & Globerson, T. (1987). Skill is not enough: The role of mindfulness in learning and transfer. *International Journal of Research in Education 11*, 623–638.

Salomon, G., & Perkins, D. N. (1989). Rocky roads to transfer: Rethinking mechanisms of a neglected phenomenon. *Educational Psychologist 24*(2), 113–142.

@Schmitt, M. C. (1988). The effects of an elaborated directed reading activity on the metacomprehension skills of third graders. In J. E. Readance & R. S. Baldwin (Eds.), *Dialogues in literacy research* (thirty-seventh yearbook of the National Reading Conference, pp. 167–181). Chicago: National Reading Conference.

@Schunk, D. H., & Rice, J. M. (1985). Verbalization of comprehension strategies: Effects on children's achievement outcomes. *Human Learning 4*(1), 1–10.

&Short, E. J., & Ryan, E. B. (1984). Metacognitive differences between skilled and less-skilled readers: Remediating deficits through story grammar and attribution training. *Journal of Educational Psychology 76*, 225–235.

!Shortland-Jones, B. (1986). *The development and testing of an instructional strategy for improving reading comprehension based on schema and metacognitive theories.* Unpublished doctoral dissertation, University of Oregon.

&Simpson, P. S. (1989). *The effects of direct training in active comprehension on reading achievement, self-concepts, and reading attitudes of at-risk sixth grade students.* Unpublished doctoral dissertation, Texas Tech University.

$Singer, H., & Dolan, D. (1982). Active comprehension: Problem solving schema with question generation for comprehension of complex short stories. *Reading Research Quarterly 17*, 166–186.

&Smith, N. J. (1977). *The effects of training teachers to teach students at different reading ability levels to formulate three types of questions on reading comprehension and question generation ability.* Unpublished doctoral dissertation, University of Georgia.

!&Taylor, B. M., & Frye, B. J. (1992). Comprehension strategy instruction in the intermediate grades. *Reading Research and Instruction 92*, 39–48.

@Trabasso, T., & Magliano, J. P. (1996). How do children understand what they read and what can we do to help them? In M. Graves, P. van den Broek, & B. Taylor (Eds.), *The first r: A right of all children* (pp. 160–188). New York: Teachers College Press.

&Weiner, C. J. (1978). *The effect of training in questioning and student question-generation on reading achievement.* Paper presented at the Annual Meeting of the American Educational Research Association, Toronto, Ontario, Canada.

$Williams, J. P. (1986a). Extracting information from text. In J. A. Niles & R. V. Lalik (Eds.), *Solving problems in literacy: Learners, teachers, and researchers* (thirty-fifth yearbook of the National Reading Conference, pp. 11–29). Rochester, NY: National Reading Conference.

$Williams, J. P. (1986b). Research and instructional development on main idea skills. In J. F. Baumann (Ed.), *Teaching main idea comprehension* (pp. 73–95). Newark, DE: International Reading Association.

!&Williamson, R. A. (1989). *The effects of reciprocal teaching on student performance gains in third grade basal reading instructions.* Unpublished doctoral dissertation, Texas A&M University.

$Winigrad, P. N., & Bridge, C. A. (1986). The comprehension of important information in written prose. In J. B. Baumann (Ed.), *Teaching main idea comprehension* (pp. 18–48). Newark, DE: International Reading Association.

!&Wong, B. Y. L., & Jones, W. (1982). Increasing metacomprehension in learning disabled and normally achieving students through self-questioning training. *Learning Disability Quarterly 5*, 228–239.

II

The Time Dimension

In addition to the effective instructional strategies in Part I, there are strategies that are concerned with time allocation and utilization. Additionally, many of the instructional strategies in Part I that have an effect on achievement exclusive of the time dimension, such as those associated with clarity of communication, class size, and student readiness, also have an effect on time allocation and utilization. Academic achievement is strongly affected by the amount of time spent on teaching and learning. The dimension must be taken into account and managed wisely if learning is to be enhanced. Three chapters on time allocation and management follow.

The first is "Providing Ample Learning Time." Ample learning time needs to be estimated during instructional planning. And if students are unable to learn in the time allocated, additional learning time needs to be allocated until students are able to learn. The evidence shows that all but the most psychologically handicapped students can learn everything they are assigned to learn through high school. The primary difference between one student and another is the amount of time and instruction it takes for them to learn it (Bloom 1968; Block & Anderson 1975).

The second chapter, "Keeping Students on Task," deals with a related but slightly different time issue. Although sufficient time may be allotted for students to learn, they must stay focused on assigned learning tasks in order to learn. If students do not attend to assigned learning tasks, they can't possibly learn to perform them. Consequently, every effort must be made to keep students focused on tasks they are assigned to learn.

The third chapter, "Providing Ample Teaching Time," deals with the third time dimension pertinent to learning. Student learning is substantially affected by the amount of time they are taught, as opposed to learning on their own. That is, student learning is enhanced when sufficient time is spent guiding and facilitating their performance of learning tasks.

Although ample learning time, time on task, and teaching time are not independent of each other, it is beneficial to conceive of them as separate but related time factors that have a profound impact on learning. The following three chapters should clarify their relationship and their importance to learning.

13

Providing Ample Learning Time

INTRODUCTION

Students must be allowed the time necessary to correctly perform tasks they are assigned if they are to achieve the desired level of performance. Students need time to contemplate their performance beforehand, to test the behaviors they hypothesize will result in correct performance, to evaluate the results of their performance, and to make refinements if need be. Students need time for trial and error. Excessively restricting the amount of time allowed for the performance of assigned tasks may lead to unnecessary student failure. Additionally, instructional planners and teachers, not students, are responsible for determining what is adequate time for the purpose of achieving the desired level of performance on tasks they are assigned to perform.

STUDENT BENEFICIARIES

The evidence indicates that allowing ample time to perform tasks correctly enhances the academic achievement of students in kindergarten, elementary, secondary, college, and adult learning classrooms. Moreover, academic achievement was improved in a wide range of content areas. No evidence could be found to suggest that allowing ample time for task performance should not be a priority in all subject areas for all types of students.

LEARNING ACHIEVED

Achievement in the content areas of mathematics, history, foreign languages, English, reading, social sciences, sciences, social studies, business, and occupational areas is enhanced when ample time is allocated for the performance of tasks.

In studies reviewed, allowing ample time for the performance of tasks was positively related to student achievement.

INSTRUCTIONAL TACTICS

The evidence well supports the need to allow students ample time for the performance of tasks. The following tactics are derived from studies that demonstrate the need to allow students ample time for the performance of tasks. Discretion has been used to interpret and reduce overlap in tactics used in different studies and to elaborate tactics.

Tactics employed are:

- Sufficient time should be allocated to permit students to perform assigned tasks correctly on an initial attempt.
- In the event a student does not perform a task correctly during the original allocated time, the student should be allowed additional time to correctly perform the task.
- Ample time for students to perform assigned tasks needs to be planned for all assigned tasks, such as in class learning activities, homework, library projects, and laboratory activities.

Elaborations of the above summary of tactics can be obtained from reading the studies that are to follow. To be most effective, the instructional tactics need to be integrated into the particular instructional program being planned or presently in use.

CAUTIONS AND COMMENTS

Allocation of time for performance of assigned tasks should be based on the instructional planner's or the teacher's assessment of the ability of most of the students, not all of the students. Additional time should be afforded those students who cannot master an assigned task during the time most of the students could be expected to perform a task. Allocation of too much time in an attempt to accommodate all students may unnecessarily slow the progress of other students.

Although some research suggests a positive relationship between achievement and homework, insufficient research has been conducted, either in this country or internationally, to support this conclusively.

GENERALIZATION: ON AMPLE LEARNING TIME

Achievement of learning objectives is enhanced when students are given ample time to perform assigned tasks.

Supportive Research on Ample Learning Time
Total number of studies covered: 168

Groups of Studies

Author: Anderson (1985)

Students: Elementary and secondary

Learning: Achievement

Instructional Tactics:

- In the event a student does not perform a task correctly during the original allocated time, the student will be allowed additional time to correctly perform the task.
- Additional time may be either inside or outside the classroom, depending on the teacher's assessment.

Other instructional tactics are employed in these studies that are applicable to other generalizations and will be presented in the appropriate chapters.

Findings: The preceding instructional tactics were found to be associated with greater achievement. Additionally, it has been found that these tactics result in as high as 80% of the students mastering a learning task for which only 20% of the students achieve a level of mastery in a more traditional time allocation. Allocation of additional time to perform assigned tasks was *not* found to be related to an increase in off-task behavior.

Groups of studies reviewed in this logical synthesis of research did not provide statistical evidence. However, many of the individual studies included in the logical synthesis of research do contain statistical evidence. In the event that a reader wishes to view this evidence, an extensive listing of the individual studies reviewed is provided in the reference list at the end of the chapter (the studies are identified by the symbol %).

Author: Marliave & Filby (1985)

Students: Elementary and secondary

Learning: Reading and mathematics achievement

Instructional Tactics:

- The pace should be appropriate to the student and the subject matter.
- Students who do not perform a task correctly the first time are allowed additional time to correctly perform the task.

Other instructional tactics are employed in these studies that are applicable to other generalizations and will be presented in the appropriate chapters.

Findings: The preceding instructional tactics were found to be related to greater student achievement.

Groups of studies reviewed in this logical synthesis of research did not provide statistical evidence.

However, many of the individual studies included in the logical synthesis of research do contain statistical evidence. In the event that a reader wishes to view this evidence, an extensive listing of the individual studies reviewed is provided in the reference list (the studies are identified by the symbol !).

Author: Anderson (1994)

Students: Kindergarten, elementary, secondary, college, and other adult students

Learning: Achievement

Instructional Tactics: The following tactics associated with readiness and mastery learning are also presented in Bloom (1985), Block (1980), and others. Other tactics associated with Mastery Learning are applicable to other generalizations and are covered in the appropriate chapters.

- In the event a student does not perform a task correctly during the original allocated time, the student will be allowed additional time to correctly perform the task.

Findings: Positive achievement gains associated with Mastery Learning were seen in 90% of the studies reviewed in the seven meta-analyses.

Individual studies analyzed by these meta-analyses are identified in the reference list by the following symbols:

Kulik et al. (1990a) *

Kulik et al. (1990b) #

Slavin (1990) @

Guskey & Pigott (1988) $

Guskey & Gates (1986) &

Block & Burns (1976) +

Individual Studies

Author: Gettinger (1984)

Students: Grades 4 and 5

Learning: Reading and spelling achievement

Instructional Tactics:

- One group of students was told to work on a task until they had achieved 100% accuracy.
- A second group of students was told the goal was to achieve 100% accuracy and allowed to determine the time they needed to work on the task on their own.

Findings: The group of students that worked on the learning tasks until they achieved 100% accuracy scored an average 12.49 points higher on a spelling retention test and 12.80 points higher on a reading test than the group that was allowed to determine how much time they should spend on the assigned tasks.

REFERENCE LIST

*+Abraham, F. J., & Newton, J. M (1974). *The interview technique as a personalized system of instruction for economics: The Oregon experience*. Paper presented at the National Conference on Personalized Instruction in Higher Education, Washington, DC.

$Anania, J. (1981). *The effects of quality of instruction on the cognitive and affective learning of students*. Unpublished doctoral dissertation, University of Chicago.

+Anderson, L. W. (1973). *Time and school learning*. Unpublished doctoral dissertation, University of Chicago.

$&Anderson, L. W. (1975a). *Time to criterion: An experimental study*. Paper presented at the annual meeting of the American Educational Research Association, Washington, DC. (ERIC Document Reproduction Service No. ED 108 006)

*$&Anderson, L. W. (1975b). Student involvement in learning and school achievement. *California Journal of Educational Research 26*, 53–62.

*$&+Anderson, L. W. (1976). An empirical investigation of individual differences in time to learn. *Journal of Educational Psychology 68*, 226–233.

Anderson, L. W. (1985). Time and timing. In C. W. Fisher & D. C. Berliner (Eds.), *Perspectives on instructional time* (pp. 157–168). White Plains, NY: Longman.

*#@$&Anderson, L. W., Scott, C., & Hutlock, N. (1976, April). *The effects of a mastery learning program on selected cognitive, affective, and ecological variables in grades 1 through 6*. Paper presented at the annual meeting of the American Educational Research Association, San Francisco.

+Anderson, O. T., & Artman, R. A. (1972). A self-paced independent study, introductory physics sequence-description and evaluation. *American Journal of Physics 40*, 1737–1742.

Anderson, S. A. (1994). *Synthesis of research on mastery learning*. (Information Analysis). (ERIC Document Reproduction Service No. ED 382 567)

%Arlin, M., & Webster, J. (1983). Time costs of mastery learning. *Journal of Educational Psychology 75*, 187–195.

*$&Arlin, M., & Westbury, I. (1976). The leveling effect of teacher pacing on science content mastery. *Journal of Research on Science Teaching 13*, 213–219.

*Austin, S. M., & Gilbert, K. E. (1973). Student performance in a Keller-Plan course in introductory electricity and magnetism. *American Journal of Physics 41*, 12–18.

*Badia, P., Stutts, C., & Harsh, J. (1978). Do methods of instruction and measures of different abilities and study habits interact? In J. G. Sherman, R. S. Ruskin, & R. M. Lazar (Eds.), *Personalized instruction in education today* (pp. 113–128). San Francisco: San Francisco Press.

!Barr, R. (1974). Instructional pace differences and their effect on reading acquisition. *Reading Research Quarterly 9*, 526–554.

!Barr, R. (1975). How children are taught to read: Grouping and pacing. *School Review 83*, 479–498.

*Benson, J. S., & Yeany, R. H. (1980, April). *Generalizability of diagnostic-prescriptive teaching strategies across student locus of control and multiple instructional units.* Paper presented at the annual meeting of the American Educational Research association, Boston. (ERIC Document Reproduction Service No. 187 534)

*+Billings, D. B. (1974). PSI versus the lecture course in the principles of economics: a quasi-controlled experiment. In R. S. Ruskin & S. F. Bono (Eds.), *Personalized instruction in higher education* (pp. 30–37). Washington, DC: Center for Personalized Instruction.

*$Blackburn, K. T., & Nelson, D. (1985, April). *Differences between a group using a traditional format with mastery learning and a group using a traditional format only in developmental mathematics courses at the university level: Implications for teacher education programs.* Paper presented at the annual meeting of the American Educational Research Association, Chicago. (ERIC Document Reproduction Service No. ED 258 948)

*Blasingame, J. W. (1975). Student attitude and performance in a personalized system of instruction course in business administration—Correlates performance with personality traits. *Dissertation Abstracts International 36*, 3840 (University Microfilms No. 75-2834).

$&+Block, J. H. (1972). Student learning and the setting of mastery performance standards. *Educational Horizons 50*, 183–191.

+Block, J. H. (1973). *Mastery performance standards and student learning.* Unpublished study, University of California, Santa Barbara.

Block, J. H. (1980). Success rate. In C. Denham & A. Lieberman (Eds.), *Time to learn* (pp. 95–106). Washington, DC: U.S. Government Printing Office.

Block, J. H. & Anderson, L. W. (1975). *Mastery learning in classroom instruction.* New York: Macmillan.

Block, J. H., & Burns, R. B. (1976). Mastery learning. In L. Schulman (Ed.), *Review of research in education* (Vol. 4, pp. 3–49). Itasca, IL: F. E. Peacock.

$+Block, J. H., & Tierney, M. (1974). An exploration of two correction procedures used in mastery learning approaches to instruction. *Journal of Educational Psychology 66*, 962–967.

Bloom, B. S. (1968). Learning for mastery. (UCLA-CSEIP) *Evaluation Comment 1*(2), 1–12.

Bloom, B. S. (1985). Learning for mastery. In C. W. Fisher & D. C. Berliner (Eds.), *Perspectives on instructional time.* White Plains, NY: Longman.

*+Born, D. G., & Davis, M. L. (1974). Amount and distribution of study in a personalized instruction course and in a lecture course. *Journal of Applied Behavior Analysis 7*, 365–375.

*+Born, D. G., Gledhill, S. M., & Davis, M. L. (1972). Examination performance in lecture-

discussion and personalized instruction courses. *Journal of Applied Behavior Analysis 5*, 33–43.

*+Breland, N. S., & Smith, M. P. (1974). A comparison of PSI and traditional methods of instruction for teaching introduction to psychology. In R. S. Ruskin & S. F. Bono (Eds.), *Personalized instruction in higher education* (pp. 21–25). Washington, DC: Center for Personalized Instruction.

*$Bryant, N. D., Payne, H. R., & Gettinger, M. (1982). Applying the mastery model to sight word instruction for disabled readers. *Journal of Experimental Education 50*, 116–121.

$Burke, A. (1983). *Students' potential for learning contrasted under tutorial and group approaches to instruction.* Unpublished doctoral dissertation, University of Chicago.

$&+Burrows, C. K., & Okey, J. R. (1975). *The effects of a mastery learning strategy on achievement.* Paper presented at the annual meeting of the American Educational Research Association, Washington, DC.

*#@$Cabezon, E. (1984). *The effects of marked changes in student achievement patterns on the students, their teachers, and their parents: The Chilean case.* Unpublished doctoral dissertation, University of Chicago.

$Chiappetta, E. L., & McBride, J. W. (1980). Exploring the effects of general remediation on ninth-graders' achievement of the mole concept. *Science Education 6*, 609–614.

*$Clark, C. P., Guskey, T. P., & Benninga, J. S. (1983). The effectiveness of mastery learning strategies in undergraduate education courses. *Journal of Educational Research 76*, 210–214.

*Clark, S. G. (1975). An innovation for introductory sociology: Personalized system of instruction. In J. M. Johnston (Ed.), *Behavior research and technology in higher education* (pp. 117–124). Springfield, IL: Charles C. Thomas.

*+Coldeway, D. O., Santowski, M., O'Brien, R., & Lagowski, V. (1975). Comparison of small group contingency management with the personalized system of instruction and the lecture system. In J. M. Johnston (Ed.), *Research and technology in college and university teaching* (pp. 215–224). Gainesville: University of Florida.

*+Cole, C., Martin, S., & Vincent, J. (1975). A comparison of two teaching formats at the college level. In J. M. Johnston (Ed.), *Behavior research and technology in higher education* (pp. 61–74). Springfield, IL: Charles C. Thomas.

*Condo, P. (1974, April). *The analysis and evaluation of a self-paced course in calculus.* Paper presented at the National Conference on Personalized Instruction in Higher Education, Washington, DC.

*+Cooper, J. L., & Greiner, J. M. (1971). Contingency management in an introductory psychology course produces better retention. *Psychological Record 21*, 391–400.

*Corey, J. R., & McMichael, J. S. (1974). Retention in a PSI introductory psychology course. In J. G. Sherman (Ed.), *PSI germinal papers* (pp. 17–19). Washington, DC: Center for Personalized Instruction.

+Corey, J. R., McMichael, J. S., & Tremont, P. J. (1970, April). *Long-term effects of personalized instruction in an introductory psychology course.* Paper presented at the meeting of the Eastern Psychology Association, Atlantic City.

*Cote, J. D. (1976). Biology by PSI in a community college. In B. A. Green, Jr. (Ed.), *Personalized instruction in higher education* (pp. 67–72). Washington, DC: Center for Personalized Instruction.

*Cross, M. Z., & Semb, G. (1976). An analysis of the effects of personalized instruction on students at different initial performance levels in an introductory college nutrition course. *Journal of Personalized Instruction 1*, 47–50.

*Decker, D. F. (1976). *Teaching to achieve learning mastery by using retesting techniques.* (ERIC Document Reproduction Service No. ED 133 002)

$Denton, W. L., Ory, J. C., Glassnap, D. R., & Poggio, J. P. (1976). *Grade expectations within a mastery learning strategy.* Paper presented at the annual meeting of the American Educational Research Association, San Francisco. (ERIC Document Reproduction Service No. ED 126 105).

*$Dillashaw, F. G., & Okey, J. R. (1983). Effects of a modified mastery learning strategy on achievement, attitudes, and on-task behavior of high school chemistry students. *Journal of Research in Science Teaching 20*, 203–211.

$Duby, P. B. (1981). *Attributions and attribution change: Effects of a mastery learning instructional approach.* Paper presented at the annual meeting of the American Educational Research Association, Los Angeles. (ERIC Document Reproduction Service No. ED 200 640)

*#@Fagan, J. S. (1976). Mastery learning: The relationship of mastery procedures and aptitude to the achievement and retention of transportation-environment concepts by seventh grade students. *Dissertation Abstracts International 36*, 5981. (University Microfilms No. 76-6402)

*Fehlen, J. E. (1976). Mastery learning techniques in the traditional classroom setting. *School Science and Mathematics 76*, 241–245.

*Fernald, P. S., & DuNann, D. H. (1975). Effects of Individualized instruction upon low- and high-achieving students' study behavior and students' evaluation of mastery. *Journal of Experimental Education 43*, 27–34.

$&+Fiel, R. L., & Okey, J. R. (1974). The effects of formative evaluation and remediation on mastery of intellectual skill. *Journal of Educational Research 68*, 253–255.

%Fisher, C. W., Berliner, D. C., Filby, N. N., Marliave, R., Cahen, L. S., & Dishaw, M. M. (1980). Teaching behaviors, academic learning time, and student achievement: An overview. In C. Denham & A. Lieberman (Eds.), *Time to learn* (pp. 7–32). Washington, DC: U.S. Government Printing Office.

%Fitzpatrick, K. A. (1981). *An investigation of secondary classroom material strategies for increasing student academic engaged time.* Doctoral dissertation, University of Illinois at Urbana–Champaign.

%Fitzpatrick, K. A. (1982). *The effect of a secondary classroom management training program on teacher and student behavior.* Paper presented at the annual meeting of the American Educational Research Association, New York.

$&Fitzpatrick, K. A. (1985, April). *Group-based mastery learning: A Robin Hood approach to instruction?* Paper presented at the annual meeting of the American Educational Research Association, Chicago.

$&Frederick, W., & Walberg, H. (1979). *Learning as a function of time.* Paper presented at the annual meeting of the American Educational Research Association, San Francisco.

Gettinger, M. (1984). Achievement as a function of time spent in learning and time needed for learning. *American Educational Research Journal 21*(3), 617–628.

+Glassnapp, D. R., Poggio, J. P., & Ory, J. C. (1975, March–April). *Cognitive and affective consequences of mastery and non-mastery instructional strategies.* Paper presented at the annual meeting of the American Educational Research Association, Washington, DC.

*Goldwater, B. C., & Acker, L. E. (1975). Instructor-paced, mass-testing for mastery performance in an introductory psychology course. *Teaching of Psychology 2*, 152–155.

!Good, T., Ebmeier, H., & Beckerman, T. (1978). Curriculum pacing: Some empirical data in mathematics. *Journal of Curriculum Studies 10*, 75–81.

*Gregory, I., Smeltzer, D. J., Knopp, W., & Gardner, M. (1976). *Teaching of psychiatry by PSI: Impact on National Board Examination scores.* Unpublished manuscript, Ohio State University, Columbus.

*$&Guskey, T. R. (1982). The effects of staff development on teachers' perceptions about effective teaching. *Journal of Educational Research 78*, 378–381.

*$&Guskey, T. R. (1984). The influence of changes in instructional effectiveness upon the affective characteristics of teachers. *American Educational Research Journal 21*, 245–259.

$Guskey, T. R. (1985). The effects of staff development on teachers' perceptions about effective teaching. *Journal of Educational Research 79*, 378–381.

*$Guskey, T. R., Benninga, J. S., & Clark, C. B. (1984). Mastery learning and students' attributions at the college level. *Research in Higher Education 20*, 491–498.

Guskey, T. R., & Gates, S. L. (1986). Synthesis of research on the effects of mastery learning in elementary and secondary classrooms. *Educational Leadership 33*(8), 73–80.

*$Guskey, T. R., & Monsaas, J. A. (1979). Mastery learning: A model for academic success in urban junior colleges. *Research in Higher Education 11*, 263–274.

Guskey, T. R., & Pigott,T. D. (1988). Research on group-based mastery learning programs: A meta-analysis. *Journal of Educational Research 81*(4), 197–216.

*Hardin, L. D. (1977). A study of the influence of a physics personalized system of instruction versus lecture on cognitive reasoning, achievement, attitudes and critical thinking. *Dissertation Abstracts International 38*, 4711A–4712A. (University Microfilms No. 77-30826)

*Hecht, L. W. (1980, April). *Stalking mastery learning in its natural habitat.* Paper presented at the annual meeting of the American Educational Research Association, Boston.

*Heffley, P. D. (1974). The implementation of the personalized system of instruction in the freshman chemistry course at Censius College. In R. S. Ruskin & S. F. Bono (Eds.), *Personalized instruction in higher education* (pp. 140–145). Washington, DC: Center for Personalized Instruction.

*Herring, B. G. (1975, December). *Cataloguing and classification.* Austin: University of Texas.

*Herring, B. G. (1977). *The written PSI study guide in a non-PSI course.* Austin: University of Texas.

*Herrmann, T. (1984, August). *TELIDON as an enhancer of student interest and performance.* Paper presented at the annual meeting of the American Psychological Association, Toronto. (ERIC Document Reproduction Service No. ED 251 004)

*Hindman, C. D. (1974). Evaluation of three programming techniques in introductory psychology courses. In R. S. Ruskin & S. F. Bono (Eds.), *Personalized instruction in higher education* (pp. 38–42). Washington, DC: Center for Personalized Instruction.

*Honeycutt, J. K. (1974, April). *The effect of computer managed instruction on content learning of undergraduate students.* Paper presented at the annual meeting of the American Educational Research Association, Chicago. (ERIC Document Reproduction Service No. ED 089 682)

*Hymel, G. M. (1974). *An investigation of John B. Carrol's model of school learning as a theoretical basis for the organizational structuring of schools* (Final Report, NIE Project No. 3-1359). University of New Orleans, New Orleans, LA.

*Hymel, G. M., & Mathews, G. (1980). Effects of a mastery approach on social studies achievement and unit evaluation. *Southern Journal of Educational Research 14*, 191–204.

*Jackman, L. E. (1982). Evaluation of a modified Keller method in a biochemistry laboratory course. *Journal of Chemical Education 59*, 225–227.

*Jacko, E. J. (1974). Lecture instruction versus a personalized system of instruction: Effects on individuals with differing achievement anxiety and academic achievement. *Dissertation Abstracts International 35*, 3521. (University Microfilms No. AAD 74-27211)

+Johnston, J. M., & Pennypacker, H. S. (1971). A behavioral approach to college teaching. *American Psychologist 26*, 219–244.

*#@$&Jones, B. F., Monsaas, J. A., & Katims, M. (1979, April). *Improving reading comprehension: Embedding diverse learning strategies within a mastery learning instructional framework.* Paper presented at the annual meeting of the American Educational Research Association, San Francisco. (ERIC Document Reproduction Service No. ED 170 698)

$+Jones, E. L., Gordon, H. A., & Stectman, G. L. (1975). *Mastery learning: A strategy for academic success in a community college.* Los Angeles: ERIC Clearinghouse for Junior Colleges. (ERIC Document Reproduction Service No. ED 115 315)

+Jones, F. G. (1974). *The effects of mastery and aptitude on learning, retention, and time.* Unpublished doctoral dissertation, University of Georgia.

+Karlin, B. M. (1972). The Keller method of instruction compared to the traditional method of instruction in a Lafayette College history course. Unpublished paper, Lafayette College, Lafayette, PA.

*#@Katims, M., Smith, J. K., Steele, C., & Wick, J. W. (1977, April). *The Chicago mastery learning reading program: An interim evaluation.* Paper presented at the annual meeting of the American Educational Research Association, New York. (ERIC Document Reproduction Service No. ED 137 737)

*#@Kersh, M. E. (1970). *A strategy of mastery learning in fifth grade arithmetic.* Unpublished doctoral dissertation, University of Chicago.

+Kim, Y., Cho, G., Park, J., & Park, M. (1974). *An application of a new instructional model* (Research Report No. 8). Seoul, Korea: Korean Educational Development Institute.

*Knight, J. M., Williams, J. D., & Jardon, M. L. (1975). The effects of contingency avoidance on programmed student achievement. *Research in Higher Education 3*, 11–17.

*Kulik, C., & Kulik, J. (1976). PSI and the mastery model. In B. A. Green, Jr. (Ed.), *Personalized instruction in higher education* (pp. 155–159). Washington, DC: Center for Personalized Instruction.

Kulik, C., Kulik, J., & Bangert-Drowns, R. (1990a). Effectiveness of mastery learning programs: A meta-analysis. *Review of Educational Research 60*(2), 265–269.

Kulik, J., Kulik, C., & Bangert-Drowns, R. (1990b). Is there better evidence on mastery learning? A response to Slavin. *Review of Educational Research 60*(2), 303–307.

+Kulik, J. A., Kulik, C. , & Carmichael, K. (1974). The Keller Plan in science teaching. *Science 183*, 379–383.

+Lee, Y. D., Kim, C. S., Kim, H., Park, B. Y., Yoo, H. K., Chang, S. M., & Kim, S. C. (1971). *Interaction improvement studies of the Mastery Learning Project* (Final Report on the Mastery Learning Project, April–November 1971). Seoul, Korea: Educational Research Center, Seoul National University.

*Leppmann, P. K., & Herrman, T. F. (1981, August). *PSI—What are the critical elements?* Paper presented at the annual meeting of the American Psychological Association, Los Angeles. (ERIC Document Reproduction Service No. ED 214 502)

$+Levin, T. (1975). *The effect of content prerequisites and process-oriented experiences on application ability in the learning of probability.* Unpublished doctoral dissertation, University of Chicago.

*Lewis, E. W. (1984). The effects of a mastery learning strategy and an interactive computerized quiz strategy on student achievement and attitude in college trigonometry. *Dissertation Abstracts International 45*, 2430A. (University Microfilms No. DA84-24589)

*Leyton, F. S. (1983). *The extent to which group instruction supplemented by mastery of initial cognitive prerequisites approximates the learning effectiveness of one-to-one tutorial methods.* Unpublished doctoral dissertation, University of Chicago.

*Locksley, N. (1977). The Personalized System of Instruction (PSI) in a university mathematics class. *Dissertation Abstracts International 37*, 4194. (University Microfilms No. ADD76-28194)

%Lomax, R., & Colley, W. (1979). *The student achievement–instructional time relationship.* Paper presented at the annual meeting of the American Educational Research Association, San Francisco.

#@Long, J. C., Okey, J. R., & Yeany, R. H. (1978). The effects of diagnosis with teacher on student directed remediation on science achievement and attitudes. *Journal of Research in Science Teaching 15*, 505–511.

*Lu, M. C. (1976). The retention of material learned by PSI in a mathematics course. In B. A. Green, Jr. (Ed.), *Personalized instruction in higher education* (pp. 151–154). Washington, DC: Center for Personalized Instruction.

*Lu, P. H. (1976). Teaching human growth and development by the Personalized System for Instruction. *Teaching of Psychology 3*, 127–128.

*Lubkin, J. L. (1974). Engineering statistics: A Keller Plan course with novel problems and novel features. In R. S. Ruskin and S. F. Bono (Eds.), *Personalized instruction in higher education* (pp. 153–161). Washington, DC: Center for Personalized Instruction.

*#@Lueckmeyer, C. L., & Chiappetta, W. L. (1981). An investigation into the effects of a modified mastery learning strategy on achievement in a high school human physiology unit. *Journal of Research in Science Teaching 18*, 269–273.

*Malec, M. A. (1975). PSI: A brief report and reply to Francis. *Teaching Sociology 2*, 212–217.

Marliave, R., & Filby, N. N. (1985). Success rate: A measure of task appropriateness. In C. W. Fisher & D. C. Berliner (Eds.), *Perspectives on instructional time* (pp. 217–235). White Plains, NY: Longman.

*Martin, R. R., & Srikameswaran, K. (1974). Correlation between frequent testing and student performance. *Journal of Chemical Education 51*, 485–486.

$Mathews, G. S. (1982). *Effects of a mastery learning strategy on the cognitive knowledge and unit evaluation of students in high school social studies.* Unpublished doctoral dissertation, University of Southern Mississippi.

*McFarland, B. (1976). An individualized course in elementary composition for the marginal student. In B. A. Green, Jr. (Ed.), *Personalized instruction in higher education* (pp. 45–52). Washington, DC: Center for Personalized Instruction.

*+McMichael, J., & Corey, J. R. (1969). Contingency management in an introductory psychology course produces better learning. *Journal of Applied Behavior Analysis 2*, 79–83.

*#@Mevarech, Z. R. (1980). *The role of teaching-learning strategies and feedback-corrective procedures in developing higher cognitive achievement.* Unpublished doctoral dissertation, University of Chicago.

*&Mevarech, Z. R. (1981, April). *Attaining mastery on higher cognitive achievement.* Paper presented at the annual meeting of the American Educational Research Association, Los Angeles.

*Mevarech, Z. R. (1985). The effects of cooperative mastery learning strategies on mathematical achievement. *Journal of Educational Research 78*, 372–377.

*#@Mevarech, Z. R. (1986). The role of feedback corrective procedure in developing mathematics achievement and self-concept in desegregated classrooms. *Studies in Educational Evaluation 12*, 197–203.

*Mevarech, Z. R., & Werner, S. (1985). Are mastery learning strategies beneficial for developing problem solving skills? *Higher Education 14*, 425–432.

*Meyers, R. R. (1976). The effects of mastery and aptitude on achievement and attitude in an introductory college geography course. *Dissertation Abstracts International 36*, 5874. (University Microfilms No. 76-6436)

*+Morris, C., & Kimbrill, G. (1972). Performance and attitudinal effects of the Keller method in an introductory psychology course. *Psychological Record 22*, 523–530.

*Nation, J. R., Knight, J. M., Lamberth, J., & Dyck, D. (1974). Programmed student achievement: A test of the avoidance hypothesis. *Journal of Experimental Education 42*, 57–61.

*Nation, J. R., Massad, P., & Wilkerson, P. (1977). Student performance in introductory psychology following termination of the programmed achievement contingency at mid-semester. *Teaching of Psychology 4*, 116–119.

*Nation, J. R., & Roop, S. S. (1975). A comparison of two mastery approaches to teaching introductory psychology. *Teaching of Psychology 2*, 108–111.

*+Nazzaro, J. R., Todorov, J. C., & Nazzaro, J. N. (1972). Student ability and individualized instruction. *Journal of College Science Teaching 2*, 29–30.

*Nord, S. B. (1975). Comparative achievement and attitude in individualized and class instructional settings. *Dissertation Abstracts International 35*, 5129A. (University Microfilms No. 75-02314)

$Nordin, A. B. (1979). *The effects of different qualities of instruction on selected cognitive, affective, and time variables.* Unpublished doctoral dissertation, University of Chicago.

*$+Okey, J. R. (1974). Altering teacher and pupil behavior with mastery teaching. *Social Science and Mathematics 74*, 530–535.

+Okey, J. R. (1975). *Development of mastery teaching materials* (Final Evaluation Report, USOE G-74-2990). Bloomington: Indiana University.

$&Okey, J. R. (1977). The consequences of training teachers to use a mastery learning strategy. *Journal of Teacher Education 28*(5), 57–62.

*$Omelich, C. L., & Covington, M. V. (1981). *Do the learning benefits of behavioral instruction outweigh the psychological costs?* Paper presented at the annual meeting of the Western Psychological Association, Los Angeles.

*Pascarella, E. T. (1977, April). *Aptitude-treatment interaction in a college calculus course taught in personalized system of instruction and conventional formats.* Paper presented at the annual meeting of the American Educational Research Association, New York. (ERIC Document Reproduction Service No. ED 137 137)

*Peluso, A., & Baranchik, A. J. (1977). Self-paced mathematics instruction: A statistical comparison with traditional teaching. *The American Mathematical Monthly 84*, 124–129.

*+Phillippas, M. A., & Sommerfeldt, R. W. (1972). Keller vs. lecture method in general physics instruction. *American Journal of Physics 40*, 1800.

+Poggio, (1976, April). *Long-term cognitive retention resulting from the mastery learning paradigm.* Paper presented at the annual meeting of the American Educational Research Association, San Francisco.

*Pollack, N. F., & Roeder, P. W. (1975). Individualized instruction in an introductory government course. *Teaching Political Science 8*, 18–36.

*+Rosati, P. A. (1975). A comparison of the personalized system of instruction with the lecture method in teaching elementary dynamics. In J. M. Johnston (Ed.), *Behavior research and technology in higher education* (pp. 90–101). Springfield, IL: Charles C. Thomas.

+Roth, C. H., Jr. (1973). Continuing effectiveness of personalized self-paced instruction in digital systems engineering. *Engineering Education 63*(6), 447–450.

*Roth, C. H., Jr. (1975, December). *Electrical engineering laboratory I* (One of a series of reports on the projects titled Expansion of Keller Plan Instruction in Engineering and Selected Other Disciplines). Austin: University of Texas.

*Saunders-Harris, R. L., & Yeany, R. H. (1981). Diagnosis, remediation, and locus of control: Effects of immediate and retained achievement and attitude. *Journal of Experimental Education 49*, 220–224.

*Schielack, V. P., Jr. (1983). A personalized system of instruction versus a conventional method in a mathematics course for elementary education majors. *Dissertation Abstracts International 43*, 2267. (University Microfilms No. 82-27717)

*Schimpfhauser, F., Horrocks, L., Richardson, K., Alben, J., Schumm, D., & Sprecher, H. (1974). The personalized system of instruction as an adaptable alternative within the traditional structure of medical basic sciences. In R. S. Ruskin and S. F. Bono (Eds.), *Personalized instruction in higher education* (pp. 61–69). Washington, DC: Center for Personalized Instruction.

*Schwartz, P. L. (1981). Retention of knowledge in clinical biochemistry and the effect of the Keller Plan. *Journal of Medical Education 56*, 778–781.

*Sharples, D. K., Smith, D. J., & Strasler, G. M. (1976). *Individually-paced learning in civil engineering technology: An approach to mastery.* Columbia: South Carolina State Board for Technical and Comprehensive Education. (ERIC Document Reproduction Service No. ED 131 870)

*$Sheldon, M. S., & Miller, E. D. (1973). *Behavioral objectives and mastery learning applied to two areas of junior college instruction.* Los Angeles: University of California at Los Angeles. (ERIC Document Reproduction Service No. ED 082 730)

*Sheppard, W. C., & MacDermott, H. G. (1970). Design and evaluation of a programmed course in introductory psychology. *Journal of Applied Behavior Analysis 3*, 5–11.

*Siegfried, J. J., & Strand, S. H. (1976). An evaluation of the Vanderbilt-JCEE experimental PSI course in elementary economics. *The Journal of Economic Education 8*, 9–26.

*+Silberman, R., & Parker, B. (1974). Student attitudes and the Keller Plan. *Journal of Chemical Education 51*, 393.

Slavin, R. E. (1990). Mastery learning re-considered. *Review of Educational Research 60*(2), 300–302.

*#@$&Slavin, R. E., & Karweit, N. L. (1984). Mastery learning and student teams: A factorial

experiment in urban general mathematics classes. *American Educational Research Journal 21*, 725–736.

*Smiernow, G. A., & Lawley, A. (1980). Decentralized sequenced instruction (DSI) at Drexel. *Engineering Education 70*, 423–426.

*Smith, J. E. (1976). A comparison of the traditional method and a personalized system of instruction in college mathematics. *Dissertation Abstracts International 37*, 904. (University Microfilms No. AAD76-18370)

*Spector, L. C. (1976). The effectiveness of personalized system of instruction in economics. *Journal of Personalized Instruction 1*, 118–122.

*Spevack, H. M. (1976). A comparison of the personalized system of instruction with the lecture recitation system for nonsciene oriented chemistry students at an open enrollment community college. *Dissertation Abstracts International 36*, 4385A–4386A. (University Microfilms No. 76-01757)

*Steele, W. F. (1974). *Mathematics 101 at Heidleberg College—PSI vs. tradition.* Paper presented at the National Conference on Personalized Instruction in Higher Education, Washington, DC.

*Stout, L. J. (1978). A comparison of four different pacing strategies of personalized system of instruction and a traditional lecture format. *Dissertation Abstracts International 38*, 6205. (University Microfilms No. AAD78-08600)

*$Strasler, G. M. (1979, April). *The process of transfer in a learning for mastery setting.* Paper presented at the annual meeting of the American Educational Research Association, San Francisco. (ERIC Document Reproduction Service No. ED 174 642)

*$&Swanson, D. H., & Denton, J. J. (1976). Learning for Mastery versus Personalized System of Instruction: A comparison of remediation strategies with secondary school chemistry students. *Journal of Research in Science Teaching 14*, 515–524.

*Taylor, V. (1977, April). *Individualized calculus for the "life-long" learner: A two semester comparison of attitudes and effectiveness.* Paper presented at the Fourth National Conference of the Center for Personalized Instruction, San Francisco.

$Tenenbaum, G. (1982). *A method of group instruction which is as effective as one-to-one tutorial instruction.* Unpublished doctoral dissertation, University of Chicago.

*&Thompson, S. B. (1980). Do individualized mastery and traditional instructional systems yield different course effects in college calculus? *American Educational Research Journal, 17*, 361–375.

*Tietenberg, T. H. (1975). Teaching intermediate microeconomics using the personalized system of instruction. In J. M. Johnston (Ed.), *Behavior research and technology in higher education* (pp. 75–89). Springfield, IL: Charles C. Thomas.

*Toepher, C., Shaw, D., & Moniot, D. (1972). *The effect of item exposure in a contingency management system.* Paper presented at the annual meeting of the American Psychological Association, Honolulu, HI.

*Vandenbroucke, A. C., Jr. (1974, April). *Evaluation of the use of a personalized system of instruction in general chemistry.* Paper presented at the National Conference on Personalized Instruction in Higher Education, Washington, DC.

*Van Verth, J. E., & Dinan, F. J. (1974). A Keller Plan course in organic chemistry. In R. S. Ruskin and S. F. Bono (Eds.), *Personalized instruction in higher education* (pp. 162–168). Washington, DC: Center for Personalized Instruction.

*Walsh, R. G., Sr. (1977). The Keller Plan in college introductory physical geology: A comparison with the conventional teaching method. *Dissertation Abstracts International 37*, 4257. (University Microfilms No. AAD76-30292)

$&+Wentling, T. L. (1973), Mastery versus nonmastery instruction with varying test item feedback treatments. *Journal of Educational Psychology 65*, 50–58.

*White, M. E. (1974). Different equations by PSI. In R. S. Ruskin and S. F. Bono (Eds.), *Personalized instruction in higher education* (pp. 169–171). Washington, DC: Center for Personalized Instruction.

Willent, J., Yamashita, J., & Anderson, R. (1983). A meta-analysis of instructional systems applied in science teaching. *Journal of Research in Science Teaching 20*(5), 405–417.

$Wire, D. R. (1979). *Mastery learning program at Durham College: Report on progress during the first year, September 1, 1978–August 31, 1979.* Durham, NC. (ERIC Document Reproduction Service No. ED 187 387)

*Witters, D. R., & Kent, G. W. (1972). Teaching without lecturing—Evidence in the case for individualized instruction. *The Psychological Record 22*, 169–175.

$Wortham, S. C. (1980). *Mastery learning in secondary schools: A first year report.* San Antonio, TX. (ERIC Document Reproduction Service No. ED 194 453)

*Yeany, R. H., Dost, R. J., & Matthew, R. W. (1980). The effects of diagnostic-prescriptive instruction and locus of control on the achievement and attitudes of university students. *Journal of Research in Science Teaching 17*, 537–545.

$Yildren, G. (1977). *The effects of level of cognitive achievement on selected learning criteria under mastery learning and normal classroom instruction.* Unpublished doctoral dissertation, University of Chicago.

14

Keeping Students on Task

INTRODUCTION

The evidence shows quite conclusively that the more time students spend focused on the performance of assigned tasks that enable achievement of learning objectives without distractions, the more likely it is they will achieve the learning objectives. Although students' bodily presence may be mandated and coerced, students control what they attend to and learn, and will not continue to focus on the performance of assigned tasks if they do not want to. Instructional planners and teachers must make every effort to ensure that students are ready to perform assigned tasks, that their interest in performing assigned tasks is stimulated, that the learning environment is conducive to performing assigned tasks, and that they are given every opportunity to succeed in performing assigned tasks. Students who do not attend to assigned learning tasks fail to learn and may eventually become student dropouts. Student time focused on assigned tasks is fundamental.

STUDENT BENEFICIARIES

The evidence indicates that students spending more time focused on performance of assigned tasks that enable achievement of learning objectives have greater success achieving the objectives in elementary and secondary classrooms. No evidence could be found to suggest that students' spending more time focused on performance of assigned tasks should not be stressed in all subject areas for all types of students, including students in military, community, business, and adult education settings.

LEARNING ACHIEVED

Students' spending more time on task has been shown to lead to greater achievement in mathematics, reading, English, and biology. It may be reasonable to expect that achievement may be enhanced in other content areas as well. In studies reviewed, student achievement was shown to be positively related to time on task.

INSTRUCTIONAL TACTICS

The benefits of students focusing more time on performance of assigned tasks that enable achievement of the learning objectives is well supported by the evidence. However, there is a need for instructional planners and teachers to know the particular tactics that can be used to ensure that students are focusing more time on performance of assigned tasks. The following tactics are derived from the studies that demonstrate the benefits of students focusing more time on performance of assigned tasks. Discretion has been used to interpret and reduce overlap in tactics used in different studies and to elaborate tactics.

Tactics that ensure that students spend more time focused on performance of assigned tasks that enable achievement of the learning objectives are:

- Assign only learning tasks that are relevant to achievement of the learning objective.
- Assign only learning tasks that students possess the readiness capabilities to perform. If this is not adhered to, students will be unable to perform assigned tasks, time will be wasted, and students may be dissuaded from learning.
- Make sure that instruction is well planned and organized.
- Spend more time on demonstration and guided practice (as opposed to independent student practice).
- Make sure the students are ready to work alone before assigning independent learning tasks.
- Make sure that independent learning tasks are directly relevant to prior demonstration and guided practice.
- Assign independent learning tasks to immediately follow guided practice activities.
- Provide detailed instructions on how to perform learning tasks.
- Use question-and-answer instruction to ensure that students understand instructions for performance of assigned tasks.
- Supervise independent activity.
- Minimize disruptions, distractions, and interruptions.

Elaborations of the above summary of tactics can be obtained from reading the studies that are to follow. To be most effective, the instructional tactics need to be integrated into the particular instructional program being planned or presently in use.

CAUTIONS AND COMMENTS

Tactics not mentioned above apparently affect the time students stay focused on assigned tasks. For instance, the relationship between motivation and behavior has, in general, been established. The hypothesis needs to be tested asserting that students' *interest* in performing an assigned task is directly related to the amount of time they spend attending to and attempting to master the performance of the task. Meanwhile, based on general research, it might be a good idea to take students' interests into account when assigning tasks and to make an effort to stimulate their interest in assigned tasks.

Threats to personal safety often prevent students from focusing on the performance of assigned tasks. In schools where violence is commonplace students are frequently preoccupied with self-protection, which precludes their attending to assigned tasks. Although providing for student safety is not an instructional function, threats of bodily harm can make effective instruction difficult if not impossible. Student safety is prerequisite to effective instruction.

GENERALIZATION: ON STUDENT TIME ON TASK

Achievement of learning objectives is enhanced when students spend more time attending to tasks formulated to enable them to achieve the learning objectives.

Supportive Research on Student Time on Task
Total number of studies covered: 64

Groups of Studies

Author: Brophy & Good (1986)

Students: Elementary and secondary

Learning: Reading, mathematics, English, and biology achievement

Instructional Tactics:

- Learning tasks are assigned that are relevant to achievement of the learning objective.

- Learning tasks are formulated in accordance with the teacher's diagnosis of the students' readiness characteristics.

- The teacher controls formulation and assignment of tasks (as opposed to students being left to their own devices).

- The teacher spends more time on demonstration and guided practice (as opposed to independent student practice).

- The teacher makes sure the students are ready to work alone before assigning independent learning tasks.

- Independent learning tasks are assigned to immediately follow guided practice activities.
- The teacher supervises independent activity.

Other instructional tactics are employed in these studies that are applicable to other generalizations and will be presented in the appropriate chapters.

Individual studies included in this research synthesis are identified by the symbol * in the reference list at the end of the chapter.

Findings: Use of the above instructional tactics was found to:

- Lead to greater student engagement time in the performance of tasks they are assigned.
- Lead to greater achievement than for students who did not have the benefit of the above instructional tactics.

The following are more specific findings associated with the use of the above instructional tactics:

- Teacher control of student behavior was shown to be positively related to student achievement and student engaged time.
- Supervision of seatwork was positively related to student achievement.
- Students being expected to manage their learning on their own is negatively related to student achievement.
- Achievement gains were maximized when students consistently completed their work with few interruptions due to confusion or the need for help (achieved by selection of appropriate tasks and explaining thoroughly prior to assigning students to independent work).
- High rates of questioning of nonvolunteers leading to incorrect or no response was found to be negatively associated with achievement.
- Student engaged time was higher in classes where teachers were well organized. Student engaged time and teachers being well organized were found to be positively related to student achievement.
- The teacher's ability to predict the difficulty students will have with particular items and the appropriateness of tasks they assign to students was found to be positively associated with student achievement.
- Amount of time spent working without supervision was found to be associated with low achievement gains.
- The percentage of assigned problems attempted by students was found to be related to achievement.

- Selection of appropriate goals and objectives was found to be positively associated with student achievement.

- Poor classroom management was found to be negatively related to student achievement.

- Achievement gain was found to be related to classroom management techniques that maximize task engagement and minimize interruptions.

- The number of student-relevant responses to teacher questions was found to be associated with student achievement.

Author: Rosenshine & Stevens (1986)

Students: Elementary and secondary

Learning: Mathematics and reading achievement

Instructional Tactics:

- The teacher spends more time in demonstration and guided practice.
- The teacher makes sure that students are ready to work alone.
- The seatwork activity follows directly the guided practice.
- The seatwork activities are directly relevant to the demonstration and guided practice activities.

Other instructional tactics are employed in these studies that are applicable to other generalizations and will be presented in the appropriate chapters.

Individual studies included in this research synthesis are identified by the symbol # in the reference list.

Findings: Use of the above instructional tactics was found to be positively related to student achievement.

REFERENCE LIST

*Acland, H. (1976). Stability of teacher effectiveness: A replication. *Journal of Educational Research 69*, 289–292.

*#Anderson, L. M., Evertson, C. M., & Brophy, J. E. (1979). An experimental study of effective teaching in first-grade reading groups. *The Elementary School Journal 79*, 193–222.

*#Anderson, L. M., Evertson, C. M., & Brophy, J. E. (1982). *Principles of small group instruction* (Occasional paper no. 32). East Lansing: Michigan State University, Institute for Research on Teaching.

*Arehart, J. (1979). Student opportunity to learn related to student achievement of objectives in a probability unit. *Journal of Educational Research 72*, 253–269.

#Becker, W. C. (1977). Teaching reading and language to the disadvantaged—What we have learned from field research. *Harvard Educational Review 47*, 518–543.

*Berliner, D., Fisher, C., Filby, N., & Marliave, R. (1978). *Executive summary of Beginning Teacher Evaluation Study*. San Francisco: Far West Laboratory.

*Brophy, J. (1973). Stability of teacher effectiveness. *American Educational Research Journal 10*, 245–252.

*Brophy, J., & Evertson, C. (1974a). *Process–product correlations in the Texas Teacher Effectiveness Study: Final report* (Research Report 74-4). Austin: Research and Development Center for Teacher Education, University of Texas. (ERIC Document Reproduction No. ED 091 094)

*Brophy, J., & Evertson, C. (1974b). *The Texas Teacher Effectiveness Project: Presentation of non-linear relationships and summary discussion* (Research Report 74-6). Austin: Research and Development Center for Teacher Education, University of Texas. (ERIC Document Reproduction No. ED 099 345)

*#Brophy, J., & Evertson, C. (1976). *Learning from teaching: A developmental perspective*. Boston: Allyn and Bacon.

Brophy, J., & Good, T. (1986). Teacher behavior and student achievement. In M. C. Wittrock (Ed.), *Handbook of research on teaching* (pp. 328–375). New York: Macmillan.

*Coker, H., Medley, D., & Soar, R. (1980). How valid are expert opinions about effective teaching? *Phi Delta Kappan 62*, 131–134, 149.

*Crawford, J. (1983). A study of instructional processes in Title I classes: 1981–82. *Journal of Research and Evaluation of the Oklahoma City Public Schools 13*(1).

*Dunkin, M. J. (1978). Student characteristics, classroom processes, and student achievement. *Journal of Educational Psychology 70*, 998–1009.

*Ebmier, H., & Good, T. (1979). The effects of instructing teachers about good teaching on mathematics achievement of fourth grade students. *American Educational Research Journal 16*, 1–16.

*Emmer, E., Evertson, C., & Anderson, L. (1980). Effective classroom management at the beginning of the school year. *Elementary School Journal 80*, 219–231.

*Emmer, E., Evertson, C., & Brophy, J. (1979). Stability of teacher effects in junior high classrooms. *American Educational Research Journal 16*, 71–75.

#Emmer, E. T., Evertson, C., Sanford, J., & Clements, B. (1982). *Improving classroom management: An experimental study in junior high classrooms*. Austin: Research and Development Center for Teacher Education, University of Texas.

#Evertson, C. (1982). Differences in instructional activities in higher and lower achieving junior high English and mathematics classrooms. *Elementary School Journal 82*, 329–351.

*#Evertson, C., Anderson, C., Anderson, L., & Brophy, J. (1980). Relationships between classroom behaviors and student outcomes in junior high mathematics and English classes. *American Educational Research Journal 17*, 43–60.

*Evertson, C., Anderson, L., & Brophy, J. (1978). *Texas Junior High School Study: Final report of process–outcome relationship* (Report No. 4061). Austin: Research and Development Center for Teacher Education, University of Texas.

*Evertson, C., & Brophy, J. (1973). High-inference behavioral ratings as correlates of teacher effectiveness. *JSAS Catalog of Selected Documents in Psychology 3*, 97.

*Evertson, C., & Brophy, J. (1974). *Texas Teacher Effectiveness Project: Questionnaire and interview data* (Research Report No. 74-5). Austin: Research and Development Center for Teacher Education, University of Texas.

*#Evertson, C., Emmer, E., & Brophy, J. (1980). Predictors of effective teaching in junior high mathematics classrooms. *Journal for Research in Mathematics Education 11*, 167–178.

#Evertson, C. M., Emmer, E. T., Sanford, J. P., & Clements, B. S. (1983). Improving classroom management: An experiment in elementary classrooms. *Elementary School Journal 84*, 173–188.

*#Fisher, C. W., Berliner, D. C., Filby, N. N., Marliave, R., Cahen, L. S., & Dishaw, M. M. (1980). Teaching behaviors, academic learning time, and student achievement: An overview. In C. Denham & A. Lieberman (Eds.), *Time to learn* (pp. 7–32). Washington, DC: U.S. Government Printing Office.

#Fitzpatrick, K. A. (1981). *An investigation of secondary classroom material strategies for increasing student academic engaged time.* Doctoral dissertation, University of Illinois at Urbana–Champaign.

#Fitzpatrick, K. A. (1982). *The effect of a secondary classroom management training program on teacher and student behavior.* Paper presented at the annual meeting of the American Educational Research Association, New York.

*Good, T., Ebmeier, H., & Beckerman, T. (1978) Teaching mathematics in high and low SES classrooms: An empirical comparison. *Journal of Teacher Education 29*, 85–90.

*Good, T., Grouws, D., & Beckerman, T. (1978). Curriculum pacing: Some empirical data in mathematics. *Journal of Curriculum Studies 10*, 75–81.

*#Good, T., Grouws, D., & Ebmeier, M. (1983). *Active mathematics teaching.* New York: Longman.

*#Good, T. L., & Grouws, D. A. (1977). Teaching effects: a process-product study in fourth grade mathematics classrooms. *Journal of Teacher Education 28*(3), 49–54.

*Good, T. L., & Grouws, D. A. (1979a). *Experimental study of mathematics instruction in elementary schools* (Final Report, National Institute of Education Grant No. NIE-G-79-0103). Columbia: University of Missouri, Center for the Study of Social Behavior.

*#Good, T. L., & Grouws, D. A. (1979b). The Missouri mathematics effectiveness project. *Journal of Educational Psychology 71*, 355–362.

*Good, T. L., & Grouws, D. A. (1981). *Experimental research in secondary mathematics* (Final Report, National Institute of Education Grant No. NIE-G-79-0103). Columbia: University of Missouri, Center for the Study of Social Behavior.

*Hughes, D. (1973). An experimental investigation of the effect of pupil responding and teacher reacting on pupil achievement. *American Educational Research Journal 10*, 21–37.

*Kounin, J. (1970). *Discipline and group management in classrooms.* New York: Holt, Reinhart, & Winston.

*Larrivee, B., & Algina, J. (1983, April). *Identification of teaching behaviors which predict success for mainstream students.* Paper presented at the annual meeting of the American Educational Research Association, Montreal.

*McConnel, J. (1977). *Relationship between selected teacher behaviors and attitudes/ achievements of algebra classes.* Paper presented at the annual meeting of the American Educational Research Association, New York.

*McDonald, F. (1976). Report on Phase II of the Beginning Teacher Evaluation Study. *Journal of Teacher Education 27*(1), 39–42.

*McDonald, F. (1977). Research on teaching: Report on Phase II of the Beginning Teacher Evaluation Study. In G. Borich and K. Fenton (Eds.), *The appraisal of teaching: Concepts and process.* Reading, MA: Addison-Wesley.

*McDonald, F., & Elias, P. (1976). *Executive Summary Report: Beginning Teacher Evaluation Study, Phase II.* Princeton, NJ: Educational Testing Service.

*Nuthall, G., & Church, J. (1973). Experimental studies of teaching behavior. In G. Chanan

(Ed.), *Towards a science of teaching* (pp. 9–25). London: National Foundation for Educational Research.

#Reid, E. R. (1978–1982). *The Reader Newsletter*. Salt Lake City: Exemplary Center for Reading Instruction.

Rosenshine, B., & Stevens, R. (1986). Teaching Functions. In M. C. Wittrock (Ed.), *Handbook of research on teaching* (3rd ed., pp. 376–391). New York: Macmillan.

*Schuck, R. (1981). The impact of set induction on student achievement and retention. *Journal of Educational Research 74*, 227–232.

*Soar, R. S. (1966). *An integrative approach to classroom learning* (Report for NIMH Projects No. 5-R11 MH 01096 and R-11 MH 02045). Philadelphia: Temple University. (ERIC Document Reproduction Service No. ED 033 749)

*Soar, R. S. (1968). Optimum teacher–pupil interaction for pupil growth. *Educational Leadership 26*, 275–280.

*Soar, R. S. (1973). *Follow-Through Classroom Process Measurement and Pupil Growth (1970–1971) Final Report*. Gainesville: College of Education, University of Florida.

*Soar, R. S. (1977). An integration of findings from four studies of teacher effectiveness. In G. Borich and K. Fenton (Eds.), *The appraisal of teaching: Concepts and process*. Reading, MA: Addison-Wesley.

*Soar, R. S., & Soar, R. M. (1972). An empirical analysis of selected Follow Through Programs: An appraisal of a process approach to evaluation. In G. Borich and K. Fenton (Eds.), *The appraisal of teaching: Concepts and process*. Reading, MA: Addison-Wesley.

*Soar, R. S., & Soar, R. M. (1973). Classroom behavior, pupil characteristics, and pupil growth for the school year and the summer. Gainesville: University of Florida, Institute for Development of Human Resources.

*Soar, R. S., & Soar, R. M. (1978). *Setting variables, classroom interaction, and multiple pupil outcomes* (Final Report, Project No. 6-0432, Grant No. NIE-G-76-0100). Washington, DC: National Institute of Education.

*Soar, R. S., & Soar, R. M. (1979). Emotional climate and management. In P. Peterson and H. Walberg (Eds.), *Research on teaching: Concepts, findings, and implications* (pp. 97–119). Berkeley, CA: McCutchan.

*Solomon, D., & Kendall, A. (1979). *Children in classrooms: An investigation of person–environment interaction*. New York: Praeger.

*Stallings, J. (1980). allocated academic learning time revisited, or beyond time on task. *Educational Researcher 8*(11), 11–16.

*#Stallings J., Corey, R., Fairweather, J., & Needles, M. (1977). *Early Childhood Education classroom evaluation*. Menlo Park, CA: SRI International.

*#Stallings, J. A., & Kaskowitz, D. (1974). *Follow-Through Classroom Observation*. Menlo Park, CA: SRI International.

*#Stallings, J., Needles, M., & Staybrook, N. (1979). *The teaching of basic reading skills in secondary schools, Phase II and Phase III*. Menlo Park, CA: SRI International.

*Tobin, K., & Caple, W. (1982). Relationships between classroom process variables and middle-school science achievement. *Journal of Educational Psychology 74*, 441–454.

15

Providing Ample Teaching Time

INTRODUCTION

The more guidance and facilitation students receive, the more likely they are to achieve the learning objectives. It is beneficial for students to receive guidance before performing tasks they are assigned to perform and for students to be given guidance while attempting to perform tasks they have been assigned to perform. When students receive more guidance and facilitation they are more likely to perform assigned tasks correctly and to achieve the learning objective. Leaving them to their own devices in the performance of learning tasks may lead to incorrect or diminished performance as a result of lack of understanding or the temptation to engage in off-task behavior.

Achievement of learning objectives over time requires that teaching continually facilitates task performance and keeps students focused on tasks that enable the achievement of the learning objectives. Time spent on or dealing with activities such as administrative interruptions, socializing with students, returning papers or other assignments, moving students from place to place, music, arts and crafts, dance, and student disruptions directs time away from pursuit of the learning objectives. Such distractions are to be avoided if the learning objectives are to be achieved.

STUDENT BENEFICIARIES

The evidence indicates that the amount of time spent engaged in teaching activities enhances the academic achievement of students in elementary and secondary classrooms in the subject areas of English, reading, and mathematics. No evidence could be found to suggest that maximizing teaching time should not be stressed in all subject areas for all types of students, including students in college, military, community, business, and adult education settings.

LEARNING ACHIEVED

Achievement in the content areas of English, reading, and mathematics is enhanced when more teaching time is devoted to the pursuit of intended learning objectives. It may be reasonable to expect that achievement may be enhanced in other content areas as well. In studies reviewed, student achievement was shown to be positively related to the amount of teaching time devoted to the pursuit of the learning objectives.

INSTRUCTIONAL TACTICS

The benefits of increasing the amount of time teachers engage in teaching activities is well supported by the evidence. There is a need for instructional planners and teachers to know the particular tactics that can be used to maximize teaching time. The following tactics are derived from the studies that demonstrate the benefits of increasing teaching time. Discretion has been used to interpret and reduce overlap in tactics used in different studies and to elaborate tactics.

Academic achievement is enhanced when teachers:

- Operate their classroom as a learning environment and spend most of their time on teacher-directed academic activities. In addition to providing the information necessary for students to accomplish tasks they are assigned to perform, the teacher should monitor students as they perform their assigned tasks.
- Minimize or avoid assigning students to independent activities, such as silent reading, written assignments, and other independent task performance. Students are more likely to daydream, doodle, or socialize with other students during independent activities than if they are guided by the teacher during the task performance.
- Avoid assigning students to "busy work" or other activities designed to "kill time."
- Devote time available for teaching to teaching and not to getting organized. Be well prepared and plan daily activities productively. Use available teacher planning time wisely to this end.
- Avoid nonacademic student activities, such as group sharing, socializing, arts and crafts, music, and dance, during the teaching of academic subjects. Such activities reduce the amount of time available to teach the academic subjects. Increasing the amount of time students are engaged in these activities has been shown to be negatively associated with student academic achievement. Although important, nonacademic activities should be scheduled in nonacademic settings and should not reduce the time needed for academic instruction.

- Except in the case of emergency, administrative intrusions into scheduled teaching time, whether in person or over a loudspeaker, should be restricted to normally scheduled break times.

Elaborations of the above summary of tactics can be obtained from reading the studies that are to follow. To be most effective, the instructional tactics need to be integrated into the particular instructional program being planned or presently in use.

CAUTIONS AND COMMENTS

Although increasing the time a teacher teaches is related to greater student achievement, the benefits may be low or nonexistent for an ineffective teacher. Increasing teaching time and emphasis on the effectiveness of teaching during teaching time may be necessary to ensure greater student achievement. Information on what constitutes effective teaching is the subject of many other chapters in this handbook.

GENERALIZATION: ON AMPLE TEACHING TIME

Achievement of learning objectives is enhanced when more teaching time is devoted to students to guide and facilitate their performance of academic tasks they are assigned to perform (rather than students performing tasks on their own, teachers dealing with outside intrusions, or students being assigned to nonacademic tasks).

Supportive Research on Ample Teaching Time
Total number of studies covered: 63

Groups of Studies

Author: Brophy & Good (1986)

Students: Elementary and secondary

Learning: English, reading, and mathematics achievement

Instructional Tactics:

- Teachers operate their classroom as a learning environment and spend most of their time on teacher-directed academic activities.
- Avoid or minimize nonacademic student activities such as group sharing, socializing, arts and crafts, music, and dance.
- Outside intrusions should be minimized.
- Time is devoted to teaching and not to getting organized. Be well prepared and plan daily activities proactively.
- Minimize or avoid assigning students to independent activities, such as si-

lent reading and written assignments, to be conducted during time that could be used for teaching.

Other instructional tactics are employed in these studies that are applicable to other generalizations and will be presented in the appropriate chapters.

Findings: Students who spent most of their time being taught by their teachers and less of their time engaged in games, group sharing, or socializing experienced greater gains in achievement. Time spent in nonacademic activities such as dance, music, arts and crafts, and storytelling was found to be negatively related to achievement. Teachers getting organized rather than teaching was found to be negatively related to achievement. Students working independently on activities such as silent reading and written assignments is negatively associated with student achievement.

Individual studies included in this logical synthesis of research are identified by the symbol * in the reference list at the end of the chapter.

Author: Anderson (1995)

Students: Elementary and secondary

Learning: Achievement

Instructional Tactics:

- Minimize time spent taking attendance, disciplining students, cleaning up and putting away, and movement from activity to activity.
- Maximize the amount of time spent actively teaching in relation to the amount of time available for teaching.

Other instructional tactics are employed in these studies that are applicable to other generalizations and will be presented in the appropriate chapters.

Findings: Teaching time is positively related to student achievement. In one study, the difference between allocated time for teaching and teaching time was 25% for high-achieving schools and 50% for low-achieving schools.

Individual studies included in this logical synthesis of research are identified by the symbol # in the reference list.

REFERENCE LIST

*Acland, H. (1976). Stability of teacher effectiveness: A replication. *Journal of Educational Research 69*, 289–292.

*Anderson, L. M., Evertson, C. M., & Brophy, J. E. (1979). An experimental study of effective teaching in first-grade reading groups. *The Elementary School Journal 79*, 193–222.

*Anderson, L. M., Evertson, C. M., & Brophy, J. E. (1982). *Principles of small group instruction* (Occasional paper no. 32). East Lansing: Michigan State University, Institute for Research on Teaching.

Anderson, L. W. (1995). Time, allocated and instructional. In L. W. Anderson (Ed.), *International encyclopedia of teaching and teacher education* (2nd ed., pp. 204–207). Oxford: Pergamon Press.

#Anderson, L. W. (1994). What time tells us. In L. W. Anderson and H. J. Walberg (Eds.), *Time piece: Extending and enhancing learning time* (pp. 15–31). Reston, VA: National Association of Secondary School Principals.

#Anderson, L. W., & Postlethwaite, T. N. (1989). What IEA studies say about teachers and teaching. In A. C. Purvis (Ed.), *International comparisons and educational reform.* Reston, VA: Association for Supervision and Curriculum Development.

#Anderson, L. W., Ryan, D. W., & Shapiro, B. J. (1989). *The IEA Classroom Environment Study.* Oxford: Pergamon Press.

*Arehart, J. (1979). Student opportunity to learn related to student achievement of objectives in a probability unit. *Journal of Educational Research 72*, 253–269.

*Berliner, D., & Tikunoff, W. (1976). The California Beginning Teacher Evaluation Study: Overview of the ethnographic study. *Journal of Teacher Education 27*(1), 24–30.

*Berliner, D., & Tikunoff, W. (1977). Ethnography in the classroom. In G. Borich and K. Fenton (Eds.), *The appraisal of teaching: Concepts and process.* Reading, MA: Addison-Wesley.

*Borg, W. (1979). Teacher coverage of academic content and pupil achievement. *Journal of Educational Psychology 71*, 635–645.

*Borg, W. (1980). Time and school learning. In C. Denham and A. Lieberman (Eds.), *Time to learn* (pp. 33–72). Washington, DC: National Institute of Education.

*Brophy, J. (1973). Stability of teacher effectiveness. *American Educational Research Journal 10*, 245–252.

*Brophy, J. (1981). Teacher behavior and its effects. *Journal of Educational Psychology 71*, 733–750.

*Brophy, J., & Evertson, C. (1974a). *Process–product correlations in the Texas Teacher Effectiveness Study: Final Report* (Research Report 74-4). Austin: Research and Development Center for Teacher Education, University of Texas. (ERIC Document Reproduction Service No. ED 091 094)

*Brophy, J., & Evertson, C. (1974b). *The Texas Teacher Effectiveness Project: Presentation of non-linear relationships and summary discussion* (Research Report 74-6). Austin: Research and Development Center for Teacher Education, University of Texas. (ERIC Document Reproduction Service No. ED 099 345)

*Brophy, J., & Evertson, C. (1976). *Learning from teaching: A developmental perspective.* Boston: Allyn and Bacon.

Brophy, J., & Good, T. (1986). Teacher behavior and student achievement. In M. C. Wittrock (Ed.), *Handbook of research on teaching* (pp. 328–375). New York: Macmillan.

*Chang, S., & Rath, J. (1971). The schools' contribution to the cumulating deficit. *Journal of Educational Research 64*, 272–276.

*Comber, L., & Keeves, J. (1973). *Science education in nineteen countries.* New York: Halsted Press.

*Cooley, W., & Leinhardt, G. (1980). The Instructional Dimensions Study. *Educational Evaluation and Policy Analysis 2*, 7–25.

*Crawford, J. (1983). A study of instructional processes in Title I classes: 1981–82. *Journal of Research and Evaluation of the Oklahoma City Public Schools 13*(1).

*Dunkin, M. J. (1978). Student characteristics, classroom processes, and student achievement. *Journal of Educational Psychology 70*, 998–1009.

#Durkin, D. (1978–1979). What classroom observations reveal about reading comprehension instruction. *Reading Research Quarterly 14*(4), 481–533.

*Ebmier, H., & Good, T. (1979). The effects of instructing teachers about good teaching on mathematics achievement of fourth grade students. *American Educational Research Journal 16*, 1–16.

*Emmer, E., Evertson, C., & Anderson, L. (1980). Effective classroom management at the beginning of the school year. *Elementary School Journal 80*, 219–231.

*Emmer, E., Evertson, C., & Brophy, J. (1979). Stability of teacher effects in junior high classrooms. *American Educational Research Journal 16*, 71–75.

*Evertson, C., Anderson, C., Anderson, L., & Brophy, J. (1980). Relationships between classroom behaviors and student outcomes in junior high mathematics and English classes. *American Educational Research Journal 17*, 43–60.

*Evertson, C., Anderson, L., & Brophy, J. (1978). *Texas Junior High School Study: Final report of process–outcome relationship* (Report No. 4061). Austin: Research and Development Center for Teacher Education, University of Texas.

*Evertson, C., & Emmer, E. (1982). Effective management at the beginning of the school year in junior high classes. *Journal of Educational Psychology 74*, 485–498.

*Evertson, C., Emmer, E., & Brophy, J. (1980). Predictors of effective teaching in junior high mathematics classrooms. *Journal for Research in Mathematics Education 11*, 167–178.

Fisher, C. W., & Berliner, D. C. (Eds.). (1985). *Perspectives on instructional time.* New York: Longman.

*Fisher, C. W., Berliner, D. C., Filby, N. N., Marliave, R., Cahen, L. S., & Dishaw, M. M. (1980). Teaching behaviors, academic learning time, and student achievement: An overview. In C. Denham & A. Lieberman (Eds.), *Time to learn.* Washington, DC: U.S. Government Printing Office.

#Fogelman, K. (1978). School attendance, attainment, and behavior. *British Journal of Educational Psychology 48*, 148–158.

#Frederick, W. C. (1980). Instructional time. *Evaluation of Education 4*, 117–118.

#Fuller, B. (1987). What factors raise achievement in the third world? *Review of Educational Research 57*, 255–292.

*Gage, N., & Coladarci, T. (1980). *Replication of an experiment with a research-based inservice teacher education program.* Stanford, CA: Stanford University, Center for Educational Research, Program on Teaching Effectiveness.

*Good, T., Ebmeier, H., & Beckerman, T. (1978) Teaching mathematics in high and low SES classrooms: An empirical comparison. *Journal of Teacher Education 29*, 85–90.

*Good, T., Grouws, D., & Beckerman, T. (1978). Curriculum pacing: Some empirical data in mathematics. *Journal of Curriculum Studies 10*, 75–81.

*Good, T., Grouws, D., & Ebmeier, M. (1983). *Active mathematics teaching.* New York: Longman.

*Good, T. L., & Grouws, D. A. (1977). Teaching effects: a process-product study in fourth grade mathematics classrooms. *Journal of Teacher Education 28*(3), 49–54.

*Good, T. L., & Grouws, D. A. (1979a). *Experimental study of mathematics instruction in elementary schools* (Final Report, National Institute of Education Grant No. NIE-G-79-0103), Columbia: University of Missouri, Center for the Study of Social Behavior.

*Good, T. L., & Grouws, D. A. (1979b). The Missouri mathematics effectiveness project. *Journal of Educational Psychology 71*, 355–362.

*Good, T. L., & Grouws, D. A. (1981). *Experimental research in secondary mathematics* (Final Report, National Institute of Education Grant No. NIE-G-79-0103). Columbia: University of Missouri, Center for the Study of Social Behavior.

*Harris, A., & Serwer, B. (1966). The CRAFT Project: Instructional time in reading research. *Reading Research Quarterly 2*, 27–57.

*Husen, T. (Ed.). (1967). *International study of achievement in mathematics* (Vol. 1). New York: Wiley.

*Kounin, J. (1970). *Discipline and group management in classrooms.* New York: Holt, Reinhart, & Winston.

*Larrivee, B., & Algina, J. (1983, April). *Identification of teaching behaviors which predict success for mainstream students.* Paper presented at the annual meeting of the American Educational Research Association, Montreal.

#MacKay, A. (1979). *Project Quest: Teaching strategies and pupil achievement* (Research Report No. 79-1-3). Edmonton: University of Alberta, Centre for Research in Teaching, Faculty of Education.

*McConnel, J. (1977). *Relationship between selected teacher behaviors and attitudes/ achievements of algebra classes.* Paper presented at the annual meeting of the American Educational Research Association, New York.

*McDonald, F. (1976). Report on Phase II of the Beginning Teacher Evaluation Study. *Journal of Teacher Education 27*(1), 39–42.

*McDonald, F. (1977). Research on teaching: Report on Phase II of the Beginning Teacher Evaluation Study. In G. Borich and K. Fenton (Eds.), *The appraisal of teaching: Concepts and process.* Reading, MA: Addison-Wesley.

*McDonald, F., & Elias, P. (1976). *Executive Summary Report: Beginning Teacher Evaluation Study, Phase II.* Princeton, NJ: Educational Testing Service.

*Nuthall, G., & Church, J. (1973). Experimental studies of teaching behavior. In G. Chanan (Ed.), *Towards a science of teaching.* London: National Foundation for Educational Research.

#Porter, A. (1989). A curriculum out of balance: The case of elementary school mathematics. *Educational Researcher 18*(5), 9–15.

*Ramp, E., & Rhine, W. (1981). Behavior analysis model. In W. Rhine (Ed.), *Making schools more effective: New directions from Follow Through* (pp. 155–197). New York: Academic Press.

#Reynolds, A. J., & Walberg, H. J. (1991). A structural model of science achievement. *Journal of Educational Psychology 83*(1), 97–107.

*Rosenshine, B. (1971). *Teaching behaviors and student achievement.* London: National Foundation for Educational Research.

#Sanford, J. P., & Evertson, C. M. (1983). Time use and activities in junior high classes. *Journal of Educational Research 76*(3), 140–147.

*Smith, L. (1979). Task-oriented lessons and student achievement. *Journal of Educational Research 73*, 16–19.

#Smythe, W. J. (1987). Time. In M. J. Dunkin (Ed.), *The international encyclopedia of teaching and teacher education.* Oxford: Pergamon Press.

*Stallings J., Corey, R., Fairweather, J., & Needles, M. (1977). *Early Childhood Education classroom evaluation.* Menlo Park, CA: SRI International.

*Stallings, J., Needles, M., & Staybrook, N. (1979). *The teaching of basic reading skills in secondary schools, Phase II and Phase III.* Menlo Park, CA: SRI International.

*Stallings, J. A., & Kaskowitz, D. (1974). *Follow-Through Classroom Observation.* Menlo Park, CA: SRI International.

*Veldman, D., & Brophy, J. (1974). Measuring teacher effects on pupil achievement. *Journal of Educational Psychology 66*, 319–324.

#Walberg, H. J., & Frederick, W. C. (1991). *Extending learning time.* Washington, DC: U.S. Department of Education, Office of Educational Research and Improvement.

#Welsh, W. W., Anderson, R. E., & Harris, L. J. (1982). The effects of schooling on mathematics achievement. *American Educational Research Journal 19*, 145–153.

III

Instructional Alerts

In this part of the handbook, readers' attention is drawn to promising instructional strategies presented in Chapter 16 and questionable instructional strategies presented in Chapter 17. The promising instructional strategies are distinct from the fifteen effective instructional strategies presented in Parts I and II. Although there is limited research to support their effectiveness, the research to date is favorable. Additional research may further verify their effectiveness and support their adoption. Additional instructional strategies that complement the fifteen effective strategies presented earlier and are supported by research evidence are difficult to find. Hopefully, more can be identified and included in subsequent editions of the handbook. Recommendations will be appreciated.

Questionable instructional strategies also need to be brought to educators' attention. Many of them are in common use, even though their adoption is not warranted by research evidence. The number of studies conducted to test the efficacy of each questionable strategy varies considerably. The evidence will be presented so that readers can draw their own conclusions. The use of questionable strategies continues, despite the lack of evidence to support their use. This may be partly because educational decisions are all too seldom based on evidence. In addition, although the strategies are not effective, they do no ostensible damage to people. They simply do not produce learning. Deleterious side effects are rarely noticeable.

When a medication is banned, it is usually because it has harmful side effects that can ruin people's health. The problem with ineffective instructional programs is that they are a waste of time and money and are responsible for the many uneducated and undereducated people in America and elsewhere. It's time educators base more of their decisions on evidence.

16

Promising Instructional Strategies

In Parts I and II, effective instructional strategies were reviewed. These strategies were deemed effective because from 50 to over 200 research studies which were cited supported their effectiveness. Consequently, there was no hesitancy to recommend their adoption in existing instructional programs or programs being planned, taking into account the caveats described in the "Cautions and Comments" sections of each strategy.

In this chapter, promising instructional strategies are described. There is some research support for these strategies, but not nearly the support that there is for those instructional strategies labeled effective. In some cases there may be substantial research support for promising instructional strategies in related fields, but less support with regard to instructional effectiveness.

Instructional strategies listed as promising should not be adopted without further research to support their effectiveness. However, it is quite appropriate for particular educational institutions to pilot test a promising strategy on their students. Then, if it proves to be effective, its adoption might be considered. It would take, however, many additional studies across many educational settings to establish the *generalizability* of a promising strategy. Nevertheless, with further validation, promising strategies could prove to have a significant effect on student achievement.

Promising strategies are not presented in as much detail as effective strategies, but ample references are provided for greater detail as well as statistical findings.

Enlisting the Control Motive

INTRODUCTION

Motivation determines what people will pursue and what they will try to avoid. Since in free societies it is generally illegal to coerce people to do one's bidding against their will, there is great interest in inducing people to do willingly what one wants them to do. As a result, huge sums of money are spent on motivational research. Businesses and industries want to know how to entice people to buy their goods and services and how to encourage employees to be more productive. Welfare agencies want to determine how to get people on welfare to want to work. Charities want to know how to entice people to donate more money. Crime prevention agencies would like to know how to get convicts to choose to obey the law. Parents want to know how to induce their children to cooperate without undue coercion. And educational institutions would like to find ways to enlist students' interest in pursuing the learning objectives they are assigned to achieve.

Students control what they will attend to, focus on, and try to learn. Consequently, an effort must be made to enlist their motivation to learn the knowledge and skills they are assigned to learn. Instruction would be so much easier and more successful if educators were able to induce students to learn eagerly what they are assigned to learn.

The challenge is to identify a motive that can be enlisted to induce students to achieve assigned learning objectives. Such a motive would need to meet certain conditions: (1) it must be a motive that can be enlisted to enhance the pursuit of learning objectives in educational settings without harmful side effects; (2) it must be a stable, prevalent motive inherent in most students most of the time so that it can be reliably enlisted and worked with in group instruction.

Sex is an example of a prevalent motive that cannot be satisfied in a school setting to induce students to achieve learning objectives without deleterious side effects. People are asked to restrain their sexual urges in the workplace and in schools because, as you know, the unbridled expression and satisfaction of the sex motive can be disruptive to achieving both work and learning objectives. Moreover, the open public expression of the sex motive is most often illegal. Hunger is another motive that is not enlisted and satisfied during work and instruction. In free, modern societies people are generally not starving, and it is illegal to starve them. And eating can interfere with work and learning. There are times and places set aside for eating and other times and places set aside for work and formal education.

Other motives are transient. They are not sufficiently prevalent to be reliable. They are here one minute and gone the next. For example, anger is frequently fleeting. A parent may be angry with his child one minute and be forgiving the next. Avarice, too, is often fleeting. A child may want a toy and be satisfied when given the toy. If not, the child might be distracted or soon become interested in some other attraction. In addition, bribing children to complete assignments by offering a gift can have adverse side effects. They learn to expect rewards for doing assignments instead of doing assignments because the learning that accrues is inherently beneficial.

Although knowledge of human motivation is still quite primitive, one motive has been emerging that seems to meet instructional requirements—the *control motive*. It appears to be reliably present and can be worked with to induce students to pursue instructional objectives without deleterious side effects. For our purposes, *the control motive is defined as the penchant to improve the control of outcomes.*

Unlike many other motives, satisfying the control motive is compatible with the pursuit of fundamental instructional objectives. Education is the primary means for developing productive citizens, and the development of control is essential to productive citizenship. To be productive, people must be able to exercise sufficient control to take care of themselves and to work successfully. People who are unable to exercise sufficient control become social wards.

Moreover, achieving most instructional objectives requires the control of outcomes. Writing a composition requires control of one's handwriting and descriptive ability. In school, control is exercised in laboratory experiments. In math, control is needed to execute the appropriate formula to solve problems. Additionally, the acquisition of knowledge requires control: finding facts requires control, memorizing facts requires control, as does recalling facts (see the chapter on reminders). Now that the compatibility of satisfying the control motive and pursuing learning objectives has been discussed, we need to demonstrate the presence of the control motive as a force that reliably directs people's behavior.

There is mounting evidence that when people improve their control they derive personal satisfaction. Moreover, when they perceive that they can control the achievement of an outcome they will pursue it, and when they do not perceive that they can control the achievement of an outcome their interest in pursuing the outcome diminishes and they may not try.

A great deal of evidence demonstrating the importance of the control motive has been amassed in the field of health. People who perceive that they have control over outcomes in their life fare much better healthwise (O'Leary, 1985). Nursing home studies show that inducing perceptions of control in older patients improves their well-being, including a reduction in both disease and mortality rate (Langer & Rodin, 1976; Schultz & Hoyer, 1976; Langer et al., 1979; Banzinger & Roush, 1983). So people who perceive that they have control over their life enjoy better health. And when people who have lost control are made to perceive that they are more in control, their health improves. Furthermore, people who perceive that they are more in control take better care of themselves. They take greater responsibility for their health needs (Wallston et al., 1976), they learn more about their illnesses (Toner & Manuck, 1979), and they are more likely to benefit from health education programs (Walker & Bates, 1992). They also are less withdrawn, have a more active social life, and feel better about their life and environment (Lemke & Moos, 1981; Moos, 1981; Moos & Ingra, 1980; Hickson, Housely, & Boyle, 1988). The evidence becomes more compelling as research accumulates.

Evidence demonstrating the relationship between the control motive and academic achievement is not yet compelling, but it is mounting. People who perceive that they can control outcomes obtain higher scores on measures of academic achievement and also process information more efficiently than people who do not (Lefcourt, 1973, 1982). Additional research shows that people who perceive that they can control outcomes perform better in problem solving situations (Wolk & DuCette, 1974). Stipek & Weisz (1981) also provide evidence indicating that perceived control of outcomes is related to academic achievement. Gordon (1977) shows that perceived control is related to higher self-esteem as well as greater academic achievement.

The above evidence makes working with the control motive to enhance educational achievement worth considering, as well as indicating the need for further research on the relationship.

STUDENT BENEFICIARIES

From a societal and educational perspective, enlisting the control motive to facilitate the achievement of learning objectives students are assigned to achieve will benefit all students. The students will be learning the knowledge and skills educational establishments deem necessary to equip them to succeed and to make social contributions.

To enlist the control motive, it would be necessary to design instruction to satisfy the control motive as well as to achieve other learning objectives. Under these conditions, students should get more satisfaction from pursuing and achieving learning objectives.

LEARNING ACHIEVED

In addition to achieving the learning objectives they are assigned to achieve, students would be increasing their ability to control outcomes. And as indicated, in large measure society benefits from citizens that can control outcomes. Citizens who cannot control outcomes become burdens to society.

INSTRUCTIONAL TACTICS

Three types of instructional tactics need to be employed:

1. Students need to be taught about control. Since people often have difficulty understanding and coping with their own motivation, it is important to clarify for them the control motive and how it affects behavior.
2. Students need to be taught how to improve their control.
3. The control motive should be enlisted to enhance achievement of learning objectives.
4. Instruction must be designed to engender perceptions of control in students.

CLARIFYING MOTIVATION TO CONTROL

As soon as they are old enough to understand, it can be explained to students that while we tend to be acutely aware of our intense motives, such as hunger and sex urges, other motives are important not because of their intensity but because of their prevalence. Those motives are prompting our behavior a great deal of the time. A most prevalent motive is our motivation to improve our control. Most of the time we are attempting to improve our control of something—be it our weight, our mood, our cholesterol level, other people, or getting food, a car, or money. Unlike many very intense motives, we are not always aware of our motivation to control. When eating delicious food to satisfy our hunger, we are aware of the delightful taste of the food; we are much less aware of our desire to control the acquisition of food, that is, getting the food to our mouths and providing for our future meals.

The important thing to realize is that whatever we may want at the time, be it food, companionship, or a car, we want to control its acquisition. If we are able to control its acquisition, we can make certain that it is available when we want it again in the future. We are interested in controlling all sources of satisfaction. Although the particular things we want change from time to time, we spend most of our waking hours trying to control something. That is why our motivation to control is so prevalent.

We not only want to control to get things, we find improving our control satisfying in itself. We feel good about ourselves when we are a "take control" person—in control of our lives. We feel more competent, more capable. Every time we set a goal and control its achievement we are satisfied with ourselves.

To succeed in improving our control it is necessary to understand the nature of control. *By control we mean influencing things or people, including oneself, to bring about desired outcomes.*

For one thing, we are intensely interested in controlling our environment so we can get from it the things we want when we want them. Physical objects we usually control by physically manipulating them—we turn on a stove, ride a bicycle, and close a door through physical manipulation.

People themselves are sometimes controlled by physical manipulation. For example, parents physically manipulate infants to diaper and feed them. Criminals are sometimes controlled by physical manipulation; they are handcuffed and forced into jail. However, when we are dealing with people who can understand what we say, we usually attempt to control them by talking to them. When people are dealing with subordinates, they often give them orders. In the army, drill sergeants give marching orders to their troops. Parents give orders to their children when they tell them to finish their food or go to bed. Teachers give orders when they give homework assignments or tell their class to be quiet.

On the other hand, when we are dealing with people who are under no obligation to take orders from us, we control them by asking and persuading them to do what we want them to do. If we want to make a date with someone, we ask the person for a date. If a person has something we want, we ask the person for it; for example, we may ask to borrow a pencil from a friend or ask a teacher to answer a question.

Quite often we need to work with others to control an outcome. Then, cooperation is required. Such is the case when we join a team—members of a sports team must cooperate to win games, and members of work teams must cooperate to manufacture products. If the team we join is to be successful in controlling desired outcomes, team members must place cooperation above conflicting personal preferences.

It is important to realize that self-control is a prerequisite to environmental control. If we want to drive a car, we must control our actions to start the car, shift the gears, and steer the car. If we want to make friends, we must do and say things that are appealing to other people. The bottom line is that if we can't control ourselves, we can't control anything else.

Self-control can have personal as well as environmental benefits. It is required when we want to diet to lose weight, or we want to exercise to build strength, or when we want to rest to recuperate when we are weary.

It is through education that people learn to control outcomes. Learning to speak enables children to ask adults to help them control things they cannot control themselves; learning hygiene and how to obtain medical assistance enables people to control their health; learning how to drive enables people to control a car; and learning an occupation enables people to get and hold a job. People can learn to control some primitive outcomes by themselves, such as crawling, but it is through education that people learn how to control the outcomes primarily responsible for achieving personal aspirations, whatever they may be, and succeeding in society.

TEACHING STUDENTS HOW TO CONTROL OUTCOMES

Students' motivation to control is elicited. To capture students' interest they are informed that they are about to be taught a technique that will help them control the achievement of any outcome they may want to achieve. Learning the technique will help them get what they want, whatever that may be.

Students are taught to behave purposefully. Students are informed that the technique they are about to learn is how to behave purposefully. Purposeful behavior has four defining characteristics. Purposeful behavior is (1) directed toward an outcome rather than aimless, (2) based on learning rather than instincts, (3) based on prediction rather than hindsight or ideas of the moment, and (4) selected rather than predetermined or imposed. Students are informed that the technique involves first selecting an outcome they want to pursue at the time, and then selecting a behavior to achieve the outcome as follows.

SELECTING AN OUTCOME TO ACHIEVE

The first step in behaving purposefully is to select an outcome to pursue at the time—be it obtaining money, a bicycle, a pet, a car, or taking a vacation. Although people may want to achieve many outcomes, to be successful they need to establish their preferences and plan to pursue one outcome at a time. Otherwise, they might become confused and ineffectual.

SELECTING A BEHAVIOR PREDICTED TO ACHIEVE THE OUTCOME

A behavior is selected because it is predicted to achieve the outcome. It must be made clear to students that they frequently and routinely predict the outcomes of their behavior. When turning the page of a novel they predict the story will continue on the next page. They predict that washing will make them and other things clean, that drinking will quench their thirst, that dating a particular person will be satisfying, that dieting and exercise will result in weight loss, that following a particular route will lead them to school. Because particular behaviors have frequently achieved particular outcomes in the past, they have learned to predict with confidence that the behaviors will achieve the outcomes in the future. When their learning does not enable confident predictions, they can consult libraries and data banks to find out whether cumulative learning recorded over the years enables them to make confident predictions. In addition, they can learn statistics to estimate probability in order to make more accurate predictions.

Students must be made aware that when they behave purposefully to control outcomes, they are taking an active part in shaping their own destiny through foresight and preparation, rather than reacting to things that are imposed upon them. When they behave purposefully they are more apt to make things turn out as they choose.

ENLISTING THE CONTROL MOTIVE TO FACILITATE ACHIEVEMENT OF LEARNING OBJECTIVES

Most important, the control motive should be enlisted during instruction to achieve the learning objective being pursued. In order to enlist motivation to control, students would need to be shown how pursuing an assigned learning objective can improve their control of outcomes. In general, this can be accomplished by translating assigned tasks designed to achieve a learning objective into behavior $\rightarrow$ outcome units. The performance of all tasks requires students to execute behaviors to achieve specified outcomes. Breaking down assigned tasks into behavior $\rightarrow$ outcome units during instruction not only conveys to students how their behavior can control outcomes, it simplifies the teaching of task performance. The task of performing long division can be broken down into component behavior $\rightarrow$ outcome units, and so can shopping, developing a household budget, driving a car, writing a composition, and so on. The performance of almost all tasks can be taught in behavior $\rightarrow$ outcome units. Even if students are not especially interested in achieving a particular assigned learning objective, they are interested in improving their control. Hence, if they can see that they are learning behaviors to control outcomes, thereby improving their control, the achievement of the assigned learning objective will be more attractive to them.

Motivation to control can be enlisted when teaching in any subject area, provided students are shown how the to-be-learned subject matter can improve their control of outcomes. It has been said that making instruction relevant to students' lives increases their enthusiasm for learning. By eliciting the control motive in teaching subject matter, the subject matter is not only made relevant to students' lives, it is made useful and important to them because they are being shown how to improve their control of outcomes.

Following are examples of how motivation to control can be enlisted while teaching in a subject area. When teaching social studies, students can be shown how voting (behavior) elects candidates for office (outcome), how writing to a congressman (behavior) can initiate the enactment of a law (outcome), and how breaking the law (behavior) can result in being arrested (outcome). In teaching language arts, students can be shown how learning to write (behavior) enables them to send a message to people they are not in face-to-face contact with (outcome), and how reading books (behavior) can bring them enjoyment (outcome). When teaching science, students can be shown that conducting a lab experiment (behavior) increases their ability to manipulate physical matter (outcome), and how studying the scientific method (behavior) enables them to make discoveries (outcome). In math, students can be shown how learning arithmetic (behavior) enables them to check the change they receive when shopping (outcome), and that learning how to measure (behavior) enables them to follow recipes when cooking (outcome).

ENGENDERING PERCEPTIONS OF CONTROL IN STUDENTS

When students are assigned tasks to perform, it is most important that they perceive that they can control the achievement of the tasks. If they do not, they may well not try at all or they may make a feeble effort to perform the tasks. It is incumbent upon instructional planners and teachers to engender in students the perception that they can control the achievement of assigned tasks so that they will persist in attempting to perform the tasks.

One factor that contributes to students perceiving that they can perform assigned tasks is that they have often performed them successfully in the past. This gives them confidence that they will succeed in the future. Instructional planners and teachers can inspire confidence in students by ensuring student success. This can be accomplished by making certain (1) that students have the readiness ability to perform assigned tasks, (2) that earlier tasks in a task sequence enable the performance of subsequent tasks, and (3) that task sequences are designed in small graded steps or increments.

Second, in providing students feedback on their task performance, they are given a clear understanding of their strengths and weaknesses, they are commended on their efforts and achievements as appropriate, and they are told that they have the ability to perform the next assigned tasks, if they make a concerted effort, and they will be given the assistance they need to succeed. These assurances must not be in vain or when students fail they will rightfully blame and mistrust the instructional system and refuse to cooperate.

The above explanation of how purposeful behavior is used to improve control explains in part why the instructional tactics prescribed in the chapter on decision-making enhance student achievement.

CAUTIONS AND COMMENTS

The foregoing description of the control motive and its use in achieving assigned tasks is only an introduction. A more complete presentation is made in *Taking Control: Vitalizing Education* (Friedman, 1993). Moreover, to be most effective the instructional tactics described need to be adapted to the particular instructional program in use or being planned. Although the control motive has been enlisted to achieve goals in other fields, more research needs to be done on its use in education. Meanwhile, its application in education should be restricted to pilot testing.

Enlisting the control motive to achieve learning objectives requires that behavior $\rightarrow$ outcome relationships be emphasized in instruction. In this way students will be learning how to plan their behavior to control outcomes, thereby improving their control. As a result they will be motivated to achieve the learning objectives. This instructional emphasis mandates against the teaching of isolated facts, so prevalent in many curricula. Facts should be incorporated in the teaching of behavior, or procedures to guide behaviors, to achieve particular outcomes.

Teaching facts in isolation does not satisfy the control motive because students cannot see the relationship between the facts and the improvement of their control. However, it is often the case that facts can be taught as components of a procedure used to control the achievement of a particular kind of outcome. For example, scientific method can be taught as a procedure for increasing knowledge. The components of scientific method can be taught as parts of the procedure. Then students can be guided in the execution of scientific method to enable them to see for themselves that it works. When they do, they will see that their ability to control outcomes has been improved, and they will be gratified.

REFERENCE LIST

Banziger, G., & Roush, S. 1983. Nursing home for the birds: A control relevant intervention test with bird feeders. *Gerontologists 23*(5), 527–531.

Friedman, M. I. 1993. *Taking control: Vitalizing education.* Westport, CT: Praeger.

Gordon, D. 1977. Children's beliefs in internal-external and self-esteem as related to academic achievement. *Journal of Personality Assessment 41*(4), 333–336.

Hickson, J., Housely, W. F., & Boyle, C. 1988. The relationship of locus of control to life satisfaction and death anxiety in older persons. *International Journal of Aging and Human Development 26*(3), 191–199.

Langer, E., & Rodin, J. 1976. The effects of choice and enhanced personal responsibility for the aged: A field experiment in an institutional setting. *Journal of Personality and Social Psychology 34*(2), 191–198.

Langer, E., Rodin, J., Beck, P., Weinman, C., & Spitzer, L. 1979. Environmental determinants of memory improvement in late adulthood. *Journal of Personality and Social Psychology 37*, 2003–2013.

Lefcourt, H. M. (1973). The function of the illusions of control and freedom. *American Psychologist 28*, 417–425.

Lefcourt, H. M. (1982). Locus of control: Current trends in theory and research. Hillsdale, NJ: Erlbaum.

Lemke, S., & Moos, R. 1981. The suprapersonal environments of sheltered care settings. *Journal of Gerontology 36*(2), 233–243.

Moos, R. 1981. Environmental choice and control in community care settings for older people. *Journal of Applied Social Psychology 11*(1), 23–43.

Moos, R., & Ingra, A. 1980. Detriments of the social environments of sheltered care settings. *Journal of Health and Social Behavior 21*, 88–98.

O'Leary, A. 1985. Self-efficacy and health. *Journal of Behavior Research and Therapy 23*, 437–451.

Schultz, N. R., Jr., & Hoyer, W. J. 1976. Feedback effects on spatial egocentrism in old age. *Journal of Gerontology 31*(1), 72–75.

Stipek, D. J., & Weisz, J. R. 1981. Perceived personal control and academic achievement. *Review of Educational Research 51*(1), 101–137.

Toner, J., & Manuck, S. B. 1979. Health locus of control and health related information seeking at hypertension screening. *Journal of Social Science and Medicine (Medical Psychology and Medical Sociology) 13A*(6), 823–825.

Walker, K., & Bates, R. 1992. Health locus and self-efficacy beliefs in a healthy elderly sample. *American Journal of Health Promotion 6*(4), 302–309.

Wallston, B., Wallston, K., Kaplan, G., & Maides, S. 1976. Development and validation of the health locus of control scale. *Journal of Consulting and Clinical Psychology 44*(4), 580–585.

Wolk, S., & DuCette, J. 1974. Intentional performance and incidental learning as a function of personality and task dimensions. *Journal of Personality and Social Psychology 29*, 90–101.

Providing Predictive Ability Instruction

INTRODUCTION

Predictive ability is defined as the ability to accurately forecast outcomes from antecedent conditions. To appreciate the value of predictive ability in improving academic achievement and achieving other goals, whatever they may be, it is helpful to understand that it has many applications. It not only involves ability to predict that something will happen again because it has a history of happening in a particular pattern; predictive ability also involves being able to predict what might happen in the future that has never happened before and being able to predict ways of making it happen or preventing it from happening.

Predictive ability is largely responsible for discovery and invention as well as academic and everyday achievements. Sports coaches must be able to predict strategies that will win games or they will be replaced. Students must be able to predict that study and test-taking skills will yield higher grades or they will fail in school. Businessmen must be able to predict how to realize a profit or they will go under. And to avoid accidents, drivers must be able to predict how to avoid cars and other obstacles.

In addition to its general contribution to goal achievement of any kind, there is evidence that predictive ability enhances academic achievement, and that students' predictive ability can be improved through instruction. Research corroborates predictive ability's relationship to academic achievement. Several studies indicate that good readers are good predictors (Benz & Rosemier. 1966; Greeno & Noreen, 1974; Henderson & Long, 1968; Freeman, 1982; Zinar, 1990). In a more general context, Dykes (1997) demonstrated that predictive ability contributes substantially to academic success in high school. In many cases predictive ability proves to be a better predictor of success in general and learning in particular than I.Q. (Friedman, 1974; Dykes, 1997).

A number of studies show that instruction designed to enhance predictive ability improves academic achievement (Denner & McGinley, 1990; Walker & Mohr, 1985; Hunt & Joseph, 1990; Reutzel & Fawson, 1991; Chia, 1995; Hurst & Milkent, 1994; Nolan, 1991; Friedman & Maddock, 1980).

STUDENT BENEFICIARIES

Research shows that predictive ability is related to academic achievement in high school and elementary school and for retarded students as well as students of average intelligence and above. Predictive ability has also been shown to be related to achievement in the military and in industry. Instruction designed to enhance predictive ability has been related to increased academic achievement beyond the fourth grade but not earlier.

LEARNING ACHIEVED

Instruction that enhances predictive ability has been related to increased academic achievement in the areas of reading, physics, biology, and language arts as well as the content areas covered by the Comprehensive Test of Basic Skills.

INSTRUCTIONAL TACTICS

Instructional tactics involve teaching the prediction cycle (shown at the top of the following page) as an effective means of problem solving in all academic areas as well as daily living.

First, students are given an overview of the prediction cycle so that they can see the parts/whole relationships and how the functions in the cycle are coordinated to solve problems.

Problem solving begins when motivation is aroused and presses for satisfaction.

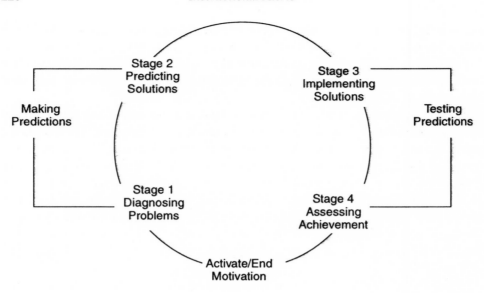

Motivation activates the activities in the prediction cycle which consists of four stages. Stage 1, Diagnosing Problems, and Stage 2, Predicting Solutions, involve making predictions. Stage 3, Implementing Solutions, and Stage 4, Assessing Achievement, involve testing predictions, as shown in the diagram of the prediction cycle. A brief overview and example of the process follows.

PROVIDING AN OVERVIEW OF THE PREDICTION CYCLE

Motivation

People are motivated to satisfy their desires, without knowing initially what to do about them. For example, a student is worried about failing science and is motivated to do something about the situation.

Making Predictions

The student needs to predict a way to alleviate this worry. To proceed the student (1) diagnoses the problem as a basis for (2) predicting a solution.

Stage 1, Diagnosing Problems

Defining the Problem. To satisfy desires it is advantageous to define them as problems. A problem can be defined as a discrepancy between an existing state and a desired state. To continue with our example, existing state: The student is earning a grade of "F" in science. Desired state: The student wants to earn a "B" in science by the end of the school term.

Once the problem is defined, the solution becomes clear: to progress from a grade of "F" to a grade of "B." To complete the diagnosis, factors that need to be controlled to achieve a solution are determined.

Factors to Be Controlled. Factors that need to be controlled are those factors that must be attended to or manipulated to generate progress from the existing state to the desired state.

For example, the student must identify the particular tasks that must be performed competently to raise the science grade to a "B." A conference with the teacher might reveal the following factors to be controlled.

- Earn a "B" on the science project.
- Improve performance on weekly quizzes.
- Earn a "B" on the final exam.

Constraints. In addition to defining the problem and identifying factors to be controlled, constraints are identified so that realistic limitations can be dealt with. Continuing with the example, one constraint would be earning a "B" by the end of the school term.

Stage 2, Predicting Solutions

Once factors to be controlled and constraints are identified to solve the problem, an attempt is made to predict a solution by (1) identifying means of controlling the factors, providing for the constraints and (2) prescribing procedures to apply the means.

Means of Controlling the Factors.

- Means of controlling the factors are identified through recall and research, if need be.
- Common elements of previous science projects that won awards are identified, and a similar science project is selected.
- Engage a tutor to improve the student's understanding of science and to teach test-taking skills.
- Increase study time.

Prescribing Procedures. A procedure is prescribed to coordinate the means of controlling the factors providing for constraints. For instance, a procedure is derived to implement the science project, engage a tutor and schedule tutoring lessons, and increase study time in time to raise the student's grade to a "B" within the school term.

Testing Predictions

After the problem is diagnosed at Stage 1 and a solution is predicted in Stage 2, it is necessary to test the prediction that the proposed solution will solve the problem. This entails implementing the solution and then assessing the outcome.

Stage 3, Implementing Solutions

To implement solutions, the prescribed procedure is executed according to specifications. For example, the procedure prescribed for completing the science project, being tutored, and increasing study time are implemented exactly as planned.

Stage 4, Assessing Achievement

After implementing the solution, observations are made of the outcome. Then the outcome is compared to the desired state to see the extent to which the desired state has been achieved. If it is achieved, the implemented solution would be considered to be effective. Side effects are also observed, as well as efficiency factors, such as costs of implementing the solution. For instance, at the end of the school term the student notes the grade on their report card to see if they earned the final grade of "B" as desired. They also determine the final cost of the tutoring they received, as well as side effects. Improved study tactics taught by their tutor might have improved their grades in other courses.

This completes the initial execution of the prediction cycle.

Motivation

After the completion of each prediction cycle, motivation is revisited and reappraised. If the desired state is achieved the problem might be considered solved, and there might not be any motivation to continue. In this case, attention would be turned to other problems which people are motivated to solve. This would constitute the end of this problem-solving mission. For example, the student might earn a final grade of "B" and turn their attention elsewhere to solve other disturbing problems they are motivated to solve. On the other hand, the desired state might be achieved and there might be motivation to recycle to increase efficiency: for example, to reduce the time and money that was required to implement the solution the first time; or recycling might be initiated to remove an undesirable side effect. To recycle people, move to Stage 1 again to diagnose the problem anew and then proceed through the remaining stages to complete the prediction cycle another time.

If the desired state is not achieved, there might be motivation to recycle to try again to solve the problem. Many problems are not solved on the first attempt. Rather, they are solved by successive approximation, when one cycle after another is executed until the problem is solved. Each time the cycle is completed, something new can be learned that makes it more likely that a solution will be achieved on a subsequent attempt. In contrast, there may be no motivation to continue to try to solve the problem. The pursuit might be abandoned because there is no longer any interest in solving the problem or resources are insufficient to continue pursuing a solution.

For whatever reason motivation is sufficient to recycle, the motivation activates the recycling and the four stages of the cycle are repeated in order.

Demonstrating the Relevance of the Prediction Cycle

Once an overview of the prediction cycle is presented to students and they understand the parts/whole relationships of the cycle, the relevance of the cycle to solving problems in all subject areas and daily living are demonstrated for the students. This can be achieved by showing students how the prediction cycle can be applied to solve problems in science, math, language arts, and social studies as well as in their daily lives.

Detailing Each Stage of the Prediction Cycle

After students understand how the cycle can be used to solve any kind of problem, it is necessary to teach them how to perform each stage of the cycle in detail. It takes more than a general understanding of the cycle to be able to apply it. Students must become proficient in performing each stage of the cycle. Following are some of the nuances and details students need to learn.

Stage 1, Diagnosing Problems

Defining Problems. Students are taught the advantages of defining a problem as a discrepancy between an existing state and a desired state, rather than just specifying a desired state as a goal or objective. Defining an existing state as a starting point as well as a desired state facilitates predicting solutions at Stage 2 and assessing achievement at Stage 4. It is advantageous to know both the existing state or starting point and the desired state when planning a solution, rather than knowing only the desired state, since the solution must produce progress from the existing to the desired state. It is also advantageous to know both the existing state and the desired state when constructing an observation instrument to detect progress from the existing to the desired state, rather than just knowing the desired state.

Factors to Be Controlled. Many factors that need to be controlled to generate progress from the existing to the desired state are causal agents. Students need to learn about cause–effect relationships so that they can understand that causal agents may need to be identified when the effect being pursued is a specified desired state.

Constraints. Students are taught that desired states cannot be pursued without considering constraints. It is often necessary to avoid harmful side effects when solving problems, and it is often necessary to attempt to solve problems with limited resources.

After students understand in detail how problems are diagnosed, they are assigned to diagnose problems in various subject areas and in their daily lives until they become competent.

Stage 2, Predicting Solutions

To become competent at predicting solutions, students must be able to identify means of controlling the factors that were identified in Stage 1 and prescribe procedures for solving the problem.

Means of Controlling the Factors. Students must be taught how to conduct research to identify means of controlling factors they are interested in controlling. They need to be taught how to access and locate information in libraries and computer data banks. Sophistication can be developed gradually over time.

Prescribing Procedures. Initially students should be taught to find appropriate procedures by searching libraries and data banks. Later they can be taught methods of deriving procedures when standard operating procedures are not available.

Many methods for planning procedures are available: for instance, Project Evaluation and Review Technique (PERT) as well as various methods of deriving computer and other programs. Students are also taught that a predicted solution might be to do nothing but wait. Such is the case when it is predicted that the problem will dissipate with the passage of time.

Students' ability to predict solutions is tested in the various content areas and daily living and remediated as needed until they become proficient.

Stage 3, Implementing Solutions

Students are taught that unless predicted solutions are implemented as prescribed according to specifications, the effectiveness of the solution in solving the problem cannot be tested. Every effort must be made to detect and correct deviations from predicted solution specifications. When predicted solutions are complicated, training is often necessary to ensure that the solution is implemented as prescribed. During training, performance is monitored and corrected until it can be certified as proficient. Monitoring devices such as video and audio recorders can be used to monitor and analyze performance.

Once students understand how to implement solutions, their ability to implement solutions to problems in science, math, language arts, social studies, and daily living is tested and remediated as needed until they become proficient. Initially, assignments should not require knowledge of monitoring devices or how to estimate the resources needed to implement solutions. Students should eventually learn how to estimate the resources needed to implement solutions.

Stage 4, Assessing Achievement

Students are taught how to make observations of existing states, both quantitative observations by means of measurement and qualitative observations. They should eventually become familiar with the various kinds of instruments that can be used to make observations and how to assess their accuracy (validity, reliability, and objectivity). Students are also taught how to compare existing states with desired states to determine any discrepancies that might be present. Eventually, students should be taught to determine the probability that a derived discrepancy is a chance factor and the importance of a discrepancy (effect size). This requires knowledge of statistics. Students should also eventually learn how to assess side effects and efficiency factors, such as costs.

When students understand how to assess achievement, their ability to assess achievement in science, math, language arts, social studies, and daily living is tested and remediated until they become proficient. Initially, students should not need to know how to use sophisticated instruments to make observations, statistics, or how to assess side effect or efficiency factors.

Developing Student Proficiency in Applying the Prediction Cycle

After students have been presented an overview of how the prediction cycle is applied and have become proficient in administering the four stages individually, they are taught how to coordinate the stages in applying the entire cycle. Their ability to apply the cycle to identify and solve problems in science, math, language arts, social studies, and daily living is then tested and remediated as needed until they become proficient.

Student proficiency includes estimating achievement, side effects, and available resources after each cycle is completed as a basis for deciding whether to recycle. Ultimately, it is the authorized decision-maker(s) who use the estimates to decide whether or not to recycle. The decision depends on their motivation, after they are fully informed. Initial applications of the cycle should be kept simple, not requiring students to estimate side effects and available resources or to use sophisticated observation instruments or statistics to estimate achievement.

CAUTIONS AND COMMENTS

An advantage of teaching students to use the prediction cycle proficiently is that they can use it from then on to solve almost all problems they need to solve that require extended effort. Predictive ability instruction can be incorporated into most existing courses or taught independently in a course designed for the purpose. It is applicable whenever systematic problem-solving is required.

SUPPORTIVE RESEARCH ON PREDICTIVE ABILITY

Groups of studies on predictive ability have not been attempted as yet. Descriptions of two individual studies follow. The first study indicates the relationship between predictive ability and general academic achievement; the second study shows the effectiveness of predictive ability instruction in enhancing general academic achievement.

Author: Dykes (1997)

Students: High school seniors

Learning: Grade point ratio

Findings: In general, predictive ability was related to academic achievement. High school seniors who had high scores on a predictive ability test also had higher GPRs. Predictive ability was a better predictor of high school success than an I.Q. test.

Authors: Friedman & Maddock (1980)

Students: 5th, 6th, 7th, and 8th grade students in rural, urban, and suburban public schools

Learning: Performance on the Comprehensive Test of Basic Skills (CTBS)

Instructional Tactics: An earlier version of the prediction cycle was taught to students as prescribed earlier under instructional tactics.

Findings: Students who received predictive ability instruction scored higher on the average on the CTBS than students who did not receive predictive ability instruction.

REFERENCE LIST

Benz, D., & Rosemier, R. 1966. Concurrent validity of the Gates level of comprehension test and the Bond, Clymer, Hoyt reading diagnostic tests. *Educational and Psychological Measurement 26*, 1057–1062.

Chia, T. 1995. Learning difficulty in applying notion of vector in physics among "A" level students in Singapore. (ERIC Document Reproduction Service No. ED 389 528)

Denner, P. R., & McGinley, W. J. (1990). *Effects of prediction combined with storytelling versus listing predictions as prereading activities on subsequent story comprehension.* Paper presented at the annual meeting of the National Reading Conference, Miami.

Dykes, S. 1997. *A test of proposition, of prediction theory.* Doctoral dissertation, University of South Carolina.

Freeman, R. H. (1982). *Improving comprehension of stories using predictive strategies.* Paper presented at the Annual Meeting of the International Reading Association, Chicago.

Friedman, M. I. (1974). Predictive ability tests: Verbal and nonverbal forms. Columbia, SC: M. I. Friedman.

Friedman, M. I., & Maddock, M. (1980). *Predictive ability instruction.* Research report published for participating school districts in South Carolina.

Greeno, J., & Noreen, D. (1974). Time to read semantically related sentences. *Memory and Cognition 2*(1A), 117–120.

Henderson, E., & Long, B. (1968). Correlation of reading readiness and children of varying backgrounds. *The Reading Teacher 22*, 40–44.

Hunt, J., & Joseph, D. (1990). Using prediction to improve reading comprehension of low-achieving readers. *Journal of Clinical Reading, Research and Programs 3*(2), 14–17.

Hurst, R., & Milkent, M. (1994). *Facilitating successful predictive reasoning in biology through application of skill theory.* Paper presented at the annual meeting of the National Association for Research in Science Teaching, Anaheim, CA, March 19–26. (ERIC Document Reproduction Service No. ED 368 582)

Nolan, T. (1991). Self-questioning and prediction: Combining metacognitive strategies. *Journal of Reading 35*(2), 77–101.

Reutzel, D., & Fawson, P. (1991). Literature webbing predictable books: A prediction strategy that helps below-average, first-grade children. *Reading Research and Instruction 30* (4), 20–30.

Walker, B. J., & Mohr, T. (1985). *The effects of ongoing self-directed questioning on silent comprehension.* Paper presented at the Annual Meeting of the Reading Research Conference, Seattle, WA.

Walker, K., & Bates, R. (1985). *The effects of ongoing self-directed questioning on silent comprehension.* Paper presented at the annual meeting of the Reading Research Conference, St. Petersburgh, FL.

Zinar, S. (1990). Fifth-graders' recall of proposition content and causal relationships from expository prose. *Journal of Reading Behavior 22,* 2.

17

Questionable Instructional Strategies

There are many instructional strategies that are not supported by research evidence. Some are in common use, and there are still advocates of the strategies that are promoting wider adoption. Moreover, teachers are being taught to adopt them and to use them. They are being taught in both pre-service and in-service teacher training, and familiarity with one or more of them is sometimes a prerequisite for teacher certification.

The purpose of this chapter is to review the research evidence on these questionable instructional strategies and to discuss their limitations, being careful not to "throw the baby out with the bath water." Although the evidence does not support the generalizability of the strategies discussed in this chapter, in some cases the evidence supports the effectiveness of a strategy for particular purposes. You need to evaluate the use of a strategy for your purpose.

Matching Student–Teacher Field-Dependent/ Field-Independent Cognitive Styles

INTRODUCTION

Witkin et al. (1977) identify field-dependence-independence as representing one dimension of cognitive style. They define this dimension as being

> the extent to which the person perceives part of a field as discrete from the surrounding field as a whole, rather than embedded in the field; or the extent to which the organization of the prevailing field determines the perception of its components; or, to put it in everyday terminology, the extent to which the person perceives analytically. Because at one extreme of the performance range perception is strongly dominated by the prevailing field, that mode of perception was designated "field dependent." At the other extreme, where the person experiences items as more or less separate from surrounding fields, the designation "field independent" was used. (p. 7)

Witkin et al. indicate that intelligence and ability to learn are unrelated to cognitive style. There are teachers and educators who feel matching student–teacher cognitive styles is important to enhancing student achievement. However, research has failed to demonstrate the efficacy of matching student–teacher cognitive styles for the enhancing of student achievement. There is a need to evaluate the effectiveness of matching student–teacher cognitive styles for the purposes of enhancing student learning.

STUDENT BENEFICIARIES

There is no evidence to support the use of matching student–teacher cognitive styles at any age or grade level. The limited amount of research that has been conducted has found no difference in student achievement between matching and mismatching student–teacher cognitive styles for the grades K–college. Matching student–teacher cognitive styles cannot be regarded as a generalization that is applicable to students at any level of instruction. To be applicable as a generalization, evidence would need to support the use of matching student–teacher cognitive styles to most students.

LEARNING ACHIEVED

No evidence was found to indicate that matching student–teacher cognitive styles enhances student achievement in any content area. Matching student–teacher cognitive styles should be seen as having no content area generalizability.

INSTRUCTIONAL TACTICS

Matching student–teacher cognitive styles employs the following instructional tactics regardless of grade level or content area:

- Identify students and teachers as either field-independent or field-dependent in cognitive style.
- Match field-independent students with field-independent teachers.
- Match field-dependent students with field-dependent teachers.

CAUTIONS AND COMMENTS

There is no empirical evidence to support the use of matching student-teacher cognitive styles. It is recognized that the existing body of research is very small and limited. One needs to question whether these instructional tactics may have long-term negative effects on student achievement. Witkin et al. (1977) suggests, "the possibilities that have been listed reflect the complexity of the relation between cognitive style match–mismatch and student achievement, and they provide a strong note of caution against deciding about the desirability of matching before a great deal more is known as to the consequences of matching for student learning" (p. 37). If the matching of student–teacher cognitive styles is to be further considered by teachers and educators, a great deal more research needs to be done. However, before one considers pursuing the matching of student–teacher cognitive styles further, they may wish to look at some of the practical aspects and first weigh the costs against any potential benefits. The only means found for identifying field-independent and field-dependent cognitive styles was the *Embedded Figures Test.* Witkin et al. (1977) indicate that an individual's cognitive style can change over time. Students and teachers would have to be tested and retested to maintain the homogeneity of the groups. Would it be wise to change teachers prior to the end of a term? What is to be done if there are not enough teachers of one cognitive style to match with the number of groups of students of the same cognitive style? Would one hire matching teachers and replace mismatched teachers?

REFERENCE LIST

Garlinger, D. K., & Frank, B. M. (1986). Teacher–student cognitive style and academic achievement: A review and mini-meta-analysis. *Journal of Classroom Interaction 21*(2), 2–8.

Sipe, T. A., & Curlette, W. L. (1997). A meta-analysis of factors relating to educational achievement. *International Journal of Educational Research 25*(7), 591–698.

Witkin, H. A., Moore, C. A., Goodenough, D. R., & Cox, P. W. (1977). Field-dependent and field-independent cognitive styles and their educational implications. *Review of Educational Research 47*(1), 1–64.

Ability Grouping Students

INTRODUCTION

The grouping of students according to ability level for the purpose of instruction is a tactic that has been in use, to varying degrees, throughout much of this century. Ability grouping of students has been tried in many forms for many years. In general, the evidence does not support its use. The body of research on teacher expectancy offers one explanation for the failure of ability grouping. Reviews of this body of research have shown that teachers teach to their perception of the level of ability of the student, with the result being the level of achievement that would be expected for that ability level (Dusek, 1975; Cooper, 1979; Jamieson et al., 1987; Hamachek, 1995). Studies have been conducted which have demonstrated that when teachers are led to believe that high-ability students are of low ability, the resulting student achievement is consistent with that of low-ability students and vice versa, when low-ability students were identified as high-ability (Dusek, 1975). Ability grouping of students for the purposes of enhancing student learning continues to be a common practice at most levels of education. However, decades of research have failed to provide evidence in support of the continued use of ability grouping. There is a need to curtail its use as a means of enhancing student learning.

STUDENT BENEFICIARIES

An insufficient number of studies have been conducted on ability grouping of students prior to grade 4 and subsequent to grade 9 to warrant any conclusions with regard to efficacy of ability grouping for students in the early elementary grades and high school. Research over the past 60–70 years has failed to support the use of ability grouping across all ability groups and grade levels. Research conducted during the past fifteen years has shown that, overall, there is in essence no enhancement of achievement by ability grouping of students, with one exception. Research has indicated moderate to strong effects on the enhancement of achievement for gifted and talented pull-out programs that accelerate and enrich the curriculum.

In view of the evidence that has been accumulated over the past 60–70 years, ability grouping cannot be regarded as a generalization that is applicable to most students. To be applicable to most students, ability grouping would have to consistently enhance learning in students at all grade levels and at all ability levels.

LEARNING ACHIEVED

Studies of ability grouping have involved almost all curriculum areas. There is very weak meta-analytic evidence for limited generalizability of ability grouping for the enhancement of learning in the content areas of reading (cross-grade ability grouping) and mathematics (within-grade ability grouping). However, across most curriculum areas there is no evidence that ability grouping enhances student learning. Ability grouping is not generalizable across content areas.

INSTRUCTIONAL TACTICS

The following are ability grouping instructional tactics most often studied by researchers.

- Students are grouped according to ability, and instruction is provided in separate classrooms for each ability group. Instruction may be for one, multiple, or all subjects. In high school this most often takes the form of academic, general, and vocational tracks. In middle school this frequently occurs in the form of advanced, basic, and remedial tracks (Kulik & Kulik, 1992; Slavin, 1990).
- Students from several grade levels are grouped together, regardless of their grade level, according to their level of academic achievement in a particular subject matter area. This tactic is used most often in elementary reading and is often referred to as the Joplin Plan (Kulik & Kulik, 1992; Slavin, 1987).

- Students within a single classroom are formed into groups based on ability, and the teacher provides instruction appropriate to each group's level of ability. This tactic has been used primarily for elementary school mathematics (Kulik & Kulik, 1992).
- High-ability students are placed in groups separate from other students and instructed using an enhanced curriculum.

In recent years a number of initiatives, Tech Prep and School to Work being examples, have been implemented to reduce ability grouping, or tracking, at the high school level. Although they should be seen as important steps in the right direction and their intention was to prepare all students for some form of post-secondary education, they most often have simply led to high school academic and vocational tracks, with the former group being seen as prepared for college and the latter prepared to go to work upon completion of high school. All students must be prepared for some form of post-secondary education if they are to be productive members of society.

CAUTIONS AND COMMENTS

There is only evidence on the effectiveness of ability grouping for gifted and talented pull-out programs, with curricular enhancement for students in grades 4–9. Ability grouping is not effective for most students. There is insufficient empirical evidence to support ability grouping of any kind for grades 1–3 and for high school. Seventy years of controversy should not be ignored. The evidence indicates that ability grouping is ineffective, with one exception being middle school gifted and talented programs that provide enriched curriculum for the students.

REFERENCE LIST

Cooper, H. M. (1979). Pygmalion grows up: A model for teacher expectation communication and performance influence. *Review of Educational Research 49*(3), 389–410.

Dusek, J. B. (1975). Do teachers bias children's learning? *Review of Educational Research 45*(4), 661–684.

Hamachek, D. (1995). Expectations revisited: Implications for teachers and counselors and questions for self-assessment. *Journal of Humanistic Education and Development 34*(2), 65–74.

Jamieson, D. W., Lydon, J. E., Stewart, G., & Zanna, M. P. (1987). Pygmalion revisited: New evidence for student expectancy in the classroom. *Journal of Educational Psychology 79*(4), 461–466.

Kulik, J. A., & Kulik, C. C. (1992). Meta-analytic findings on grouping programs. *Gifted Child Quarterly 36*(2), 73–77.

Sipe, T. A., & Curlette, W. L. (1997). A meta-analysis of factors relating to educational achievement. *International Journal of Educational Research 25*(7), 591–698.

Slavin, R. E. (1987). Ability grouping and student achievement in elementary schools: A best-evidence synthesis. *Review of Educational Research 57*(3), 293–336.

Slavin, R. E. (1990). Achievement effects of ability grouping in secondary schools: A best-evidence synthesis. *Review of Educational Research 60*(3), 471–499.

Providing Reinforcement

INTRODUCTION

The term *reinforcement* emanates from conditioning psychology. In this context, reinforcement entails repeatedly rewarding behavior that a trainer/conditioner considers desirable to condition a subject to perform the behavior automatically. For example, a dog trainer repeatedly gives a dog food the dog likes for sitting when the trainer gives the command to sit, until the dog sits habitually on command. Reinforcement may be the most widely researched psychological phenomenon of all. Moreover, conditioning psychologists have advocated that reinforcement be used in instruction for a long time. And many teachers have been taught in pre-service and in-service training to adopt and use reinforcement in their teaching. However, all psychological principles derived primarily from research on lower animals are not advantageously applied to human instruction and learning. There is a need to revisit and reevaluate the effectiveness of reinforcement on classroom instruction.

STUDENT BENEFICIARIES

Reinforcement appears to work with less mentally competent people. When used in the classroom it was not, in general, an effective means of producing academic achievement. It was effective primarily with young children and mentally retarded youth. This is a conclusion that the well respected educational researchers Brophy & Good (1986) drew after considering the available research. The present authors came to the same conclusion based on their independent review of the research. Thus it should not be regarded as a generalization that is applicable to most human students. To be applicable to most students reinforcement would, in addition, need to consistently enhance academic achievement in students who are not mentally retarded or very young. The majority of students are not mentally retarded or very young.

Since reinforcement has been used to shape behavior for such a long time and is advocated by so many, it is helpful to understand the limitations of its generalizability. The remainder of the discussion on reinforcement is devoted to clarifying its meanings and applications and explaining its limited generalizability.

Fundamental laws of reinforcement were derived by psychologists, ranging over time from Pavlov to Skinner, who did research using food to shape the behavior of captive starved lower animals. Such laws are as applicable to shaping the behavior of lower animals today as they ever were. And the laws appear to be applicable to mentally retarded and young children as well. This may be because reinforcement is more effective in shaping the behavior of less mentally competent animals and humans than in shaping the behavior of more mentally competent humans. More mentally competent humans are not as likely to respond as automatons to prompts. They are more capable of and are more likely to use their knowledge to deliberate alternatives before acting. More mentally competent humans are not as habit bound and are not as prone to be conditioned to react in a particular way to a particular prompt or stimulus.

Another reason laws of reinforcement have limited generalizability is because the captive lower animals used in traditional reinforcement research are placed in highly confining environments, which severely restrict their movements and choice. The environments are contrived to ensure that the desired behavior will occur so that it can be reinforced and habituated. For example, rats are conditioned to receive a food pellet by pressing a bar which has been placed in a small box with nothing obtruding but the bar in it. Because the rats are starved, they are active and will press the bar in a very short time. Such restrictiveness imposed upon human learners would be illegal in free countries that provide for free choice. Laws of reinforcement derived from such contrived, restrictive environments are not only not generalizable to human behavior, they have not been proven to be generalizable to the behavior of rats in their natural environment.

In addition, laws of reinforcement derived from rewarding starved lower animals with food are not generalizable to human learning environments in free countries because it is illegal for educators to starve human learners. In preparation for conditioning, rats are starved by depriving them of food (1) for a certain amount of time or (2) until they lose a certain amount of weight.

Moreover, the laws of reinforcement are derived from conditioning individual animals one at a time, not from conditioning groups of animals. Thus the laws are not generalizable to the group instruction of lower animals or human students. It is not only unwarranted, but impractical as well, for teachers to administer reinforcement to a class of students. The teacher would be required to reward every student in the class for the performance of every desirable behavior. Punishment is not allowed, so the teacher must await the performance of every desirable behavior from all students, say 20, and promptly reward them without being able to punish misbehavior. This is a recipe for chaos, as many classroom teachers who have been trained and required to administer reinforcement in their classrooms report.

In conclusion, "laws of reinforcement" are generalizable to the conditioning of single captive starved lower animals and mentally retarded and very young human students, but not beyond. Therefore, they do not qualify as generalizations of human instruction when the objective is academic achievement.

LEARNING ACHIEVED

Most of the learning produced by reinforcement is the learning of automatic behavior or habits. Although reinforcement evidently can be used to condition habits in young and mentally retarded students, only a small percentage of the learning objectives pursued in school pertain to the conditioning of habits. Such learning objectives would include the automatic recognition of words, numbers, letters of the alphabet, and significant others by name. In addition, while students may be expected to be able to recite the multiplication tables automatically, as well as the Pledge of Allegiance to the United States flag and to sing "The Star-Spangled Banner," such learning pertains primarily to the indoctrination of young children into society. More advanced learning such as problem solving requires students to deliberate options as the basis for choosing a solution. Young children's automatic responses are often impulsive and impair deriving tenable solutions. They are often told not to act impulsively but rather to think before they act.

The teaching of automatic behavior is much more in keeping with totalitarian governments, where people are to obey commands without questioning them, and in communist states, where individual penchants are to be sacrificed for the common good. In the United States, where students have the freedom to pursue happiness as they choose and are encouraged to think for themselves, conditioning students to perform as robots is frowned upon and is illegal when it deprives them of their legal rights to free choice.

Moreover, education pertains to more than performing desired behaviors habitually. It pertains to the acquisition of knowledge, knowledge people can apply as they deem appropriate and desirable. Conditioners are concerned primarily with the shaping of behavior, not with the acquisition of knowledge.

INSTRUCTIONAL TACTICS

The basic instructional tactic in (operant) conditioning is to repeatedly administer rewards to subjects for performing desirable behaviors until the behaviors are performed automatically or "stamped in" while neither rewarding or punishing other behaviors. The challenge is to identify rewards that are broadly applicable across students. So far the only reward found to be unambiguously generalizable is food, but only to hungry subjects. Subjects satiated with food are indifferent to it. Subjects glutted with food find food repugnant at the time.

Now porpoises and whales, which are taught to perform tricks for paying audiences, are conditioned to perform tricks using food as a reward. But those animals are captive, and their intake of food is controlled by their keepers and trainers. Consequently, they can be kept sufficiently hungry to ensure that food serves as a reward.

On the other hand, in free countries where, as indicated earlier, starving people is illegal, it is difficult to find a reinforcing agent or reward that all people are interested in most of the time. Food is rewarding when it satisfies the internal motive hunger. Most people in the United States are not hungry most of the time. And motives other than hunger cease to be motives for the time being when they are satisfied. It has been difficult to find a reward that satisfies most people's motives most of the time.

The would-be rewards that have been tried on students have not been nearly as successful as the food used to condition hungry lower animals. Oral forms of reinforcement, such as words of praise and encouragement, as well as indulgent attention for desired behavior, have achieved mixed, inconsistent results on humans. On reflection, it can be understood that attention and praise in general are not rewarding. Praise from a white teacher to a black student or from a female teacher to a male teenager in the company of his gang may not be rewarding. Moreover, repeated praise is often regarded as insincere.

To ensure that students will be motivated to receive offerings, tokens are offered as rewards for desired behavior. The tokens can be cashed in for one of a number of options of the students' choice. Tokens seem to work best when students can choose from among a wide variety of attractive options so that students are more certain to find an option they consider rewarding. The rationale is akin to the "Green Stamp" promotion that allowed customers to choose merchandise from a vast array of options in a catalog. This is hardly feasible in a school setting. Besides, the "Green Stamp" fad has faded. Stores have opted for reducing their prices instead of offering merchandise for green stamps.

It might be more effective to offer money to students as a reward for desired behavior. Money is certain to be more rewarding to students than tokens; students can trade the money for a much greater variety of treats and merchandise. However, many consider giving money to students for achieving learning objectives to be bribery, more so than giving tokens. Other professionals feel that learning is intrinsically rewarding because it empowers students, and that offering extrinsic rewards like candy, praise, or attention for achieving learning objectives is diverting and subverting to the learning process and to schooling.

It is exceedingly important not to confuse feedback, as described in the generalization on "remediation," and reinforcement. Some professionals contend that feedback provides, or at least should provide, reinforcement if done appropriately. They believe that it is reinforcing for students to find out that their response is correct, and that encouraging students to proceed with their next assigned task, whether they succeeded or failed in performing their last task, is also reinforcing. This blunts and perverts the important distinction between the functions of feedback and reinforcement. The purpose of reinforcing a behavior is to increase the probability that the behavior will recur. Typically, the desired behavior is rewarded repeatedly until it becomes a habit. To be reinforcing the offering given or said to a student must satisfy an internal motive, as food satisfies the hunger motive. However, as indicated, the verbal endorsement of a behavior cannot be relied upon to satisfy students' motives, so it is doubtful that telling students anything will reliably act as reinforcement.

The purpose of feedback is quite different from reinforcement. The purpose of feedback is to impart to students one of two things: (1) their behavior is correct and they are ready to attempt to perform the next more advanced task, or (2) their behavior is incorrect and they need to perform remedial tasks until they master the behavior. In both cases the underlying purpose is to advance the knowledge and skills of students.

In short, the function of reinforcement is to induce habits. The function of feedback is to enable students to continually advance their capabilities.

One reason reinforcement and feedback become intermingled, if not confused, is because the difference in the ability of humans and lower animals is not fully appreciated and taken into account. Humans are more intelligent than infrahumans and capable of understanding more sophisticated linguistic communication. Consequently, when people perform correctly they can be informed through language that they have performed correctly and are ready for the next challenge, and when they perform incorrectly they can be informed of their incorrect behavior. In addition, and most significant, they can be informed of and shown how to perform the desired behavior.

In contrast, reinforcement of a correct behavior of a porpoise encourages the porpoise to repeat the behavior to be reinforced again. This may be said, in a sense, to inform a porpoise that it has performed correctly. In addition, punishment of a porpoise for incorrect or undesirable behavior will tend to dissuade the porpoise from repeating the behavior. However, in contrast to humans, and most important, conditioners cannot communicate clearly to a porpoise what the correct behavior is and how to perform the correct behavior. This explains in part why conditioners use reward in conditioning animals, but not punishment. Reward communicates to them that their behavior is desirable. Punishment communicates that their behavior is undesirable but does not indicate the desired behavior. Moreover, continuous punishment can be harmful and can cause the animal to flee or attack.

Humans and lower animals are quite different, and their difference needs to be taken into account for instruction to be successful. Punishment that is painful and harmful should not be used on humans. It can injure them and cause them to be hostile and rebellious. There is evidence indicating that continued intense corporal punishment has long-term deleterious effects on youth. In teaching youth it is necessary to keep in mind that the aim is to discourage undesirable behavior and to encourage and instill desirable behavior by means of remediation. Undesirable behavior needs to be discouraged rather than punished. This often can be accomplished by telling the youth that their behavior is undesirable and explaining why, and then immediately telling them what the desirable behavior is and showing them how to execute it. This is the essence of remediation, which has been shown previously to be a most valuable instructional strategy for humans. Discouragement, not punishment, is used because the aim is to dissuade undesirable behavior, not to inflict pain and perhaps incite youth to rebel and spitefully increase the undesirable behavior. Most important, the performance of undesirable behavior is the signal to the sophisticated teacher to initiate the remediation process. When discouragement is used students must immediately be encouraged to perform remedial tasks with assurance that the remedial tasks will enable them to succeed.

It is also important not to confuse reinforcement (such as food) used to condition captive lower creatures to do what the conditioners desire with the sophisticated tactics used by free humans to influence other people to do what they desire. For instance, doing favors for others influences them to return favors, and complimenting others tends to be ingratiating and influences them to do one's bidding, while insulting others tends to alienate them. However, compliments are not equivalent to reinforcements such as food, nor are insults equivalent to punishments such as intense electric shock. In the final analysis, efforts to persuade free people to do one's bidding and to discourage them from doing what one dislikes will succeed only if they want to comply or they are obligated to comply.

In instruction it is more productive to refer to task performance as either correct or incorrect, rather than behavior that the teacher desires or does not desire. This places the emphasis where it belongs, on performing tasks correctly in order to achieve a learning objective, rather than on pleasing the teacher, even though the two may often be congruent. In addition, the emphasis should be on encouraging students to try to perform the next assigned task correctly in order to achieve the learning objective. When completing a task, students who perform it correctly may be complimented on their success and encouraged to meet the next challenge. Students who perform the task incorrectly cannot be complimented on their achievement. This would be encouraging them to fail. When they strive to succeed but fail, they can be complimented on their effort and encouraged to undertake remedial tasks with assurances that they will succeed. This presupposes that the teacher has had success in the past when using the remedial tasks. It would also be helpful if the teacher showed students how achieving the learning objective benefits and empowers them.

CAUTIONS AND COMMENTS

In conclusion, research results confirm conclusively that reinforcing captive, starved, individual lower animals repeatedly with food for performing behavior the conditioner deems desirable will condition the animals to perform the desired behavior. However, these reinforcement conditions do not have sufficient generalizability to be applicable to the education of most children and adults when the goal is academic achievement. Moreover, the conditions have virtually no generalizability to the educational environments of humans living in free modern nations such as England, Switzerland, and the United States, to name a few. Other so-called reinforcements such as toys, praise, attention, candy, and tokens have not been consistently effective on human students when used as reinforcing agents to achieve learning objectives. Moreover, bribing students to achieve learning objectives might dissuade them from learning for personal advantage and empowerment. Students who are bribed to learn come to expect rewards for doing what others want them to do.

REFERENCE LIST

Brophy, J., & Good, T. L. (1986). Teacher behavior and student achievement. In M. C. Wittrock (Ed.), *Handbook of Research on Teaching* (3rd ed., pp. 328–375). New York: Macmillan.

Providing Whole Language Instruction

INTRODUCTION

Whole language approaches to language instruction are characterized as indirect and unsystematic. They explicitly avoid the use of skill sequences in the organization of instruction. Individual word recognition and sound symbol relationships are not taught unless they are in the context of the whole text. It is difficult to formulate a specific example, or definition, as the proponents consider whole language instruction to be a philosophy rather than a specific method of instruction. Whole language forms of instruction have been in use for the past three decades with, as compared to other forms of instruction, only a small amount of research being conducted. Many pre-service and in-service teacher education programs today continue to emphasize the whole language approach to language instruction. However, research has failed to support the continued use of whole language approaches. There is a need to reevaluate the effectiveness of whole language instruction as a means of teaching language.

STUDENT BENEFICIARIES

There is weak support for the use of whole language instruction in the beginning stages (kindergarten in most regions of the United States) of language arts instruction. As the students move beyond beginning stages, the direction of the evidence shifts in favor of traditional approaches to instruction. Research has fairly consistently found no difference between whole language and traditional forms of language arts instruction for student achievement in grades K–6. Therefore, whole language cannot be regarded as a generalization that is applicable to most students. To be applicable to most students, whole language instruction would need to consistently enhance learning in most students—not just students in kindergarten, or first grade in regions where this is the beginning of formal instruction. Even for this category of students, the evidence is weak at best. No evidence is provided, one way or the other, for students beyond the 6th grade.

LEARNING ACHIEVED

Whole language instruction is intended to enhance student learning in the language arts of reading, writing, speaking, and listening. There is weak evidence in support of whole language instruction for initial reading and writing instruction as well as for word recognition. In terms of reading comprehension, the evidence shifts in favor of traditional forms of instruction. No evidence was found concerning writing mechanics such as sentence construction, punctuation, or spelling. In essence, whole language instruction should be seen as having limited generalizability to only beginning language instruction. However, the evidence supporting beginning language instruction should be seen as sufficiently weak to raise serious questions as to any generalizability. Proponents of whole language, in their preoccupation with the whole, would seem to have neglected the important relationships the parts have to the whole.

INSTRUCTIONAL TACTICS

Proponents' insistence that whole language instruction is a philosophy rather than a method of instruction makes it difficult to arrive at a list of employed instructional tactics. However, the following derived tactics appear to be utilized by many, if not most, whole language approaches to language arts instruction.

- Skill sequences are not used to organize instruction.
- Children move from oral to written language using words they know the meaning of.
- Individual words and sound–symbol relationships are taught only if they are needed to understand the whole lesson and not in isolation.
- Children are encouraged to use invented spelling.
- The interrelationships among and the interdependence of reading, writing, speaking, and listening are stressed.

CAUTIONS AND COMMENTS

In essence, the empirical evidence does not support the continued use of whole language instruction for the teaching of language. The evidence associated with limited student and content area (beginning language arts instruction) generalizability is at best weak. Evidence in support of generalizability beyond students in beginning language instruction is nonexistent. Although whole language instruction stresses the importance of the parts/whole relationships of reading, writing, speaking, and listening to the overall whole of communication, it neglects the important parts/whole relationships within each of these areas of communication. Does not a competent writer understand fundamental relationships among the component acts of writing? Does not problem solving in any area require that students be able to see the relationship between specific tactics necessary to the solution of a problem? Could not whole language deprive students of a thorough understanding of individual communication skills and impair their performance on verbal standardized achievement tests?

REFERENCE LIST

Sipe, T. A., & Curlette, W. L. (1997). A meta-analysis of factors relating to educational achievement. *International Journal of Educational Research 25*(7), 591–698.

Stahl, S. A., & Miller, P. D. (1989). Whole language and language experience approaches for beginning reading: A quantitative research synthesis. *Review of Educational Research 59*(1), 87–116.

18

Statistical Findings

INTRODUCTION

This chapter presents the statistical findings used as evidence in support of the instructional tactics associated with each generalization, or chapter, presented in this handbook. The findings were derived from reviews of groups of research studies and, in some cases, individual studies. A total of 50 individual studies, representing a combination of reviews of groups of studies and individual studies, was considered the minimum necessary to be considered sufficient research evidence in support of a generalization. There are from 50 to over 200 studies supporting the generalizations.

TYPES OF STUDIES

Reviews of research studies took two forms, one being the logical synthesis of research in which experts in the field look at the results of many individual research studies that pertain to a particular instructional strategy to determine the effect the strategy has on student achievement. To arrive at their conclusions, they look for patterns in the findings across the many studies. The second form of review of research is that of the meta-analysis. Here researchers calculate statistical measures of the effect instructional strategies have on achievement across many studies. It should be noted that quite often both types of review tend to arrive at the same conclusions with respect to the efficacy of instructional strategies on student achievement.

The statistical findings presented, whether from individual studies or meta-analysis of studies, were derived basically from two types of research studies: correlational and group comparison. Correlational studies are used to determine the percentage of variation in students' achievement scores that an instructional strategy accounts for and whether that variation is associated meaningfully with student achievement. Quite typically, many instructional strategies are correlated with a large group of students' achievement scores to determine how much the individual tactics are associated with that particular group of students' achievement. It should be noted that this group of students can represent more than one group of students being analyzed in combination. Group comparison studies are designed to compare the achievement scores of two or more groups of students to determine if differences in instructional strategies employed are likely to generate any meaningful difference in student achievement. They usually compare a group or groups of students being taught using some new instructional strategy to a group of control students being taught using a traditional strategy.

STATISTICAL PROCEDURES

Correlational studies employ basically two types of procedures. Simple correlational procedures such as Pearson's r and multiple correlation procedures such as factor analysis, multiple regression, and path analysis. Simple correlation procedures correlate student achievement scores for students who were taught using a new instructional strategy with student achievement scores for students not taught using the new instructional strategy. The result produces a measure of the degree to which new instructional strategies are associated with an effect on student achievement. Multiple correlational procedures correlate multiple instructional strategies with a group or groups of students' achievement scores to measure the degree to which the individual strategies are associated with the students' achievement scores and the degree to which two or more strategies might share in the effect on student achievement scores.

Group comparison studies employ procedures designed to determine the likelihood that any differences measured in student achievement for two or more groups of students are meaningful. In the case of more than two groups of students, the procedures most often used were analysis of variance (ANOVA) and analysis of covariance (ANCOVA). Both procedures provide the researcher information on the likelihood that differences exist in the level of student achievement between the groups of students. Additionally, ANCOVA attempts to control for differences between the groups in such things as student ability and prior achievement. For both procedures, when it was determined that there were likely meaningful differences among the groups, the groups were then analyzed in pairs to determine which group(s) were likely to be meaningfully different from the others in terms of effects on student achievement. The appropriate procedures used most often were t-test, Tukey, and Scheffé pairwise comparison procedures.

Meta-analyses employ statistical procedures to transform the findings of many correlational and group comparison studies into an estimated measure of the effect innovative instructional strategies, in relation to traditional instructional strategies, have on student achievement. Statistical procedures are available to transform any type of statistic into a standardized estimated measure of the effect an instructional strategy has on student achievement. Basically, a group of related research studies is located and estimated measures of the effect on student achievement are calculated for each individual study. The calculated measures are then pooled to arrive at a single measure of estimated effect on student achievement across all of the studies. For the purposes of this handbook, a criterion of 0.5 was used in determining whether the evidence was sufficient to support a generalization. Cohen (1988) identifies an effect size of 0.2 as small, 0.5 as medium, and 0.8 as large, with 0.5 being an important finding in social science research. The following basic descriptions of the most commonly utilized procedures for calculating standardized measures of effect size in meta-analyses were derived from Rosenthal (1994). The most common procedure is the Glass's Δ, where the difference in the mean scores for two groups is divided by the control groups standard deviation. Variations sometimes employed are Cohen's d and Hedges's g, which are similar to Glass's Δ except that they pool the standard deviations for the two groups. Significance tests such as the t-test can be mathematically transformed into Glass's Δ, Hedges's g, or Cohen's d. Cohen's q utilizes the difference between Fisher Zr transformations of correlations of two groups scores to arrive at a standardized estimate of effect size. Probit d utilizes the difference in standard normal transformed proportions for two groups. Further information on these and additional procedures may be found in Rosenthal (1994), Hedges & Olkin (1985), and Glass et al. (1981).

CAUTIONS AND COMMENTS

Much of the evidence used in support of the generalizations presented in this handbook was derived from reviews of research. Some reviewed correlational studies, some reviewed group comparison studies, and some reviewed a combination thereof. Many researchers consider the findings of group comparison studies to be superior to correlational studies in demonstrating the effects of an independent variable on a dependent variable. However, this position often overlooks the importance of replication of findings across many studies. When a finding keeps recurring across many correlational studies, it should be seen as being important and as evidence in support of the primary relationship between an instructional strategy and learning. Some researchers feel that much of the "experimental research" conducted in education is likewise limited in terms of the strength of the evidence produced because true experiments are seldom possible in natural school settings. As a result, researchers have arrived at the concept of meta-analysis. Although meta-analyses can include correlational studies, they most often are limited to experimental or group comparison–type studies. This review procedure produces a standardized statistical measure of effect across many studies. In essence, a measure of the degree of replication of findings.

Statistical Evidence on Taking Student Readiness into Account

GENERALIZATION TESTED: ON STUDENT READINESS—CHAPTER 1

Achievement of learning objectives is enhanced when students possess the readiness capabilities necessary to achieve the learning objectives.

Total number of studies covered: 171

Table 18.1.1
Obando & Hymel (1991)
Mean and Adjusted Mean Criterion Scores—Simple Statistics

	N	Mean	SD	Adjusted Mean
Test #1				
Experimental	22	79.23	8.94	79.30
Control	19	72.53	8.52	72.43
Test #2				
Experimental	22	81.14	7.38	82.45
Control	19	75.57	7.54	74.06
National Spanish Exam				
Experimental	22	35.41	4.34	35.05
Control	19	30.47	4.95	30.73

N = number of students; SD = standard deviation

Table 18.1.2
Obando & Hymel (1991)
ANCOVA

	Source	SS	df	MS	F	p
Test #1						
	Main Effect	350.64	1	350.64	4.35	< .05
	Covariates	192.72	3	64.24		
	Error	2903.03	36	80.64		
	Total	3448.39	40	86.16		
Test #2						
	Main Effect	522.63	1	522.63	9.27	< .05
	Covariates	22.70	3	7.57		
	Error	1934.78	36	53.74		
	Total	2480.10	40	62.00		
National Spanish Exam						
	Main Effect	296.67	1	296.67	13.88	< .05
	Covariates	20.31	3	6.77		
	Error	769.41	36	21.37		
	Total	1086.39	40	27.16		

SS = sums of squares; df = degrees of freedom; MS = mean square

Table 18.1.3
Anderson (1994)
Synthesis of Mastery Learning (Meta-analyses) Achievement Outcomes

Study	Percent Positive	Total N	ES	Grade Level
Kulik et al. (1990a)	93.2%	NR	.52	K–College
Slavin (1990)	NR	NR	.27	K–12
Kulik et al. (1990b)	63.6%	NR	.40	K–12
Guskey & Pigott (1988)	89.1%	11,532	.41 Psych	K–12
			.50 Science	
			.53 Soc. Stud.	
			.60 Lang. Arts	
			.70 Math	
			.94 Elementary	
			.48 High School	
			.41 College	
Willett et al. (1983)	NR		.64	K–12
Guskey & Gates (1985)	92.2%	8,074	.65–.94	K–College
Block & Burns (1976)	89.0%	2,767	.83	K–college

N = number of students; ES = effect size

Individual studies analyzed by these meta-analyses are identified in the reference list by the following symbols:

Kulik et al. (1990a) *
Kulik et al. (1990b) #
Slavin (1990) @
Guskey & Pigott (1988) $
Guskey & Gates (1985) &
Block & Burns (1976) +

It was not possible to determine the individual studies for which readiness was an instructional tactic for the Willett et al. (1983) analysis.

Rosenshine & Stevens (1986)

Groups of studies reviewed in this logical synthesis of research did not provide statistical evidence. However, many of the individual studies included in the logical synthesis of research do contain statistical evidence. In the event that a reader wishes to view this evidence, an extensive listing of the individual studies reviewed is provided in the reference list (the studies are identified by the symbol %).

Statistical Evidence on Defining Instructional Expectations

**GENERALIZATION TESTED: ON DEFINING
INSTRUCTIONAL EXPECTATIONS—CHAPTER 2**

Student achievement of learning objectives is enhanced when prior to instruction, (1) learning objectives are defined for students, (2) procedures to be used in the performance of tasks to achieve the objectives are identified, and (3) student outcomes designating achievement of the objectives are defined.

Total number of studies covered: 169

Table 18.2.1
Anderson (1994)
Synthesis of Mastery Learning (Meta-analyses) Achievement Outcomes

Study	Percent Positive	Total N	ES	Grade Level
Kulik et al. (1990a)	93.2%	NR	.52	K–College
Slavin (1990)	NR	NR	.27	K–12
Kulik et al. (1990b)	63.6%	NR	.40	K–12
Guskey & Pigott (1988)	89.1%	11,532	.41 Psych.	K–12
			.50 Science	
			.53 Soc. Stud.	
			.60 Lang. Arts	
			.70 Math	
			.94 Elementary	
			.48 High School	
			.41 College	
Willett et al. (1983)	NR		.64	K–12
Guskey & Gates (1985)	92.2%	8,074	.65–.94	K–College
Block & Burns (1976)	89.0%	2,767	.83	K–College

N = number of students; ES = effect size

Individual studies analyzed by these meta-analyses are identified in the reference list by the following symbols:

Kulik et al. (1990a) *
Kulik et al. (1990b) #
Slavin (1990) @
Guskey & Pigott (1988) $

Guskey & Gates (1985) &
Block & Burns (1976) +

It was not possible to determine the individual studies for which defining instructional expectations was an instructional tactic for the Willett et al. (1983) analysis.

Rosenshine & Stevens (1986)

Groups of studies reviewed in this logical synthesis of research did not provide statistical evidence. However, many of the individual studies included in the logical synthesis of research do contain statistical evidence. In the event that a reader wishes to view this evidence, an extensive listing of the individual studies reviewed is provided in the reference list (the studies are identified by the symbol %).

Statistical Evidence on Providing Effective Evaluation and Remediation

GENERALIZATION TESTED: ON EVALUATION AND REMEDIATION—CHAPTER 3

Achievement of learning objectives is enhanced when appropriate remediation is provided: (1) evaluation procedures and remedial tasks are formulated when task sequences are planned; (2) student task performance is frequently evaluated; (3) feedback on evaluation is given to students without delay; and (4) incorrect performance is immediately remediated, based on evaluation results.

Total number of studies covered: 219

Table 18.3.1
Obando & Hymel (1991)
Mean and Adjusted Mean Criterion Scores—Simple Statistics

	N	Mean	SD	Adjusted Mean
Test #1				
Experimental	22	79.23	8.94	79.30
Control	19	72.53	8.52	72.43
Test #2				
Experimental	22	81.14	7.38	82.45
Control	19	75.57	7.54	74.06
National Spanish Exam				
Experimental	22	35.41	4.34	35.05
Control	19	30.47	4.95	30.73

N = number of students; SD = standard deviation

Table 18.3.2
Obando & Hymel (1991)
ANCOVA

	Source	SS	df	MS	F	p
Test #1						
	Main Effect	350.64	1	350.64	4.35	< .05
	Covariates	192.72	3	64.24		
	Error	2903.03	36	80.64		
	Total	3448.39	40	86.16		
Test #2						
	Main Effect	522.63	1	522.63	9.27	< .05
	Covariates	22.70	3	7.57		
	Error	1934.78	36	53.74		
	Total	2480.10	40	62.00		
National Spanish Exam						
	Main Effect	296.67	1	296.67	13.88	< .05
	Covariates	20.31	3	6.77		
	Error	769.41	36	21.37		
	Total	1086.39	40	27.16		

SS = sums of squares; df = degrees of freedom; MS = mean square

Table 18.3.3
Anderson (1994)
Synthesis of Mastery Learning (Meta-analyses) Achievement Outcomes

Study	Percent Positive	Total N	ES	Grade Level
Kulik et al. (1990a)	93.2%	NR	.52	K–College
Slavin (1990)	NR	NR	.27	K–12
Kulik et al. (1990b)	63.6%	NR	.40	K–12
Guskey & Pigott (1988)	89.1%	11,532	.41 Psych.	K–12
			.50 Science	
			.53 Soc. Stud.	
			.60 Lang. Arts	
			.70 Math	
			.94 Elementary	

(continued)

Table 18.3.3 (continued)

Study	Percent Positive	Total N	ES	Grade Level
			.48 High School	
			.41 College	
Willett et al. (1983)	NR	.64		K–12
Guskey & Gates (1985)	92.2%	8,074	.65–.94	K–College
Block & Burns (1976)	89.0%	2,767	.83	K–College

N = number of students; ES = effect size

Individual studies analyzed by these meta-analyses are identified in the reference list by the following symbols:

Kulik et al. (1990a) *
Kulik et al. (1990b) #
Slavin (1990) @
Guskey & Pigott (1988) $
Guskey & Gates (1985) &
Block & Burns (1976) +

It was not possible to determine the individual studies for which readiness was an instructional tactic for the Willett et al. (1983) analysis.

Brophy & Good (1986); Rosenshine & Stevens (1986)

Groups of studies reviewed in these logical syntheses of research did not provide statistical evidence. However, many of the individual studies included in these logical syntheses of research do contain statistical evidence. In the event that a reader wishes to view this evidence, an extensive listing of the individual studies reviewed is provided in the reference list. Studies reviewed by Brophy & Good (1986) are identified by the symbol ! and studies reviewed by Rosenshine and Stevens (1986) are identified by the symbol %.

Statistical Evidence on Providing Contiguity

GENERALIZATION TESTED: ON CONTIGUITY—CHAPTER 4

Achievement of learning objectives is enhanced when events students are to associate are presented to them close together in time and space.

Total number of studies covered: 178

Table 18.4.1
Anderson (1994)
Synthesis of Mastery Learning (Meta-analyses) Achievement Outcomes

Study	Percent Positive	Total N	ES	Grade Level
Kulik et al. (1990a)	93.2%	NR	.52	K–College
Slavin (1990)	NR	NR	.27	K–12
Kulik et al. (1990b)	63.6%	NR	.40	K–12
Guskey & Pigott (1988)	89.1%	11,532	.41 Psych.	K–12
			.50 Science	
			.53 Soc. Stud.	
			.60 Lang. Arts	
			.70 Math	
			.94 Elementary	
			.48 High School	
			.41 College	
Willett et al. (1983)	NR		.64	K–12
Guskey & Gates (1985)	92.2%	8,074	.65–.94	K–College
Block & Burns (1976)	89.0%	2,767	.83	K–College

N = number of students; ES = effect size

Individual studies analyzed by these meta-analyses are identified in the reference list by the following symbols:

Kulik et al. (1990a) *
Kulik et al. (1990b) #
Slavin (1990) @
Guskey & Pigott (1988) $
Guskey & Gates (1985) &
Block & Burns (1976) +

It was not possible to determine the individual studies for which readiness was an instructional tactic for the Willett et al. (1983) analysis.

Rosenshine & Stevens (1986)

Groups of studies reviewed in this logical synthesis of research did not provide statistical evidence. However, many of the individual studies included in the logical synthesis of research do contain statistical evidence. In the event that a reader wishes to view this evidence, an extensive listing of the individual studies reviewed is provided in the reference list (the studies are identified by the symbol %).

Statistical Evidence on Utilizing Repetition Effectively

GENERALIZATION TESTED: ON REPETITION—
CHAPTER 5

Achievement of learning objectives is enhanced when there is repetition in instruction and in tasks students are assigned to perform.

Total number of studies covered: 66

Table 18.5.1
Ausubel & Youseff (1965)
Retention Test Scores of Experimental and Control Groups on Learning Passage

Group	Treatment	Mean	SD
Experimental	Repetition	24.25	5.79
Control	No Repetition	19.65	5.26

Calculated effect size = .88; SD = standard deviation

An unspecified test for difference of the means was reported significant at the .001 level.

Table 18.5.2
Kulik et al. (1984) Meta-analysis
Means and Standard Errors of Effect Sizes for Different Numbers of Practice Tests

Number of Practice Tests	Identical Tests			Parallel Tests		
	Number of Studies	Effect Size M	SE	Number of Studies	Effect Size M	SE
1	19	.42	.08	21	.23	.04
2	6	.70	.30	5	.32	.04
3	5	.96	.37	4	.35	.07
4	3	1.35	.60	3	.47	.18
5	3	1.42	.59	2	.52	.16
6	2	1.94	.79	1	.73	
7	2	1.89	.86	1	.74	

M = mean effect size; SE = standard error

Studies associated with this meta-analysis are identified by the symbol * in the reference list.

Table 18.5.3
Nelson (1977) Experiment 1
Mean Percentage of Correct Responses for Each Condition

Condition			
1 Repetition **@ 4 seconds**	**1 Repetition** **@ 8 seconds**	**2 Repetitions** **(Same)** **@ 4 seconds**	**2 Repetitions** **(Different)** **@ 4 seconds**
25	23	33	32

Table 18.5.4
Nelson (1977)
Three Planned Orthogonal Comparisons (constructed from data presented in results)

Comparison	**F**	**p**
The two two-repetition groups to the two one-repetition groups	30.42	< .005
One repetition @ 4 seconds to one repetition @ 8 seconds	< 1.00	> .10
(Same) two-repetition groups to (different) two-repetition group	< 1.00	> .10

Table 18.5.5
Nelson (1977) Experiment 2
Mean Percentage of Correct Responses for Each Condition

One Repetition	Two Repetitions				
	Massed	Spaced			
		Lag 7	Lag 11	Lag 15	Ave.
24	40	46	47	50	48

Lag = number of seconds between presentations

Table 18.5.6
Nelson (1977) Experiment 2
Scheffé Post-Hoc Comparisons (p values not given) (created from data reported in results)

Comparison	F
Two back-to-back repetitions to one repetition	8.05*
Two spaced repetitions to one repetition	17.85*
Two back-to-back repetitions to two spaced repetitions	1.92**
Comparison of spaced intervals	< 1.00**

* Reported as significant; ** Reported as not significant

Nelson (1977) Experiment 3
Repetition and Depth of Processing

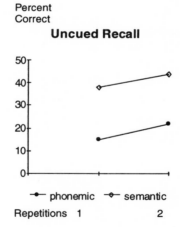

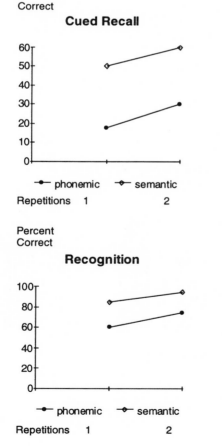

Table 18.5.7
Nelson (1977) Experiment 3
Anova Statistics (Tables created from statistics presented in results)

Uncued

Variable	df	F	(p values not given)
Repetition	1, 92	11.83	
Processing	1, 92	129.56	
Repetition × Processing	not given	< 1.00	

Cued

Variable	df	F	(p values not given)
Repetition	1, 92	10.13	
Processing	1, 92	108.81	
Repetition × Processing	not given	< 1.00	

Recognition

Variable	df	F	(p values not given)
Repetition	1, 92	23.96	
Processing	1, 92	87.95	
Repetition × Processing	1, 92	23.96	

*Analysis of simple effects indicated two repetitions produced a larger effect for both the semantic and phonemic conditions.

Peterson et al. (1935)

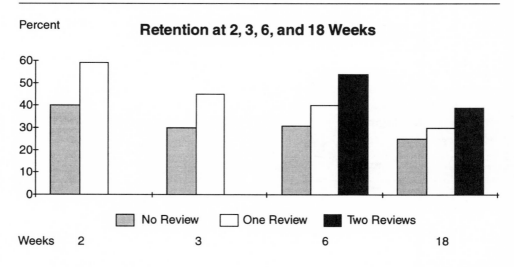

Percent — **Retention at 2, 3, 6, and 18 Weeks**

No Review   One Review   Two Reviews

Weeks 2   3   6   18

(continued)

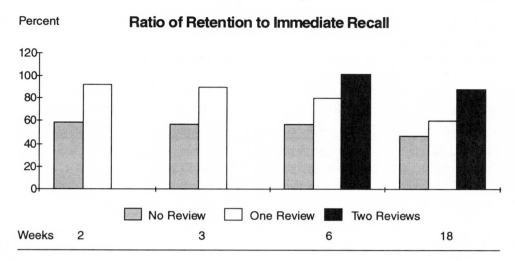

Ratio of Retention to Immediate Recall

Percent

Legend: No Review, One Review, Two Reviews

Weeks: 2, 3, 6, 18

Table 18.5.8
Petros & Hoving (1980)
Mean Proportion of Idea Units Correctly Recalled

	Delayed Recall				
Importance Level	Group 1	Group 2	Group 3	Group 4	Group 5
High	.455	.366	.374	.264	.387
Medium	.347	.268	.243	.175	.237
Low	.327	.196	.170	.138	.263
Total	.376	.276	.262	.192	.296

Table 18.5.9
Watkins & Kerkar (1985)
Percentage of Items Recalled

	Once-Presented Items	Twice-Presented Items		
Experiment		Observed	Predicted*	Superadditivity
1	17.67	45.89	31.81	14.08**
2	17.22	43.89	31.11	12.78**
3	26.67	56.08	45.46	10.62**

*Calculated by an equation intended to correct for the probability of guessing an item correctly; ** $p < .001$

Table 18.5.10
Hines et al. (1985)
Relationships between Measures of Teacher Behaviors and Student Outcomes

Level of Measurement	Measurement Source	Canonical Analysis Correlation	Regression Analysis Achievement
Low-inference	observers	.75	.72*
	students	.95**	.69*
	teachers	.67*	.53
Intermediate-inference	observers	.70**	.67**
			Zero-Order Correlation
High-inference	observers	.65**	.63**
	students	.73**	.53**
	teachers	.45*	.34*

*p < .05; **p < .01

Rosenshine (1986)

Groups of studies reviewed in this logical synthesis of research did not provide statistical evidence. However, many of the individual studies included in the logical synthesis of research do contain statistical evidence. In the event that a reader wishes to view this evidence, an extensive listing of the individual studies reviewed is provided in the reference list at the end of the chapter (the studies are identified by the symbol #).

Statistical Evidence on Clarifying Communication

GENERALIZATION TESTED: ON CLARIFYING COMMUNICATION—CHAPTER 6

Achievement of learning objectives is enhanced when information on learning objectives, tasks, and evaluations are clearly communicated to students over time.

Total number of studies covered: 111

Table 18.6.1
Land (1985)
Vagueness Terms and Student Achievement

Experimental Studies

Study	Significance	Content	Grade Level	N
Smith & Edmond 1978	0.05	Mathematics	College	204 students
Land & Smith 1979a	0.05	Mathematics	College	50 students
Land & Smith 1979b	0.07	Mathematics	College	160 students
Smith & Cotton 1980	0.001	Mathematics	Elementary	100 students
Smith & Bramblett 1981	0.05	Biology	High school	48 students

Table 18.6.2
Land (1985)
Correlational Studies

Study	Significance	Content	Grade Level	N
Hiller et al. 1969	0.01 to 0.001	Social Studies	High school	32 teachers 672 students
Smith 1977	0.05	Mathematics	High school	20 teachers 455 students
Dunkin 1978	ns	Social Studies	Elementary	29 teachers 827 students
Dunkin & Doenau 1980	0.05	Social Studies	Elementary	28 teachers 723 students
Dunkin & Doenau 1980	ns	Social Studies	Elementary	26 teachers 741 students

Table 18.6.3

Land (1985)

Correlational Studies: Clusters of Low-Inference Clarity Variables and Student Achievement

Study	Variables	Significance	Content	Grade Level	N
Hiller et al. 1969	Teacher verbal fluency: (average sentence length, comma proportions, utterances of "uh")	0.01 0.05	Social Studies Social Studies	High school High school	32 classes 23 classes
Clark et al. 1979	Teacher structuring: (Reviewing main ideas and facts, stating objectives, outining lesson content signaling transitions, indicating important points, summarizing)	ns	Science	Elementary	408
Dunkin 1978		0.05	Social studies	Elementary	827
Denham & Land 1981	Clarity: (verbal mazes, vagueness terms, emphasis, transitions, additional unexplained content)	0.001	Psychology	College	129
Land 1979		0.01	Psychology	College	78
Land 1980		0.02	Psychology	College	77
Land & Smith 1981	Clarity: (verbal mazes, vagueness terms)	ns	Social Studies	College	80
Land 1981		0.05	Mathematics	College	84
Hines et al. 1982	29 Clarity variables	0.03	Mathematics	College	32

Table 18.6.4
Hines et al. (1985)
Relationships between Measures of Teacher Behaviors and Student Outcomes

Level of Measurement	Measurement Source	Canonical Analysis Correlation	Regression Analysis Achievement
Low-inference	observers	.75	.72*
	students	.95**	.69*
	teachers	.67*	.53
Intermediate-inference	observers	.70**	.67**
			Zero-Order Correlation
High-inference	observers	.65**	.63**
	students	.73**	.53**
	teachers	.45*	.34*

*p < .05; **p < .01

Table 18.6.5
Land & Smith (1979) *Summarized in Land (1985)
Scores for Clear and Unclear Treatment

Condition	Mean Score	Standard Dev
Clear instruction, no mazes or vagueness terms	8.10	3.45
Mazes and vagueness terms present	5.25	3.08

Smith & Cotton (1980) *Summarized in Land (1985)
Student Achievement Scores

Condition	Mean Score	Standard Dev
Clear instruction, no vagueness and no discontinuity	8.68	5.87
Vagueness and discontinuity present	2.80	1.02

Brophy & Good (1986)

Groups of studies reviewed in this logical synthesis of research did not provide statistical evidence. However, many of the individual studies included in the logical synthesis of research do contain statistical evidence. In the event that a reader wishes to view this evidence, an extensive listing of the individual studies reviewed is provided in the reference list (the studies are identified by the symbol *).

Statistical Evidence on Reducing Student/Teacher Ratio

GENERALIZATION: ON STUDENT/TEACHER RATIO—CHAPTER 7

Achievement of learning objectives is enhanced when there is a lower student-to-teacher ratio in teaching situations.

Total number of studies covered: 101

Table 18.7.1
Glass et al. (1982) Meta-analysis
Data on the Relationship of Class Size and Achievement from Studies Using Random Assignment of Pupils

Study Number	Size of Larger Class	Size of Smaller Class	loge(L/S)	Effect Size
1	25	1	3.22	.32
2	3	1	1.10	.22
2	25	1	3.22	1.52
2	25	3	2.12	1.22
3	35	17	.72	−.29
4	112	28	1.39	−.03
5	2	1	.69	.36
5	5	1	1.61	.52
5	23	1	3.14	.83
5	5	2	.92	.22
5	23	2	2.44	.57
5	23	5	1.53	.31
6	30	15	.69	.17
7	23	16	.36	.05
7	30	16	.63	.04
7	37	16	.84	.08
7	30	23	.27	.04
7	37	23	.48	.04
7	37	30	.21	0.00
8	28	20	.33	.15
9	50	26	.65	.29
10	32	1	3.46	.65
11	37	15	.90	.40
11	60	15	1.38	1.25
11	60	37	.48	.65

(continued)

Table 18.7.1 (continued)

Study Number	Size of Larger Class	Size of Smaller Class	loge(L/S)	Effect Size
12	8	1	2.08	.30
13	45	15	1.10	.07
14	14	1	2.64	.72
14	30	1	3.40	.78
14	30	14	.76	.17
		Average:	1.42	.38

Studies analyzed in this meta-analysis are identified by the symbol * in the reference list.

Table 18.7.2
McGivern et al. (1989) Meta-analysis
Estimate of Effect Sizes—PRIMETIME

Test	School/ Subject	Control			PRIMETIME			Pooled SD	Effect Size
		X	s	n	X	s	n		
1:	School System A								
ITBS	Reading	46.07	15.02	27	67.96	13.41	24	14.29	1.53
	Math	32.46	19.86	26	76.43	19.30	23	19.60	2.24
	Composite	44.25	13.62	25	70.70	16.68	23	15.16	1.74
2:	School System B								
SAT	Reading	50.97	20.24	54	47.66	20.50	47	20.36	−.16
	Math	56.99	22.68	54	52.20	23.24	47	22.94	−.21
3:	School System C								
ITBS	Reading	54.50	23.10	164	68.90	25.10	145	24.22	.59
	Math	63.10	24.10	164	66.40	24.40	145	24.40	.14
	Composite	63.20	21.90	164	71.40	22.80	145	22.47	.36
4:	School System D								
ITBS	Reading	52.78	21.09	131	54.29	18.89	131	20.02	.07
	Math	53.36	19.64	131	58.71	17.13	131	18.43	.29
	Composite	54.35	20.48	131	57.04	18.33	131	19.43	.14
5:	School System E School E1:								
ITBS	Reading	102.80	11.65	56	96.73	10.06	44	10.98	−.55
CAT	Composite	99.80	15.24	55	101.26	14.76	74	14.97	.10

(continued)

Table 18.7.2 (continued)

Test	School/ Subject	Control X	s	n	PRIMETIME X	s	n	Pooled Effect SD	Size
6: CAT	School E2: Composite	102.47	11.59	58	96.50	10.24	44	11.03	−.54
7: CAT	School E3: Composite	99.06	12.28	49	98.32	13.84	57	13.14	−.74
8:	School System F School F1:								
ITBS	Reading	60.8	2.90	81	62.3	6.10	84	4.80	.31
	Math	63.9	4.00	81	69.8	2.40	84	3.28	.52
	Composite	64.4	2.00	81	67.2	4.70	84	3.44	.29
9:	School F2:								
ITBS	Reading	60.8	4.30	69	58.6	3.00	63	3.74	−.59
	Math	63.9	4.80	69	59.9	8.00	63	6.52	−.61
	Composite	64.4	4.30	69	61.9	5.10	63	4.70	−.53
10:	School F3:								
ITBS	Reading	52.2	2.80	96	57.4	4.10	96	3.51	1.48
	Math	50.2	4.80	96	55.2	5.50	96	5.16	.97
	Composite	52.5	5.00	96	59.0	5.00	96	5.00	1.30

ITBS = Iowa Tests of Basic Skills; SAT = Stanford Achievement Test; CAT = Cognitive Abilities Test; X = mean score; s = standard deviation; n = number of classes; SD = standard deviation

Word et al. (1990)

Groups of studies reviewed in this logical synthesis of research did not provide statistical evidence. However, many of the individual studies included in the logical synthesis of research do contain statistical evidence. In the event that a reader wishes to view this evidence, an extensive listing of the individual studies reviewed is provided in the reference list (the studies are identified by the symbol #).

Table 18.7.3
Mosteller (1995)
Estimates of Mean Effect Sizes, 1985–1989

	SAT Reading	BSF Reading	SAT Math	BSF Math
Comparision of class size 13–17:1 to 22–25:1	.23	.21	.27	.13
Comparison of class size 22–25:1 with an aide to class size 22–25:1 without an aide	.14	.08	.10	.05

Percentile Ranks of Average Scores Based on National Test Norms

Grade Level	Percentile			
	K	1	2	3
Total Reading SAT				
Small Classes	59	64	61	62
Regular without an aide	53	53	52	55
Regular with an aide	54	58	54	54
Total Math SAT				
Small Classes	66	59	76	76
Regular without an aide	61	48	68	69
Regular with an aide	61	51	69	68

SAT = Stanford Achivement Test
Percentile ranks are based on Stanford's multilevel norms

Statistical Evidence on Providing Reminders Instruction

GENERALIZATION TESTED: ON REMINDERS INSTRUCTION— CHAPTER 8

Achievement of learning objectives is enhanced when reminders are used to cue the recall of information needed to perform assigned tasks.

Total number of studies covered: 89

Belleza (1996)
Levin (1994)
Carney et al. (1993)
Levin (1988)

Groups of studies reviewed in these logical syntheses of research did not provide statistical evidence. However, many of the individual studies included in these logical syntheses of research do contain statistical evidence. In the event that a reader wishes to view this evidence, an extensive listing of the individual studies reviewed is provided in the reference. Studies reviewed by Belleza (1996) are identified by the symbol *; studies reviewed by Levin (1994) are identified by the symbol #; studies reviewed by Carney et al. (1993) are identified by the symbol $; and studies reviewed by Levin (1988) are identified by the symbol @.

Table 18.8.1
Griffith (1979)
Table of Studies Reviewed (created from the text); Significant Findings p < .05
Although Students Not Given for Most Studies (Griffith states most studies used
college students)

Author	Mnemotechnic	Students	Findings
Croninger (1971) (1971)	Method of Loci	College	Recall superior to a control group at 1 week and 5 weeks.
Robertson et al. (1976)	Method of Loci	Senior citizens	Higher pretest-posttest recall than a control group.

Four other Method of Loci studies reviewed that were criticized for lack of control group

Author	Mnemotechnic	Students	Findings
Smith & Nobel (1965)	Pegword	not given*	No significant difference during learning phase. Significantly enhanced recall at 24 hours as compared to a control group.
Senter & Hauser (1968)	Hook (pegword)	not given	Effective for recall at two association levels as compared to control subjects.
Berla et al. (1969)	Pegword	not given	The word list was learned significantly faster by students in the experimental condition.
Perensky & Senter (1969)	Pegword	not given	Two pegword conditions performed significantly better on immediate recall and 24-hour delayed recall.
Bugelski et al. (1968)	Pegword	not given	No significant enhancement at a 2-second rate. Significant enhancement at 4- and 8-

(continued)

Table 18.8.1 (continued)

Author	Mnemotechnic	Students	Findings
			second rates as compared to a rhyme control and standard control groups.
Bugelski (1968)	Pegword	not given	On final recall the mnemonic group recalled 63% and the control group recalled 22%.
Keppel & Zavortink (1969)	Pegword	not given	Partially replicated the findings of Bugelski (1968).
Griffith & Atkinson (1978)	Pegword	Military	Individuals with GT scores over 110 experienced significantly enhanced recall. Findings were not significant for lower GT levels.
Bower & Reitman (1972)	Compared two means of employing pegwords—no significant difference.		
Pavio (1968)			
Departo & Baker (1974)	Addressed pegword concreteness.		
Wortman & Sparling (1974)			
Wood (1967)	Linking	not given	Recall for the linking group was superior to that of a control group.
Bugelski (1974)	Linking	College, Grade 8	Serial recall was superior for linking groups as compared to control groups.
Bower & Clark (1969)	Linking	not given	No difference on immediate recall. On final recall the experimental group outperformed the control group by a factor close to 4.
Murray (1974)	Linking	not given	Significant difference in favor of the experimental group for the end of session test and for day 7 retention test. No significant

(continued)

Table 18.8.1 (continued)

Author	Mnemotechnic	Students	Findings
			difference for day 14 and day 28 retention tests.
Gamst & Freund (1978)	Linking	not given	No significant findings for 2 experiments.
Ott et al. (1973)	Keyword	not given	Experimental group performed significantly better than controls on learning and retention tests. No significant difference on delayed retention.
Raugh & Atkinson (1974, 1975)	Keyword	not given	*Experiment 1*: Experimental group final test score 88% correct as compared to 28% correct for the control group. *Experiment 2*: Final test score was 59% correct for the experimental group and 30% correct for the control group.
Atkinson & Raugh (1975)	Keyword	not given	Average percentage correct on a comprehension test was 72% for the keyword group and 46% for the control group. On a delayed comprehension test, recall was 43% for the keyword group and 28% for the control group.
Willerman (1977)	Keyword	College	No significant findings.
Griffith & Atkinson (1978)	Pictorial	not given	No significant findings.

Statistical Evidence on Providing Subject Matter Unifiers

GENERALIZATION TESTED: ON UNIFIERS—CHAPTER 9

Achievement of learning objectives is enhanced when a scheme is used to highlight parts/whole relationships in the subject matter students are assigned to learn.

Total number of studies covered: 50

Table 18.9.1
Horton et al. (1993) Meta-analysis
Achievement Effect Sizes

	n	Median	Mean	SE
Grade Level				
Elementary	2	0.84	0.84	0.14
Middle	2	0.27	0.27	0.12
High School	9	0.11	0.31	0.23
College	5	0.52	0.63	0.27
Overall	18		0.46	0.14

n = number of studies; SE = standard error

Table 18.9.2
Fisher (1997) Meta-analysis
Effect Size Descriptive Statistics

Variable	N	Mean	St Dev	Min	Q1	Median	Q3	Max
Combined	48	0.51	0.44	−0.49	0.29	0.46	0.72	1.71
Immediate								
Recall	31	0.57	0.35	−0.12	0.32	0.54	0.76	1.46
Delayed								
Recall	17	0.40	0.56	−0.49	0.10	0.32	0.58	1.71

N = number of studies; St Dev = standard deviation; Min = minimum; Q1= first quartile;
Q3 = third quartile; Max = maximum

Table 18.9.3
Bower et al. (1969) Experiment I
Average Words Recalled over Four Trials

	Trials			
	1	2	3	4
Words Presented	112	112	112	112
Words Recalled				
Blocked	73.0	106.1	112	112
Random	20.6	38.9	52.8	70.1
Recall of Level Four Words				
Words Presented	73.5	73.5	73.5	73.5
Words Recalled				
Blocked	44.6	69.6	73.5	73.5
Random	13.2	22.8	35.2	44.8

Table 18.9.4
Experiment II (Bower et al. 1969)
Percentage of Words Recalled

	Trial	
Condition	T1	T2
Blocked		
LL	.61	.89
LN	.65	—
NL	—	.88
Random		
LL	.21	.43
LN	.29	—
NL	—	.39

Table 18.9.5
Experiment III (Bower et al. 1969)
Proportion of Clusters Recalled and Mean Words Per Recalled Cluster on Trial 2 and Final Recall Trial

	Proportion of Clusters		Words per Cluster (of 4)	
Group	Trial 2	Final	Trial 2	Final
Relevant	.84	.98	3.52	3.58
Irrelevant	.89	.99	3.20	3.35
Rest Control	.86	.98	3.40	3.42

Experiment IV (Bower et al. 1969)
Tables not provided. Blocked condition reported as exceeding the random condition on recall with all p's < .01.

Table 18.9.6
Selinger (1995)
Summary of Writing Posttest Scores

	n	Low Score	High Score	Mean Score	SD
Control	28	12	82	49.29	19
Treatment	30	53	90	74.10	9

*$F_{1, 55} = 37.25$, $p < .001$

Table 18.9.7
Dean & Kulhavy (1981) Experiment I
Means and Standard Deviations

Dependent Measure		Treatment Group	
		Map Construction	No Construction
Multiple Choice			
	M	21.50	17.15
	SD	4.27	3.77
Constructed Response			
	M	20.55	14.95
	SD	4.61	5.29
Idea Units			
	M	25.50	19.40
	SD	7.00	4.07

Table 18.9.8
Experiment II (Dean & Kulhavy 1981)
Means and Standard Deviations

Dependent Measure		Treatment Group		
		Map Construction	No Construction	Provided Map
Multiple Choice				
	M	27.25	17.83	19.15
	SD	4.13	4.69	4.25
Constructed Response				
	M	24.35	14.81	16.40
	SD	4.54	5.01	4.99
Idea Units				
	M	28.10	16.44	18.13
	SD	6.91	4.54	4.91

Statistical Evidence on Providing Transfer of Learning Instruction

GENERALIZATION TESTED: ON TRANSFER OF LEARNING INSTRUCTION—CHAPTER 10

Achievement of learning objectives is enhanced when students are taught beforehand the knowledge and skills needed to perform assigned tasks and how to determine when learned knowledge and skills can be used to perform assigned tasks.

Total number of studies covered: 73

Table 18.10.1
Marzolf & DeLoache (1994)
Mean Number of Errorless Retrievals

	Retrieval 1		Retrieval 2	
	Mean	**Std Dev**	**Mean**	**Std Dev**
Experiment 1				
Transfer Group				
Day 1	2.67	1.23	3.50	.67
Day 2	2.58	1.31	3.08	.67
Control Group				
Day 1	1.08	.90	2.92	1.00
Day 2	1.42	1.00	3.08	.79
Experiment 2				
Transfer Group				
Day 1	3.50	.71	3.50	.53
Day 2	3.50	.97	3.80	.42
Control Group				
Day 1	1.20	.79	3.30	.95
Day 2	2.60	1.08	3.80	.42

Table 18.10.2
Farrell (1988)
Transfer Test and Pretest Scores

Instruction Method	Percent Correct	Mean	Standard Deviation	z	p
Experiment 1					
Transfer Test					
Proportional	67.3	10.77	4.45	5.68	< .001
Standard	34.8	5.58	4.54		
Pretest					
Proportional	31.5	7.55	4.52	1.17	.121
Standard	26.4	6.34	5.57		
Experiment 2					
Transfer Test					
Proportional	72.4	11.58	4.33	3.39	< .001
Standard	50.4	8.07	4.76		
Pretest					
Proportional	47.4	11.36	5.98	1.87	.031
Standard	37.2	8.93	5.21		

Table 18.10.3
Gott et al. (1995)
Sherlock 2 Posttest Measures of Troubleshooting Proficiency

Group	N	Test	Mean	Std Dev
Novices		VTT3		
Control	23		59	37
Experimental	18		95	5
Masters	13		85	12
Novices		VTT4		
Control	23		58	37
Experimental	18		91	7
Masters	13		86	11
Novices		NIT		
Control	23		75	14
Experimental	18		87	12
Masters	13		86	11

Table 18.10.4
Gott et al. (1995)
Frankenstation Posttest Measures of Transfer

Novices		VTT		
Control	21		55	31
Experimental	17		82	23
Masters	12		91	22
Novices		NIT		
Control	21		72	4
Experimental	17		80	10
Masters	12		88	12

Table 18.10.5
Gott et al. (1995)
Effect Size for Postest Measures

Measure	Control			Experimental			Effect Size
	N	M	SD	N	M	SD	
Sherlock VTT3	23	59	37	18	95	5	1.27
Sherlock VTT4	23	58	37	18	91	7	1.17
Sherlock NIT	23	75	14	18	87	12	.87
Frankenstation VTT	21	55	31	17	82	23	.96
Frankenstation NIT	21	72	11	17	80	10	.76

N = number of students; M = mean score; SD = standard deviation

Table 18.10.6
Gott et al. (1995)
Frequency of Component Swapping Without Complete Testing

Group	Swaps After No Testing	Swaps After Partial Testing
Controls	50	12
Experimentals	3	13
Masters	8	15

Table 18.10.7
Gott et al. (1995)
Frequency and Quality of Self-Test Use

Group	Self-Test Use	Frequency of Inefficient Use
Controls	16	11
Experimentals	12	4
Masters	14	2

Table 18.10.8
Gott et al. (1995)
Number of Violations in Logical Sequence of Troubleshooting

Group	Number of Violations
Controls	21
Experimentals	9
Masters	20

Table 18.10.9
Gott et al. (1995)
Percentage of Solutions to Frankenstation VTT by Group

Group	Percentage Achieving Solution
Controls	63.6
Experimentals	70.6
Masters	83.3

Statistical Evidence on Providing Teamwork Instruction

GENERALIZATION TESTED: ON TEAMWORK INSTRUCTION—CHAPTER 11

Achievement of the learning objective group achievement is enhanced when students are taught to perform complementary tasks as a team in pursuit of the objective.

Total number of studies covered: 165

Table 18.11.1
Slavin (1995) Meta-analysis
Effect Sizes by Cooperative Methods

Method	Mean ES	Mean ES Standardized Tests	Percentage of Studies		
			Significantly Positive	No Difference	Significantly Negative
All Studies	.26		64	31	5
STAD	.32	.21	69	31	0
TGT	.38	.40	75	25	0
CIRC	.29	.23	100	0	0
TAI	.15	.15	100	0	0
Learning Together	.04		42	42	17
Jigsaw	.12		31	46	23
Group Investigation	.06		50	50	0
Structured Dyads	.86		100	0	0
Other	.10		29	71	0
Group Goals and Individual Accountability	.32		78	22	0
Group Goals Only	.07		22	56	22
Individual Accountability (Task specialization)	.07		35	47	18
No Group Goals or Individual Accountability	.16		56	44	0

ES = effect size

Individual studies included in this "best evidence synthesis" are identified by the symbol *
in the reference list.

Sharan (1980)

Groups of studies reviewed in this logical synthesis of research did not provide statistical evidence. However, many of the individual studies included in this logical synthesis of research do contain statistical evidence. In the event that a reader wishes to view this evidence, an extensive listing of the individual studies reviewed is provided in the reference list (the studies are identified by the symbol #).

Table 18.11.2
Johnson et al. (1981)
Meta-Analysis Findings

					Method				
	Voting			Effect Size			z score		
									Fail-
Condition	N	ND	P	M	SD	N	z	N	safe n
Cooperative vs group competitive	3	6	4	.00	.63	9	.16	13	
Cooperative vs competitive	8	36	65	.78	.99	70	16.00	84	7,859
Group competitive vs competitive	3	22	19	.37	.78	16	6.39	31	430
Cooperative vs individualistic	6	42	108	.78	.91	104	24.01	132	27,998
Group competitive vs individualistic	1	10	20	.50	.37	20	11.37	29	1,356
Competitive vs individualistic	12	38	9	.03	1.02	48	4.82	50	380

Voting: N = negative; ND = no difference; P = positive. *Effect size*: M = mean; SD = standard deviation; N = number of studies. z score: N = number of studies; fail safe n = number of students required.

Individual studies included in this meta-analysis are identified by the symbol @ in the reference list.

Statistical Evidence on Providing Decision-Making Instruction

GENERALIZATION TESTED: ON DECISION-MAKING INSTRUCTION—CHAPTER 12

Achievement of learning objectives is enhanced when students are shown how to use decision-making tactics to consider and select procedures to perform assigned tasks.

Total number of studies covered: 79

Table 18.12.1
Rosenshine & Meister (1994) Meta-analysis
Effect Sizes Based on Quality of Study

	Standardized Test	Short-Answer Test	Summarization Test	Experimenter Developed Test
All studies	.32	1.00	.85	.88
High quality	.31	1.00	.77	.86
Middle quality	.36	1.06	1.10	.87
Low quality	−.12			

Table 18.12.2
Rosenshine et al. (1996) Meta-analysis
Overall Effect Sizes by Type of Test

	Instructional Approach		
Type of test	Reciprocal Teaching (n = 9)	Regular Instruction (n = 17)	Combined (n = 26)
Standardized	0.34 (6)	0.35 (7)	0.36 (13)
Exp. short answer	1.00 (5)	0.88 (11)	0.87 (16)
Summary	0.85 (3)	0.81 (2)	0.85 (5)

Number in parentheses refers to the number of studies used to compute the effect size.

Salomon & Perkins (1989)

Groups of studies reviewed in this logical synthesis of research did not provide statistical evidence. However, many of the individual studies included in the logical synthesis of research do contain statistical evidence. In the event that a reader wishes to view this evidence, an extensive listing of the individual studies reviewed is provided in the reference list (the studies are identified by the symbol *).

Prawat (1989)

Groups of studies reviewed in this logical synthesis of research did not provide statistical evidence. However, many of the individual studies included in the logical synthesis of research do contain statistical evidence. In the event that a reader wishes to view this evidence, an extensive listing of the individual studies reviewed is provided in the reference list (the studies are identified by the symbol #).

Kucan & Beck (1997)

Groups of studies reviewed in this logical synthesis of research did not provide statistical evidence. However, many of the individual studies included in the logical synthesis of research do contain statistical evidence. In the event that a reader wishes to view this evidence, an extensive listing of the individual studies reviewed is provided in the reference list (the studies are identified by the symbol @).

Dole et al. (1991)

Groups of studies reviewed in this logical synthesis of research did not provide statistical evidence. However, many of the individual studies included in the logical synthesis of research do contain statistical evidence. In the event that a reader wishes to view this evidence, an extensive listing of the individual studies reviewed is provided in the reference list (the studies are identified by the symbol $).

Statistical Evidence on Providing Ample Learning Time

GENERALIZATION TESTED: ON AMPLE LEARNING TIME—CHAPTER 13

Achievement of learning objectives is enhanced when students are given ample time to perform assigned tasks.

Total number of studies covered: 168

Table 18.13.1
Anderson (1994)
Synthesis of Mastery Learning (Meta-analyses) Achievement Outcomes

Study	Number of Studies	Percent Positive	Total N	ES	Grade Level
Kulik et al. (1990a)	103	93.2%	NR	.52	K–College
Slavin (1990)	17	NR	NR	.27	K–12
Kulik et al. (1990b)	11	63.6%	NR	.40	K–12
Guskey & Pigott (1988)	46	89.1%	11,532	.41 Psych.	K–12
				.50 Science	
				.53 Soc. Stud.	
				.60 Lang. Arts	
				.70 Math	
				.94 Elementary	
				.48 High School	
				.41 College	
Willett et al. (1983)	13	NR		.64	K–12
Guskey & Gates (1985)	38	92.2%	8,074	.65–.94	K–College
Block & Burns (1976)	51	89.0%	2,767	.83	K–College

N = number of students; ES = effect size

Individual studies analyzed by these meta-analyses are identified in the reference list by the following symbols:

Kulik et al. (1990a) *
Kulik et al. (1990b) #
Slavin (1990) @
Guskey & Pigott (1988) $
Guskey & Gates (1985) &
Block & Burns (1976) +

Table 18.13.2
Gettinger (1984)
Means and Standard Deviations for Retention

Variable	Reading Task		Spelling Task	
	M	**SD**	**M**	**SD**
Time Spent Learning	80.08	18.38	72.39	18.29
Time Needed to Learn	92.99	12.49	84.88	17.88

M = mean score; SD = standard deviation

Anderson (1985)

Groups of studies reviewed in this logical synthesis of research did not provide statistical evidence. However, many of the individual studies included in the logical synthesis of research do contain statistical evidence. In the event that a reader wishes to view this evidence, an extensive listing of the individual studies reviewed is provided in the reference list (the studies are identified by the symbol %).

Marliave & Filby (1985)

Groups of studies reviewed in this logical synthesis of research did not provide statistical evidence. However, many of the individual studies included in the logical synthesis of research do contain statistical evidence. In the event that a reader wishes to view this evidence, an extensive listing of the individual studies reviewed is provided in the reference list (the studies are identified by the symbol !).

Statistical Evidence on Keeping Students on Task

GENERALIZATION TESTED: ON STUDENT TIME ON TASK—CHAPTER 14

Achievement of learning objectives is enhanced when students spend more time attending to tasks formulated to enable them to achieve the learning objectives.

Total number of studies covered: 64

Brophy & Good (1986); Rosenshine & Stevens (1986)

Groups of studies reviewed in these logical syntheses of research did not provide statistical evidence. However, many of the individual studies included in these logical syntheses of research do contain statistical evidence. In the event that a reader wishes to view this evidence, an extensive listing of the individual studies reviewed is provided in the reference list. Studies reviewed by Brophy & Good (1986) are identified by the symbol * and studies reviewed by Rosenshine & Stevens (1986) are identified by the symbol #.

Statistical Evidence on Providing Ample Teaching Time

GENERALIZATION TESTED: ON AMPLE TEACHING TIME—CHAPTER 15

Achievement of learning objectives is enhanced when more teaching time is devoted to students to guide and facilitate their performance of academic tasks they are assigned to perform (rather than students performing tasks on their own, teachers dealing with outside intrusions, or students being assigned to nonacademic tasks).

Total number of studies covered: 63

Brophy & Good (1986); Anderson (1995)

Groups of studies reviewed in these logical syntheses of research did not provide statistical evidence. However, many of the individual studies included in these logical syntheses of research do contain statistical evidence. In the event that a reader wishes to view this evidence, an extensive listing of the individual studies reviewed is provided in the reference list. Studies associated with Brophy & Good (1986) are identified by the symbol * and studies associated with Anderson (1995) are identified by the symbol #.

Statistical Evidence on Providing Predictive Ability Instruction

PROMISING INSTRUCTIONAL STRATEGY—CHAPTER 16

Table 18.16.1
Dykes (1997)
Direct and Indirect Effects of Predictive Ability on Achievement from Path Analysis

Independent Variable	Direct Effect on Achievement	Indirect Effect on Achievement
Predictive Ability	.31	.13
IQ	.20	.20
Self-Confidence	.09	.13
Attendance	.12	.05

n = 88 students

Table 18.16.2
Dykes (1997)
Correlation Analysis for Cases Used in Path Analysis

Variable	Predictive Ability	IQ	Self-Confidence	Attendance
Predictive Ability				
IQ	.5135 (p = .000)			
Self-Confidence	.2195 (p = .040)	.2410 (p = .024)		
Attendance	.0359 (p = .740)	.1433 (p = .183)	.1502 (p = .162)	
Achievement	.4350 (p = .000)	.3974 (p = .000)	.2234 (p = .036)	.1705 (p = .112)

n = 88

Statistical Evidence on Ability Grouping Students

QUESTIONABLE INSTRUCTIONAL STRATEGY—CHAPTER 17

Total number of studies covered: 127

Table 18.17.1
Sipe & Curlette (1997)
Reported Mean Effect Size on Achievement by Meta-Analysis

Study	n	Effect Size
Slavin (1990)		
Total	20	−.038
Slavin (1987)		
Overall		.224
Comprehensive ability grouping		−.038
Regrouping reading and math		.182
Joplin Plan		.434
Within-class ability grouping		.335
Kulik & Kulik (1992)		
Overall	127	.253
Multilevel classes	51	.03
Joplin Plan	14	.30

(continued)

Table 18.17.1 (continued)

Study	n	Effect Size
With in-class grouping	11	.25
Enriched classes for the gifted	25	.41
Accelerated classes for the gifted	23	.87

n = number of studies

Statistical Evidence on Matching Student–Teacher Field-Dependent/Field-Independent Cognitive Styles

QUESTIONABLE INSTRUCTIONAL STRATEGY—CHAPTER 17

Total number of studies covered: 5

Sipe & Curlette (1997)

Mean effect size for the five studies analyzed was .03.

Statistical Evidence on Providing Whole Language Instruction

QUESTIONABLE INSTRUCTIONAL STRATEGY—CHAPTER 17

Total number of studies covered: 34

Table 18.17.2
Sipe & Curlette (1997)
Meta-analysis

Type Study	n	Construct	Effect Size
USOE cooperative first grade	19	Word recognition	.17
		Comprehension	.09
Non-USOE	15	Word recognition	.33
		Comprehension	−.42
Overall	34		.09

REFERENCE LIST

Glass, G. V., McGaw, B., & Smith, M. L. (1981). *Meta-analysis in social research*. Newbury Park, CA: Sage.

Hedges, L. V., & Olkin, I. (1985). *Statistical methods for meta-analysis*. Boston: Academic Press.

Rosenthal, R. (1994). Parametric measures of effect size. In H. Cooper & L. V. Hedges (Eds.), *The handbook of research synthesis* (pp. 231–244). New York: Russell Sage.

IV

Instructional Aids

Two instructional aids are presented in Part IV: guidelines for instructional deci-sion-making and a glossary. The guidelines present key instructional decisions that need to be made in a concise format to facilitate decision-making and to provide a context for understanding relationships among strategies discussed in the hand-book. The glossary is constructed to clarify the meaning of terms in the handbook. The strategies are presented so that they can be understood without benefit of the guidelines or glossary. However, the glossary can be used to further clarify the meaning of terms, and the guidelines should facilitate the application of the strate-gies.

19

Guidelines for Making Instructional Decisions

In this chapter, a simple conceptualization of the instructional process is presented, within which major instructional decision-making points are identified. This framework provides a basis for specifying guidelines for instructional decision-making. The guidelines enable the reader to consider and utilize the fifteen effective instructional strategies described earlier in the handbook to make cogent decisions that will improve instruction and, therefore, learning. The strategies need to be considered in the decision-making of educators if they are to beneficially effect instructional practice.

Afterward, instructional failures are systematically reviewed in the context of the decision-making process previously described, highlighting possible breakdowns in the process that can result from faulty decision-making. In the final section of the chapter, a summary of both the instructional decision-making points and the fifteen effective instructional strategies is presented. After a particular strategy is summarized, decision-making points are mentioned where the strategy is relevant and should be considered in arriving at decisions.

The instructional process described in this chapter was used to derive internally consistent definitions of key terms used in the book, as well as to provide an orienting frame of reference whenever clarifications were sought. The instructional process described can serve as an orienting instructional frame of reference for the reader as well. There are so many terms associated with instruction and so many complicated renditions of the instructional process that it is very easy to become confused. The instructional process described in this chapter identifies and relates primary functions of the instructional process in a relatively simple yet non-simplistic way. Jargon is avoided as well as attempts to arbitrarily assign functions to positions such as teacher, administrator, or curriculum planner. The functions assigned to those positions vary enormously from educational institution to educational institution. Although there may not be a need to standardize the assignment of functions to positions, there is a pressing need to clarify the functions of the instructional process.

POLICY OBJECTIVES

Although educational policy objectives are not a part of instruction, they serve to initiate and guide the formulation of instruction. Policy objectives are desired student outcomes to be achieved by means of instruction. Policy objectives are established by policy-makers, such as legislatures and school boards. The setting of policy objectives is prerequisite to instructional decision-making but is not a part of it.

INSTRUCTIONAL PLANNING

Five major decision-making points in instructional planning are: (1) deriving learning objectives, (2) planning instructional tasks, (3) planning evaluation, (4) planning task assignments, and (5) planning teaching.

Deriving Learning Objectives

Learning objectives are terminal tasks students are to achieve. Since policy objectives may not be stated in learning objective form, it behooves those responsible for deriving learning objectives to work with policy-makers to translate policy objectives into learning objective form. This amounts to translating a policy objective into tasks it is desirable for students to be able to perform. In this way the policy objective becomes the ultimate learning objective to be achieved.

The decisions to be made at this decision point are: What learning objective corresponds to the policy objective being pursued? How can the learning objective best be stated to enhance student understanding of the objective?

Planning Instructional Tasks

Tasks are student/subject matter interactions formulated for students to perform to enable them to achieve learning objectives. Task planning is the organizing of a continuum of tasks students are to perform, leading progressively from minimal entry-level tasks that are designed for students with particular readiness abilities to tasks that represent achievement of a learning objective. Task planning includes the planning of *remedial tasks* for students who fail to perform *progressive tasks* on the continuum. Thus, task planning involves the planning of both progressive tasks and remedial tasks.

The decisions to be made at this decision point are:

1. What should be the entry-level readiness requirements for students assigned to pursue the learning objective?

2. What continuum of progressive tasks should be designed, leading from the first task to the achievement of the learning objective?

3. What remedial tasks should be designed for students who fail in performing each progressive task?

4. What student/subject matter interactions should be prescribed for each task?

Attendant questions are: Is the subject matter prescribed in each task appropriate for the student's readiness characteristics? Are task demands appropriate for the student's readiness characteristics?

Planning Evaluation

Evaluation is defined as the comparison of actual task performance to criteria specifying competent task performance and the diagnosis of insufficiencies in task performance. Planning evaluations consists of (1) developing a procedure to identify actual task performance, (2) establishing criteria of competent task performance, (3) specifying a procedure for comparing actual and competent task performance, and (4) developing a procedure for diagnosing insufficiencies in task performance. It is necessary to diagnose causes of insufficiencies in order to remediate them.

The primary decision to be made is: How can the accuracy of evaluation procedures be established? Technically speaking, this requires that the validity, reliability, and objectivity of the evaluation procedures be demonstrated.

Planning Task Assignments

Tasks are assigned to students based on their performance on the evaluation instruments. The plan is to assign students to perform *progressive tasks,* that is, more advanced tasks, when they perform tasks on the continuum successfully. When they do not they are assigned *remedial tasks* to perform until they are able to perform the failed tasks on the continuum correctly. In all cases the aim is to match tasks with student abilities. When a match is made it may be said that students are ready to perform the task. Thus *readiness* is defined as possessing the knowledge, skills, and disposition necessary to perform a task.

The major decision to be made in planning tasks is: How can a match between task demands and student readiness characteristics be assured? Attendant questions are: Do students have the knowledge, skills, and disposition necessary to successfully perform the assigned tasks being considered?

Planning Teaching

Teaching is defined as guiding and facilitating task performance in order to achieve a learning objective. Thus, planning teaching entails planning conditions that will enhance student task performance. Such conditions as teaching aids, noise level, accessibility to needed books and equipment, allotted learning time, and class size must be taken into account.

The primary decision to be made is: How can instructional conditions be arranged to optimize students' opportunity to perform assigned tasks successfully? Attendant questions might be: How can disruption be minimized? What publications, equipment, and facilities can be provided to enhance task performance? Is sufficient time being allotted for students to successfully perform assigned tasks? Is the proposed class size conducive to successful task performance? Are students safe in the instructional environment?

INSTRUCTION

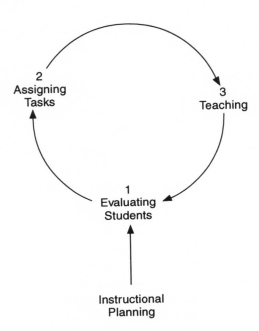

As the above cycle shows, instruction begins after instructional planning to achieve a learning objective has been completed. Instructional planning is in preparation for instruction. First, students are evaluated to determine their readiness to perform tasks on the continuum leading to the achievement of the learning objective. Second, they are assigned progressive or remedial tasks based on the evaluation. Third, teaching ensues, that is, student task performance is guided and facilitated. The cycle is repeated over and over until the learning objective being pursued is achieved.

As can be seen, the process defines a feedback loop, which can be used as the basic unit for analyzing instruction.

INSTRUCTIONAL FAILURES

Instructional failures occur because of failures in instruction, which may in turn be indirectly attributable to failures in instructional planning.

FAILURE TO ACHIEVE THE LEARNING OBJECTIVE

Since the primary purpose of instruction is to achieve learning objectives, the ultimate failure of instruction is failure to achieve a learning objective being pursued.

FAILURES IN INSTRUCTION

Failure to achieve a learning objective manifests itself in the learning process during the evaluation phase, when student ability to perform assigned tasks that signify achievement of the learning objective are evaluated. Failures during each of the three phases of instruction (evaluating students, assigning tasks, teaching) can contribute to the failure to achieve a learning objective as follows.

Failure in Evaluating Students

Failure in evaluating students may be due to inadequacies in the procedures used (1) to assess and compare student task performance to criteria of competent task performance, and/or (2) to diagnose student insufficiencies in task performance. Incorrectly assessing and comparing student task performance to criteria of competent performance would result in the incorrect assignment of a progressive or remedial task to a student. Incorrectly diagnosing student failure to perform a task would result in an incorrect remedial task being assigned to a student.

Failure in Assigning Tasks to Students

If evaluation procedures are accurate, failure to assign students to perform tasks that match or are appropriate for their readiness capabilities may be responsible for students not achieving the learning objective being pursued.

Failure in Teaching

Both evaluation and task assignment may be accurate, and students may fail to achieve the learning objective because teaching is ineffective. That is, student performance of assigned tasks may not be adequately guided and facilitated.

FAILURES IN INSTRUCTIONAL PLANNING

Although failures in instruction may be directly responsible for failure to achieve a learning objective, instructional planning may be indirectly responsible. Failures in instructional planning may be attributable to failure in (1) deriving appropriate learning objectives, (2) planning instructional tasks, (3) planning task assignments, (4) planning evaluations, and/or (5) planning teaching. Failures in instructional planning handicap the instructional process.

Failure in Deriving Appropriate Learning Objectives

Since learning objectives are or should be defined for students with specified readiness characteristics to achieve, mistakes can be made in projecting learning objectives for students. The students may be incapable of achieving objectives they are expected to achieve. Moreover, students may not achieve a policy objective because the policy objective was not accurately translated into learning objective form. In this case, students might achieve an ultimate learning objective and not achieve a corresponding policy objective. For example, a school board that set a policy objective might not be satisfied with the performance of students who are supposed to have achieved the policy objective.

Failure in Planning Instructional Tasks

Derived learning objectives may be appropriate for students' readiness characteristics, and students may fail to achieve the learning objectives because the progressive tasks formulated and sequenced to lead from the specified readiness state of students to the achievement of the learning objectives are inappropriately formulated and/or sequenced; or, planned remedial tasks do not remediate students' inadequacies in performing tasks.

Failure in Planning Task Assignments

The deriving of learning objectives and the planning of tasks may be successful, yet students may fail to achieve a learning objective because the planning of task assignments was inadequate. Inadequate plans may have been made for matching student readiness characteristics with task demands.

Failure in Planning Evaluations

The deriving of learning objectives and the planning of instructional tasks and task assignments may be adequate, yet students may fail to achieve a learning objective because of the planning of faulty evaluation procedures. For instance, evaluation procedures that were developed may not accurately assess and compare students' task performance to criteria of competent task performance.

Failure in Planning Teaching

Although learning objectives, instructional tasks, task assignments, and evaluations may have been planned appropriately, students may fail to achieve a learning objective because of the poor planning of teaching. That is, ways of guiding and facilitating student task performance may not have been adequately planned. For instance, an insufficient amount of time may have been allotted for students to practice and become competent in performing assigned tasks.

UTILIZING EFFECTIVE INSTRUCTIONAL STRATEGIES IN MAKING INSTRUCTIONAL DECISIONS

Following is a summary of the instructional decision-making points that were discussed and the fifteen effective instructional strategies. The strategies are summarized by repeating the generalizations pertaining to each strategy. Applicability of the strategies at the decision-making points is indicated by listing relevant decision-making points after each strategy is summarized.

SUMMARY OF DECISION-MAKING POINTS

Instructional Planning

- Deriving learning objectives
- Planning instructional tasks
- Planning evaluations
- Planning task assignments
- Planning teaching

Instruction

- Evaluating students
- Assigning tasks
- Teaching

SUMMARY OF EFFECTIVE INSTRUCTIONAL STRATEGIES

Taking Student Readiness into Account

Generalization: Achievement of learning objectives is enhanced when students possess the readiness capabilities to achieve learning objectives.

Relevant decision-making points: Planning instructional tasks, planning task assignments, evaluating students, assigning tasks, teaching.

Defining Instructional Expectations

Generalization: Student achievement of learning objectives is enhanced when prior to instruction (1) learning objectives are derived for students, (2) procedures to be used in the performance of tasks to achieve the objectives are identified, and (3) student outcomes designating achievement of the objectives are defined.

Relevant decision-making points: Deriving learning objectives, planning instructional tasks, planning evaluations, teaching.

Providing Effective Evaluation and Remediation

Generalization: Achievement of learning objectives is enhanced when appropriate remediation is provided: (1) evaluation procedures and remedial tasks are formulated when task sequences are planned, (2) student task performance is frequently evaluated, (3) feedback on evaluation is given to students without delay, and (4) incorrect performance is immediately remediated, based on evaluation results.

Relevant decision-making points: Planning instructional tasks, planning evaluations, planning task assignments, planning teaching, evaluating students, assigning
tasks, teaching.

Providing Contiguity

Generalization: Achievement of learning objectives is enhanced when events
students are to associate are presented to them close together in time and space.
Relevant decision-making points: Planning instructional tasks, planning teaching, assigning tasks, teaching.

Utilizing Repetition Effectively

Generalization: Achievement of learning objectives is enhanced when there is
repetition in instruction and tasks students are assigned to perform.
Relevant decision-making points: Planning instructional tasks, planning task assignments, planning teaching, assigning tasks, teaching.

Clarifying Communication

Generalization: Achievement of learning objectives is enhanced when information on objectives, tasks, and evaluations is clearly communicated to students.
Relevant decision-making points: Deriving learning objectives, planning instructional tasks, planning evaluations, planning teaching, evaluating students, teaching.

Reducing Student/Teacher Ratio

Generalization: Achievement of learning objectives is enhanced when there is a
lower student-to-teacher ratio in teaching situations.
Relevant decision-making points: Planning instructional tasks, planning evaluations, planning teaching, evaluating students, teaching.

Providing Reminders Instruction

Generalization: Achievement of learning objectives is enhanced when reminders are used to cue the recall of information needed to perform assigned tasks.
Relevant decision-making points: Planning instructional tasks, planning evaluations, planning teaching, teaching.

Providing Subject Matter Unifiers

Generalization: Achievement of learning objectives is enhanced when a scheme
is used to highlight parts/whole relationships in the subject matter students are
assigned to learn.

Relevant decision-making points: Deriving learning objectives, planning instructional tasks, planning teaching, assigning tasks, teaching.

Providing Transfer of Learning Instruction

Generalization: Achievement of learning objectives is enhanced when students are taught beforehand the knowledge and skills needed to perform assigned tasks and how to determine when learned knowledge and skills can be used to perform assigned tasks.

Relevant decision-making points: Planning instructional tasks, planning evaluations, planning task assignments, planning teaching, assigning tasks, teaching.

Providing Teamwork Instruction

Generalization: Achievement of the learning objective *group achievement* is enhanced when students are taught to perform complementary tasks as a team in pursuit of the objective.

Relevant decision-making points: Deriving learning objectives, planning instructional tasks, planning evaluations, planning task assignments, planning teaching, evaluating students, assigning tasks, teaching.

Providing Decision-Making Instruction

Generalization: Achievement of learning objectives is enhanced when students are shown how to use decision-making tactics to consider and select procedures to perform assigned tasks.

Relevant decision-making points: Deriving learning objectives, planning instructional tasks, planning evaluations, planning task assignments, evaluating students, assigning tasks, teaching.

Providing Ample Learning Time

Generalization: Achievement of learning objectives is enhanced when students are given ample learning time to perform tasks.

Relevant decision-making points: Planning instructional tasks, planning evaluations, planning task assignments, planning teaching, evaluating students, assigning tasks, teaching.

Keeping Students on Task

Generalization: Achievement of learning objectives is enhanced when students spend more time *attending* to tasks formulated to enable them to achieve the learning objective.

Relevant decision-making points: Planning instructional tasks, planning teaching, teaching.

Providing Ample Teaching Time

Generalization: Achievement of learning objectives is enhanced when more teaching time is devoted to students to guide and facilitate the performance of academic tasks they are assigned to perform (rather than students performing tasks on their own, teachers dealing with outside intrusions, or students being assigned to non-academic tasks).

Relevant decision-making points: Planning instructional tasks, planning evaluations, planning teaching, evaluating students, teaching.

An effective instructional strategy may be more closely related to some decisions than to others. Whenever any relevancy could be seen between an effective instructional strategy and a decision-making point, the relevancy was reported. However, the reader may see relevancy between strategies and decision-making points that were not reported.

Glossary

The definitions in the following glossary are relevant to instruction and pertain to instructional contexts and settings. Some of the terms defined in the glossary are key terms in the "guidelines for instructional decision-making"; others are key terms in the strategies that are presented. The terms may well have other definitions in other contexts and disciplines and in dictionaries of the English language.

ability grouping   The grouping of students according to their ability level for the purpose of instruction.

contiguity   The proximity of to-be-associated events in space and time.

control motive   The penchant to improve the control of outcomes.

decision-making   Selecting a course of action.

evaluation   See **instructional evaluation.**

expectations   See **instructional expectations.**

field-dependent/field independent cognitive style   The tendency to perceive events as either (1) independent of their surrounding field or (2) dependent upon their surrounding field.

instruction   A process in which educators evaluate students, assign tasks to students based on the evaluations, and teach students to perform assigned tasks in order to achieve a learning objective.

instructional conditions   Assignment conditions that can affect students' task performance, such as class size, disruptions, equipment, time allowed for task performance, and safety.

instructional cycle   The cyclical execution of the acts of evaluating → assigning tasks → teaching in order to achieve a learning objective. It may be necessary to repeat the cycle a number of times to achieve a learning objective.

instructional evaluation   The comparison of the performance of an instructional task with criteria of competent performance, and the diagnosis of insufficiencies in task performance.

instructional expectations   (1) Objectives students are assigned to achieve, (2) procedures to be followed to achieve the objectives, and (3) criteria specifying successful achievement of the objectives.

instructional planning   The process of (1) deriving learning objectives, (2) planning instructional tasks, (3) planning evaluations, (4) planning task assignments, and (5) planning teaching.

instructional strategies   Procedures used to enhance the achievement of learning objectives.

instructional units   Units of instruction consisting of a sequence of evaluation, task assignment, and teaching tactics leading progressively to the achievement of a unit learning objective. A number of unit objectives are achieved as a means of achieving a policy objective.

learning objectives   Terminal tasks students are to learn to perform by means of instruction.

learning time   Time allotted to students for performing assigned tasks.

objectives   See **learning objectives** and **policy objectives.**

planning   See **instructional planning.**

policy objectives   Desired student outcomes to be achieved by educators. Policy objectives are established by policy-makers, such as school boards, for educators to achieve.

predictive ability   The ability to forecast outcomes from antecedent conditions.

progressive tasks   A continuum of tasks leading progressively from entry-level tasks appropriate for students with specified readiness characteristics to the achievement of a learning objective.

readiness   Student knowledge, skills, and disposition necessary to perform a task.

reinforcement   The attempt to increase the probability that a desired assigned task will be performed by providing for the satisfaction of a motive when the desired task is performed.

remedial tasks   Tasks formulated to remediate students' failure to adequately perform a task.

remediation   The correction of inadequate task performance.

reminders   Memory joggers or mnemonics designed and used to facilitate and improve recall of to-be-learned information or skills.

repetition   The repeated presentation of to-be-learned material to students and/or student repetition of to-be-learned skills.

strategies   See **instructional strategies.**

student/teacher ratio   The proportion of teachers to students the teachers are assigned to teach.

students   People being taught.

subject matter   The content to be learned by students.

subject matter unifiers   Presentations of the parts/whole relationships in subject matter students are assigned to learn to enhance their learning of the subject matter.

task planning   The formulating and organizing of progressive tasks and remedial tasks to achieve a learning objective based on student readiness characteristics.

tasks   Student/subject matter interactions formulated to enable students to achieve learning objectives.

teaching   Guiding and facilitating student task performance in order to achieve a learning objective.

teaching time   The proportion of learning time spent guiding and facilitating student performance of assigned tasks.

teamwork   Cooperation among people to achieve a common objective.

time on task   The amount of time students spend focused on the performance of assigned tasks.

transfer of learning   The application of prior learning to enable the performance of new tasks.

unifiers   See **subject matter unifiers.**

Index of Researchers

Subject Index

Note: An effort has been made to provide a complete index by subject of the plain-English terminology used in this handbook. Additionally, we have attempted, as completely as possible, to cross-reference the terminology used in the handbook with corresponding professional terminology used by educational psychologists and educators.

About the Authors

MYLES I. FRIEDMAN is Professor of Educational Research and Gambrell Chair at the University of South Carolina. A renowned educator and author, Dr. Friedman's books include *Rational Behavior*, *Teaching Reading and Thinking Skills*, *Improving Teacher Education: Resources and Recommendations*, *Teaching Higher Order Thinking Skills to Gifted Students*, and *Taking Control: Vitalizing Education*. Professor Friedman has spent 20 years conducting and applying research to improve education.

STEVEN P. FISHER is a doctoral candidate in the Program for Educational Research at the University of South Carolina. He has earned a degree of Master of Education, awarded by the University of South Carolina. Mr. Fisher has five years' experience teaching and managing an associate degree program at Technical College of the Low Country in Beaufort, South Carolina.